Charles Lamb, Alfred Ainger

The essays of Elia. With introd. and notes by Alfred Ainger

Charles Lamb, Alfred Ainger

The essays of Elia. With introd. and notes by Alfred Ainger

ISBN/EAN: 9783337858612

Printed in Europe, USA, Canada, Australia, Japan

Cover: Foto ©ninafisch / pixelio.de

More available books at **www.hansebooks.com**

THE ESSAYS OF ELIA

MACMILLAN AND CO., Limited
LONDON · BOMBAY · CALCUTTA
MELBOURNE

THE MACMILLAN COMPANY
NEW YORK · BOSTON · CHICAGO
ATLANTA · SAN FRANCISCO

THE MACMILLAN CO. OF CANADA, Ltd.
TORONTO

THE

ESSAYS OF ELIA

WITH INTRODUCTION AND NOTES

BY

ALFRED AINGER

MACMILLAN AND CO., LIMITED
ST. MARTIN'S STREET, LONDON
1910

This Edition of the Essays of Elia was first printed in 1883
Reprinted 1884, 1887, 1888, 1889, 1891, 1892, 1894, 1896, 1898, 1899, 1903, 1906
1910

INTRODUCTION.

THE two volumes of miscellaneous writings by Charles Lamb, published by the Olliers in 1818, contained a variety of prose sufficient to prove once more that the study and practice of verse is one of the best trainings for a prose style. In his dedication of the poetical volume to Coleridge, Lamb half apologises for having forsaken his old calling, and for having "dwindled into prose and criticism." The apology, as I have elsewhere remarked, was hardly needed. If we except the lines to Hester Savary and a few of the sonnets and shorter pieces, there was little in the volume to weigh against the two essays on Hogarth and the tragedies of Shakspere. It was the result of the miscellaneous and yet thorough character of Lamb's reading from a boy that the critical side of his mind was the first to mature. The shorter papers contributed by Lamb to Leigh Hunt's *Reflector* in 1811— the year to which belong the two critical essays just mentioned—more or less framed on the model of the *Tatler* and its successors, give by comparison little promise of the richness and variety of the Elia series of ten years later. On the other hand, there are passages in the critical essays, such as that on *Lear*, as represented on the stage, and the vindication of Hogarth as a moral teacher, which represent Lamb at his highest.

On the republication of these miscellanies in 1818, it could not be overlooked that a prose writer of something like genius was coming to the front. One of the younger critics of the day, Henry Nelson Coleridge, reviewing the volumes in the fifth number of the *Etonian*, in 1821, does not hesitate to declare that " Charles Lamb writes the best, the purest, and most genuine English of any man living," and adds the following acute remark :— " For genuine Anglicism, which amongst all other essentials of excellence in our native literature, is now recovering itself from the leaden mace of the *Rambler*, he is quite a study : his prose is absolutely perfect, it conveys thought, without smothering it in blankets." Lamb was indeed to do more than any man of his time to remove the Johnsonian incubus from our periodical literature. But the full scope of the writer's powers was not known, perhaps even to himself, till the opportunity afforded him by the establishment of the *London Magazine* in 1820. It did credit to the discernment of the editors of that publication, that no control seems to have been exercised over the matter or manner of Lamb's contributions. The writer had not to see all that made the individuality of his style disappear under the editor's hand, as his review of the *Excursion* in the *Quarterly* had suffered under Gifford's. To " wander at its own sweet will " was the first necessity of Lamb's genius. And this miscellaneousness of subject and treatment is the first surprise and delight felt by the reader of Lamb. It seems as if the choice of subject came to him almost at haphazard,—as if, like Shakspeare, he found the first plot that came to hand suitable, because the hand that was to deal with it was absolutely secure of its power to transmute the most unpromising material into gold. *Roast Pig*, *The Praise of Chimney-Sweepers*, *A Bachelor's Complaint of the Conduct of Married People*, *Grace before Meat*—the incongruity of the titles at once declares the humorist's confidence in the certainty of his touch. To have been commonplace on such topics would have been certain failure.

In the *Character of the late Elia, by a Friend* which Lamb wrote in the interval between the publication of the first and second series of essays, he hits off the characteristics of his style in a tone half contemptuous, half apologetic, which yet contains a criticism of real value. "I am now at liberty to confess," he writes, "that much which I have heard objected to my late friend's writings was well founded. Crude, they are, I grant you—a sort of unlicked, incondite things—villainously pranked in an affected array of antique words and phrases. They had not been *his*, if they had been other than such; and better it is that a writer should be natural in a self-pleasing quaintness than to affect a naturalness (so called) that should be strange to him." No better text could be found from which to discourse on Charles Lamb's English. The plea put forth almost as a paradox is nevertheless a simple truth. What appears to the hasty reader artificial in Lamb's style was natural to *him*. For in this matter of style he was the product of his reading, and from a child his reading had lain in the dramatists, and generally in the great imaginative writers of the sixteenth and seventeenth centuries. Shakspeare and Milton he knew almost by heart: Beaumont and Fletcher, Massinger, Ford, and Webster, were hardly less familiar to him; and next to these, the writers of the so-called metaphysical school, the later developments of the Euphuistic fashion, had the strongest fascination for him. Where the Fantastic vein took the pedantic-humorous shape, as in Burton; or the metaphysical-humorous, as in Sir Thomas Browne; or where it was combined with true poetic sensibility, as in Wither and Marvell,—of these springs Lamb had drunk so deeply that his mind was saturated with them. His own nature became "subdued to what it worked in." For him to bear, not only on his style, but on the cast of his mind and fancy, the mark of these writers, and many more in whom genius and eccentricity went together, was no matter of choice. It was this that constituted the "self-pleasing quaintness" of his literary manner. The phrase could not be improved. Affectation is a manner put on to impress others. Lamb's manner pleased himself and that is why, to use a familiar phrase, he was "happy in it."

To one of the writers just named Lamb stands in a special relation. Sir Thomas Browne was at once a scholar, a mystic, and a humorist. His humour is so grave that, when he is enunciating one of those paradoxes he loves so well, it is often impossible to tell whether or not he wears a smile upon his face. To Lamb this combination of characters was irresistible, for in it he saw a reflection of himself. He knew the writings of Browne so well that not only does he quote him more often than any other author, but whenever he has to confront the mysteries of life and death his mental attitude at once assimilates to Browne's, and his English begins to dilate and to become sombre. The dominant influence on Lamb in his reflective mood is Browne. His love of paradox, and the colour of his style, derived from the use of Latinised words never thoroughly acclimatised, is also from the same source—a use which, in the hands of a less skilful Latinist than Lamb, might have been hazardous. We do not resent his use of such words as *agnize*, *arride*, *reluct*, *reduce* (in the sense of "bring back"), or even such portentous creations as *sciential*, *cognition*, *intellectuals*, and the like. Lamb could not have lived so long among the writers of the Renascence without sharing their fondness for word-coinage. And the flavour of the antique in style he felt to be an almost indispensable accompaniment to the antique in fancy.

Another feature of his style is its allusiveness. He is rich in quotations, and in my notes I have succeeded in tracing most of them to their source, a matter of some difficulty in Lamb's case, for his inaccuracy is all but perverse. But besides those avowedly introduced as such, his style is full of quotations held—if the expression may be allowed—in solution. One feels, rather than recognises, that a phrase or idiom or turn of expression is an echo of something that one has heard or read before. Yet such is the use made of his material, that a charm is added by the very fact that we are thus continually renewing our experience of an older day. His style becomes aromatic, like the perfume of faded rose-leaves in a china jar. With such allusiveness as this, I need not say that I have not meddled in my notes. Its whole charm lies in our recognising it for ourselves. The "prosperity" of an allusion, as of a jest, "lies in the ear of him that hears it," and it were doing a poor service to Lamb or his readers to draw out and arrange in order the threads he has wrought into the very fabric of his English.

But although Lamb's style is essentially the product of the authors he had made his own, nothing would be more untrue than to say of him that he read nature, or anything else, "through the spectacles of books." Wordsworth would never have called to *him* to leave his books that he might come forth, and bring with him a heart

"That watches and receives."

It is to his own keen insight and intense sympathy that we owe everything of value in his writing. His observation was his own, though when he gave it back into the world, the manner of it was the creation of his reading. Where, for instance, he describes (and it is seldom) the impression produced on him by country sights and sounds, there is not a trace discoverable of that conventional treatment of nature which had been so common with mere book-men, before Burns and Wordsworth. Lamb did not care greatly for the country and its associations. Custom had made the presence of society, streets and crowds, the theatre and the picture gallery, an absolute necessity. Yet if he has to reproduce a memory of rural life, it is with the precision and tenderness of a Wordsworth. Take, as an example, this exquisite glimpse of a summer afternoon at Blakesware:—"The cheerful store-room, in whose hot window-seat I used to sit and read Cowley, with the grass-plot before, and the hum and flappings of that one solitary wasp that ever haunted it, about me—it is in mine ears now, as oft as summer returns:" or again, the sweet garden scene from *Dream Children*, where the spirit of Wordsworth seems to contend for mastery with the fancifulness of Marvell, "because I had more pleasure in strolling about among the old melancholy-looking yew-trees, or the firs, and picking up the red berries and the fir apples, which were good for nothing but to look at—or in lying about upon the fresh grass, with all the fine garden smells around me—or basking in the orangery, till I could almost fancy myself ripening too along with the oranges and limes in that grateful warmth—or in watching the dace that darted to and fro in the fish pond at the bottom of the garden, with here and there a great sulky pike hanging midway down the water in silent state, as if it mocked at their impertinent friskings." It is hard to say whether the poet's eye or the painter's is more surely exhibited here. The "solitary wasp" and the "sulky pike" are master-touches; and in the following passage it is perhaps as much of Cattermole as of Goldsmith or Gray, that we are reminded:—"But would'st thou know the beauty of holiness?—go alone on some week-day, borrowing the keys of good Master Sexton, traverse the cool aisles of some country church: think of the piety that has kneeled there—the meek pastor—the docile parishioner. With no disturbing emotions, no cross conflicting comparisons, drink in the tranquillity of the place, till thou thyself become as fixed and motionless as the marble effigies that kneel and weep around thee."

The idea that some readers might derive from the casual titles and subjects of these essays, and the discursiveness of their treatment, that they are hasty things thrown off in a moment of high spirits, is of course erroneous. Lamb somewhere writes of the essay just quoted, as a "futile effort wrung from him with slow pain." Perhaps this was an extreme case, but it is clear that most of the essays are the result of careful manipulation. They are elaborate studies in style, and even in colour. Nothing is more remarkable about the essays

than the contrasts of colour they present—another illustration of Lamb's sympathy with the painter's art. The essay on the *Chimney-Sweepers* is a study in black :—
"I like to meet a sweep—understand me—not a grown sweeper—old chimney-sweepers are by no means attractive—but one of those tender novices, blooming through their first nigritude, the maternal washings not quite effaced from the cheek—such as come forth with the dawn, or somewhat earlier, with their little professional notes sounding like the *peep peep* of a young sparrow; or liker to the matin lark, shall I pronounce them, in their aerial ascents not seldom anticipating the sunrise? I have a kindly yearning towards those dim specks— poor blots—innocent blacknesses— I reverence these young Africans of our own growth—these almost clergy imps, who sport their cloth without assumption."

And if one would understand Lamb's skill as a colourist, let him turn as a contrast to the essay on *Quakers*, which may be called a study in dove-colour :—" The very garments of a Quaker seem incapable of receiving a soil; and cleanliness in them to be something more than the absence of its contrary. Every Quakeress is a lily; and when they come up in bands to their Whitsun conferences, whitening the easterly streets of the metropolis, from all parts of the United Kingdom, they show like troops of the Shining Ones."

The essay on *Chimney-Sweepers* is one blaze of wit, which yet may pass unobserved from the very richness of its setting. How surprising, and at the same time how picturesque, is the following :—" I seem to remember having been told that a bad sweep was once left in the stack with his brush, to indicate which way the wind blew. It was an awful spectacle, certainly, not much unlike the old stage direction in *Macbeth*, where the 'apparition of a child crowned, with a tree in his hand, rises.'" Lamb's wit, original as it is, shows often enough the influence of particular models. Of all old writers, none had a firmer hold on his affection than

Fuller. Now and then he has passages in deliberate imitation of Fuller's manner. The descriptions, in detached sentences, of the *Poor Relation* and the *Convalescent* are Fuller all over. When Lamb writes of the Poor Relation—" He entereth smiling and embarrassed. He holdeth out his hand to you to shake, and draweth it back again. He casually looketh in about dinner-time, when the table is full,"—and so on, there can be no doubt that he had in mind such characterisation as Fuller's in the *Good Yeoman*, or the *Degenerous Gentleman*. The manner is due originally, of course, to Theophrastus, but it was from Fuller, I think, that Lamb derived his fondness for it. And throughout his writings the influence of this humorist is to be traced. How entirely in the vein of Fuller, for instance, is the following :—" They (the sweeps), from their little pulpits (the tops of chimneys), preach a lesson of patience to mankind ;" or this, again, from the essay *Grace Before Meat:*—" Gluttony and surfeiting are no proper occasions for thanksgiving. When Jeshurun waxed fat, we read that he kicked ;" or, once more, this fine comment on the stillness of the Quaker's worship :—" For a man to refrain even from good words and to hold his peace, it is commendable ; but for a multitude, it is great mastery.".

But Lamb's wit, like his English, is Protean, and just as we think we have fixed its character and source, it escapes into new forms. In simile he finds opportunity for it that is all his own. What, for instance, can be more surprising in its unexpectedness than the description in *The Old Margate Hoy* of the ubiquitous sailor on board : —" How busily didst thou ply thy multifarious occupation, cook, mariner, attendant, chamberlain ; here, there, *like another Ariel*, flaming at once about all parts of the deck "? Again, what wit—or shall we call it humour —is there in the gravity of his detail, by which he touches springs of delight unreached even by Defoe or Swift ; as in *Roast Pig*, where he says that the " father and son were summoned to take their trial at Pekin, *then an inconsiderable assize town;*" or more delightful still, later on:—" Thus this custom of firing houses continued, till in process of time, says my manuscript, a sage arose; *like our Locke*, who made a discovery that the flesh of swine, or indeed of any other animal, might be cooked (burnt, as they called it) without the necessity of consuming a whole house to dress it." Or, for another vein, take the account of the mendacious traveller he affects to remember as a fellow-passenger on his early voyage in the old Margate Hoy, who assures his admiring listeners that, so far from the Phœnix being a unique bird, it was by no means uncommon " in some parts of Upper Egypt," where the whole episode is not one jot the less humorous because it is clear to the reader, not that the traveller invented his facts, but that Lamb invented the traveller: Or yet once more, how exquisitely unforeseen, and how rich in tenderness, is the following remark as to the domestic happiness of himself and his "cousin Bridget," in *Mackery End:*—"We are generally in harmony, with occasional bickerings—as it should be among near relations." What is the name for this antithesis of irony— this hiding of a sweet aftertaste in a bitter word? Whatever its name, it is a dominant flavour in Lamb's humour. There are two features, I think, of Lamb's method which distinguish him from so many humorists of to-day. He takes homely and familiar things, and makes them fresh and beautiful. The fashion of to-day is to vulgarise great and noble things by burlesque associations. The humorist's contrast is obtained in both cases; only that in the one it elevates the commonplace, and in the other it degrades the excellent. And, secondly, in this generation, when what is meant to raise a laugh has, nine times out of ten, its root in cynicism, it should be refreshing to turn again and dwell in the humane atmosphere of these essays of Elia.

To many other qualities that go to make up that highly composite thing, Lamb's humour—to that feature of it that consists in the unabashed display of his own unconventionality—his difference from other people, and to that "metaphysical" quality of his wit which belongs to him in a far truer sense than as applied to Cowley and his school, it is sufficient to make a passing reference. But the mention of Cowley, by whom with Fuller, Donne, and the rest, his imagination was assuredly shaped, reminds us once more of the charm that belongs to the "old and antique" strain heard through all his more earnest utterances. As we listen to Elia the moralist, now with the terse yet stately egotism of one old master, now in the long-drawn-out harmonics of another, we live again with the thinkers and dreamers of two centuries ago. Sometimes he confides to us weaknesses that few men are bold enough to avow, as when he tells how he dreaded death and clung to life. "I am not content to pass away 'like a weaver's shuttle.' These metaphors solace me not, nor sweeten the unpalatable draught of mortality. I care not to be carried with the tide, and reluct at the inevitable course of destiny. I am in love with this green earth; the face of town and country; the unspeakable rural solitudes, and the sweet security of streets." There is an essay by Lamb's friend Hazlitt on the *Fear of Death*, which it is interesting to compare with this. The one essay may have been possibly suggested by the other. Hazlitt is that one of Lamb's contemporaries with whom it is natural to compare him. There are, indeed, obvious points of resemblance between them. Hazlitt wrote a vigorous and flexible style; he could quote Shakspeare and Milton as copiously as Lamb; he wrote on Lamb's class of subjects; he shared his love of paradoxes and his frank egotistical method. But here all likeness ends. Hazlitt's essay is on the text that, since it does not pain us to reflect that there was once a time when we did not exist, so it should be no pain to think that at some future time the same state of things shall be. But this light-hearted attempt at consolation is found to be more depressing than the melancholy of Lamb, for it lacks the two things needful, the accent of absolute sincerity, and a nature unsoured by the world.

But Lamb had his serener moods, and in one of these let us part from him. The essay on the *Old Benchers of the Inner Temple* is one of the most varied and beautiful pieces of prose that English literature can boast. Eminently, moreover, does it show us Lamb as the product of two different ages—the child of the Renascence of the sixteenth century and of that of the nineteenth. It is as if both Spenser and Wordsworth had laid hands of blessing upon his head. This is how he writes of his childhood, when the old lawyers paced to and fro before him on the Terrace Walk, making up to his childish eyes "the mythology of the Temple :"—

"In those days I saw Gods, as 'old men covered with a mantle,' walking upon the earth. Let the dreams of classic idolatry perish—extinct be the fairies and fairy trumpery of legendary fabling—in the heart of childhood there will for ever spring up a well of innocent or wholesome superstition—the seeds of exaggeration will be busy there, and vital, from everyday forms educing the unknown and the uncommon. In that little Goshen there will be light when the grown world flounders about in the darkness of sense and materiality. While childhood, and while dreams reducing childhood, shall be left, imagination shall not have spread her holy wings totally to fly the earth."

It is in such passages as these that Lamb shows himself, what indeed he is, the last of the Elizabethans. He had "learned their great language," and yet he had early discovered, with the keen eye of a humorist, how effective for his purpose was the touch of the pedantic and the fantastical from which the noblest of them were not wholly free. He was thus able to make even their weaknesses a fresh source of delight, as he dealt with them from the vantage ground of two centuries. It may seem strange, on first thoughts, that the fashion of Lamb's style should not have grown, in its turn, old-fashioned ;

that, on the contrary, no literary reputation of sixty years' standing should seem more certain of its continuance. But it is not the antique manner — the "self-pleasing quaintness" — that has embalmed the substance. Rather is there that in the substance which ensures immortality for the style. It is one of the rewards of purity of heart that, allied with humour, it has the promise of perennial charm. "Saint Charles!" exclaimed Thackeray one day, as he finished reading once more the original of one of Lamb's letters to Bernard Barton. There was much in Lamb's habits and manners that we do not associate with the saintly ideal; but patience under suffering and a boundless sympathy hold a large place in that ideal, and in Charles Lamb these were not found wanting.

I would add a few words on the kind of information I have sought to furnish in my Notes. The impertinence of criticism or comment, I hope has been almost entirely avoided. But there was a certain waywardness and love of practical joking in Charles Lamb that led him often to treat matters of fact with deliberate falsification. His essays are full of autobiography, but often purposely disguised, whether to amuse those who were in the secret, or to perplex those who were not, it is impossible to say. In his own day, therefore, corrections of fact would have been either superfluous, or would have spoiled the jest; but now that Lamb's contemporaries are all but passed away, much of the humour of his method is lost without some clue to the many disguises and perversions of fact with which the essays abound. They are full, for instance, of references to actual persons, by means of initials or other devices. To readers fairly conversant with the literary history of Lamb's time, many of these disguises are transparent enough; but for others, notes here and there are indispensable. We have an authentic clue to most of the initials or asterisks employed in the first series of Elia. There is in existence a list of these initials drawn up by some unknown hand, and filled in with the real names by Lamb himself. Through the kindness of its possessor, Mr. Alexander Ireland of Manchester, the original of this interesting relic has been in my hands, and I can vouch for the handwriting, phraseology, and (it may be added) the spelling, being indubitably Lamb's.

There is much information in these essays, more or less disguised, about Lamb's relatives, and I have tried to illustrate these points by details of his family history for which I had not space in my Memoir of Lamb. In a few instances I have permitted myself to repeat some sentences from that memoir, where the same set of circumstances had to be narrated again. But apart from changes of names and incidents in the essays, there is in Lamb's humour the constant element of a mischievous love of hoaxing. He loves nothing so much as to mingle romance with reality, so that it shall be difficult for the reader to disentangle them. Sometimes he deals with fiction as if it were fact; and sometimes, after supplying literal facts, he ends with the insinuation that they are fictitious. And besides these deliberate mystifications, there is found also in Lamb a certain natural incapacity for being accurate—an inveterate turn for the opposite. "What does Elia care for dates?" he asks in one of his letters, and indeed about accuracy in any such trifles he did not greatly care. In the matter of quotation, as already remarked, this is curiously shown. He seldom quotes even a hackneyed passage from Shakspeare or Milton correctly; and sometimes he half-remembers a passage from some old author, and re-writes it, to suit the particular subject he wishes it to illustrate. I have succeeded in tracing all but two or three of the many quotations occurring in the essays, and they serve to show the remarkable range and variety of his reading.

It is generally known that when Lamb collected his essays, for publication in book form, from the pages of the *London* and other magazines, he omitted certain passages. These I have thought it right, as a rule, not to restore. In most cases the reason for their omission is obvious. They were excrescences or digressions, injuring the effect of the essay as a whole. In the few instances in which I have retained a note, or other short passage, from the original versions of the essays, I have shown that this is the case by enclosing it in brackets.

I have to thank many friends, and many known to me only by their high literary reputation, for courteous and ready help in investigating points connected with Lamb's writings. Among these I would mention Mr. Alexander Ireland of Manchester; Mr. Richard Garnett of the British Museum; and, as before, my friend Mr. J. E. Davis, counsel to the Commissioners of Police, who has given many valuable suggestions and constant assistance of other kinds. I must also express my acknowledgments to Mr. W. J. Jeaffreson, of Folkestone, and to the family of the late Mr. Arthur Loveday of Wardington, Banbury, for permission to make extracts from unpublished letters of Lamb's in their possession.

1883.

NOTE TO NEW EDITION.

SEVERAL corrections and additions have been made in the Notes to the present Edition.

Jan. 1887.

PREFACE TO THE LAST ESSAYS.

BY A FRIEND OF THE LATE ELIA.

This poor gentleman, who for some months past had been in a declining way, hath at length paid his final tribute to nature.

To say truth, it is time he were gone. The humour of the thing, if ever there was much in it, was pretty well exhausted; and a two years' and a half existence has been a tolerable duration for a phantom.

I am now at liberty to confess, that much which I have heard objected to my late friend's writings was well founded. Crude they are, I grant you—a sort of unlicked, incondite things—villainously pranked in an affected array of antique modes and phrases. They had not been *his*, if they had been other than such; and better it is, that a writer should be natural in a self-pleasing quaintness, than to affect a naturalness (so called) that should be strange to him. Egotistical they have been pronounced by some who did not know, that what he tells us, as of himself, was often true only (historically) of another; as in a former Essay (to save many instances)—where under the *first person* (his favourite figure) he shadows forth the forlorn estate of a country-boy placed at a London school, far from his friends and connections—in direct opposition to his own early history. If it be egotism to imply and twine with his own identity the griefs and affections of another—making himself many, or reducing many unto himself—then is the skilful novelist, who all along brings in his hero or heroine, speaking of themselves, the greatest egotist of all; who yet has never, therefore, been accused of that narrowness. And how shall the intenser dramatist escape being faulty, who, doubtless under cover of passion uttered by another, oftentimes gives blameless vent to his most inward feelings, and expresses his own story modestly?

My late friend was in many respects a singular character. Those who did not like him, hated him; and some, who once liked him, afterwards became his bitterest haters. The truth is, he gave himself too little concern what he uttered, and in whose presence. He observed neither time nor place, and would e'en out with what came uppermost. With the severe religionist he would pass for a free-thinker; while the other faction set him down for a bigot, or persuaded themselves that he belied his sentiments. Few understood him; and I am not certain that at all times he quite understood himself. He too much affected that dangerous figure—irony. He sowed doubtful speeches, and reaped plain, unequivocal hatred. He would interrupt the gravest discussion with some light jest; and yet, perhaps, not quite irrelevant in ears that could understand it. Your long and much talkers hated him. The informal habit of his mind, joined to an inveterate impediment of speech, forbade him to be an orator; and he seemed determined that no one else should play that part when he was present. He was *petit* and ordinary in his person and appearance. I have seen him sometimes in what is called good company, but where he has been a stranger, sit silent, and be suspected for an odd fellow; till some unlucky occasion provoking it, he would stutter out some senseless pun (not altogether senseless, perhaps, if rightly taken), which has stamped his character for the evening. It was hit or miss with him; but nine times out of ten he contrived by this device to send away a whole company his enemies. His conceptions rose kindlier than his utterance, and his happiest *impromptus* had the appearance of effort. He has been accused of trying to be witty, when in truth he was but struggling to give his poor thoughts articulation. He chose his companions for some individuality of character which they manifested. Hence, not many persons of science, and few professed *literati*, were of his councils. They were, for the most part, persons of an uncertain fortune; and, as to such people commonly nothing is more obnoxious than a gentleman of settled (though moderate) income, he passed with most of them for a great miser. To my knowledge this was a mistake. His *intimados*, to confess a truth, were in the world's eye a ragged regiment. He found them floating on the surface of society; and the colour, or something else, in the weed pleased him. The burrs stuck to him—but they were good and loving burrs for all that. He never greatly cared for the society of what are called good people. If any of these were scandalised (and offences were sure to arise) he could not help it. When he has been remonstrated with for not making more concessions to the feelings of good people, he would retort by asking, what one point did these good people ever concede to him? He was temperate in his meals and diversions, but always kept a little on this side of abstemiousness. Only in the use of the Indian weed he might be thought a little excessive. He took it, he would say, as a solvent of speech. Marry—as the friendly vapour ascended, how his prattle would curl up sometimes with it! the ligaments which tongue-tied him were loosened, and the stammerer proceeded a statist!

I do not know whether I ought to bemoan or rejoice that my old friend is departed. His jests were beginning to grow obsolete, and his stories to be found out. He felt the approaches of age; and while he pretended to cling to life, you saw how slender were the ties left to bind him. Discoursing with him latterly on this subject, he expressed himself with a pettishness, which I thought unworthy of him. In our walks about his suburban retreat (as he called it) at Shacklewell, some children belonging to a school of industry had met us, and bowed and curtseyed, as he thought, in an especial manner to *him*. "They take me for a visiting governor," he muttered earnestly. He had a horror, which he carried to a foible, of looking like anything important and parochial. He thought that he approached nearer to that stamp daily. He had a general aversion from being treated like a grave or respectable character, and kept a wary eye upon the advances of age that should so entitle him. He herded always, while it was possible, with people younger than himself. He did not conform to the march of time, but was dragged along in the procession. His manners lagged behind his years. He was too much of the boy-man. The *toga virilis* never sate gracefully on his shoulders. The impressions of infancy had burnt into him, and he resented the impertinence of manhood. These were weaknesses; but such as they were, they are a key to explicate some of his writings.

CONTENTS.

FIRST SERIES.

The South-Sea House
Oxford in the Vacation
Christ's Hospital Five and Thirty Years Ago
The Two Races of Men
New Year's Eve
Mrs. Battle's Opinions on Whist
A Chapter on Ears
All Fools' Day
A Quakers' Meeting
The Old and the New Schoolmaster
Imperfect Sympathies
Witches and other Night Fears
Valentine's Day
My Relations
Mackery End in Hertfordshire
My First Play
Modern Gallantry
The Old Benchers of the Inner Temple
Grace Before Meat

CONTENTS.

	PAGE
Dream-Children; A Reverie	137
Distant Correspondents	142
The Praise of Chimney-Sweepers	148
A Complaint of the Decay of Beggars in the Metropolis	156
A Dissertation upon Roast Pig	164
A Bachelor's Complaint of the Behaviour of Married People	172
On Some of the Old Actors	180
On the Artificial Comedy of the Last Century	192
On the Acting of Munden	201

LAST ESSAYS.

Blakesmoor in H——shire	205
Poor Relations	210
Detached Thoughts on Books and Reading	218
Stage Illusion	225
To the Shade of Elliston	229
Ellistoniana	231
The Old Margate Hoy	237
The Convalescent	246
Sanity of True Genius	251
Captain Jackson	254
The Superannuated Man	259
The Genteel Style in Writing	267
Barbara S——	272

CONTENTS.

FIRST SERIES.

The South-Sea House
Oxford in the Vacation
Christ's Hospital Five and Thirty Years Ago
The Two Races of Men
New Year's Eve
Mrs. Battle's Opinions on Whist
A Chapter on Ears
All Fools' Day
A Quakers' Meeting
The Old and the New Schoolmaster
Imperfect Sympathies
Witches and other Night Fears
Valentine's Day
My Relations
Mackery End in Hertfordshire
My First Play
Modern Gallantry
The Old Benchers of the Inner Temple
Grace Before Meat

CONTENTS.

	PAGE
Dream-Children: a Reverie	137
Distant Correspondents	142
The Praise of Chimney-Sweepers	148
A Complaint of the Decay of Beggars in the Metropolis	156
A Dissertation upon Roast Pig	164
A Bachelor's Complaint of the Behaviour of Married People	172
On Some of the Old Actors	180
On the Artificial Comedy of the Last Century	192
On the Acting of Munden	201

LAST ESSAYS.

Blakesmoor in H——shire	205
Poor Relations	210
Detached Thoughts on Books and Reading	218
Stage Illusion	225
To the Shade of Elliston	229
Ellistoniana	231
The Old Margate Hoy	237
The Convalescent	246
Sanity of True Genius	251
Captain Jackson	254
The Superannuated Man	259
The Genteel Style in Writing	267
Barbara S——	272

CONTENTS. XXV

	PAGE
The Tombs in the Abbey	278
Amicus Redivivus	281
Some Sonnets of Sir Philip Sydney	286
Newspapers Thirty-Five Years Ago	295
Barrenness of the Imaginative Faculty in the Productions of Modern Art	303
The Wedding	315
Rejoicings upon the New Year's Coming of Age	321
Old China	327
The Child Angel; A Dream	333
Confessions of a Drunkard	336
Popular Fallacies:	
I. That a Bully is always a Coward	346
II. That Ill-Gotten Gain never prospers	347
III. That a Man must not laugh at his own Jest	347
IV. That Such a one shows his Breeding.—That it is easy to perceive he is no Gentleman	348
V. That the Poor copy the Vices of the Rich	349
VI. That Enough is as good as a Feast	350
VII. Of Two Disputants, the Warmest is generally in the Wrong	351
VIII. That Verbal Allusions are not Wit, because they will not bear a Translation	352
IX. That the Worst Puns are the Best	353
X. That Handsome is that Handsome does	355

POPULAR FALLACIES:

 XI. THAT WE MUST NOT LOOK A GIFT HORSE IN THE MOUTH 358

 XII. THAT HOME IS HOME THOUGH IT IS NEVER SO HOMELY 360

 XIII. THAT YOU MUST LOVE ME AND LOVE MY DOG 365

 XIV. THAT WE SHOULD RISE WITH THE LARK 369

 XV. THAT WE SHOULD LIE DOWN WITH THE LAMB 371

 XVI. THAT A SULKY TEMPER IS A MISFORTUNE . 373

NOTES 377

THE ESSAYS OF ELIA.

THE SOUTH-SEA HOUSE.

READER, in thy passage from the Bank—where thou hast been receiving thy half-yearly dividends (supposing thou art a lean annuitant like myself)—to the Flower Pot, to secure a place for Dalston, or Shacklewell, or some other thy suburban retreat northerly—didst thou never observe a melancholy-looking, handsome, brick and stone edifice, to the left, where Threadneedle Street abuts upon Bishopsgate? I dare say thou hast often admired its magnificent portals ever gaping wide, and disclosing to view a grave court, with cloisters and pillars, with few or no traces of goers-in or comers-out—a desolation something like Balclutha's.[1]

This was once a house of trade—a centre of busy interests. The throng of merchants was here—the quick pulse of gain—and here some forms of business are still kept up, though the soul be long since fled. Here are still to be seen stately porticoes; imposing staircases, offices roomy as the state apartments in palaces—deserted, or thinly peopled with a few straggling clerks; the still more sacred interiors of court and committee rooms, with venerable faces of beadles, door-keepers—directors seated in form on solemn days (to proclaim a dead dividend) at long worm-eaten tables, that have been mahogany, with tarnished gilt-leather coverings, support-

[1] I passed by the walls of Balclutha, and they were desolate.—OSSIAN.

ing massy silver inkstands long since dry;—the oaken wainscots hung with pictures of deceased governors and sub-governors, of Queen Anne, and the two first monarchs of the Brunswick dynasty;—huge charts, which subsequent discoveries have antiquated;—dusty maps of Mexico, dim as dreams, and soundings of the Bay of Panama! The long passages hung with buckets, appended, in idle row, to walls, whose substance might defy any, short of the last, conflagration: with vast ranges of cellarage under all, where dollars and pieces of eight once lay, an "unsunned heap," for Mammon to have solaced his solitary heart withal—long since dissipated, or scattered into air at the blast of the breaking of that famous BUBBLE.——

Such is the SOUTH-SEA HOUSE. At least such it was forty years ago, when I knew it—a magnificent relic! What alterations may have been made in it since, I have had no opportunities of verifying. Time, I take for granted, has not freshened it. No wind has resuscitated the face of the sleeping waters. A thicker crust by this time stagnates upon it. The moths, that were then battening upon its obsolete ledgers and day-books, have rested from their depredations, but other light generations have succeeded, making fine fretwork among their single and double entries. Layers of dust have accumulated (a superfœtation of dirt!) upon the old layers, that seldom used to be disturbed, save by some curious finger, now and then, inquisitive to explore the mode of book-keeping in Queen Anne's reign; or, with less hallowed curiosity, seeking to unveil some of the mysteries of that tremendous HOAX, whose extent the petty peculators of our day look back upon with the same expression of incredulous admiration and hopeless ambition of rivalry as would become the puny face of modern conspiracy contemplating the Titan size of Vaux's superhuman plot.

Peace to the manes of the BUBBLE! Silence and destitution are upon thy walls, proud house, for a memorial!

Situated, as thou art, in the very heart of stirring and living commerce—amid the fret and fever of speculation—with the Bank, and the 'Change, and the India House about thee, in the heyday of present prosperity, with their important faces, as it were, insulting thee, their *poor neighbour out of business*—to the idle and merely contemplative—to such as me, old house! there is a charm in thy quiet:—a cessation—a coolness from business—an indolence almost cloistral—which is delightful! With what reverence have I paced thy great bare rooms and courts at eventide! They spoke of the past:—the shade of some dead accountant, with visionary pen in ear, would flit by me, stiff as in life. Living accounts and accountants puzzle me. I have no skill in figuring. But thy great dead tomes, which scarce three degenerate clerks of the present day could lift from their enshrining shelves—with their old fantastic flourishes and decorative rubric interlacings—their sums in triple columniations, set down with formal superfluity of ciphers—with pious sentences at the beginning, without which our religious ancestors never ventured to open a book of business, or bill of lading—the costly vellum covers of some of them almost persuading us that we are got into some *better library*—are very agreeable and edifying spectacles. I can look upon these defunct dragons with complacency. Thy heavy odd-shaped ivory-handled penknives (our ancestors had everything on a larger scale than we have hearts for) are as good as anything from Herculaneum. The pounce-boxes of our days have gone retrograde.

The very clerks which I remember in the South-Sea House—I speak of forty years back—had an air very different from those in the public offices that I have had to do with since. They partook of the genius of the place!

They were mostly (for the establishment did not admit of superfluous salaries) bachelors. Generally (for they had not much to do) persons of a curious and speculative turn of mind. Old-fashioned, for a reason mentioned before; humourists, for they were of all descriptions; and, not having been brought together in early life (which has a tendency to assimilate the members of corporate bodies to each other), but, for the most part, placed in this house in ripe or middle age, they necessarily carried into it their separate habits and oddities, unqualified, if I may so speak, as into a common stock. Hence they formed a sort of Noah's ark. Odd fishes. A lay-monastery. Domestic retainers in a great house, kept more for show than use. Yet pleasant fellows, full of chat—and not a few among them had arrived at considerable proficiency on the German flute.

The cashier at that time was one Evans, a Cambro-Briton. He had something of the choleric complexion of his countrymen stamped on his visage, but was a worthy, sensible man at bottom. He wore his hair, to the last, powdered and frizzed out, in the fashion which I remember to have seen in caricatures of what were termed, in my young days, *Maccaronies*. He was the last of that race of beaux. Melancholy as a gib-cat over his counter all the forenoon, I think I see him making up his cash (as they call it) with tremulous fingers, as if he feared every one about him was a defaulter; in his hypochondry, ready to imagine himself one; haunted, at least, with the idea of the possibility of his becoming one: his tristful visage clearing up a little over his roast neck of veal at Anderton's at two (where his picture still hangs, taken a little before his death by desire of the master of the coffee-house which he had frequented for the last five-and-twenty years), but not attaining the meridian of its animation till evening brought on the hour of tea and visiting. The simultaneous sound of his well-known rap at the door with the stroke of the clock announcing six, was a topic of never-failing mirth in the families which this dear old bachelor gladdened with his presence. Then was his *forte*, his glorified hour! How would he chirp and expand over a muffin! How would he dilate into secret history! His countryman, Pennant himself, in particular, could not be more eloquent than he in relation to old and new London—the site of old theatres, churches, streets gone to decay—where Rosamond's pond stood—the Mulberry-gardens—and the Conduit in Cheap—with many a pleasant anecdote, derived from paternal tradition, of those grotesque figures which Hogarth has immortalized in his picture of *Noon*—the worthy descendants of those heroic confessors, who, flying to this country from the wrath of Louis the Fourteenth and his dragoons, kept alive the flame of pure religion in the sheltering obscurities of Hog Lane and the vicinity of the Seven Dials!

Deputy, under Evans, was Thomas Tame. He had the air and stoop of a nobleman. You would have taken him for one, had you met him in one of the passages leading to Westminster Hall. By stoop, I mean that gentle bending of the body forwards, which, in great men, must be supposed to be the effect of an habitual condescending attention to the applications of their inferiors. While he held you in converse, you felt strained to the height in the colloquy. The conference over, you were at leisure to smile at the comparative insignificance of the pretensions which had just awed you. His intellect was of the shallowest order. It did not reach to a saw or a proverb. His mind was in its original state of white paper. A sucking babe might have posed him. What was it then? Was he rich? Alas, no! Thomas Tame was very poor. Both he and his wife looked outwardly gentlefolks, when I fear all was not well at all times within. She had a neat meagre person, which it was evident she had not sinned in over-pampering; but in its veins was noble blood. She traced her descent, by some labyrinth of relationship, which I never thoroughly understood, much less can explain with any heraldic certainty at this time of day, to the illustrious but unfortunate house of Derwentwater. This was the secret of Thomas's stoop. This was the thought—the sentiment—the bright solitary star of your lives,—ye mild and happy pair,—which cheered you in the night of intellect, and in the obscurity of your station! This was to you instead of riches, instead of rank, instead of glittering attainments: and it was worth them all together. You insulted none with it; but, while you wore it as a piece of defensive armour only, no insult likewise could reach you through it. *Decus et solamen.*

Of quite another stamp was the then accountant, John Tipp. He neither pretended to high blood, nor in good truth cared one fig about the matter. He "thought an accountant the greatest character in the world, and himself the greatest accountant in it." Yet John was not without his hobby. The fiddle relieved his vacant hours. He sang, certainly, with other notes than to the Orphean lyre. He did, indeed, scream and scrape most abominably. His fine suite of official rooms in Threadneedle Street, which, without anything very substantial appended to them, were enough to enlarge a man's notions of himself that lived in them (I know not who is the occupier of them now [1]), resounded fortnightly to the notes of a concert of "sweet breasts," as our ancestors would have called them, culled from club-rooms, and orchestras—chorus singers—first and second violoncellos—double basses—and clarionets—who ate his cold mutton and drank his punch and praised his ear. He sat like Lord Midas among them. But at the desk Tipp was quite another sort of creature. Thence all ideas, that were purely ornamental, were banished. You could not speak of anything romantic without rebuke. Politics were excluded. A newspaper was thought too refined and abstracted. The whole duty of man consisted in writing off dividend warrants. The striking of the annual balance in the company's books (which, perhaps, differed from the

[1] [I have since been informed, that the present tenant of them is a Mr. Lamb, a gentleman who is happy in the possession of some choice pictures, and among them a rare portrait of Milton, which I mean to do myself the pleasure of going to see, and at the same time to refresh my memory with the sight of old scenes. Mr. Lamb has the character of a right courteous and communicative collector.]

balance of last year in the sum of £25 : 1 : 6) occupied his days and nights for a month previous. Not that Tipp was blind to the deadness of *things* (as they called them in the city) in his beloved house, or did not sigh for a return of the old stirring days when South-Sea hopes were young (he was indeed equal to the wielding of any the most intricate accounts of the most flourishing company in these or those days) : but to a genuine accountant the difference of proceeds is as nothing. The fractional farthing is as dear to his heart as the thousands which stand before it. He is the true actor, who, whether his part be a prince or a peasant, must act it with like intensity. With Tipp form was everything. His life was formal. His actions seemed ruled with a ruler. His pen was not less erring than his heart. He made the best executor in the world : he was plagued with incessant executorships accordingly, which excited his spleen and soothed his vanity in equal ratios. He would swear (for Tipp swore) at the little orphans, whose rights he would guard with a tenacity like the grasp of the dying hand that commended their interests to his protection. With all this there was about him a sort of timidity (his few enemies used to give it a worse name) —a something which, in reverence to the dead, we will place, if you please, a little on this side of the heroic. Nature certainly had been pleased to endow John Tipp with a sufficient measure of the principle of self-preservation. There is a cowardice which we do not despise, because it has nothing base or treacherous in its elements ; it betrays itself, not you : it is mere temperament ; the absence of the romantic and the enterprising ; it sees a lion in the way, and will not, with Fortinbras, "greatly find quarrel in a straw," when some supposed honour is at stake. Tipp never mounted the box of a stage-coach in his life ; or leaned against the rails of a balcony ; or walked upon the ridge of a parapet ; or looked down a precipice ; or let off a gun ; or went upon a water-party ; or would willingly let you go if he could have helped it :

neither was it recorded of him, that for lucre, or for intimidation, he ever forsook friend or principle.

Whom next shall we summon from the dusty dead, in whom common qualities become uncommon? Can I forget thee, Henry Man, the wit, the polished man of letters, the *author*, of the South-Sea House? who never enteredst thy office in a morning or quittedst it in midday (what didst *thou* in an office?) without some quirk that left a sting! Thy gibes and thy jokes are now extinct, or survive but in two forgotten volumes, which I had the good fortune to rescue from a stall in Barbican, not three days ago, and found thee terse, fresh, epigrammatic, as alive. Thy wit is a little gone by in these fastidious days—thy topics are staled by the "new-born gauds" of the time:—but great thou used to be in Public Ledgers, and in Chronicles, upon Chatham, and Shelburne, and Rockingham, and Howe, and Burgoyne, and Clinton, and the war which ended in the tearing from Great Britain her rebellious colonies,—and Keppel, and Wilkes, and Sawbridge, and Bull, and Dunning, and Pratt, and Richmond—and such small politics.——

A little less facetious, and a great deal more obstreperous, was fine rattling, rattleheaded Plumer. He was descended,—not in a right line, reader (for his lineal pretensions, like his personal, favoured a little of the sinister bend)—from the Plumers of Hertfordshire. So tradition gave him out: and certain family features not a little sanctioned the opinion. Certainly old Walter Plumer (his reputed author) had been a rake in his days, and visited much in Italy, and had seen the world. He was uncle, bachelor-uncle, to the fine old whig still living, who has represented the county in so many successive parliaments, and has a fine old mansion near Ware. Walter flourished in George the Second's days, and was the same who was summoned before the House of Commons about a business of franks, with the old Duchess of Marlborough. You may read of it in Johnson's Life of Cave. Cave came off cleverly in that business. It is

certain our Plumer did nothing to discountenance the
rumour. He rather seemed pleased whenever it was,
with all gentleness insinuated. But besides his family
pretensions, Plumer was an engaging fellow, and sang
gloriously.——

Not so sweetly sang Plumer as thou sangest, mild,
child-like, pastoral M——; a flute's breathing less divinely
whispering than thy Arcadian melodies, when, in tones
worthy of Arden, thou didst chant that song sung by
Amiens to the banished duke, which proclaims the winter
wind more lenient than for a man to be ungrateful. Thy
sire was old surly M——, the unapproachable church-
warden of Bishopsgate. He knew not what he did, when
he begat thee, like spring, gentle offspring of blustering
winter:—only unfortunate in thy ending, which should
have been mild, conciliatory, swan-like.——

Much remains to sing. Many fantastic shapes rise
up, but they must be mine in private:—already I have
fooled the reader to the top of his bent; else could I
omit that strange creature Woollett, who existed in trying
the question, and *bought litigations!*—and still stranger,
inimitable, solemn Hepworth, from whose gravity Newton
might have deduced the law of gravitation. How pro-
foundly would he nib a pen—with what deliberation
would he wet a wafer!——

But it is time to close—night's wheels are rattling
fast over me—it is proper to have done with this solemn
mockery.

Reader, what if I have been playing with thee all this
while—peradventure the very *names*, which I have summoned up before thee, are fantastic—insubstantial—like
Henry Pimpernel, and old John Naps of Greece:——

Be satisfied that something answering to them has had
a being. Their importance is from the past.

OXFORD IN THE VACATION.

CASTING a preparatory glance at the bottom of this article—as the very connoisseur in prints, with cursory eye (which, while it reads, seems as though it read not), never fails to consult the *quis sculpsit* in the corner, before he pronounces some rare piece to be a Vivares, or a Woollet—methinks I hear you exclaim, Reader, *Who is Elia?*

Because in my last I tried to divert thee with some half-forgotten humours of some old clerks defunct, in an old house of business, long since gone to decay, doubtless you have already set me down in your mind as one of the self-same college—a votary of the desk—a notched and cropt scrivener—one that sucks his sustenance, as certain sick people are said to do, through a quill.

Well, I do agnise something of the sort. I confess that it is my humour, my fancy — in the fore-part of the day, when the mind of your man of letters requires some relaxation (and none better than such as at first sight seems most abhorrent from his beloved studies)—to while away some good hours of my time in the contemplation of indigos, cottons, raw silks, piece-goods, flowered or otherwise. In the first place   *   *   * and then it sends you home with such increased appetite to your books   *   *   *   *   *   * not to say, that your outside sheets, and waste wrappers of foolscap, do receive into them, most kindly and naturally, the impression of sonnets, epigrams, *essays*—so that the very parings of a counting-house are, in some sort, the settings up of an author. The enfranchised quill, that has plodded all the morning among the cart-rucks of figures and ciphers, frisks and curvets so at its ease over the flowery carpet-ground of a midnight dissertation.— It feels its promotion.   *   *   *   *

So that you see, upon the whole, the literary dignity of *Elia* is very little, if at all, compromised in the condescension.

Not that, in my anxious detail of the many commodities incidental to the life of a public office, I would be thought blind to certain flaws, which a cunning carper might be able to pick in this Joseph's vest. And here I must have leave, in the fulness of my soul, to regret the abolition, and doing-away-with altogether, of those consolatory interstices, and sprinklings of freedom, through the four seasons,—the *red-letter days*, now become, to all intents and purposes, *dead-letter days*. There was Paul, and Stephen, and Barnabas—

Andrew and John, men famous in old times

—we were used to keep all their days holy, as long back as when I was at school at Christ's. I remember their effigies, by the same token, in the old Baskett Prayer Book. There hung Peter in his uneasy posture—holy Bartlemy in the troublesome act of flaying, after the famous Marsyas by Spagnoletti.—I honoured them all, and could almost have wept the defalcation of Iscariot—so much did we love to keep holy memories sacred:—only methought I a little grudged at the coalition of the *better Jude* with Simon—clubbing (as it were) their sanctities together, to make up one poor gaudy-day between them—as an economy unworthy of the dispensation.

These were bright visitations in a scholar's and a clerk's life—"far off their coming shone." I was as good as an almanac in those days. I could have told you such a saint's-day falls out next week, or the week after. Peradventure the Epiphany, by some periodical infelicity, would, once in six years, merge in a Sabbath. Now am I little better than one of the profane. Let me not be thought to arraign the wisdom of my civil superiors, who have judged the further observation of these holy tides to be papistical, superstitious. Only in a custom of such long standing, methinks, if their Holinesses the Bishops had, in decency, been first sounded—but I am wading out of my depths. I am not the man to decide the limits of civil and ecclesiastical authority—I am plain Elia—no Selden, nor Archbishop Usher—though at present in the thick of their books, here in the heart of learning, under the shadow of the mighty Bodley.

I can here play the gentleman, enact the student. To such a one as myself, who has been defrauded in his young years of the sweet food of academic institution, nowhere is so pleasant, to while away a few idle weeks at, as one or other of the Universities. Their vacation, too, at this time of the year, falls in so pat with *ours*. Here I can take my walks unmolested, and fancy myself of what degree or standing I please. I seem admitted *ad eundem*. I fetch up past opportunities. I can rise at the chapel-bell, and dream that it rings for *me*. In moods of humility I can be a Sizar, or a Servitor. When the peacock vein rises, I strut a Gentleman Commoner. In graver moments, I proceed Master of Arts. Indeed I do not think I am much unlike that respectable character. I have seen your dim-eyed vergers, and bed-makers in spectacles, drop a bow or a curtsy, as I pass, wisely mistaking me for something of the sort. I go about in black, which favours the notion. Only in Christ Church reverend quadrangle I can be content to pass for nothing short of a Seraphic Doctor.

The walks at these times are so much one's own,—the tall trees of Christ's, the groves of Magdalen! The halls deserted, and with open doors, inviting one to slip in unperceived, and pay a devoir to some Founder, or noble or royal Benefactress (that should have been ours) whose portrait seems to smile upon their over-looked beadsman, and to adopt me for their own. Then, to take a peep in by the way at the butteries, and sculleries, redolent of antique hospitality: the immense caves of kitchens, kitchen fireplaces, cordial recesses ; ovens whose first pies were baked four centuries ago; and spits which have cooked for Chaucer! Not the meanest minister among the dishes but is hallowed to me through his imagination, and the Cook goes forth a Manciple.

Antiquity! thou wondrous charm, what art thou? that, being nothing, art everything! When thou *wert*, thou wert not antiquity — then thou wert nothing, but hadst a remoter *antiquity*, as thou calledst it, to look back to with blind veneration; thou thyself being to thyself flat, jejune, *modern!* What mystery lurks in this retroversion? or what half Januses[1] are we, that cannot look forward with the same idolatry with which we for ever revert! The mighty future is as nothing, being everything! the past is everything, being nothing!

What were thy *dark ages?* Surely the sun rose as brightly then as now, and man got him to his work in the morning? Why is it we can never hear mention of them without an accompanying feeling, as though a palpable obscure had dimmed the face of things, and that our ancestors wandered to and fro groping!

Above all thy rarities, old Oxenford, what do most arride and solace me, are thy repositories of mouldering learning, thy shelves——

What a place to be in is an old library! It seems as though all the souls of all the writers, that have bequeathed their labours to these Bodleians, were reposing here, as in some dormitory, or middle state. I do not want to handle, to profane the leaves, their winding-sheets. I could as soon dislodge a shade. I seem to inhale learning, walking amid their foliage; and the odour of their old moth-scented coverings is fragrant as the first bloom of those sciential apples which grew amid the happy orchard.

Still less have I curiosity to disturb the elder repose of MSS. Those *variæ lectiones*, so tempting to the more erudite palates, do but disturb and unsettle my faith. I am no Herculanean raker. The credit of the three

---

[1] Januses of one face. Sir Thomas Browne.

witnesses might have slept unimpeached for me. I leave these curiosities to Porson, and to G. D.—whom, by the way, I found busy as a moth over some rotten archive, rummaged out of some seldom-explored press, in a nook at Oriel. With long poring, he is grown almost into a book. He stood as passive as one by the side of the old shelves. I longed to new-coat him in russia, and assign him his place. He might have mustered for a tall Scapula.

D. is assiduous in his visits to these seats of learning. No inconsiderable portion of his moderate fortune, I apprehend, is consumed in journeys between them and Clifford's Inn—where, like a dove on the asp's nest, he has long taken up his unconscious abode, amid an incongruous assembly of attorneys, attorneys' clerks, apparitors, promoters, vermin of the law, among whom he sits, "in calm and sinless peace." The fangs of the law pierce him not—the winds of litigation blow over his humble chambers—the hard sheriff's officer moves his hat as he passes—legal nor illegal discourtesy touches him—none thinks of offering violence or injustice to him—you would as soon "strike an abstract idea."

D. has been engaged, he tells me, through a course of laborious years, in an investigation into all curious matter connected with the two Universities; and has lately lit upon a MS. collection of charters, relative to C——, by which he hopes to settle some disputed points—particularly that long controversy between them as to priority of foundation. The ardour with which he engages in these liberal pursuits, I am afraid, has not met with all the encouragement it deserved, either here or at C——. Your caputs, and heads of colleges, care less than anybody else about these questions.—Contented to suck the milky fountains of their Alma Maters, without inquiring into the venerable gentlewomen's years, they rather hold such curiosities to be impertinent—unreverend. They have their good glebe lands *in manu*, and care not much to rake into the title-deeds. I gather at least so much from other sources, for D. is not a man to complain.

D. started like an unbroken heifer, when I interrupted him. *A priori* it was not very probable that we should have met in Oriel. But D. would have done the same, had I accosted him on the sudden in his own walks in Clifford's Inn, or in the Temple. In addition to a provoking short-sightedness (the effect of late studies and watchings at the midnight oil) D. is the most absent of men. He made a call the other morning at our friend M.'s in Bedford Square; and, finding nobody at home, was ushered into the hall, where, asking for pen and ink, with great exactitude of purpose he enters me his name in the book which ordinarily lies about in such places, to record the failures of the untimely or unfortunate visitor—and takes his leave with many ceremonies, and professions of regret. Some two or three hours after, his walking destinies returned him into the same neighbourhood again, and again the quiet image of the fireside circle at M.'s—Mrs. M. presiding at it like a Queen Lar, with pretty A. S. at her side—striking irresistibly on his fancy, he makes another call (forgetting that they were "certainly not to return from the country before that day week"), and disappointed a second time, inquires for pen and paper as before: again the book is brought, and in the line just above that in which he is about to print his second name (his re-script)—his first name (scarce dry) looks out upon him like another Sosia, or as if a man should suddenly encounter his own duplicate! The effect may be conceived. D. made many a good resolution against any such lapses in future. I hope he will not keep them too rigorously.

For with G. D.—to be absent from the body, is sometimes (not to speak it profanely) to be present with the Lord. At the very time when, personally encountering thee, he passes on with no recognition—or, being stopped, starts like a thing surprised—at that moment, Reader, he is on Mount Tabor—or Parnassus—or co-sphered with Plato—or, with Harrington, framing "immortal commonwealths"—devising some plan of amelioration to thy country, or thy species —peradventure meditating some individual kindness or courtesy, to be done to *thee thyself*, the returning consciousness of which made him to start so guiltily at thy obtruded personal presence.

[D. commenced life, after a course of hard study in the house of "pure Emanuel," as usher to a knavish fanatic schoolmaster at * * *, at a salary of eight pounds per annum, with board and lodging. Of this poor stipend, he never received above half in all the laborious years he served this man. He tells a pleasant anecdote, that when poverty, staring out at his ragged knees, has sometimes compelled him, against the modesty of his nature, to hint at arrears, Dr. * * * would take no immediate notice, but after supper, when the school was called together to evensong, he would never fail to introduce some instructive homily against riches, and the corruption of the heart occasioned through the desire of them—ending with "Lord, keep Thy servants, above all things, from the heinous sin of avarice. Having food and raiment, let us therewithal be content. Give me Agur's wish"—and the like—which, to the little auditory, sounded like a doctrine full of Christian prudence and simplicity, but to poor D. was a receipt in full for that quarter's demand at least.

And D. has been under-working for himself ever since; —drudging at low rates for unappreciating booksellers, —wasting his fine erudition in silent corrections of the classics, and in those unostentatious but solid services to learning which commonly fall to the lot of laborious scholars, who have not the heart to sell themselves to the best advantage. He has published poems, which do not sell, because their character is unobtrusive, like his own, and because he has been too much absorbed in ancient literature to know what the popular mark in poetry is, even if he could have hit it. And, therefore, his verses are properly, what he terms them, *crotchets;* voluntaries; odes to liberty and spring; effusions; little tributes and offerings, left behind him upon tables and window-seats at parting from friends' houses; and from all the inns of hospitality, where he has been courteously (or but tolerably) received in his pilgrimage. If his muse of kindness halt a little behind the strong lines in fashion in this excitement-loving age, his prose is the best of the sort in the world, and exhibits a faithful transcript of his own healthy, natural mind, and cheerful, innocent tone of conversation.]

D. is delightful anywhere, but he is at the best in such places as these. He cares not much for Bath. He is out of his element at Buxton, at Scarborough, or Harrowgate. The Cam and the Isis are to him "better than all the waters of Damascus." On the Muses' hill he is happy, and good, as one of the Shepherds on the Delectable Mountains; and when he goes about with you to show you the halls and colleges, you think you have with you the Interpreter at the House Beautiful.

CHRIST'S HOSPITAL

FIVE AND THIRTY YEARS AGO.

In Mr. Lamb's "Works," published a year or two since, I find a magnificent eulogy on my old school,[1] such as it was, or now appears to him to have been, between the years 1782 and 1789. It happens, very oddly, that my own standing at Christ's was nearly corresponding with his; and, with all gratitude to him for his enthusiasm for the cloisters, I think he has contrived to bring together whatever can be said in praise of them, dropping all the other side of the argument most ingeniously.

I remember L. at school; and can well recollect that he had some peculiar advantages, which I and others of his schoolfellows had not. His friends lived in town, and were near at hand; and he had the privilege of going to

[1] Recollections of Christ's Hospital

see them, almost as often as he wished, through some invidious distinction, which was denied to us. The present worthy sub-treasurer to the Inner Temple can explain how that happened. He had his tea and hot rolls in a morning, while we were battening upon our quarter of a penny loaf—our *crug*—moistened with attenuated small beer, in wooden piggins, smacking of the pitched leathern jack it was poured from. Our Monday's milk porritch, blue and tasteless, and the pease soup of Saturday, coarse and choking, were enriched for him with a slice of "extraordinary bread and butter," from the hot-loaf of the Temple. The Wednesday's mess of millet, somewhat less repugnant (we had three banyan to four meat days in the week)—was endeared to his palate with a lump of double-refined, and a smack of ginger (to make it go down the more glibly) or the fragrant cinnamon. In lieu of our *half-pickled* Sundays, or *quite fresh* boiled beef on Thursdays (strong as *caro equina*), with detestable marigolds floating in the pail to poison the broth—our scanty mutton scrags on Fridays—and rather more savoury, but grudging, portions of the same flesh, rotten-roasted or rare, on the Tuesdays (the only dish which excited our appetites, and disappointed our stomachs, in almost equal proportion)—he had his hot plate of roast veal, or the more tempting griskin (exotics unknown to our palates), cooked in the paternal kitchen (a great thing), and brought him daily by his maid or aunt! I remember the good old relative (in whom love forbade pride) squatting down upon some old stone in a by-nook of the cloisters, disclosing the viands (of higher regale than those cates which the ravens ministered to the Tishbite); and the contending passions of L. at the unfolding. There was love for the bringer; shame for the thing brought, and the manner of its bringing; sympathy for those who were too many to share in it; and, at top of all, hunger (eldest, strongest of the passions!) predominant, breaking down the stony fences of shame, and awkwardness, and a troubling over-consciousness.

I was a poor friendless boy. My parents, and those who should care for me, were far away. Those few acquaintances of theirs, which they could reckon upon as being kind to me in the great city, after a little forced notice, which they had the grace to take of me on my first arrival in town, soon grew tired of my holiday visits. They seemed to them to recur too often, though I thought them few enough; and, one after another, they all failed me, and I felt myself alone among six hundred playmates.

O the cruelty of separating a poor lad from his early homestead! The yearnings which I used to have towards it in those unfledged years! How, in my dreams, would my native town (far in the west) come back, with its church, and trees, and faces! How I would wake weeping, and in the anguish of my heart exclaim upon sweet Calne in Wiltshire!

To this late hour of my life, I trace impressions left by the recollection of those friendless holidays. The long warm days of summer never return but they bring with them a gloom from the haunting memory of those *whole-day leaves*, when, by some strange arrangement, we were turned out, for the live-long day, upon our own hands, whether we had friends to go to, or none. I remember those bathing-excursions to the New River, which L. recalls with such relish, better, I think, than he can—for he was a home-seeking lad, and did not much care for such water-pastimes:—How merrily we would sally forth into the fields; and strip under the first warmth of the sun; and wanton like young dace in the streams; getting us appetites for noon, which those of us that were penniless (our scanty morning crust long since exhausted) had not the means of allaying—while the cattle, and the birds, and the fishes, were at feed about us, and we had nothing to satisfy our cravings—the very beauty of the day, and the exercise of the pastime, and the sense of liberty, setting a keener edge upon them!—How faint and languid, finally, we would return, towards night-fall, to our desired morsel, half-rejoicing, half-reluctant, that the hours of our uneasy liberty had expired!

It was worse in the days of winter, to go prowling about the streets objectless—shivering at cold windows of print shops, to extract a little amusement; or haply, as a last resort, in the hopes of a little novelty, to pay a fifty-times repeated visit (where our individual faces should be as well known to the warden as those of his own charges) to the Lions in the Tower—to whose levée, by courtesy immemorial, we had a prescriptive title to admission.

L.'s governor (so we called the patron who presented us to the foundation) lived in a manner under his paternal roof. Any complaint which he had to make was sure of being attended to. This was understood at Christ's, and was an effectual screen to him against the severity of masters, or worse tyranny of the monitors. The oppressions of these young brutes are heart-sickening to call to recollection. I have been called out of my bed, and *waked for the purpose*, in the coldest winter nights—and this not once, but night after night—in my shirt, to receive the discipline of a leathern thong, with eleven other sufferers, because it pleased my callow overseer, when there has been any talking heard after we were gone to bed, to make the six last beds in the dormitory, where the youngest children of us slept, answerable for an offence they neither dared to commit, nor had the power to hinder. — The same execrable tyranny drove the younger part of us from the fires, when our feet were perishing with snow; and, under the cruellest penalties, forbade the indulgence of a drink of water, when we lay in sleepless summer nights, fevered with the season and the day's sports.

There was one H——, who, I learned in after days, was seen expiating some maturer offence in the hulks. (Do I flatter myself in fancying that this might be the planter of that name, who suffered—at Nevis, I think, or St. Kitts,—some few years since? My friend Tobin was the benevolent instrument of bringing him to the gallows.) This petty Nero actually branded a boy, who had offended him, with a red-hot iron ; and nearly starved forty of us, with exacting contributions, to the one half of our bread, to pamper a young ass, which, incredible as it may seem, with the connivance of the nurse's daughter (a young flame of his) he had contrived to smuggle in, and keep upon the leads of the *ward*, as they called our dormitories. This game went on for better than a week, till the foolish beast, not able to fare well but he must cry roast meat—happier than Caligula's minion, could he have kept his own counsel—but, foolisher, alas! than any of his species in the fables—waxing fat, and kicking, in the fulness of bread, one unlucky minute would needs proclaim his good fortune to the world below ; and, laying out his simple throat, blew such a ram's horn blast, as (toppling down the walls of his own Jericho) set concealment any longer at defiance. The client was dismissed, with certain attentions, to Smithfield ; but I never understood that the patron underwent any censure on the occasion. This was in the stewardship of L.'s admired Perry.

Under the same *facile* administration, can L. have forgotten the cool impunity with which the nurses used to carry away openly, in open platters, for their own tables, one out of two of every hot joint, which the careful matron had been seeing scrupulously weighed out for our dinners? These things were daily practised in that magnificent apartment, which L. (grown connoisseur since, we presume) praises so highly for the grand paintings "by Verrio and others," with which it is "hung round and adorned." But the sight of sleek well-fed blue-coat boys in pictures was, at that time, I believe, little consolatory to him, or us, the living ones, who saw the better part of our provisions carried away before our faces by harpies ; and ourselves reduced (with the Trojan in the hall of Dido)

To feed our mind with idle portraiture.

L. has recorded the repugnance of the school to *gags*, or the fat of fresh beef boiled ; and sets it down to some superstition. But these unctuous morsels are never grateful to young palates (children are universally fat-haters), and in strong, coarse, boiled meats, *unsalted*, are detestable. A *gag-eater* in our time was equivalent to a *goule*, and held in equal detestation. —— suffered under the imputation :

> . . . . 'Twas said
> He ate strange flesh.

He was observed, after dinner, carefully to gather up the remnants left at his table (not many, nor very choice fragments, you may credit me)—and, in an especial manner, these disreputable morsels, which he would convey away, and secretly stow in the settle that stood at his bedside. None saw when he ate them. It was rumoured that he privately devoured them in the night. He was watched, but no traces of such midnight practices were discoverable. Some reported, that, on leave-days, he had been seen to carry out of the bounds a large blue check handkerchief, full of something. This then must be the accursed thing. Conjecture next was at work to imagine how he could dispose of it. Some said he sold it to the beggars. This belief generally prevailed. He went about moping. None spake to him. No one would play with him. He was excommunicated ; put out of the pale of the school. He was too powerful a boy to be beaten, but he underwent every mode of that negative punishment, which is more grievous than many stripes. Still he persevered. At length he was observed by two of his schoolfellows, who were determined to get at the secret, and had traced him one leave-day for that purpose, to enter a large worn-out building, such as there exist specimens of in Chancery Lane, which are let out to various scales of pauperism, with open door, and a common staircase. After him they silently slunk in, and followed by stealth up four flights, and saw him tap at a poor wicket, which was opened by an aged woman, meanly clad. Suspicion was now ripened into certainty. The informers had secured their victim. They had him in their toils. Accusation was formally preferred, and retribution most signal was looked for. Mr. Hathaway, the then steward (for this happened a little after my time), with that patient sagacity which tempered all his conduct, determined to investigate the matter, before he proceeded to sentence. The result was, that the supposed mendicants, the receivers or purchasers of the mysterious scraps, turned out to be the parents of ——, an honest couple come to decay,—whom this seasonable supply had, in all probability, saved from mendicancy: and that this young stork, at the expense of his own good name, had all this while been only feeding the old birds!—The governors on this occasion, much to their honour, voted a present relief to the family of ——, and presented him with a silver medal. The lesson which the steward read upon RASH JUDGMENT, on the occasion of publicly delivering the medal to ——, I believe, would not be lost upon his auditory.—I had left school then, but I well remember ——. He was a tall, shambling youth, with a cast in his eye, not at all calculated to conciliate hostile prejudices. I have since seen him carrying a baker's basket. I think I heard he did not do quite so well by himself as he had done by the old folks.

I was a hypochondriac lad; and the sight of a boy in fetters, upon the day of my first putting on the blue clothes, was not exactly fitted to assuage the natural terrors of initiation. I was of tender years, barely turned of seven; and had only read of such things in books, or seen them but in dreams. I was told he had *run away*. This was the punishment for the first offence. As a novice I was soon after taken to see the dungeons. These were little, square, Bedlam cells, where a boy could just lie at his length upon straw and a blanket—a mattress, I think, was afterwards substituted—with a peep of light, let in askance, from a prison-orifice at top, barely enough to read by. Here the poor boy was locked in by himself all day, without sight of any but the porter who brought him his bread and water—who *might not speak to him ;*—or of the beadle, who came twice a week to call him out to receive his periodical chastisement, which was almost welcome, because it separated him for a brief interval from solitude: —and here he was shut up by himself *of nights*, out of the reach of any sound, to suffer whatever horrors the weak nerves, and superstition incident to his time of life, might subject him to.[1] This was the penalty for the second offence. Wouldst thou like, Reader, to see what became of him in the next degree?

The culprit, who had been a third time an offender, and whose expulsion was at this time deemed irreversible, was brought forth, as at some solemn *auto da fé*, arrayed in uncouth and most appalling attire, all trace of his late "watchet-weeds" carefully effaced, he was exposed in a jacket, resembling those which London lamplighters formerly delighted in, with a cap of the same. The effect of this divestiture was such as the ingenious devisers of it could have anticipated. With his pale and frightened features, it was as if some of those disfigurements in Dante had seized upon him. In this disguisement he was brought into the hall (*L.'s favourite state-room*), where awaited him the whole number of his schoolfellows, whose joint lessons and sports he was thenceforth to share no more ; the awful presence of the steward, to be seen for the last time ; of the executioner beadle, clad in his state robe for the occasion ; and of two faces more, of direr import, because never but in these extremities visible. These were governors ; two of whom, by choice, or charter, were always accustomed to officiate at these *Ultima Supplicia* ; not to mitigate (so at least we understood it), but to enforce the uttermost stripe. Old Bamber Gascoigne, and Peter Aubert, I remember, were colleagues on one occasion, when the beadle turning rather pale, a glass of brandy was

[1] One or two instances of lunacy, or attempted suicide, accordingly, at length convinced the governors of the impolicy of this part of the sentence, and the midnight torture to the spirits was dispensed with.— This fancy of dungeons for children was a sprout of Howard's brain ; for which (saving the reverence due to Holy Paul) methinks I could willingly spit upon his statue.

ordered to prepare him for the mysteries. The scourging was, after the old Roman fashion, long and stately. The lictor accompanied the criminal quite round the hall. We were generally too faint with attending to the previous disgusting circumstances to make accurate report with our eyes of the degree of corporal suffering inflicted. Report, of course, gave out the back knotty and livid. After scourging, he was made over, in his *San Benito*, to his friends, if he had any (but commonly such poor runagates were friendless), or to his parish officer, who, to enhance the effect of the scene, had his station allotted to him on the outside of the hall gate.

These solemn pageantries were not played off so often as to spoil the general mirth of the community. We had plenty of exercise and recreation *after* school hours; and, for myself, I must confess, that I was never happier than *in* them. The Upper and the Lower Grammar Schools were held in the same room: and an imaginary line only divided their bounds. Their character was as different as that of the inhabitants on the two sides of the Pyrenees. The Rev. James Boyer was the Upper Master, but the Rev. Matthew Field presided over that portion of the apartment, of which I had the good fortune to be a member. We lived a life as careless as birds. We talked and did just what we pleased, and nobody molested us. We carried an accidence, or a grammar, for form; but, for any trouble it gave us, we might take two years in getting through the verbs deponent, and another two in forgetting all that we had learned about them. There was now and then the formality of saying a lesson, but if you had not learned it, a brush across the shoulders (just enough to disturb a fly) was the sole remonstrance. Field never used the rod; and in truth he wielded the cane with no great good will—holding it "like a dancer." It looked in his hands rather like an emblem than an instrument of authority; and an emblem, too, he was ashamed of. He was a good easy man, that did not care to ruffle his own peace, nor perhaps set any great consideration upon the value of juvenile time. He came among us, now and then, but often staid away whole days from us; and when he came, it made no difference to us—he had his private room to retire to, the short time he staid, to be out of the sound of our noise. Our mirth and uproar went on. We had classics of our own, without being beholden to " insolent Greece or haughty Rome," that passed current among us— Peter Wilkins—The Adventures of the Hon. Captain Robert Boyle—the Fortunate Blue-coat Boy—and the like. Or we cultivated a turn for mechanic and scientific operations; making little sun-dials of paper; or weaving those ingenious parentheses, called *cat-cradles;* or making dry peas to dance upon the end of a tin pipe; or studying the art military over that laudable game " French and English," and a hundred other such devices to pass away the time— mixing the useful with the agreeable—as would have made the souls of Rousseau and John Locke chuckle to have seen us.

Matthew Field belonged to that class of modest divines who affect to mix in equal proportion the *gentleman*, the *scholar*, and the *Christian:* but, I know not how, the first ingredient is generally found to be the predominating dose in the composition. He was engaged in gay parties, or with his courtly bow at some episcopal levée, when he should have been attending upon us. He had for many years the classical charge of a hundred children, during the four or five first years of their education; and his very highest form seldom proceeded further than two or three of the introductory fables of Phædrus. How things were suffered to go on thus, I cannot guess. Boyer, who was the proper person to have remedied these abuses, always affected, perhaps felt, a delicacy in interfering in a province not strictly his own. I have not been without my suspicions, that he was not altogether displeased at the contrast we presented to his end of the school. We were a sort of Helots to his young Spartans. He would sometimes, with ironic deference, send to borrow a rod of the Under Master, and then, with Sardonic grin, observe to one of his upper boys, "how neat and fresh the twigs looked." While his pale students were battering their brains over Xenophon and Plato, with a silence as deep as that enjoined by the Samite, we were enjoying ourselves at our ease in our little Goshen. We saw a little into the secrets of his discipline, and the prospect did but the more reconcile us to our lot. His thunders rolled innocuous for us; his storms came near, but never touched us; contrary to Gideon's miracle, while all around were drenched, our fleece was dry.[1] His boys turned out the better scholars; we, I suspect, have the advantage in temper. His pupils cannot speak of him without something of terror allaying their gratitude; the remembrance of Field comes back with all the soothing images of indolence, and summer slumbers, and work like play, and innocent idleness, and Elysian exemptions, and life itself a "playing holiday."

Though sufficiently removed from the jurisdiction of Boyer, we were near enough (as I have said) to understand a little of his system. We occasionally heard sounds of the *Ululantes*, and caught glances of Tartarus. B. was a rabid pedant. His English style was crampt to barbarism. His Easter anthems (for his duty obliged him to those periodical flights) were grating as scrannel pipes.[2] —He would laugh—ay, and heartily—but then it must be at Flaccus's quibble about *Rex*—— or at the *tristis severitas in vultu*, or *inspicere in patinas*, of Terence— thin jests, which at their first broaching could hardly have had *vis* enough to move a Roman muscle.—He had two

---

[1] Cowley.
[2] In this and everything B. was the antipodes of his coadjutor. While the former was digging his brains for crude anthems, worth a pig-nut, F. would be recreating his gentlemanly fancy in the more flowery walks of the Muses. A little dramatic effusion of his, under the name of Vertumnus and Pomona, is not yet forgotten by the chroniclers of that sort of literature. It was accepted by Garrick, but the town did not give it their sanction.—B. used to say of it, in a way of half-compliment, half-irony, that it was *too classical for representation*.

wigs, both pedantic, but of different omen. The one
serene, smiling, fresh powdered, betokening a mild day.
The other, an old discoloured, unkempt, angry caxon, denoting frequent and bloody execution. Woe to the school,
when he made his morning appearance in his *passy*, or
passionate wig. No comet expounded surer.—J. B. had
a heavy hand. I have known him double his knotty fist
at a poor trembling child (the maternal milk hardly dry
upon its lips) with a "Sirrah, do you presume to set your
wits at me?"—Nothing was more common than to see
him make a headlong entry into the school-room, from his
inner recess, or library, and, with turbulent eye, singling
out a lad, roar out, "Od's my life, sirrah" (his favourite
adjuration), "I have a great mind to whip you,"—then,
with as sudden a retracting impulse, fling back into his
lair—and, after a cooling lapse of some minutes (during
which all but the culprit had totally forgotten the context)
drive headlong out again, piecing out his imperfect sense,
as if it had been some Devil's Litany, with the expletory
yell—"*and I* WILL *too.*"—In his gentler moods, when
the *rabidus furor* was assuaged, he had resort to an ingenious method, peculiar, for what I have heard, to himself, of whipping the boy, and reading the Debates, at the
same time; a paragraph and a lash between; which in
those times, when parliamentary oratory was most at a
height and flourishing in these realms, was not calculated
to impress the patient with a veneration for the diffuser
graces of rhetoric.

Once, and but once, the uplifted rod was known to fall
ineffectual from his hand—when droll squinting W——
having been caught putting the inside of the master's desk
to a use for which the architect had clearly not designed
it, to justify himself, with great simplicity averred, that
he did not know that the thing had been forewarned. This
exquisite irrecognition of any law antecedent to the *oral*
or *declaratory*, struck so irresistibly upon the fancy of all
who heard it (the pedagogue himself not excepted) that
remission was unavoidable.

L. has given credit to B.'s great merits as an instructor. Coleridge, in his literary life, has pronounced a more intelligible and ample encomium on them. The author of the Country Spectator doubts not to compare him with the ablest teachers of antiquity. Perhaps we cannot dismiss him better than with the pious ejaculation of C.— when he heard that his old master was on his death-bed: "Poor J. B.!—may all his faults be forgiven; and may he be wafted to bliss by little cherub boys, all head and wings, with no *bottoms* to reproach his sublunary infirmities."

Under him were many good and sound scholars bred. First Grecian of my time was Lancelot Pepys Stevens, kindest of boys and men, since Co-grammar-master (and inseparable companion) with Dr. T-----e. What an edifying spectacle did this brace of friends present to those who remembered the anti-socialities of their predecessors! —You never met the one by chance in the street without a wonder, which was quickly dissipated by the almost immediate subappearance of the other. Generally arm-in-arm, these kindly coadjutors lightened for each other the toilsome duties of their profession, and when, in advanced age, one found it convenient to retire, the other was not long in discovering that it suited him to lay down the fasces also. Oh, it is pleasant, as it is rare, to find the same arm linked in yours at forty, which at thirteen helped it to turn over the *Cicero De Amicitiâ*, or some tale of Antique Friendship, which the young heart even then was burning to anticipate!—Co-Grecian with S. was Th——, who has since executed with ability various diplomatic functions at the Northern courts. Th— was a tall, dark, saturnine youth, sparing of speech, with raven locks.—Thomas Fanshaw Middleton followed him (now Bishop of Calcutta), a scholar and a gentleman in his teens. He has the reputation of an excellent critic; and is author (besides the Country Spectator) of a Treatise on the Greek Article, against Sharpe. M. is said to bear his mitre high in India, where the *regni novitas* (I dare say) sufficiently justifies the bearing. A humility quite as primitive as that of Jewel or Hooker might not be exactly fitted to impress the minds of those Anglo-Asiatic diocesans with a reverence for home institutions, and the church which those fathers watered. The manners of M. at school, though firm, were mild and unassuming.—Next to M. (if not senior to him) was Richards, author of the Aboriginal Britons, the most spirited of the Oxford Prize Poems; a pale, studious Grecian.—Then followed poor S——, ill-fated M——! of these the Muse is silent.

> Finding some of Edward's race
> Unhappy, pass their annals by.

Come back into memory, like as thou wert in the day-spring of thy fancies, with hope like a fiery column before thee—the dark pillar not yet turned—Samuel Taylor Coleridge—Logician, Metaphysician, Bard!—How have I seen the casual passer through the Cloisters stand still, entranced with admiration (while he weighed the disproportion between the *speech* and the *garb* of the young Mirandula), to hear thee unfold, in thy deep and sweet intonations, the mysteries of Jamblichus, or Plotinus (for even in those years thou waxedst not pale at such philosophic draughts), or reciting Homer in his Greek, or Pindar—— while the walls of the old Grey Friars re-echoed to the accents of the *inspired charity-boy!*—Many were the "wit-combats" (to dally awhile with the words of old Fuller), between him and C. V. Le G——, "which two I behold like a Spanish great galleon, and an English man of war: Master Coleridge, like the former, was built far higher in learning, solid, but slow in his performances. C. V. L., with the English man of war, lesser in bulk, but lighter in sailing, could turn with all times, tack about, and take advantage of all winds, by the quickness of his wit and invention."

Nor shalt thou, their compeer, be quickly forgotten, Allen, with the cordial smile, and still more cordial laugh, with which thou wert wont to make the old Cloisters shake, in thy cognition of some poignant jest of theirs ; or the anticipation of some more material, and peradventure practical one, of thine own. Extinct are those smiles, with that beautiful countenance, with which (for thou wert the *Nireus formosus* of the school), in the days of thy maturer waggery, thou didst disarm the wrath of infuriated town-damsel, who, incensed by provoking pinch, turning tigress-like round, suddenly converted by thy angel-look, exchanged the half-formed terrible "*bl*——," for a gentler greeting—"*bless thy handsome face!*"

Next follow two, who ought to be now alive, and the friends of Elia—the junior Le G—— and F——; who impelled, the former by a roving temper, the latter by too quick a sense of neglect—ill capable of enduring the slights poor Sizars are sometimes subject to in our seats of learning—exchanged their Alma Mater for the camp; perishing, one by climate, and one on the plains of Salamanca :—Le G——, sanguine, volatile, sweet-natured ; F——, dogged, faithful, anticipative of insult, warm-hearted, with something of the old Roman height about him.

Fine, frank-hearted Fr——, the present master of Hertford, with Marmaduke T——, mildest of Missionaries —and both my good friends still—close the catalogue of Grecians in my time.

THE TWO RACES OF MEN.

THE human species, according to the best theory I can form of it, is composed of two distinct races, *the men who borrow, and the men who lend.* To these two original diversities may be reduced all those impertinent classifications of Gothic and Celtic tribes, white men, black men, red men. All the dwellers upon earth, " Parthians, and Medes, and Elamites," flock hither, and do naturally fall in with one or other of these primary distinctions.

The infinite superiority of the former, which I chose to designate as the *great race*, is discernible in their figure, port, and a certain instinctive sovereignty. The latter are born degraded. "He shall serve his brethren." There is something in the air of one of this cast, lean and suspicious; contrasting with the open, trusting, generous manners of the other.

Observe who have been the greatest borrowers of all ages—Alcibiades—Falstaff—Sir Richard Steele—our late incomparable Brinsley—what a family likeness in all four!

What a careless, even deportment hath your borrower! what rosy gills! what a beautiful reliance on Providence doth he manifest,—taking no more thought than lilies! What contempt for money,—accounting it (yours and mine especially) no better than dross! What a liberal confounding of those pedantic distinctions of *meum* and *tuum!* or rather, what a noble simplification of language (beyond Tooke), resolving these supposed opposites into one clear, intelligible pronoun adjective!—What near approaches doth he make to the primitive *community,*— to the extent of one half of the principle at least.

He is the true taxer who "calleth all the world up to be taxed;" and the distance is as vast between him and *one of us*, as subsisted between the Augustan Majesty and the poorest obolary Jew that paid it tribute-pittance at Jerusalem! His exactions, too, have such a cheerful, voluntary air! So far removed from your sour parochial or state-gatherers, those ink-horn varlets, who carry their want of welcome in their faces! He cometh to you with a smile, and troubleth you with no receipt; confining himself to no set season. Every day is his Candlemas, or his feast of Holy Michael. He applieth the *lene tormentum* of a pleasant look to your purse,—which to that gentle warmth expands her silken leaves, as naturally as the cloak of the traveller, for which sun and wind contended! He is the true Propontic which never ebbeth! The sea which taketh handsomely at each man's hand. In vain the victim, whom he delighteth to honour, struggles with destiny; he is in the net. Lend therefore cheerfully, O man ordained to lend—that thou lose not in the end, with thy worldly penny, the reversion promised. Combine not preposterously in thine own person the penalties of Lazarus and of Dives!—but, when thou seest the proper authority coming, meet it smilingly, as it were half-way. Come, a handsome sacrifice! See how light *he* makes of it! Strain not courtesies with a noble enemy.

Reflections like the foregoing were forced upon my mind by the death of my old friend, Ralph Bigod, Esq., who parted this life on Wednesday evening; dying, as he had lived, without much trouble. He boasted himself a descendant from mighty ancestors of that name, who heretofore held ducal dignities in this realm. In his actions and sentiments he belied not the stock to which he pretended. Early in life he found himself invested with ample revenues; which, with that noble disinterestedness which I have noticed as inherent in men of the *great race*, he took almost immediate measures entirely to dissipate and bring to nothing: for there is something revolting in the idea of a king holding a private purse; and the thoughts of Bigod were all regal. Thus furnished, by the very act of disfurnishment; getting rid of the cumbersome luggage of riches, more apt (as one sings)

> To slacken virtue, and abate her edge,
> Than prompt her to do aught may merit praise,

he set forth, like some Alexander, upon his great enterprise, "borrowing and to borrow!"

In his periegesis, or triumphant progress throughout this island, it has been calculated that he laid a tythe part of the inhabitants under contribution. I reject this estimate as greatly exaggerated:—but having had the honour of accompanying my friend, divers times, in his perambulations about this vast city, I own I was greatly struck at first with the prodigious number of faces we met, who claimed a sort of respectful acquaintance with us. He was one day so obliging as to explain the phenomenon. It seems, these were his tributaries; feeders of his exchequer; gentlemen, his good friends (as he was pleased to express himself), to whom he had occasionally been beholden for a loan. Their multitudes did no way disconcert him. He rather took a pride in numbering them; and, with Comus, seemed pleased to be "stocked with so fair a herd."

With such sources, it was a wonder how he contrived to keep his treasury always empty. He did it by force of an aphorism, which he had often in his mouth, that "money kept longer than three days stinks." So he made use of it while it was fresh. A good part he drank away (for he was an excellent toss-pot), some he gave away, the rest he threw away, literally tossing and hurling it violently from him—as boys do burrs, or as if it had been infectious,—into ponds, or ditches, or deep holes, inscrutable cavities of the earth;—or he would bury it (where he would never seek it again) by a river's side under some bank, which (he would facetiously observe) paid no interest—but out away from him it must go peremptorily, as Hagar's offspring into the wilderness, while it was sweet. He never missed it. The streams were perennial which fed his fisc. When new supplies became necessary, the first person that had the felicity to fall in with him, friend or stranger, was sure to contribute to the deficiency. For Bigod had an *undeniable* way with him. He had a cheerful, open exterior, a quick jovial eye, a bald forehead, just touched with grey (*cana fides*). He anticipated no excuse, and found none. And, waiving for a while my theory as to the *great race*, I would put it to the most untheorising reader, who may at times have disposable coin in his pocket, whether it is not more repugnant to the kindliness of his nature to refuse such a one as I am describing, than to say *no* to a poor petitionary rogue (your bastard borrower), who, by his mumping visnomy, tells you that he expects nothing better; and, therefore, whose preconceived notions and expectations you do in reality so much less shock in the refusal.

When I think of this man; his fiery glow of heart; his swell of feeling; how magnificent, how *ideal* he was; how great at the midnight hour; and when I compare with him the companions with whom I have associated since, I grudge the saving of a few idle ducats, and think that I am fallen into the society of *lenders*, and *little* men.

To one like Elia, whose treasures are rather cased in leather covers than closed in iron coffers, there is a class of alienators more formidable than that which I have touched upon; I mean your *borrowers of books*—those mutilators of collections, spoilers of the symmetry of shelves, and creators of odd volumes. There is Comberbatch, matchless in his depredations!

That foul gap in the bottom shelf facing you, like a great eye-tooth knocked out—(you are now with me in my little back study in Bloomsbury, Reader!)—with the huge Switzer-like tomes on each side (like the Guildhall giants, in their reformed posture, guardant of nothing) once held the tallest of my folios, Opera Bonaventuræ, choice and massy divinity, to which its two supporters (school divinity also, but of a lesser calibre,—Bellarmine, and Holy Thomas), showed but as dwarfs,—itself an Ascapart!—*that* Comberbatch abstracted upon the faith of a theory he holds, which is more easy, I confess, for me to suffer by than to refute, namely, that "the title to property in a book (my Bonaventure, for instance) is in exact ratio to the claimant's powers of understanding and appreciating the same." Should he go on acting upon this theory, which of our shelves is safe?

The slight vacuum in the left-hand case—two shelves from the ceiling—scarcely distinguishable but by the quick eye of a loser—was whilom the commodious resting-place of Browne on Urn Burial. C. will hardly allege that he knows more about that treatise than I do, who introduced it to him, and was indeed the first (of the moderns) to discover its beauties—but so have I known a foolish lover to praise his mistress in the presence of a rival more qualified to carry her off than himself.—Just below, Dodsley's dramas want their fourth volume, where Vittoria Corombona is! The remainder nine are as distasteful as Priam's refuse sons, when the Fates *borrowed* Hector. Here stood the Anatomy of Melancholy, in sober state.—There loitered the Complete Angler; quiet as in life, by some stream side. In yonder nook, John Buncle, a widower-volume, with "eyes closed," mourns his ravished mate.

One justice I must do my friend, that if he sometimes, like the sea, sweeps away a treasure, at another time, sea-like, he throws up as rich an equivalent to match it. I have a small under-collection of this nature (my friend's gatherings in his various calls), picked up, he has forgotten at what odd places, and deposited with as little memory at mine. I take in these orphans, the twice-deserted. These proselytes of the gate are welcome as the true Hebrews. There they stand in conjunction; natives, and naturalised. The latter seem as little disposed to inquire out their true lineage as I am.—I charge no warehouse-room for these deodands, nor shall ever put myself to the ungentlemanly trouble of advertising a sale of them to pay expenses.

To lose a volume to C. carries some sense and meaning in it. You are sure that he will make one hearty meal on your viands, if he can give no account of the platter after it. But what moved thee, wayward, spiteful K., to be so importunate to carry off with thee, in spite of tears and adjurations to thee to forbear, the Letters of that princely woman, the thrice noble Margaret Newcastle—knowing at the time, and knowing that I knew also, thou most assuredly wouldst never turn over one leaf of the illustrious folio:—what but the mere spirit of contradiction, and childish love of getting the better of thy friend?—Then, worst cut of all! to transport it with thee to the Gallican land—

Unworthy land to harbour such a sweetness,
A virtue in which all ennobling thoughts dwelt,
Pure thoughts, kind thoughts, high thoughts, her sex's wonder!

——hadst thou not thy play-books, and books of jests and fancies, about thee, to keep thee merry, even as thou keepest all companies with thy quips and mirthful tales? Child of the Green-room, it was unkindly done of thee. Thy wife, too, that part-French, better-part-Englishwoman!—that *she* could fix upon no other treatise to bear away, in kindly token of remembering us, than the works of Fulke Greville, Lord Brook—of which no Frenchman, nor woman of France, Italy, or England, was ever by nature constituted to comprehend a tittle! *Was there not Zimmerman on Solitude?*

Reader, if haply thou art blessed with a moderate collection, be shy of showing it; or if thy heart overfloweth to lend them, lend thy books; but let it be to such a one as S. T. C.—he will return them (generally anticipating the time appointed) with usury; enriched with annotations, tripling their value. I have had experience. Many are these precious MSS. of his—(in *matter* oftentimes, and almost in *quantity* not unfrequently, vying with the originals) in no very clerkly hand—legible in my Daniel; in old Burton: in Sir Thomas Browne; and those abstruser cogitations of the Greville, now, alas! wandering in Pagan lands.— I counsel thee, shut not thy heart, nor thy library, against S. T. C.

NEW YEAR'S EVE.

EVERY man hath two birth-days: two days at least, in every year, which set him upon revolving the lapse of time, as it affects his mortal duration. The one is that which in an especial manner he termeth *his*. In the gradual desuetude of old observances, this custom of solemnizing our proper birth-day hath nearly passed away, or is left to children, who reflect nothing at all about the matter, nor understand anything in it beyond cake and orange. But the birth of a New Year is of an interest too wide to be pretermitted by king or cobbler. No one ever regarded the First of January with indifference. It is that from which all date their time, and count upon what is left. It is the nativity of our common Adam.

Of all sound of all bells—(bells, the music nighest bordering upon heaven)—most solemn and touching is the peal which rings out the Old Year. I never hear it without a gathering-up of my mind to a concentration of all the images that have been diffused over the past twelvemonth; all I have done or suffered, performed or neglected, in that regretted time. I begin to know its worth, as when a person dies. It takes a personal colour; nor was it a poetical flight in a contemporary, when he exclaimed—

> I saw the skirts of the departing Year.

It is no more than what in sober sadness every one of us seems to be conscious of, in that awful leave-taking. I am sure I felt it, and all felt it with me, last night; though some of my companions affected rather to manifest an exhilaration at the birth of the coming year, than any very tender regrets for the decease of its predecessor. But I am none of those who—

> Welcome the coming, speed the parting guest.

I am naturally, beforehand, shy of novelties; new books, new faces, new years,—from some mental twist which makes it difficult in me to face the prospective. I have almost ceased to hope; and am sanguine only in the prospects of other (former years). I plunge into foregone visions and conclusions. I encounter pell-mell with past disappointments. I am armour-proof against old discouragements. I forgive, or overcome in fancy, old adversaries. I play over again *for love*, as the gamesters phrase it, games for which I once paid so dear. I would scarce now have any of those untoward accidents and events of my life reversed. I would no more alter them than the incidents of some well-contrived novel. Methinks, it is better that I should have pined away seven of my goldenest years, when I was thrall to the fair hair, and fairer eyes, of Alice W——n, than that so passionate a love adventure should be lost. It was better that our family should have missed that legacy, which old Dorrell cheated us of, than that I should have at this moment two thousand pounds *in banco*, and be without the idea of that specious old rogue.

In a degree beneath manhood, it is my infirmity to look back upon those early days. Do I advance a paradox when I say, that, skipping over the intervention of forty years, a man may have leave to love *himself*, without the imputation of self-love?

If I know aught of myself, no one whose mind is introspective—and mine is painfully so—can have a less respect for his present identity than I have for the man Elia. I know him to be light, and vain, and humoursome; a notorious * * * ; addicted to * * *; averse from counsel, neither taking it, nor offering it;— * * * besides; a stammering buffoon; what you will; lay it on, and spare not; I subscribe to it all, and much more, than thou canst be willing to lay at his door —but for the child Elia—that "other me," there, in the background—I must take leave to cherish the remembrance of that young master—with as little reference, I protest, to his stupid changeling of five-and-forty, as if it had been a child of some other house, and not of my parents. I can cry over its patient small-pox at five, and rougher medicaments. I can lay its poor fevered head upon the sick pillow at Christ's, and wake with it in surprise at the gentle posture of maternal tenderness hanging over it, that unknown had watched its sleep. I know how it shrank from any the least colour of falsehood.—God help thee, Elia, how art thou changed!—

Thou art sophisticated. — I know how honest, how courageous (for a weakling) it was — how religious, how imaginative, how hopeful! From what have I not fallen, if the child I remember was indeed myself, — and not some dissembling guardian, presenting a false identity, to give the rule to my unpractised steps, and regulate the tone of my moral being!

That I am fond of indulging, beyond a hope of sympathy, in such retrospection, may be the symptom of some sickly idiosyncrasy. Or is it owing to another cause: simply, that being without wife or family, I have not learned to project myself enough out of myself; and having no offspring of my own to dally with, I turn back upon memory, and adopt my own early idea, as my heir and favourite? If these speculations seem fantastical to thee, Reader (a busy man, perchance), if I tread out of the way of thy sympathy, and am singularly conceited only, I retire, impenetrable to ridicule, under the phantom cloud of Elia.

The elders, with whom I was brought up, were of a character not likely to let slip the sacred observance of any old institution; and the ringing out of the Old Year was kept by them with circumstances of peculiar ceremony. —In those days the sound of those midnight chimes, though it seemed to raise hilarity in all around me, never failed to bring a train of pensive imagery into my fancy. Yet I then scarce conceived what it meant, or thought of it as a reckoning that concerned me. Not childhood alone, but the young man till thirty, never feels practically that he is mortal. He knows it indeed, and, if need were, he could preach a homily on the fragility of life; but he brings it not home to himself, any more than in a hot June we can appropriate to our imagination the freezing days of December. But now, shall I confess a truth?—I feel these audits but too powerfully. I begin to count the probabilities of my duration, and to grudge at the expenditure of moments and shortest periods, like misers' farthings. In proportion as the years both lessen and shorten, I set more count upon their periods, and would fain lay my ineffectual finger upon the spoke of the great wheel. I am not content to pass away "like a weaver's shuttle." Those metaphors solace me not, nor sweeten the unpalatable draught of mortality. I care not to be carried with the tide, that smoothly bears human life to eternity; and reluct at the inevitable course of destiny. I am in love with this green earth; the face of town and country; the unspeakable rural solitudes, and the sweet security of streets. I would set up my tabernacle here. I am content to stand still at the age to which I am arrived; I, and my friends: to be no younger, no richer, no handsomer. I do not want to be weaned by age; or drop, like mellow fruit, as they say, into the grave.—Any alteration, on this earth of mine, in diet or in lodging, puzzles and discomposes me. My household-gods plant a terrible fixed foot, and are not rooted up without blood. They do not willingly seek Lavinian shores. A new state of being staggers me.

Sun, and sky, and breeze, and solitary walks, and summer holidays, and the greenness of fields, and the delicious juices of meats and fishes, and society, and the cheerful glass, and candle-light, and fireside conversations, and innocent vanities, and jests, and *irony itself*—do these things go out with life?

Can a ghost laugh, or shake his gaunt sides, when you are pleasant with him?

And you, my midnight darlings, my Folios; must I part with the intense delight of having you (huge armfuls) in my embraces? Must knowledge come to me, if it come at all, by some awkward experiment of intuition, and no longer by this familiar process of reading?

Shall I enjoy friendships there, wanting the smiling indications which point me to them here,—the recognisable face—the "sweet assurance of a look"?

In winter this intolerable disinclination to dying—to give it its mildest name—does more especially haunt and beset me. In a genial August noon, beneath a swelter-

ing sky, death is almost problematic. At those times do
such poor snakes as myself enjoy an immortality. Then
we expand and burgeon. Then we are as strong again,
as valiant again, as wise again, and a great deal taller.
The blast that nips and shrinks me, puts me in thoughts
of death. All things allied to the insubstantial, wait
upon that master feeling; cold, numbness, dreams, perplexity; moonlight itself, with its shadowy and spectral
appearances,—that cold ghost of the sun, or Phœbus'
sickly sister, like that innutritious one denounced in the
Canticles :—I am none of her minions—I hold with the
Persian.

Whatsoever thwarts, or puts me out of my way, brings
death unto my mind. All partial evils, like humours,
run into that capital plague-sore.—I have heard some
profess an indifference to life. Such hail the end of their
existence as a port of refuge; and speak of the grave
as of some soft arms, in which they may slumber as on
a pillow. Some have wooed death —— but out upon
thee, I say, thou foul, ugly phantom! I detest, abhor,
execrate, and (with Friar John) give thee to six score
thousand devils, as in no instance to be excused or
tolerated, but shunned as an universal viper; to be
branded, proscribed, and spoken evil of! In no way
can I be brought to digest thee, thou thin, melancholy
Privation, or more frightful and confounding *Positive!*

Those antidotes, prescribed against the fear of thee,
are altogether frigid and insulting, like thyself. For
what satisfaction hath a man, that he shall "lie down
with kings and emperors in death," who in his lifetime
never greatly coveted the society of such bed-fellows?—
or, forsooth, that "so shall the fairest face appear"?—
why, to comfort me, must Alice W—n be a goblin?
More than all, I conceive disgust at those impertinent and
misbecoming familiarities, inscribed upon your ordinary
tombstones. Every dead man must take upon himself
to be lecturing me with his odious truism, that "Such as
he now is I must shortly be." Not so shortly, friend,

perhaps, as thou imaginest. In the meantime I am alive. I move about. I am worth twenty of thee. Know thy betters! Thy New Years' days are past. I survive, a jolly candidate for 1821. Another cup of wine—and while that turncoat bell, that just now mournfully chanted the obsequies of 1820 departed, with changed notes lustily rings in a successor, let us attune to its peal the song made on a like occasion, by hearty, cheerful Mr. Cotton.

THE NEW YEAR.

HARK, the cock crows, and yon bright star
Tells us, the day himself's not far;
And see where, breaking from the night,
He gilds the western hills with light.
With him old Janus doth appear,
Peeping into the future year,
With such a look as seems to say
The prospect is not good that way.
Thus do we rise ill sights to see,
And 'gainst ourselves to prophesy;
When the prophetic fear of things
A more tormenting mischief brings,
More full of soul-tormenting gall
Than direst mischiefs can befall.
But stay! but stay! methinks my sight,
Better informed by clearer light,
Discerns sereneness in that brow
That all contracted seemed but now.
His revers'd face may show distaste,
And frown upon the ills are past;
But that which this way looks is clear,
And smiles upon the New-born Year.
He looks too from a place so high,
The year lies open to his eye;
And all the moments open are
To the exact discoverer.
Yet more and more he smiles upon
The happy revolution.
Why should we then suspect or fear
The influences of a year,
So smiles upon us the first morn,
And speaks us good so soon as born?
Plague on't! the last was ill enough,

This cannot but make better proof;
Or, at the worst, as we brush'd through
The last, why so we may this too;
And then the next in reason shou'd
Be superexcellently good:
For the worst ills (we daily see)
Have no more perpetuity
Than the best fortunes that do fall;
Which also bring us wherewithal
Longer their being to support,
Than those do of the other sort:
And who has one good year in three,
And yet repines at destiny,
Appears ungrateful in the case,
And merits not the good he has.
Then let us welcome the New Guest
With lusty brimmers of the best:
Mirth always should Good Fortune meet,
And renders e'en Disaster sweet:
And though the Princess turn her back,
Let us but line ourselves with sack,
We better shall by far hold out,
Till the next year she face about.

How say you, Reader—do not these verses smack of the rough magnanimity of the old English vein? Do they not fortify like a cordial; enlarging the heart, and productive of sweet blood, and generous spirits, in the concoction? Where be those puling fears of death, just now expressed or affected?—Passed like a cloud—absorbed in the purging sunlight of clear poetry—clean washed away by a wave of genuine Helicon, your only Spa for these hypochondries. And now another cup of the generous! and a merry New Year, and many of them to you all, my masters!

MRS. BATTLE'S OPINIONS ON WHIST.

"A CLEAR fire, a clean hearth,[1] and the rigour of the game." This was the celebrated *wish* of old Sarah Battle

[[1] This was before the introduction of rugs, Reader. You must

(now with God), who, next to her devotions, loved a good game of whist. She was none of your lukewarm gamesters, your half-and-half players, who have no objection to take a hand, if you want one to make up a rubber; who affirm that they have no pleasure in winning; that they like to win one game and lose another; that they can while away an hour very agreeably at a card-table, but are indifferent whether they play or no; and will desire an adversary, who has slipped a wrong card, to take it up and play another.[1] These insufferable triflers are the curse of a table. One of these flies will spoil a whole pot. Of such it may be said that they do not play at cards, but only play at playing at them.

Sarah Battle was none of that breed. She detested them, as I do, from her heart and soul, and would not, save upon a striking emergency, willingly seat herself at the same table with them. She loved a thorough-paced partner, a determined enemy. She took, and gave, no concessions. She hated favours. She never made a revoke, nor ever passed it over in her adversary without exacting the utmost forfeiture. She fought a good fight: cut and thrust. She held not her good sword (her cards) "like a dancer." She sate bolt upright; and neither showed you her cards, nor desired to see yours. All people have their blind side—their superstitions; and I have heard her declare, under the rose, that Hearts was her favourite suit.

I never in my life—and I knew Sarah Battle many of the best years of it—saw her take out her snuff-box when it was her turn to play; or snuff a candle in the middle of a game; or ring for a servant, till it was fairly over. She never introduced, or connived at, miscellaneous conversation during its process. As she emphatically observed, cards were cards; and if I ever saw unmingled

remember the intolerable crash of the unswept cinders betwixt your foot and the marble.]

[1 As if a sportsman should tell you he liked to kill a fox one day and lose him the next.]

distaste in her fine last-century countenance, it was at the airs of a young gentleman of a literary turn, who had been with difficulty persuaded to take a hand; and who, in his excess of candour, declared, that he thought there was no harm in unbending the mind now and then, after serious studies, in recreations of that kind! She could not bear to have her noble occupation, to which she wound up her faculties, considered in that light. It was her business, her duty, the thing she came into the world to do,—and she did it. She unbent her mind afterwards—over a book.

Pope was her favourite author: his Rape of the Lock her favourite work. She once did me the favour to play over with me (with the cards) his celebrated game of Ombre in that poem; and to explain to me how far it agreed with, and in what points it would be found to differ from, tradrille. Her illustrations were apposite and poignant; and I had the pleasure of sending the substance of them to Mr. Bowles; but I suppose they came too late to be inserted among his ingenious notes upon that author.

Quadrille, she has often told me, was her first love; but whist had engaged her maturer esteem. The former, she said, was showy and specious, and likely to allure young persons. The uncertainty and quick shifting of partners—a thing which the constancy of whist abhors; the dazzling supremacy and regal investiture of Spadille—absurd, as she justly observed, in the pure aristocracy of whist, where his crown and garter give him no proper power above his brother-nobility of the Aces;—the giddy vanity, so taking to the inexperienced, of playing alone; above all, the overpowering attractions of a *Sans Prendre Vole*,—to the triumph of which there is certainly nothing parallel or approaching, in the contingencies of whist:—all these, she would say, make quadrille a game of captivation to the young and enthusiastic. But whist was the *solider* game: that was her word. It was a long meal; not like quadrille, a feast of snatches. One or two rubbers might co-extend in duration with an evening. They gave time to form rooted friendships, to cultivate steady enmities. She despised the chance-started, capricious, and ever-fluctuating alliances of the other. The skirmishes of quadrille, she would say, reminded her of the petty ephemeral embroilments of the little Italian states, depicted by Machiavel: perpetually changing postures and connexions; bitter foes to-day, sugared darlings to-morrow; kissing and scratching in a breath; —but the wars of whist were comparable to the long, steady, deep-rooted, rational antipathies of the great French and English nations.

A grave simplicity was what she chiefly admired in her favourite game. There was nothing silly in it, like the nob in cribbage—nothing superfluous. No *flushes*— that most irrational of all pleas that a reasonable being can set up:—that any one should claim four by virtue of holding cards of the same mark and colour, without reference to the playing of the game, or the individual worth or pretensions of the cards themselves! She held this to be a solecism; as pitiful an ambition at cards as alliteration is in authorship. She despised superficiality, and looked deeper than the colours of things.—Suits were soldiers, she would say, and must have a uniformity of array to distinguish them: but what should we say to a foolish squire, who should claim a merit from dressing up his tenantry in red jackets, that never were to be marshalled—never to take the field?—She even wished that whist were more simple than it is; and, in my mind, would have stripped it of some appendages, which, in the state of human frailty, may be venially, and even commendably, allowed of. She saw no reason for the deciding of the trump by the turn of the card. Why not one suit always trumps?—Why two colours, when the mark of the suit would have sufficiently distinguished them without it?

"But the eye, my dear madam, is agreeably refreshed with the variety. Man is not a creature of pure reason—

he must have his senses delightfully appealed to. We see it in Roman Catholic countries, where the music and the paintings draw in many to worship, whom your quaker spirit of unsensualising would have kept out.—You yourself have a pretty collection of paintings—but confess to me, whether, walking in your gallery at Sandham, among those clear Vandykes, or among the Paul Potters in the ante-room, you ever felt your bosom glow with an elegant delight, at all comparable to *that* you have it in your power to experience most evenings over a well-arranged assortment of the court-cards?—the pretty antic habits, like heralds in a procession—the gay triumph-assuring scarlets—the contrasting deadly-killing sables—the 'hoary majesty of spades'—Pam in all his glory!—

"All these might be dispensed with; and with their naked names upon the drab pasteboard, the game might go on very well, pictureless; but the *beauty* of cards would be extinguished for ever. Stripped of all that is imaginative in them, they must degenerate into mere gambling. Imagine a dull deal board, or drum head, to spread them on, instead of that nice verdant carpet (next to nature's), fittest arena for those courtly combatants to play their gallant jousts and turneys in!—Exchange those delicately-turned ivory markers—(work of Chinese artist, unconscious of their symbol,—or as profanely slighting their true application as the arrantest Ephesian journeyman that turned out those little shrines for the goddess) —exchange them for little bits of leather (our ancestors' money), or chalk and a slate!"—

The old lady, with a smile, confessed the soundness of my logic; and to her approbation of my arguments on her favourite topic that evening I have always fancied myself indebted for the legacy of a curious cribbage-board, made of the finest Sienna marble, which her maternal uncle (old Walter Plumer, whom I have elsewhere celebrated) brought with him from Florence:—this, and a trifle of five hundred pounds, came to me at her death.

The former bequest (which I do not least value) I

have kept with religious care; though she herself, to confess a truth, was never greatly taken with cribbage. It was an essentially vulgar game, I have heard her say,—disputing with her uncle, who was very partial to it. She could never heartily bring her mouth to pronounce "*Go*," or "*That's a go.*" She called it an ungrammatical game. The pegging teased her. I once knew her to forfeit a rubber (a five-dollar stake) because she would not take advantage of the turn-up knave, which would have given it her, but which she must have claimed by the disgraceful tenure of declaring "*two for his heels.*" There is something extremely genteel in this sort of self-denial. Sarah Battle was a gentlewoman born.

Piquet she held the best game at the cards for two persons, though she would ridicule the pedantry of the terms—such as pique—repique—the capot—they savoured (she thought) of affectation. But games for two, or even three, she never greatly cared for. She loved the quadrate, or square. She would argue thus:—Cards are warfare: the ends are gain, with glory. But cards are war, in disguise of a sport: when single adversaries encounter, the ends proposed are too palpable. By themselves, it is too close a fight; with spectators, it is not much bettered. No looker-on can be interested, except for a bet, and then it is a mere affair of money; he cares not for your luck *sympathetically*, or for your play.—Three are still worse; a mere naked war of every man against every man, as in cribbage, without league or alliance; or a rotation of petty and contradictory interests, a succession of heartless leagues, and not much more hearty infractions of them, as in tradrille.—But in square games (*she meant whist*), all that is possible to be attained in card-playing is accomplished. There are the incentives of profit with honour, common to every species—though the *latter* can be but very imperfectly enjoyed in those other games, where the spectator is only feebly a participator. But the parties in whist are spectators and principals too. They are a theatre to themselves, and a looker-on is not wanted. He is rather worse than nothing, and an impertinence. Whist abhors neutrality, or interests beyond its sphere. You glory in some surprising stroke of skill or fortune, not because a cold—or even an interested—bystander witnesses it, but because your *partner* sympathises in the contingency. You win for two. You triumph for two. Two are exalted. Two again are mortified; which divides their disgrace, as the conjunction doubles (by taking off the invidiousness) your glories. Two losing to two are better reconciled, than one to one in that close butchery. The hostile feeling is weakened by multiplying the channels. War becomes a civil game. By such reasonings as these the old lady was accustomed to defend her favourite pastime.

No inducement could ever prevail upon her to play at any game, where chance entered into the composition, *for nothing*. Chance, she would argue—and here again, admire the subtlety of her conclusion;—chance is nothing, but where something else depends upon it. It is obvious that cannot be *glory*. What rational cause of exultation could it give to a man to turn up size ace a hundred times together by himself? or before spectators, where no stake was depending?—Make a lottery of a hundred thousand tickets with but one fortunate number—and what possible principle of our nature, except stupid wonderment, could it gratify to gain that number as many times successively without a prize? Therefore she disliked the mixture of chance in backgammon, where it was not played for money. She called it foolish, and those people idiots, who were taken with a lucky hit under such circumstances. Games of pure skill were as little to her fancy. Played for a stake, they were a mere system of over-reaching. Played for glory, they were a mere setting of one man's wit,—his memory, or combination-faculty rather against another's; like a mock-engagement at a review, bloodless and profitless. She could not conceive a *game* wanting the spritely infusion of chance, the handsome excuses of good fortune. Two people playing at chess in a corner of a room, whilst

whist was stirring in the centre, would inspire her with
insufferable horror and ennui. Those well-cut similitudes
of Castles and Knights, the *imagery* of the board, she
would argue (and I think in this case justly), were entirely misplaced and senseless. Those hard-head contests
can in no instance ally with the fancy. They reject form
and colour. A pencil and dry slate (she used to say) were
the proper arena for such combatants.

To those puny objectors against cards, as nurturing the
bad passions, she would retort, that man is a gaming
animal. He must be always trying to get the better in
something or other:—that this passion can scarcely be
more safely expended than upon a game at cards: that
cards are a temporary illusion; in truth, a mere drama;
for we do but *play* at being mightily concerned, where a
few idle shillings are at stake, yet, during the illusion, we
are as mightily concerned as those whose stake is crowns
and kingdoms. They are a sort of dream-fighting; much
ado; great battling, and little bloodshed: mighty means
for disproportioned ends: quite as diverting, and a great
deal more innoxious, than many of those more serious
games of life, which men play without esteeming them to
be such.

With great deference to the old lady's judgment in
these matters, I think I have experienced some moments
in my life when playing at cards *for nothing* has even
been agreeable. When I am in sickness, or not in the
best spirits, I sometimes call for the cards, and play a game
at piquet *for love* with my cousin Bridget—Bridget Elia.

I grant there is something sneaking in it; but with a
tooth-ache, or a sprained ankle,—when you are subdued
and humble, you are glad to put up with an inferior
spring of action.

There is such a thing in nature, I am convinced, as
sick whist.

I grant it is not the highest style of man—I deprecate
the manes of Sarah Battle—she lives not, alas! to whom
I should apologise.

At such times, those *terms* which my old friend objected to, come in as something admissible — I love to get a tierce or a quatorze, though they mean nothing. I am subdued to an inferior interest. Those shadows of winning amuse me.

That last game I had with my sweet cousin (I capotted her)—(dare I tell thee, how foolish I am?)—I wished it might have lasted for ever, though we gained nothing, and lost nothing, though it was a mere shade of play: I would be content to go on in that idle folly for ever. The pipkin should be ever boiling, that was to prepare the gentle lenitive to my foot, which Bridget was doomed to apply after the game was over: and, as I do not much relish appliances, there it should ever bubble. Bridget and I should be ever playing.

A CHAPTER ON EARS.

I have no ear.—

Mistake me not, reader—nor imagine that I am by nature destitute of those exterior twin appendages, hanging ornaments, and (architecturally speaking) handsome volutes to the human capital. Better my mother had never borne me.—I am, I think, rather delicately than copiously provided with those conduits; and I feel no disposition to envy the mule for his plenty, or the mole for her exactness, in those ingenious labyrinthine inlets — those indispensable side-intelligencers.

Neither have I incurred, or done anything to incur, with Defoe, that hideous disfigurement, which constrained him to draw upon assurance—to feel "quite unabashed,"[1] and at ease upon that article. I was never, I thank my stars, in the pillory; nor, if I read them aright, is it within the compass of my destiny, that I ever should be.

When therefore I say that I have no ear, you will

[1] ["Earless on high stood, unabashed, Defoe."—*Dunciad.*]

understand me to mean—*for music*. To say that this heart never melted at the concord of sweet sounds, would be a foul self-libel. "*Water parted from the sea*" never fails to move it strangely. So does "*In infancy*." But they were used to be sung at her harpsichord (the old-fashioned instrument in vogue in those days) by a gentlewoman—the gentlest, sure, that ever merited the appellation—the sweetest—why should I hesitate to name Mrs. S——, once the blooming Fanny Weatheral of the Temple— who had power to thrill the soul of Elia, small imp as he was, even in his long coats; and to make him glow, tremble, and blush with a passion, that not faintly indicated the day-spring of that absorbing sentiment which was afterwards destined to overwhelm and subdue his nature quite for Alice W——n.

I even think that *sentimentally* I am disposed to harmony. But *organically* I am incapable of a tune. I have been practising "*God save the King*" all my life; whistling and humming of it over to myself in solitary corners; and am not yet arrived, they tell me, within many quavers of it. Yet hath the loyalty of Elia never been impeached.

I am not without suspicion, that I have an undeveloped faculty of music within me. For thrumming, in my wild way, on my friend A.'s piano, the other morning, while he was engaged in an adjoining parlour,—on his return he was pleased to say, "*he thought it could not be the maid!*" On his first surprise at hearing the keys touched in somewhat an airy and masterful way, not dreaming of me, his suspicions had lighted on *Jenny*. But a grace, snatched from a superior refinement, soon convinced him that some being—technically perhaps deficient, but higher informed from a principle common to all the fine arts—had swayed the keys to a mood which Jenny, with all her (less cultivated) enthusiasm, could never have elicited from them. I mention this as a proof of my friend's penetration, and not with any view of disparaging Jenny.

Scientifically I could never be made to understand (yet

have I taken some pains) what a note in music is ; or how one note should differ from another. Much less in voices can I distinguish a soprano from a tenor. Only sometimes the thorough-bass I contrive to guess at, from its being supereminently harsh and disagreeable. I tremble, however, for my misapplication of the simplest terms of *that* which I disclaim. While I profess my ignorance, I scarce know what to *say* I am ignorant of. I hate, perhaps, by misnomers. *Sostenuto* and *adagio* stand in the like relation of obscurity to me ; and *Sol, Fa, Mi, Re*, is as conjuring as *Baralipton.*

It is hard to stand alone in an age like this,—(constituted to the quick and critical perception of all harmonious combinations, I verily believe, beyond all preceding ages, since Jubal stumbled upon the gamut,) to remain, as it were, singly unimpressible to the magic influences of an art, which is said to have such an especial stroke at soothing, elevating, and refining the passions.—Yet, rather than break the candid current of my confessions, I must avow to you that I have received a great deal more pain than pleasure from this so cried-up faculty.

I am constitutionally susceptible of noises. A carpenter's hammer, in a warm summer noon, will fret me into more than midsummer madness. But those unconnected, unset sounds, are nothing to the measured malice of music. The ear is passive to those single strokes ; willingly enduring stripes while it hath no task to con. To music it cannot be passive. It will strive—mine at least will—spite of its inaptitude, to thrid the maze ; like an unskilled eye painfully poring upon hieroglyphics. I have sat through an Italian Opera, till, for sheer pain, and inexplicable anguish, I have rushed out into the noisiest places of the crowded streets, to solace myself with sounds, which I was not obliged to follow, and get rid of the distracting torment of endless, fruitless, barren attention ! I take refuge in the unpretending assemblage of honest common-life sounds ;—and the purgatory of the Enraged Musician becomes my paradise.

I have sat at an Oratorio (that profanation of the purposes of the cheerful playhouse) watching the faces of the auditory in the pit (what a contrast to Hogarth's Laughing Audience!) immoveable, or affecting some faint emotion—till (as some have said, that our occupations in the next world will be but a shadow of what delighted us in this) I have imagined myself in some cold Theatre in Hades, where some of the *forms* of the earthly one should be kept up, with none of the *enjoyment;* or like that

——Party in a parlour
All silent, and all DAMNED.

Above all, those insufferable concertos, and pieces of music, as they are called, do plague and embitter my apprehension.—Words are something; but to be exposed to an endless battery of mere sounds; to be long a dying; to lie stretched upon a rack of roses; to keep up languor by unintermitted effort; to pile honey upon sugar, and sugar upon honey, to an interminable tedious sweetness; to fill up sound with feeling, and strain ideas to keep pace with it; to gaze on empty frames, and be forced to make the pictures for yourself; to read a book, *all stops*, and be obliged to supply the verbal matter; to invent extempore tragedies to answer to the vague gestures of an inexplicable rambling mime—these are faint shadows of what I have undergone from a series of the ablest-executed pieces of this empty *instrumental music*.

I deny not, that in the opening of a concert, I have experienced something vastly lulling and agreeable:—afterwards followeth the languor and the oppression.—Like that disappointing book in Patmos; or, like the comings on of melancholy, described by Burton, doth music make her first insinuating approaches:—" Most pleasant it is to such as are melancholy given, to walk alone in some solitary grove, betwixt wood and water, by some brook side, and to meditate upon some delightsome and pleasant subject, which shall affect him most, *amabilis insania*, and *mentis gratissimus error.* A most incomparable delight to build castles in the air, to go smiling to themselves, acting an infinite variety of parts, which they suppose, and strongly imagine, they act, or that they see done.—So delightsome these toys at first, they could spend whole days and nights without sleep, even whole years in such contemplations, and fantastical meditations, which are like so many dreams, and will hardly be drawn from them—winding and unwinding themselves as so many clocks, and still pleasing their humours, until at the last the SCENE TURNS UPON A SUDDEN, and they being now habitated to such meditations and solitary places, can endure no company, can think of nothing but harsh and distasteful subjects. Fear, sorrow, suspicion, *subrusticus pudor*, discontent, cares, and weariness of life, surprise them on a sudden, and they can think of nothing else: continually suspecting, no sooner are their eyes open, but this infernal plague of melancholy seizeth on them, and terrifies their souls, representing some dismal object to their minds; which now, by no means, no labour, no persuasions, they can avoid, they cannot be rid of, they cannot resist."

Something like this "SCENE TURNING" I have experienced at the evening parties, at the house of my good Catholic friend *Nov*——; who, by the aid of a capital organ, himself the most finished of players, converts his drawing-room into a chapel, his week days into Sundays, and these latter into minor heavens.[1]

When my friend commences upon one of those solemn anthems, which peradventure struck upon my heedless ear, rambling in the side aisles of the dim Abbey, some five-and-thirty years since, waking a new sense, and putting a soul of old religion into my young apprehension—(whether it be *that*, in which the Psalmist, weary of the persecutions of bad men, wisheth to himself dove's wings—or *that other* which, with a like measure of sobriety and pathos, inquireth by what means the young man shall best cleanse

---

[1] I have been there, and still would go—
'Tis like a little heaven below.—DR. WATTS.

his mind)—a holy calm pervadeth me.—I am for the time
> rapt above earth,
> And possess joys not promised at my birth.

But when this master of the spell, not content to have laid a soul prostrate, goes on, in his power, to inflict more bliss than lies in her capacity to receive—impatient to overcome her " earthly " with his " heavenly,"—still pouring in, for protracted hours, fresh waves and fresh from the sea of sound, or from that inexhausted *German* ocean, above which, in triumphant progress, dolphin-seated, ride those Arions *Haydn* and *Mozart*, with their attendant Tritons, *Bach*, *Beethoven*, and a countless tribe, whom to attempt to reckon up would but plunge me again in the deeps,—I stagger under the weight of harmony, reeling to and fro at my wits' end ;—clouds, as of frankincense, oppress me—priests, altars, censers, dazzle before me—the genius of *his* religion hath me in her toils—a shadowy triple tiara invests the brow of my friend, late so naked, so ingenuous—he is Pope,—and by him sits, like as in the anomaly of dreams, a she-Pope too,—tri-coronated like himself!—I am converted, and yet a Protestant ;—at once *malleus hereticorum*, and myself grand heresiarch : or three heresies centre in my person :—I am Marcion, Ebion, and Cerinthus— Gog and Magog—what not?—till the coming in of the friendly supper-tray dissipates the figment, and a draught of true Lutheran beer (in which chiefly my friend shows himself no bigot) at once reconciles me to the rationalities of a purer faith ; and restores to me the genuine unterrifying aspects of my pleasant-countenanced host and hostess.

ALL FOOLS' DAY.

THE compliments of the season to my worthy masters, and a merry first of April to us all!

Many happy returns of this day to you—and you—and *you*, Sir—nay, never frown, man, nor put a long face upon the matter. Do not we know one another? what need of ceremony among friends? we have all a touch of *that same*—you understand me—a speck of the motley. Beshrew the man who on such a day as this, the *general festival*, should affect to stand aloof. I am none of those sneakers. I am free of the corporation, and care not who knows it. He that meets me in the forest to-day, shall meet with no wise-acre, I can tell him. *Stultus sum.* Translate me that, and take the meaning of it to yourself for your pains. What! man, we have four quarters of the globe on our side, at the least computation.

Fill us a cup of that sparkling gooseberry—we will drink no wise, melancholy, politic port on this day—and let us troll the catch of Amiens—*duc ad me—duc ad me*—how goes it?

> Here shall he see
> Gross fools as he.

Now would I give a trifle to know, historically and authentically, who was the greatest fool that ever lived. I would certainly give him in a bumper. Marry, of the present breed, I think I could without much difficulty name you the party.

Remove your cap a little further, if you please: it hides my bauble. And now each man bestride his hobby, and dust away his bells to what tune he pleases. I will give you, for my part,

> ———The crazy old church clock,
> And the bewildered chimes.

Good master Empedocles,¹ you are welcome. It is long since you went a salamander-gathering down Ætna. Worse than samphire-picking by some odds. 'Tis a mercy your worship did not singe your mustachios.

Ha! Cleombrotus!² and what salads in faith did you light upon at the bottom of the Mediterranean? You were founder, I take it, of the disinterested sect of the Calenturists.

Gebir, my old free-mason, and prince of plasterers at Babel,³ bring in your trowel, most Ancient Grand! You have claim to a seat here at my right hand, as patron of the stammerers. You left your work, if I remember Herodotus correctly, at eight hundred million toises, or thereabout, above the level of the sea. Bless us, what a long bell you must have pulled, to call your top workmen to their nuncheon on the low grounds of Shinar. Or did you send up your garlic and onions by a rocket? I am a rogue if I am not ashamed to show you our Monument on Fish-street Hill, after your altitudes. Yet we think it somewhat.

What, the magnanimous Alexander in tears?—cry, baby, put its finger in its eye, it shall have another globe, round as an orange, pretty moppet!

Mister Adams—— 'odso, I honour your coat—pray do us the favour to read to us that sermon, which you lent to Mistress Slipslop—the twenty and second in your portmanteau there—on Female Incontinence—the same —it will come in most irrelevantly and impertinently seasonable to the time of the day.

Good Master Raymund Lully, you look wise. Pray correct that error.——

Duns, spare your definitions. I must fine you a bumper, or a paradox. We will have nothing said or

[¹ ——— He who, to be deem'd
   A god, leap'd fondly into Etna flames—]
[² ——— He who, to enjoy
   Plato's Elysium, leap'd into the sea—]
[³ The builders next of Babel on the plain
   Of Senaar—]

done syllogistically this day. Remove those logical forms, waiter, that no gentleman break the tender shins of his apprehension stumbling across them.

Master Stephen, you are late.—Ha! Cokes, is it you?—Aguecheek, my dear knight, let me pay my devoir to you.—Master Shallow, your worship's poor servant to command.—Master Silence, I will use few words with you.—Slender, it shall go hard if I edge not you in somewhere.—You six will engross all the poor wit of the company to-day.—I know it, I know it.

Ha! honest R——, my fine old Librarian of Ludgate, time out of mind, art thou here again? Bless thy doublet, it is not over-new, threadbare as thy stories:—what dost thou flitting about the world at this rate?—Thy customers are extinct, defunct, bed-rid, have ceased to read long ago.—Thou goest still among them, seeing if, peradventure, thou canst hawk a volume or two.—Good Granville S——, thy last patron, is flown.

> King Pandion, he is dead,
> All thy friends are lapt in lead.—

Nevertheless, noble R——, come in, and take your seat here, between Armado and Quisada; for in true courtesy, in gravity, in fantastic smiling to thyself, in courteous smiling upon others, in the goodly ornature of well-apparelled speech, and the commendation of wise sentences, thou art nothing inferior to those accomplished Dons of Spain. The spirit of chivalry forsake me for ever, when I forget thy singing the song of Macheath, which declares that he might be *happy with either*, situated between those two ancient spinsters—when I forget the inimitable formal love which thou didst make, turning now to the one, and now to the other, with that Malvolian smile—as if Cervantes, not Gay, had written it for his hero; and as if thousands of periods must revolve, before the mirror of courtesy could have given his invidious preference between a pair of so goodly-propertied and meritorious-equal damsels.   *   *   *   *

To descend from these altitudes, and not to protract our Fools' Banquet beyond its appropriate day,—for I fear the second of April is not many hours distant—in sober verity I will confess a truth to thee, reader. I love a *Fool*—as naturally as if I were of kith and kin to him. When a child, with child-like apprehensions, that dived not below the surface of the matter, I read those *Parables* —not guessing at the involved wisdom—I had more yearnings towards that simple architect, that built his house upon the sand, than I entertained for his more cautious neighbour: I grudged at the hard censure pronounced upon the quiet soul that kept his talent; and— prizing their simplicity beyond the more provident, and, to my apprehension, somewhat *unfeminine* wariness of their competitors—I felt a kindliness, that almost amounted to a *tendre*, for those five thoughtless virgins. —I have never made an acquaintance since, that lasted: or a friendship, that answered; with any that had not some tincture of the absurd in their characters. I venerate an honest obliquity of understanding. The more laughable blunders a man shall commit in your company, the more tests he giveth you, that he will not betray or overreach you. I love the safety which a palpable hallucination warrants; the security, which a word out of season ratifies. And take my word for this, reader, and say a fool told it you, if you please, that he who hath not a dram of folly in his mixture, hath pounds of much worse matter in his composition. It is observed, that "the foolisher the fowl or fish, woodcocks,—dotterels cods'- heads, etc., the finer the flesh thereof," and what are commonly the world's received fools but such whereof the world is not worthy? and what have been some of the kindliest patterns of our species, but so many darlings of absurdity, minions of the goddess, and her white boys? Reader, if you wrest my words beyond their fair construction, it is you, and not I, that are the *April Fool*.

A QUAKERS' MEETING.

> Still-born Silence! thou that art
> Flood-gate of the deeper heart!
> Offspring of a heavenly kind!
> Frost o' the mouth, and thaw o' the mind!
> Secrecy's confidant, and he
> Who makes religion mystery!
> Admiration's speaking'st tongue!
> Leave, thy desert shades among,
> Reverend hermit's hallow'd cells,
> Where retired devotion dwells!
> With thy enthusiasms come,
> Seize our tongues, and strike us dumb![1]

READER, would'st thou know what true peace and quiet mean; would'st thou find a refuge from the noises and clamours of the multitude; would'st thou enjoy at once solitude and society; would'st thou possess the depth of thine own spirit in stillness, without being shut out from the consolatory faces of thy species; would'st thou be alone and yet accompanied; solitary, yet not desolate; singular, yet not without some to keep thee in countenance; a unit in aggregate; a simple in composite:—come with me into a Quakers' Meeting.

Dost thou love silence deep as that "before the winds were made"? go not out into the wilderness, descend not into the profundities of the earth; shut not up thy casements; nor pour wax into the little cells of thy ears, with little-faith'd self-mistrusting Ulysses.—Retire with me into a Quakers' Meeting.

For a man to refrain even from good words, and to hold his peace, it is commendable; but for a multitude it is great mastery.

What is the stillness of the desert compared with this place? what the uncommunicating muteness of fishes?—here the goddess reigns and revels.—"Boreas, and Cesias, and Argestes loud," do not with their interconfounding

---

[1] From "Poems of all sorts," by Richard Fleckno, 1653.

uproars more augment the brawl—nor the waves of the blown Baltic with their clubbed sounds—than their opposite (Silence her sacred self) is multiplied and rendered more intense by numbers, and by sympathy. She too hath her deeps, that call unto deeps. Negation itself hath a positive more and less; and closed eyes would seem to obscure the great obscurity of midnight.

There are wounds which an imperfect solitude cannot heal. By imperfect I mean that which a man enjoyeth by himself. The perfect is that which he can sometimes attain in crowds, but nowhere so absolutely as in a Quakers' Meeting. — Those first hermits did certainly understand this principle, when they retired into Egyptian solitudes, not singly, but in shoals, to enjoy one another's want of conversation. The Carthusian is bound to his brethren by this agreeing spirit of incommunicativeness. In secular occasions, what so pleasant as to be reading a book through a long winter evening, with a friend sitting by—say, a wife—he, or she, too, (if that be probable,) reading another without interruption, or oral communication?—can there be no sympathy without the gabble of words?—away with this inhuman, shy, single, shade-and-cavern-haunting solitariness. Give me, Master Zimmerman, a sympathetic solitude.

To pace alone in the cloisters or side aisles of some cathedral, time-stricken;

> Or under hanging mountains,
> Or by the fall of fountains;

is but a vulgar luxury compared with that which those enjoy who come together for the purposes of more complete, abstracted solitude. This is the loneliness "to be felt."—The Abbey Church of Westminster hath nothing so solemn, so spirit soothing, as the naked walls and benches of a Quakers' Meeting. Here are no tombs, no inscriptions.

> ———Sands, ignoble things,
> Dropt from the ruined sides of kings—

but here is something which throws Antiquity herself into the fore-ground—SILENCE—eldest of things—language of old Night—primitive discourser—to which the insolent decays of mouldering grandeur have but arrived by a violent, and, as we may say, unnatural progression.

> How reverend is the view of these hushed heads,
> Looking tranquillity!

Nothing-plotting, nought-caballing, unmischievous synod! convocation without intrigue! parliament without debate! what a lesson dost thou read to council, and to consistory!—if my pen treat of you lightly—as haply it will wander—yet my spirit hath gravely felt the wisdom of your custom, when, sitting among you in deepest peace, which some out-welling tears would rather confirm than disturb, I have reverted to the times of your beginnings, and the sowings of the seed by Fox and Dewesbury.—I have witnessed that which brought before my eyes your heroic tranquillity, inflexible to the rude jests and serious violences of the insolent soldiery, republican or royalist, sent to molest you—for ye sate betwixt the fires of two persecutions, the outcast and off-scouring of church and presbytery.—I have seen the reeling sea-ruffian, who had wandered into your receptacle with the avowed intention of disturbing your quiet, from the very spirit of the place receive in a moment a new heart, and presently sit among ye as a lamb amidst lambs. And I remember Penn before his accusers, and Fox in the bail dock, where he was lifted up in spirit, as he tells us, and "the Judge and the Jury became as dead men under his feet."

Reader, if you are not acquainted with it, I would recommend to you, above all church-narratives, to read Sewel's History of the Quakers. It is in folio, and is the abstract of the journals of Fox and the primitive Friends. It is far more edifying and affecting than anything you will read of Wesley and his colleagues. Here is nothing to stagger you, nothing to make you mistrust, no suspicion of alloy, no drop or dreg of the

worldly or ambitious spirit. You will here read the true story of that much-injured, ridiculed man (who perhaps hath been a byword in your mouth)—James Naylor: what dreadful sufferings, with what patience, he endured, even to the boring through of his tongue with red-hot irons, without a murmur; and with what strength of mind, when the delusion he had fallen into, which they stigmatised for blasphemy, had given way to clearer thoughts, he could renounce his error, in a strain of the beautifullest humility, yet keep his first grounds, and be a Quaker still!—so different from the practice of your common converts from enthusiasm, who, when they apostatize, *apostatize all*, and think they can never get far enough from the society of their former errors, even to the renunciation of some saving truths, with which they had been mingled, not implicated.

Get the writings of John Woolman by heart; and love the early Quakers.

How far the followers of these good men in our days have kept to the primitive spirit, or in what proportion they have substituted formality for it, the Judge of Spirits can alone determine. I have seen faces in their assemblies upon which the dove sate visibly brooding. Others, again, I have watched, when my thoughts should have been better engaged, in which I could possibly detect nothing but a blank inanity. But quiet was in all, and the disposition to unanimity, and the absence of the fierce controversial workings.—If the spiritual pretensions of the Quakers have abated, at least they make few pretences. Hypocrites they certainly are not, in their preaching. It is seldom, indeed, that you shall see one get up amongst them to hold forth. Only now and then a trembling, female, generally *ancient*, voice is heard—you cannot guess from what part of the meeting it proceeds—with a low, buzzing, musical sound, laying out a few words which "she thought might suit the condition of some present," with a quaking diffidence, which leaves no possibility of supposing that anything of female vanity was mixed up, where the tones were so full of tenderness, and a restraining modesty.—The men, for what I have observed, speak seldomer.

Once only, and it was some years ago, I witnessed a sample of the old Foxian orgasm. It was a man of giant stature, who, as Wordsworth phrases it, might have danced "from head to foot equipt in iron mail." His frame was of iron too. But *he* was malleable. I saw him shake all over with the spirit—I dare not say of delusion. The strivings of the outer man were unutterable—he seemed not to speak, but to be spoken from. I saw the strong man bowed down, and his knees to fail—his joints all seemed loosening—it was a figure to set off against Paul preaching—the words he uttered were few, and sound—he was evidently resisting his will—keeping down his own word-wisdom with more mighty effort than the world's orators strain for theirs. "He had been a WIT in his youth," he told us, with expressions of a sober remorse. And it was not till long after the impression had begun to wear away that I was enabled, with something like a smile, to recall the striking incongruity of the confession—understanding the term in its worldly acceptation—with the frame and physiognomy of the person before me. His brow would have scared away the Levities—the Jocos Risus-que—faster than the Loves fled the face of Dis at Enna.—By *wit*, even in his youth, I will be sworn he understood something far within the limits of an allowable liberty.

More frequently the Meeting is broken up without a word having been spoken. But the mind has been fed. You go away with a sermon not made with hands. You have been in the milder caverns of Trophonius; or as in some den, where that fiercest and savagest of all wild creatures, the TONGUE, that unruly member, has strangely lain tied up and captive. You have bathed with stillness.—O, when the spirit is sore fretted, even tired to sickness of the janglings and nonsense-noises of the world, what a balm and a solace it is to go and seat yourself for a quiet half-hour upon some undisputed corner of a bench, among the gentle Quakers!

Their garb and stillness conjoined, present a uniformity, tranquil and herd-like—as in the pasture—"forty feeding like one."—

The very garments of a Quaker seem incapable of receiving a soil; and cleanliness in them to be something more than the absence of its contrary. Every Quakeress is a lily; and when they come up in bands to their Whitsun conferences, whitening the easterly streets of the metropolis, from all parts of the United Kingdom, they show like troops of the Shining Ones.

THE OLD AND THE NEW SCHOOLMASTER.

My reading has been lamentably desultory and immethodical. Odd, out of the way, old English plays, and treatises, have supplied me with most of my notions, and ways of feeling. In everything that relates to *science*, I am a whole Encyclopædia behind the rest of the world. I should have scarcely cut a figure among the franklins, or country gentlemen, in King John's days. I know less geography than a schoolboy of six weeks' standing. To me a map of old Ortelius is as authentic as Arrowsmith. I do not know whereabout Africa merges into Asia; whether Ethiopia lie in one or other of those great divisions; nor can form the remotest conjecture of the position of New South Wales, or Van Diemen's Land. Yet do I hold a correspondence with a very dear friend in the first-named of these two Terræ Incognitæ. I have no astronomy. I do not know where to look for the Bear, or Charles's Wain; the place of any star; or the name of any of them at sight. I guess at Venus only by her brightness—and if the sun on some portentous morn were to make his first appearance in the West, I verily believe, that, while all the world were gasping

in apprehension about me, I alone should stand unterrified,
from sheer incuriosity and want of observation. Of
history and chronology I possess some vague points, such
as one cannot help picking up in the course of miscellaneous study; but I never deliberately sat down to a
chronicle, even of my own country. I have most dim
apprehensions of the four great monarchies; and some
times the Assyrian, sometimes the Persian, floats as *first*
in my fancy. I make the widest conjectures concerning
Egypt, and her shepherd kings. My friend *M.*, with
great painstaking, got me to think I understood the first
proposition in Euclid, but gave me over in despair at the
second. I am entirely unacquainted with the modern
languages; and, like a better man than myself, have
"small Latin and less Greek." I am a stranger to the
shapes and texture of the commonest trees, herbs, flowers
—not from the circumstance of my being town-born—for
I should have brought the same inobservant spirit into
the world with me, had I first seen it "on Devon's
leafy shores,"—and am no less at a loss among purely
town objects, tools, engines, mechanic processes.—Not
that I affect ignorance—but my head has not many
mansions, nor spacious; and I have been obliged to fill
it with such cabinet curiosities as it can hold without
aching. I sometimes wonder how I have passed my
probation with so little discredit in the world, as I have
done, upon so meagre a stock. But the fact is, a man
may do very well with a very little knowledge, and
scarce be found out, in mixed company; everybody is so
much more ready to produce his own, than to call for a
display of your acquisitions. But in a *tête-à-tête* there is
no shuffling. The truth will out. There is nothing
which I dread so much, as the being left alone for a
quarter of an hour with a sensible, well-informed man,
that does not know me. I lately got into a dilemma of
this sort.—

In one of my daily jaunts between Bishopsgate and
Shacklewell, the coach stopped to take up a staid-looking

gentleman, about the wrong side of thirty, who was giving his parting directions (while the steps were adjusting), in a tone of mild authority, to a tall youth, who seemed to be neither his clerk, his son, nor his servant, but something partaking of all three. The youth was dismissed, and we drove on. As we were the sole passengers, he naturally enough addressed his conversation to me; and we discussed the merits of the fare; the civility and punctuality of the driver; the circumstance of an opposition coach having been lately set up, with the probabilities of its success—to all which I was enabled to return pretty satisfactory answers, having been drilled into this kind of etiquette by some years' daily practice of riding to and fro in the stage aforesaid—when he suddenly alarmed me by a startling question, whether I had seen the show of prize cattle that morning in Smithfield? Now, as I had not seen it, and do not greatly care for such sort of exhibitions, I was obliged to return a cold negative. He seemed a little mortified, as well as astonished, at my declaration, as (it appeared) he was just come fresh from the sight, and doubtless had hoped to compare notes on the subject. However, he assured me that I had lost a fine treat, as it far exceeded the show of last year. We were now approaching Norton Folgate, when the sight of some shop-goods *ticketed* freshened him up into a dissertation upon the cheapness of cottons this spring. I was now a little in heart, as the nature of my morning avocations had brought me into some sort of familiarity with the raw material; and I was surprised to find how eloquent I was becoming on the state of the India market; when, presently, he dashed my incipient vanity to the earth at once, by inquiring whether I had ever made any calculation as to the value of the rental of all the retail shops in London. Had he asked of me what song the Syrens sang, or what name Achilles assumed when he hid himself among women, I might, with Sir Thomas Browne, have hazarded a "wide solution."[1]

[1] Urn Burial.

My companion saw my embarrassment, and, the almshouses beyond Shoreditch just coming in view, with great good-nature and dexterity shifted his conversation to the subject of public charities; which led to the comparative merits of provision for the poor in past and present times, with observations on the old monastic institutions, and charitable orders; but, finding me rather dimly impressed with some glimmering notions from old poetic associations, than strongly fortified with any speculations reducible to calculation on the subject, he gave the matter up; and, the country beginning to open more and more upon us, as we approached the turnpike at Kingsland (the destined termination of his journey), he put a home thrust upon me, in the most unfortunate position he could have chosen, by advancing some queries relative to the North Pole Expedition. While I was muttering out something about the Panorama of those strange regions (which I had actually seen), by way of parrying the question, the coach stopping relieved me from any further apprehensions. My companion getting out, left me in the comfortable possession of my ignorance; and I heard him, as he went off, putting questions to an outside passenger, who had alighted with him, regarding an epidemic disorder that had been rife about Dalston, and which my friend assured him had gone through five or six schools in that neighbourhood. The truth now flashed upon me, that my companion was a schoolmaster; and that the youth, whom he had parted from at our first acquaintance, must have been one of the bigger boys, or the usher.— He was evidently a kind-hearted man, who did not seem so much desirous of provoking discussion by the questions which he put, as of obtaining information at any rate. It did not appear that he took any interest, either, in such kind of inquiries, for their own sake; but that he was in some way bound to seek for knowledge. A greenish-coloured coat, which he had on, forbade me to surmise that he was a clergyman. The adventure gave birth to some reflections on the difference between persons of his profession in past and present times.

Rest to the souls of those fine old Pedagogues; the breed, long since extinct, of the Lilys, and the Linacres: who believing that all learning was contained in the languages which they taught, and despising every other acquirement as superficial and useless, came to their task as to a sport! Passing from infancy to age, they dreamed away all their days as in a grammar-school. Revolving in a perpetual cycle of declensions, conjugations, syntaxes, and prosodies; renewing constantly the occupations which had charmed their studious childhood; rehearsing continually the part of the past; life must have slipped from them at last like one day. They were always in their first garden, reaping harvests of their golden time, among their *Flori-* and their *Spici-legia:* in Arcadia still, but kings; the ferule of their sway not much harsher, but of like dignity with that mild sceptre attributed to king Basileus; the Greek and Latin, their stately Pamela and their Philoclea; with the occasional duncery of some untoward tyro, serving for a refreshing interlude of a Mopsa, or a clown Damœtas!

With what a savour doth the Preface to Colet's, or (as it is sometimes called) Paul's Accidence, set forth! "To exhort every man to the learning of grammar, that intendeth to attain the understanding of the tongues, wherein is contained a great treasury of wisdom and knowledge, it would seem but vain and lost labour; for so much as it is known, that nothing can surely be ended, whose beginning is either feeble or faulty; and no building be perfect whereas the foundation and groundwork is ready to fall, and unable to uphold the burden of the frame." How well doth this stately preamble (comparable to those which Milton commendeth as "having been the usage to prefix to some solemn law, then first promulgated by Solon or Lycurgus") correspond with and illustrate that pious zeal for conformity, expressed in a succeeding clause, which would fence about grammar-rules with the severity of faith-articles!—"as for the diversity of grammars, it is well profitably taken away by the King's Majesties wisdom, who foreseeing the inconvenience, and favourably providing the remedie, caused one kind of grammar by sundry learned men to be diligently drawn, and so to be set out, only everywhere to be taught for the use of learners, and for the hurt in changing of schoolmaisters." What a *gusto* in that which follows: "wherein it is profitable that he (the pupil) can orderly decline his noun and his verb." *His* noun!

The fine dream is fading away fast; and the least concern of a teacher in the present day is to inculcate grammar-rules.

The modern schoolmaster is expected to know a little of everything, because his pupil is required not to be entirely ignorant of anything. He must be superficially, if I may so say, omniscient. He is to know something of pneumatics; of chemistry; of whatever is curious or proper to excite the attention of the youthful mind; an insight into mechanics is desirable, with a touch of statistics; the quality of soils, etc., botany, the constitution of his country, *cum multis aliis*. You may get a notion of some part of his expected duties by consulting the famous Tractate on Education, addressed to Mr. Hartlib.

All these things—these, or the desire of them—he is expected to instil, not by set lessons from professors, which he may charge in the bill, but at school intervals, as he walks the streets, or saunters through green fields (those natural instructors), with his pupils. The least part of what is expected from him is to be done in school-hours. He must insinuate knowledge at the *mollia tempora fandi*. He must seize every occasion—the season of the year—the time of the day—a passing cloud—a rainbow—a waggon of hay—a regiment of soldiers going by—to inculcate something useful. He can receive no pleasure from a casual glimpse of Nature, but must catch at it as an object of instruction. He must inter-

pret beauty into the picturesque. He cannot relish a beggar-man, or a gipsy, for thinking of the suitable improvement. Nothing comes to him, not spoiled by the sophisticating medium of moral uses. The Universe—that Great Book, as it has been called—is to him, indeed, to all intents and purposes, a book out of which he is doomed to read tedious homilies to distasting schoolboys.
—Vacations themselves are none to him, he is only rather worse off than before; for commonly he has some intrusive upper-boy fastened upon him at such times; some cadet of a great family; some neglected lump of nobility, or gentry; that he must drag after him to the play, to the Panorama, to Mr. Bartley's Orrery, to the Panopticon, or into the country, to a friend's house, or his favourite watering-place. Wherever he goes this uneasy shadow attends him. A boy is at his board, and in his path, and in all his movements. He is boy-rid, sick of perpetual boy.

Boys are capital fellows in their own way, among their mates; but they are unwholesome companions for grown people. The restraint is felt no less on the one side than on the other.—Even a child, that "plaything for an hour," tires *always*. The noises of children, playing their own fancies—as I now hearken to them, by fits, sporting on the green before my window, while I am engaged in these grave speculations at my neat suburban retreat at Shacklewell— by distance made more sweet— inexpressibly take from the labour of my task. It is like writing to music. They seem to modulate my periods. They ought at least to do so—for in the voice of that tender age there is a kind of poetry, far unlike the harsh prose-accents of man's conversation.—I should but spoil their sport, and diminish my own sympathy for them, by mingling in their pastime.

I would not be domesticated all my days with a person of very superior capacity to my own—not, if I know myself at all, from any considerations of jealousy or self-comparison, for the occasional communion with such minds has constituted the fortune and felicity of my life—but the habit of too constant intercourse with spirits above you, instead of raising you, keeps you down. Too frequent doses of original thinking from others restrain what lesser portion of that faculty you may possess of your own. You get entangled in another man's mind, even as you lose yourself in another man's grounds. You are walking with a tall varlet, whose strides out-pace yours to lassitude. The constant operation of such potent agency would reduce me, I am convinced, to imbecility. You may derive thoughts from others; your way of thinking, the mould in which your thoughts are cast, must be your own. Intellect may be imparted, but not each man's intellectual frame.—

As little as I should wish to be always thus dragged upward, as little (or rather still less) is it desirable to be stunted downwards by your associates. The trumpet does not more stun you by its loudness, than a whisper teases you by its provoking inaudibility.

Why are we never quite at our ease in the presence of a schoolmaster?—because we are conscious that he is not quite at his ease in ours. He is awkward, and out of place in the society of his equals. He comes like Gulliver from among his little people, and he cannot fit the stature of his understanding to yours. He cannot meet you on the square. He wants a point given him, like an indifferent whist-player. He is so used to teaching, that he wants to be teaching *you*. One of these professors, upon my complaining that these little sketches of mine were anything but methodical, and that I was unable to make them otherwise, kindly offered to instruct me in the method by which young gentlemen in *his* seminary were taught to compose English themes. The jests of a schoolmaster are coarse, or thin. They do not *all* out of school. He is under the restraint of a formal or didactive hypocrisy in company, as a clergyman is under a moral one. He can no more let his intellect loose in society than the other can his inclinations. He is forlorn among his coevals; his juniors cannot be his friends.

"I take blame to myself," said a sensible man of this profession, writing to a friend respecting a youth who had quitted his school abruptly, "that your nephew was not more attached to me. But persons in my situation are more to be pitied than can well be imagined. We are surrounded by young, and, consequently, ardently affectionate hearts, but *we* can never hope to share an atom of their affections. The relation of master and scholar forbids this. *How pleasing this must be to you, how I envy your feelings!* my friends will sometimes say to me, when they see young men whom I have educated, return after some years' absence from school, their eyes shining with pleasure, while they shake hands with their old master, bringing a present of game to me, or a toy to my wife, and thanking me in the warmest terms for my care of their education. A holiday is begged for the boys; the house is a scene of happiness; I, only, am sad at heart.—This fine-spirited and warm-hearted youth, who fancies he repays his master with gratitude for the care of his boyish years—this young man—in the eight long years I watched over him with a parent's anxiety, never could repay me with one look of genuine feeling. He was proud, when I praised; he was submissive, when I reproved him: but he did never *love* me—and what he now mistakes for gratitude and kindness for me, is but the pleasant sensation which all persons feel at revisiting the scenes of their boyish hopes and fears; and the seeing on equal terms the man they were accustomed to look up to with reverence. My wife, too," this interesting correspondent goes on to say, "my once darling Anna, is the wife of a schoolmaster. When I married her—knowing that the wife of a schoolmaster ought to be a busy notable creature, and fearing that my gentle Anna would ill supply the loss of my dear bustling mother, just then dead, who never sat still, was in every part of the house in a moment, and whom I was obliged sometimes to threaten to fasten down in a chair, to save her from fatiguing herself to death— I expressed my fears that I was bring

ing her into a way of life unsuitable to her; and she, who loved me tenderly, promised for my sake to exert herself to perform the duties of her new situation. She promised, and she has kept her word. What wonders will not woman's love perform? —My house is managed with a propriety and decorum unknown in other schools; my boys are well fed, look healthy, and have every proper accommodation; and all this performed with a careful economy, that never descends to meanness. But I have lost my gentle *helpless* Anna! When we sit down to enjoy an hour of repose after the fatigue of the day, I am compelled to listen to what have been her useful (and they are really useful) employments through the day, and what she proposes for her to-morrow's task. Her heart and her features are changed by the duties of her situation. To the boys, she never appears other than the *master's wife*, and she looks up to me as the *boys' master;* to whom all show of love and affection would be highly improper, and unbecoming the dignity of her situation and mine. Yet *this* my gratitude forbids me to hint to her. For my sake she submitted to be this altered creature, and can I reproach her for it?"—For the communication of this letter I am indebted to my cousin Bridget.

IMPERFECT SYMPATHIES.

> I am of a constitution so general, that it consorts and sympathiseth with all things; I have no antipathy, or rather idiosyncrasy in anything. Those natural repugnancies do not touch me, nor do I behold with prejudice the French, Italian, Spaniard, or Dutch. *Religio Medici.*

THAT the author of the Religio Medici mounted upon the airy stilts of abstraction, conversant about notional and conjectural essences; in whose categories of Being the possible took the upper hand of the actual; should have overlooked the impertinent individualities of such poor concretions as mankind, is not much to be admired. It is rather to be wondered at, that in the genus of animals he should have condescended to distinguish that species at all. For myself—earth-bound and fettered to the scene of my activities,—

> Standing on earth, not rapt above the sky,

I confess that I do feel the differences of mankind, national or individual, to an unhealthy excess. I can look with no indifferent eye upon things or persons. Whatever is, is to me a matter of taste or distaste; or when once it becomes indifferent it begins to be disrelishing. I am, in plainer words, a bundle of prejudices—made up of likings and dislikings—the veriest thrall to sympathies, apathies, antipathies. In a certain sense, I hope it may be said of me that I am a lover of my species. I can feel for all indifferently, but I cannot feel towards all equally. The more purely-English word that expresses sympathy, will better explain my meaning. I can be a friend to a worthy man, who upon another account cannot be my mate or *fellow*. I cannot *like* all people alike.[1]

[1] I would be understood as confining myself to the subject of *imperfect sympathies*. To nations or classes of men there can be no direct antipathy. There may be individuals born and constellated so opposite to another individual nature, that the same sphere cannot hold them. I have met with my moral antipodes, and can believe the story of two persons meeting (who never saw one another before in their lives) and instantly fighting.

> ———We by proof find there should be
> 'Twixt man and man such an antipathy,
> That though he can show no just reason why
> For any former wrong or injury,
> Can neither find a blemish in his fame,
> Nor aught in face or feature justly blame,
> Can challenge or accuse him of no evil,
> Yet notwithstanding hates him as a devil.

The lines are from old Heywood's "Hierarchie of Angels," and he subjoins a curious story in confirmation, of a Spaniard who attempted to assassinate a king Ferdinand of Spain, and being put

I have been trying all my life to like Scotchmen, and am obliged to desist from the experiment in despair. They cannot like me—and in truth, I never knew one of that nation who attempted to do it. There is something more plain and ingenuous in their mode of proceeding. We know one another at first sight. There is an order of imperfect intellects (under which mine must be content to rank) which in its constitution is essentially anti-Caledonian. The owners of the sort of faculties I allude to, have minds rather suggestive than comprehensive. They have no pretences to much clearness or precision in their ideas, or in their manner of expressing them. Their intellectual wardrobe (to confess fairly) has few whole pieces in it. They are content with fragments and scattered pieces of Truth. She presents no full front to them—a feature or side-face at the most. Hints and glimpses, germs and crude essays at a system, is the utmost they pretend to. They beat up a little game peradventure—and leave it to knottier heads, more robust constitutions, to run it down. The light that lights them is not steady and polar, but mutable and shifting: waxing, and again waning. Their conversation is accordingly. They will throw out a random word in or out of season, and be content to let it pass for what it is worth. They cannot speak always as if they were upon their oath—but must be understood, speaking or writing, with some abatement. They seldom wait to mature a proposition, but e'en bring it to market in the green ear. They delight to impart their defective discoveries as they arise, without waiting for their full development. They are no systematizers, and would but err more by attempting it. Their minds, as I said before, are suggestive merely. The brain of a true Caledonian (if I am not mistaken) is constituted upon quite a different plan. His Minerva is

to the rack could give no other reason for the deed but an inveterate antipathy which he had taken to the first sight of the king.

―――'The cause which to that act compell'd him
Was, he ne'er loved him since he first beheld him.

born in panoply. You are never admitted to see his ideas in their growth—if, indeed, they do grow, and are not rather put together upon principles of clock-work. You never catch his mind in an undress. He never hints or suggests anything, but unlades his stock of ideas in perfect order and completeness. He brings his total wealth into company, and gravely unpacks it. His riches are always about him. He never stoops to catch a glittering something in your presence to share it with you, before he quite knows whether it be true touch or not. You cannot cry *halves* to anything that he finds. He does not find, but bring. You never witness his first apprehension of a thing. His understanding is always at its meridian—you never see the first dawn, the early streaks.—He has no falterings of self-suspicion. Surmises, guesses, misgivings, half-intuitions, semi-consciousnesses, partial illuminations, dim instincts, embryo conceptions, have no place in his brain or vocabulary. The twilight of dubiety never falls upon him. Is he orthodox—he has no doubts. Is he an infidel—he has none either. Between the affirmative and the negative there is no border-land with him. You cannot hover with him upon the confines of truth, or wander in the maze of a probable argument. He always keeps the path. You cannot make excursions with him—for he sets you right. His taste never fluctuates. His morality never abates. He cannot compromise, or understand middle actions. There can be but a right and a wrong. His conversation is as a book. His affirmations have the sanctity of an oath. You must speak upon the square with him. He stops a metaphor like a suspected person in an enemy's country. "A healthy book!"—said one of his countrymen to me, who had ventured to give that appellation to John Buncle,—"Did I catch rightly what you said? I have heard of a man in health, and of a healthy state of body, but I do not see how that epithet can be properly applied to a book." Above all, you must beware of indirect expressions before a Caledonian. Clap an extinguisher upon your irony, if you are unhappily blest with a vein of it. Remember you are upon your oath. I have a print of a graceful female after Leonardo da Vinci, which I was showing off to Mr. * * * * After he had examined it minutely, I ventured to ask him how he liked MY BEAUTY (a foolish name it goes by among my friends)—when he very gravely assured me, that "he had considerable respect for my character and talents" (so he was pleased to say), "but had not given himself much thought about the degree of my personal pretensions." The misconception staggered me, but did not seem much to disconcert him.— Persons of this nation are particularly fond of affirming a truth—which nobody doubts. They do not so properly affirm, as annunciate it. They do indeed appear to have such a love of truth (as if, like virtue, it were valuable for itself) that all truth becomes equally valuable, whether the proposition that contains it be new or old, disputed, or such as is impossible to become a subject of disputation. I was present not long since at a party of North Britons, where a son of Burns was expected ; and happened to drop a silly expression (in my South British way), that I wished it were the father instead of the son—when four of them started up at once to inform me, that "that was impossible, because he was dead." An impracticable wish, it seems, was more than they could conceive. Swift has hit off this part of their character, namely their love of truth, in his biting way, but with an illiberality that necessarily confines the passage to the margin.[1] The

[1] There are some people who think they sufficiently acquit themselves, and entertain their company, with relating facts of no consequence, not at all out of the road of such common incidents as happen every day ; and this I have observed more frequently among the Scots than any other nation, who are very careful not to omit the minutest circumstances of time or place ; which kind of discourse, if it were not a little relieved by the uncouth terms and phrases, as well as accent and gesture, peculiar to that country, would be hardly tolerable.—*Hints towards an Essay on Conversation.*

tediousness of these people is certainly provoking. I wonder if they ever tire one another!—In my early life I had a passionate fondness for the poetry of Burns. I have sometimes foolishly hoped to ingratiate myself with his countrymen by expressing it. But I have always found that a true Scot resents your admiration of his compatriot even more than he would your contempt of him. The latter he imputes to your "imperfect acquaintance with many of the words which he uses;" and the same objection makes it a presumption in you to suppose that you can admire him.—Thomson they seem to have forgotten. Smollett they have neither forgotten nor forgiven, for his delineation of Rory and his companion, upon their first introduction to our metropolis.—Speak of Smollett as a great genius, and they will retort upon you Hume's History compared with *his* Continuation of it. What if the historian had continued Humphrey Clinker?

I have, in the abstract, no disrespect for Jews. They are a piece of stubborn antiquity, compared with which Stonehenge is in its nonage. They date beyond the pyramids. But I should not care to be in habits of familiar intercourse with any of that nation. I confess that I have not the nerves to enter their synagogues. Old prejudices cling about me. I cannot shake off the story of Hugh of Lincoln. Centuries of injury, contempt, and hate, on the one side,—of cloaked revenge, dissimulation, and hate, on the other, between our and their fathers, must and ought to affect the blood of the children. I cannot believe it can run clear and kindly yet; or that a few fine words, such as candour, liberality, the light of a nineteenth century, can close up the breaches of so deadly a disunion. A Hebrew is nowhere congenial to me. He is least distasteful on 'Change—for the mercantile spirit levels all distinctions, as all are beauties in the dark. I boldly confess that I do not relish the approximation of Jew and Christian, which has become so fashionable. The reciprocal endearments have, to me, something hypocritical and unnatural in them. I do not like to see the Church and Synagogue kissing and congeeing in awkward postures of an affected civility. If *they* are converted, why do they not come over to us altogether? Why keep up a form of separation, when the life of it is fled? If they can sit with us at table, why do they keck at our cookery? I do not understand these half convertites. Jews christianizing—Christians judaizing—puzzle me. I like fish or flesh. A moderate Jew is a more confounding piece of anomaly than a wet Quaker. The spirit of the synagogue is essentially *separative*. B—— would have been more in keeping if he had abided by the faith of his forefathers. There is a fine scorn in his face, which nature meant to be of——Christians.—The Hebrew spirit is strong in him, in spite of his proselytism. He cannot conquer the Shibboleth. How it breaks out, when he sings, "The Children of Israel passed through the Red Sea!" The auditors, for the moment, are as Egyptians to him, and he rides over our necks in triumph. There is no mistaking him. B—— has a strong expression of sense in his countenance, and it is confirmed by his singing. The foundation of his vocal excellence is sense. He sings with understanding, as Kemble delivered dialogue. He would sing the Commandments, and give an appropriate character to each prohibition. His nation, in general, have not oversensible countenances. How should they?—but you seldom see a silly expression among them.—Gain, and the pursuit of gain, sharpen a man's visage. I never heard of an idiot being born among them. Some admire the Jewish female-physiognomy. I admire it—but with trembling. Jael had those full dark inscrutable eyes.

In the Negro countenance you will often meet with strong traits of benignity. I have felt yearnings of tenderness towards some of these faces—or rather masks—that have looked out kindly upon one in casual encounters in the streets and highways. I love what Fuller beautifully calls—these "images of God cut in ebony."

But I should not like to associate with them, to share my meals and my good nights with them—because they are black.

I love Quaker ways, and Quaker worship. I venerate the Quaker principles. It does me good for the rest of the day when I meet any of their people in my path. When I am ruffled or disturbed by any occurrence, the sight, or quiet voice of a Quaker, acts upon me as a ventilator, lightening the air, and taking off a load from the bosom. But I cannot like the Quakers (as Desdemona would say) " to live with them." I am all over sophisticated — with humours, fancies, craving hourly sympathy. I must have books, pictures, theatres, chit-chat, scandal, jokes, ambiguities, and a thousand whim-whams, which their simpler taste can do without. I should starve at their primitive banquet. My appetites are too high for the salads which (according to Evelyn) Eve dressed for the angel; my gusto too excited

> To sit a guest with Daniel at his pulse.

The indirect answers which Quakers are often found to return to a question put to them may be explained, I think, without the vulgar assumption, that they are more given to evasion and equivocating than other people. They naturally look to their words more carefully, and are more cautious of committing themselves. They have a peculiar character to keep up on this head. They stand in a manner upon their veracity. A Quaker is by law exempted from taking an oath. The custom of resorting to an oath in extreme cases, sanctified as it is by all religious antiquity, is apt (it must be confessed) to introduce into the laxer sort of minds the notion of two kinds of truth — the one applicable to the solemn affairs of justice, and the other to the common proceedings of daily intercourse. As truth bound upon the conscience by an oath can be but truth, so in the common affirmations of the shop and the market-place a latitude is expected and conceded upon questions wanting this solemn covenant.

Something less than truth satisfies. It is common to hear a person say, "You do not expect me to speak as if I were upon my oath." Hence a great deal of incorrectness and inadvertency, short of falsehood, creeps into ordinary conversation; and a kind of secondary or laic-truth is tolerated, where clergy-truth—oath-truth, by the nature of the circumstances, is not required. A Quaker knows none of this distinction. His simple affirmation being received upon the most sacred occasions, without any further test, stamps a value upon the words which he is to use upon the most indifferent topics of life. He looks to them, naturally, with more severity. You can have of him no more than his word. He knows, if he is caught tripping in a casual expression, he forfeits, for himself at least, his claim to the invidious exemption. He knows that his syllables are weighed—and how far a consciousness of this particular watchfulness, exerted against a person, has a tendency to produce indirect answers, and a diverting of the question by honest means, might be illustrated, and the practice justified by a more sacred example than is proper to be adduced upon this occasion. The admirable presence of mind, which is notorious in Quakers upon all contingencies, might be traced to this imposed self-watchfulness—if it did not seem rather an humble and secular scion of that old stock of religious constancy, which never bent or faltered, in the Primitive Friends, or gave way to the winds of persecution, to the violence of judge or accuser, under trials and racking examinations. "You will never be the wiser, if I sit here answering your questions till midnight," said one of those upright Justicers to Penn, who had been putting law-cases with a puzzling subtlety. "Thereafter as the answers may be," retorted the Quaker. The astonishing composure of this people is sometimes ludicrously displayed in lighter instances.—I was travelling in a stage-coach with three male Quakers, buttoned up in the straitest nonconformity of their sect. We stopped to bait at Andover, where a meal, partly tea apparatus, partly supper, was set before us. My friends confined themselves to the tea-table. I in my way took supper. When the landlady brought in the bill, the eldest of my companions discovered that she had charged for both meals. This was resisted. Mine hostess was very clamorous and positive. Some mild arguments were used on the part of the Quakers, for which the heated mind of the good lady seemed by no means a fit recipient. The guard came in with his usual peremptory notice. The Quakers pulled out their money and formally tendered it—so much for tea—I, in humble imitation, tendering mine—for the supper which I had taken. She would not relax in her demand. So they all three quietly put up their silver, as did myself, and marched out of the room, the eldest and gravest going first, with myself closing up the rear, who thought I could not do better than follow the example of such grave and warrantable personages. We got in. The steps went up. The coach drove off. The murmurs of mine hostess, not very indistinctly or ambiguously pronounced, became after a time inaudible—and now my conscience, which the whimsical scene had for a while suspended, beginning to give some twitches, I waited, in the hope that some justification would be offered by these serious persons for the seeming injustice of their conduct. To my great surprise not a syllable was dropped on the subject. They sat as mute as at a meeting. At length the eldest of them broke silence, by inquiring of his next neighbour, "Hast thee heard how indigos go at the India House?" and the question operated as a soporific on my moral feeling as far as Exeter.

WITCHES, AND OTHER NIGHT FEARS.

We are too hasty when we set down our ancestors in the gross for fools, for the monstrous inconsistencies (as they seem to us) involved in their creed of witchcraft. In the relations of this visible world we find them to have been as rational, and shrewd to detect an historic anomaly, as ourselves. But when once the invisible world was supposed to be open, and the lawless agency of bad spirits assumed, what measures of probability, of decency, of fitness, or proportion—of that which distinguishes the likely from the palpable absurd—could they have to guide them in the rejection or admission of any particular testimony?—That maidens pined away, wasting inwardly as their waxen images consumed before a fire—that corn was lodged, and cattle lamed—that whirlwinds uptore in diabolic revelry the oaks of the forest—or that spits and kettles only danced a fearful-innocent vagary about some rustic's kitchen when no wind was stirring—were all equally probable where no law of agency was understood. That the prince of the powers of darkness, passing by the flower and pomp of the earth, should lay preposterous siege to the weak fantasy of indigent eld—has neither likelihood nor unlikelihood *à priori* to us, who have no measure to guess at his policy, or standard to estimate what rate those anile souls may fetch in the devil's market. Nor, when the wicked are expressly symbolised by a goat, was it to be wondered at so much, that *he* should come sometimes in that body, and assert his metaphor.—That the intercourse was opened at all between both worlds was perhaps the mistake—but that once assumed, I see no reason for disbelieving one attested story of this nature more than another on the score of absurdity. There is no law to judge of the lawless, or canon by which a dream may be criticised.

I have sometimes thought that I could not have existed in the days of received witchcraft: that I could not have slept in a village where one of those reputed hags dwelt. Our ancestors were bolder or more obtuse. Amidst the universal belief that these wretches were in league with the author of all evil, holding hell tributary to their muttering, no simple justice of the peace seems to have scrupled issuing, or silly headborough serving, a warrant upon them—as if they should subpœna Satan!—Prospero in his boat, with his books and wand about him, suffers himself to be conveyed away at the mercy of his enemies to an unknown island. He might have raised a storm or two, we think, on the passage. His acquiescence is in exact analogy to the non-resistance of witches to the constituted powers.—What stops the Fiend in Spenser from tearing Guyon to pieces—or who had made it a condition of his prey that Guyon must take assay of the glorious bait—we have no guess. We do not know the laws of that country.

From my childhood I was extremely inquisitive about witches and witch-stories. My maid, and more legendary aunt, supplied me with good store. But I shall mention the accident which directed my curiosity originally into this channel. In my father's book-closet the history of the Bible by Stackhouse occupied a distinguished station. The pictures with which it abounds—one of the ark, in particular, and another of Solomon's temple, delineated with all the fidelity of ocular admeasurement, as if the artist had been upon the spot—attracted my childish attention. There was a picture, too, of the Witch raising up Samuel, which I wish that I had never seen. We shall come to that hereafter. Stackhouse is in two huge tomes; and there was a pleasure in removing folios of that magnitude, which, with infinite straining, was as much as I could manage, from the situation which they occupied upon an upper shelf. I have not met with the work from that time to this, but I remember it consisted of Old Testament stories, orderly set down, with the *objection* appended to each story, and the *solution* of the objection regularly tacked to that. The *objection* was a summary of whatever difficulties had been opposed to the credibility of the history by the shrewdness of ancient or modern infidelity, drawn up with an almost complimentary excess of candour. The *solution* was brief, modest, and satisfactory. The bane and antidote were both before you. To doubts so put, and so quashed, there seemed to be an end for ever. The dragon lay dead, for the foot of the veriest babe to trample on. But—like as was rather feared than realized from that slain monster in Spenser—from the womb of those crushed errors young dragonets would creep, exceeding the prowess of so tender a Saint George as myself to vanquish. The habit of expecting objections to every passage set me upon starting more objections, for the glory of finding a solution of my own for them. I became staggered and perplexed, a sceptic in long-coats. The pretty Bible stories which I had read, or heard read in church, lost their purity and sincerity of impression, and were turned into so many historic or chronologic theses to be defended against whatever impugners. I was not to disbelieve them, but—the next thing to that—I was to be quite sure that some one or other would or had disbelieved them. Next to making a child an infidel is the letting him know that there are infidels at all. Credulity is the man's weakness, but the child's strength. O, how ugly sound scriptural doubts from the mouth of a babe and a suckling!—I should have lost myself in these mazes, and have pined away, I think, with such unfit sustenance as these husks afforded, but for a fortunate piece of ill-fortune which about this time befell me. Turning over the picture of the ark with too much haste, I unhappily made a breach in its ingenious fabric—driving my inconsiderate fingers right through the two larger quadrupeds, the elephant and the camel, that stare (as well they might) out of the two last windows next the steerage in that unique piece of naval architecture. Stackhouse was henceforth locked up, and became an interdicted treasure. With the book, the *objections* and *solutions* gradually cleared out of my head, and have seldom returned since in any force to trouble me. But there was one impression which I had imbibed from Stackhouse which no lock or bar could shut out, and which was destined to try my childish nerves rather more seriously.—That detestable picture!

I was dreadfully alive to nervous terrors. The nighttime, solitude, and the dark, were my hell. The sufferings I endured in this nature would justify the expression. I never laid my head on my pillow, I suppose, from the fourth to the seventh or eighth year of my life— so far as memory serves in things so long ago—without an assurance, which realized its own prophecy, of seeing some frightful spectre. Be old Stackhouse then acquitted in part, if I say, that to this picture of the Witch raising up Samuel—(O that old man covered with a mantle!)— I owe—not my midnight terrors, the hell of my infancy —but the shape and manner of their visitation. It was he who dressed up for me a hag that nightly sate upon my pillow—a sure bedfellow, when my aunt or my maid was far from me. All day long, while the book was permitted me, I dreamed waking over his delineation, and at night (if I may use so bold an expression) awoke into sleep, and found the vision true. I durst not, even in the day-light, once enter the chamber where I slept, without my face turned to the window, aversely from the bed where my witch-ridden pillow was. Parents do not know what they do when they leave tender babes alone to go to sleep in the dark. The feeling about for a friendly arm—the hoping for a familiar voice—when they wake screaming—and find none to soothe them— what a terrible shaking it is to their poor nerves! The keeping them up till midnight, through candle-light and the unwholesome hours, as they are called,—would, I am satisfied, in a medical point of view, prove the better caution.—That detestable picture, as I have said, gave the fashion to my dreams—if dreams they were—for the scene of them was invariably the room in which I lay. Had I never met with the picture, the fears would have come self-pictured in some shape or other—

   Headless bear, black man, or ape—

but, as it was, my imaginations took that form.- It is not book, or picture, or the stories of foolish servants, which create these terrors in children. They can at most but give them a direction. Dear little T. H., who of all children has been brought up with the most scrupulous exclusion of every taint of superstition—who was never allowed to hear of goblin or apparition, or scarcely to be told of bad men, or to read or hear of any distressing story —finds all this world of fear, from which he has been so rigidly excluded *ab extra*, in his own "thick-coming fancies;" and from his little midnight pillow, this nurse-child of optimism will start at shapes, unborrowed of tradition, in sweats to which the reveries of the cell-damned murderer are tranquillity.

Gorgons, and Hydras, and Chimæras dire—stories of Celæno and the Harpies—may reproduce themselves in the brain of superstition—but they were there before. They are transcripts, types—the archetypes are in us, and eternal. How else should the recital of that, which we know in a waking sense to be false, come to affect us at all?—or

> ——Names, whose sense we see not,
> Fray us with things that be not?

Is it that we naturally conceive terror from such objects, considered in their capacity of being able to inflict upon us bodily injury?—O, least of all! These terrors are of older standing. They date beyond body—or, without the body, they would have been the same. All the cruel, tormenting, defined devils in Dante tearing, mangling, choking, stifling, scorching demons—are they one half so fearful to the spirit of a man, as the simple idea of a spirit unembodied following him—

> Like one that on a lonesome road
> Doth walk in fear and dread,
> And having once turn'd round, walks on
> And turns no more his head;
> Because he knows a frightful fiend
> Doth close behind him tread.[1]

That the kind of fear here treated of is purely spiritual

---

[1] Mr. Coleridge's Ancient Mariner.

—that it is strong in proportion as it is objectless upon earth—that it predominates in the period of sinless infancy—are difficulties, the solution of which might afford some probable insight into our ante-mundane condition, and a peep at least into the shadowland of pre-existence.

My night fancies have long ceased to be afflictive. I confess an occasional nightmare; but I do not, as in early youth, keep a stud of them. Fiendish faces, with the extinguished taper, will come and look at me; but I know them for mockeries, even while I cannot elude their presence, and I fight and grapple with them. For the credit of my imagination, I am almost ashamed to say how tame and prosaic my dreams are grown. They are never romantic, seldom even rural. They are of architecture and of buildings—cities abroad, which I have never seen and hardly have hoped to see. I have traversed, for the seeming length of a natural day, Rome, Amsterdam, Paris, Lisbon — their churches, palaces, squares, market-places, shops, suburbs, ruins, with an inexpressible sense of delight—a map-like distinctness of trace, and a day-light vividness of vision, that was all but being awake.- I have formerly travelled among the Westmoreland fells- my highest Alps,—but they are objects too mighty for the grasp of my dreaming recognition; and I have again and again awoke with ineffectual struggles of the inner eye, to make out a shape, in any way whatever, of Helvellyn. Methought I was in that country, but the mountains were gone. The poverty of my dreams mortifies me. There is Coleridge, at his will can conjure up icy domes, and pleasure-houses for Kubla Khan, and Abyssinian maids, and songs of Abara, and caverns,

> Where Alph, the sacred river, runs,

to solace his night solitudes— when I cannot muster a fiddle. Barry Cornwall has his tritons and his nereids gamboling before him in nocturnal visions, and proclaiming sons born to Neptune—when my stretch of imaginative activity can hardly, in the night season, raise up the ghost of a fish-wife. To set my failures in somewhat a mortifying light—it was after reading the noble Dream of this poet, that my fancy ran strong upon these marine spectra; and the poor plastic power, such as it is, within me set to work to humour my folly in a sort of dream that very night. Methought I was upon the ocean billows at some sea nuptials, riding and mounted high, with the customary train sounding their conchs before me, (I myself, you may be sure, the *leading god*), and jollily we went careering over the main, till just where Ino Leucothea should have greeted me (I think it was Ino) with a white embrace, the billows gradually subsiding, fell from a sea roughness to a sea calm, and thence to a river motion, and that river (as happens in the familiarization of dreams) was no other than the gentle Thames, which landed me in the wafture of a placid wave or two, alone, safe and inglorious, somewhere at the foot of Lambeth palace.

The degree of the soul's creativeness in sleep might furnish no whimsical criterion of the quantum of poetical faculty resident in the same soul waking. An old gentleman, a friend of mine, and a humorist, used to carry this notion so far, that when he saw any stripling of his acquaintance ambitious of becoming a poet, his first question would be,—"Young man, what sort of dreams have you?" I have so much faith in my old friend's theory, that when I feel that idle vein returning upon me, I presently subside into my proper element of prose, remembering those eluding nereids, and that inauspicious inland landing.

VALENTINE'S DAY.

HAIL to thy returning festival, old Bishop Valentine! Great is thy name in the rubric, thou venerable Archflamen of Hymen! Immortal Go-between; who and what manner of person art thou? Art thou but a *name*, typifying the restless principle which impels poor humans to seek perfection in union? or wert thou indeed a mortal prelate, with thy tippet and thy rochet, thy apron on, and decent lawn sleeves? Mysterious personage! Like unto thee, assuredly, there is no other mitred father in the calendar; not Jerome, nor Ambrose, nor Cyril; nor the consigner of undipt infants to eternal torments, Austin, whom all mothers hate; nor he who hated all mothers, Origen; nor Bishop Bull, nor Archbishop Parker, nor Whitgift. Thou comest attended with thousands and ten thousands of little Loves, and the air is

> Brush'd with the hiss of rustling wings.

Singing Cupids are thy choristers and thy precentors; and instead of the crosier, the mystical arrow is borne before thee.

In other words, this is the day on which those charming little missives, yclepcd Valentines, cross and intercross each other at every street and turning. The weary and all forspent twopenny postman sinks beneath a load of delicate embarrassments, not his own. It is scarcely credible to what an extent this ephemeral courtship is carried on in this loving town, to the great enrichment of porters, and detriment of knockers and bell-wires. In these little visual interpretations, no emblem is so common as the *heart*,—that little three-cornered exponent of all our hopes and fears,—the bestuck and bleeding heart; it is twisted and tortured into more allegories and affectations than an opera hat. What authority we have in history or mythology for placing the headquarters and metropolis of god Cupid in this anatomical seat rather than in any other, is not very clear; but we have got it, and it will serve as well as any other. Else we might easily imagine, upon some other system which might have prevailed for anything which our pathology knows to the contrary, a lover addressing his mistress, in perfect simplicity of feeling, "Madam, my *liver* and fortune are entirely at your disposal;" or putting a delicate question, "Amanda, have you a *midriff* to bestow?" But custom has settled these things, and awarded the seat of sentiment to the aforesaid triangle, while its less fortunate neighbours wait at animal and anatomical distance.

Not many sounds in life, and I include all urban and all rural sounds, exceed in interest a *knock at the door*. It "gives a very echo to the throne where hope is seated." But its issues seldom answer to this oracle within. It is so seldom that just the person we want to see comes. But of all the clamorous visitations the welcomest in expectation is the sound that ushers in, or seems to usher in, a Valentine. As the raven himself was hoarse that announced the fatal entrance of Duncan, so the knock of the postman on this day is light, airy, confident, and befitting one that bringeth good tidings. It is less mechanical than on other days; you will say, "That is not the post, I am sure." Visions of Love, of Cupids, of Hymens!—delightful eternal commonplaces, which "having been will always be;" which no schoolboy nor school-man can write away; having your irreversible throne in the fancy and affections—what are your transports, when the happy maiden, opening with careful finger, careful not to break the emblematic seal, bursts upon the sight of some well-designed allegory, some type, some youthful fancy, not without verses—

       Lovers all,
       A madrigal,

or some such device, not over-abundant in sense—young Love disclaims it,—and not quite silly—something between wind and water, a chorus where the sheep might almost join the shepherd, as they did, or as I apprehend they did, in Arcadia.

All Valentines are not foolish; and I shall not easily forget thine, my kind friend (if I may have leave to call you so) E. B——. E. B. lived opposite a young maiden whom he had often seen, unseen, from his parlour window in C——e Street. She was all joyousness and innocence, and just of an age to enjoy receiving a Valentine, and just of a temper to bear the disappointment of missing one with good humour. E. B. is an artist of no common powers; in the fancy parts of designing, perhaps inferior to none; his name is known at the bottom of many a well-executed vignette in the way of his profession, but no further; for E. B. is modest, and the world meets nobody half way. E. B. meditated how he could repay this young maiden for many a favour which she had done him unknown; for when a kindly face greets us, though but passing by, and never knows us again, nor we it, we should feel it as an obligation: and E. B. did. This good artist set himself at work to please the damsel. It was just before Valentine's day three years since. He wrought, unseen and unsuspected, a wondrous work. We need not say it was on the finest gilt paper with borders—full, not of common hearts and heartless allegory, but all the prettiest stories of love from Ovid, and older poets than Ovid (for E. B. is a scholar). There was Pyramus and Thisbe, and be sure Dido was not forgot, nor Hero and Leander, and swans more than sang in Cayster, with mottoes and fanciful devices, such as beseemed—a work, in short, of magic. Iris dipt the woof. This on Valentine's eve he commended to the all-swallowing indiscriminate orifice (O ignoble trust!) of the common post; but the humble medium did its duty, and from his watchful stand the next morning he saw the cheerful messenger knock, and by-and-by the precious charge delivered. He saw, unseen, the happy girl unfold the Valentine, dance about, clap her hands, as one after one the pretty emblems unfolded themselves. She danced about, not with light love, or foolish expectations, for she had no lover; or, if she had, none she knew that could have created those bright images which delighted her. It was more like some fairy present; a God-send, as our familiarly pious ancestors termed a benefit received where the benefactor was unknown. It would do her no harm. It would do her good for ever after. It is good to love the unknown. I only give this as a specimen of E. B. and his modest way of doing a concealed kindness.

Good morrow to my Valentine, sings poor Ophelia; and no better wish, but with better auspices, we wish to all faithful lovers, who are not too wise to despise old legends, but are content to rank themselves humble diocesans of old Bishop Valentine and his true church.

MY RELATIONS.

I am arrived at that point of life at which a man may account it a blessing, as it is a singularity, if he have either of his parents surviving. I have not that felicity—and sometimes think feelingly of a passage in "Browne's Christian Morals," where he speaks of a man that hath lived sixty or seventy years in the world. "In such a compass of time," he says, "a man may have a close apprehension what it is to be forgotten, when he hath lived to find none who could remember his father, or scarcely the friends of his youth, and may sensibly see with what a face in no long time OBLIVION will look upon himself."

I had an aunt, a dear and good one. She was one whom single blessedness had soured to the world. She often used to say, that I was the only thing in it which she loved; and, when she thought I was quitting it, she grieved over me with mother's tears. A partiality quite so exclusive my reason cannot altogether approve. She was from morning till night poring over good books and devotional exercises. Her favourite volumes were,

"Thomas à Kempis," in Stanhope's translation; and a Roman Catholic Prayer Book, with the *matins* and *complines* regularly set down—terms which I was at that time too young to understand. She persisted in reading them, although admonished daily concerning their Papistical tendency: and went to church every Sabbath, as a good Protestant should do. These were the only books she studied; though, I think at one period of her life, she told me, she had read with great satisfaction the "Adventures of an Unfortunate Young Nobleman." Finding the door of the chapel in Essex Street open one day—it was in the infancy of that heresy—she went in, liked the sermon, and the manner of worship, and frequented it at intervals for some time after. She came not for doctrinal points, and never missed them. With some little asperities in her constitution, which I have above hinted at, she was a steadfast, friendly being, and a fine *old Christian*. She was a woman of strong sense, and a shrewd mind—extraordinary at a *repartee;* one of the few occasions of her breaking silence—else she did not much value wit. The only secular employment I remember to have seen her engaged in, was the splitting of French beans, and dropping them into a china basin of fair water. The odour of those tender vegetables to this day comes back upon my sense, redolent of soothing recollections. Certainly it is the most delicate of culinary operations.

Male aunts, as somebody calls them, I had none to remember. By the uncle's side I may be said to have been born an orphan. Brother, or sister, I never had any to know them. A sister, I think, that should have been Elizabeth, died in both our infancies. What a comfort, or what a care, may I not have missed in her!—But I have cousins sprinkled about in Hertfordshire besides *two*, with whom I have been all my life in habits of the closest intimacy, and whom I may term cousins *par excellence*. These are James and Bridget Elia. They are older than myself by twelve, and ten, years; and neither of them seems disposed, in matters of advice and guidance, to waive any of the prerogatives which primogeniture confers. May they continue still in the same mind; and when they shall be seventy-five, and seventy-three, years old (I cannot spare them sooner), persist in treating me in my grand climacteric precisely as a stripling, or younger brother!

James is an inexplicable cousin. Nature hath her unities, which not every critic can penetrate; or, if we feel, we cannot explain them. The pen of Yorick, and of none since his, could have drawn J. E. entire—those fine Shandean lights and shades, which make up his story. I must limp after in my poor antithetical manner, as the fates have given me grace and talent. J. E. then—to the eye of a common observer at least—seemeth made up of contradictory principles. The genuine child of impulse, the frigid philosopher of prudence—the phlegm of my cousin's doctrine, is invariably at war with his temperament, which is high sanguine. With always some fire-new project in his brain, J. E. is the systematic opponent of innovation, and crier down of everything that has not stood the test of age and experiment. With a hundred fine notions chasing one another hourly in his fancy, he is startled at the least approach to the romantic in others; and, determined by his own sense in everything, commends *you* to the guidance of common sense on all occasions.—With a touch of the eccentric in all which he does or says, he is only anxious that *you* should not commit yourself by doing anything absurd or singular. On my once letting slip at table, that I was not fond of a certain popular dish, he begged me at any rate not to *say* so—for the world would think me mad. He disguises a passionate fondness for works of high art (whereof he hath amassed a choice collection), under the pretext of buying only to sell again—that his enthusiasm may give no encouragement to yours. Yet, if it were so, why does that piece of tender, pastoral Domenichino hang still by his wall?—is the ball of his sight much more dear to him?—or what picture-dealer can talk like him?

Whereas mankind in general are observed to warp their speculative conclusions to the bent of their individual humours, *his* theories are sure to be in diametrical opposition to his constitution. He is courageous as Charles of Sweden, upon instinct; chary of his person upon principle, as a travelling Quaker. He has been preaching up to me, all my life, the doctrine of bowing to the great—the necessity of forms, and manner, to a man's getting on in the world. He himself never aims at either, that I can discover,—and has a spirit that would stand upright in the presence of the Cham of Tartary. It is pleasant to hear him discourse of patience —extolling it as the truest wisdom—and to see him during the last seven minutes that his dinner is getting ready. Nature never ran up in her haste a more restless piece of workmanship than when she moulded this impetuous cousin—and Art never turned out a more elaborate orator than he can display himself to be, upon his favourite topic of the advantages of quiet and contentedness in the state, whatever it be, that we are placed in. He is triumphant on this theme, when he has you safe in one of those short stages that ply for the western road, in a very obstructing manner, at the foot of John Murray's Street—where you get in when it is empty, and are expected to wait till the vehicle hath completed her just freight—a trying three quarters of an hour to some people. He wonders at your fidgetiness,— "where could we be better than we are, *thus sitting, thus consulting?*"—"prefers, for his part, a state of rest to locomotion,"—with an eye all the while upon the coachman, till at length, waxing out of all patience, at *your want of it*, he breaks out into a pathetic remonstrance at the fellow for detaining us so long over the time which he had professed, and declares peremptorily, that "the gentleman in the coach is determined to get out, if he does not drive on that instant."

Very quick at inventing an argument, or detecting a sophistry, he is incapable of attending *you* in any chain of arguing. Indeed, he makes wild work with logic; and seems to jump at most admirable conclusions by some process not at all akin to it. Consonantly enough to this, he hath been heard to deny, upon certain occasions, that there exists such a faculty at all in man as *reason;* and wondereth how man came first to have a conceit of it—enforcing his negation with all the might of *reasoning* he is master of. He has some speculative notions against laughter, and will maintain that laughing is not natural to *him*—when peradventure the next moment his lungs shall crow like chanticleer. He says some of the best things in the world, and declareth that wit is his aversion. It was he who said, upon seeing the Eton boys at play in their grounds—*What a pity to think that these fine ingenuous lads in a few years will all be changed into frivolous Members of Parliament!*

His youth was fiery, glowing, tempestuous—and in age he discovereth no symptom of cooling. This is that which I admire in him. I hate people who meet Time half way. I am for no compromise with that inevitable spoiler. While he lives, J. E. will take his swing.—It does me good, as I walk towards the street of my daily avocation, on some fine May morning, to meet him marching in a quite opposite direction, with a jolly handsome presence, and shining sanguine face, that indicates some purchase in his eye—a Claude—or a Hobbima—for much of his enviable leisure is consumed at Christie's and Phillips's—or where not, to pick up pictures, and such gauds. On these occasions he mostly stoppeth me, to read a short lecture on the advantage a person like me possesses above himself, in having his time occupied with business which he *must* do—assureth me that he often feels it hang heavy on his hands—wishes he had fewer holidays—and goes off—Westward Ho!—chanting a tune, to Pall Mall—perfectly convinced that he has convinced me—while I proceed in my opposite direction tuneless.

It is pleasant, again, to see this Professor of Indifference doing the honours of his new purchase, when he has fairly housed it. You must view it in every light, till *he* has found the best—placing it at this distance, and at that, but always suiting the focus of your sight to his own. You must spy at it through your fingers, to catch the aërial perspective—though you assure him that to you the landscape shows much more agreeable without that artifice. Woe be to the luckless wight who does not only not respond to his rapture, but who should drop an unseasonable intimation of preferring one of his anterior bargains to the present!—The last is always his best hit —his "Cynthia of the minute."—Alas! how many a mild Madonna have I known to *come in*—a Raphael!—keep its ascendency for a few brief moons—then, after certain intermedial degradations, from the front drawing-room to the back gallery, thence to the dark parlour,—adopted in turn by each of the Carracci, under successive lowering ascriptions of filiation, mildly breaking its fall—consigned to the oblivious lumber-room, *go out* at last a Lucca Giordano, or plain Carlo Maratti!—which things when I beheld — musing upon the chances and mutabilities of fate below hath made me to reflect upon the altered condition of great personages, or that woeful Queen of Richard the Second-

-set forth in pomp,
She came adorned hither like sweet May;
Sent back like Hallowmass or shortest day.

With great love for *you*, J. E. hath but a limited sympathy with what you feel or do. He lives in a world of his own, and makes slender guesses at what passes in your mind. He never pierces the marrow of your habits. He will tell an old established play-goer, that Mr. Such-a-one, of So-and-so (naming one of the theatres), is a very lively comedian —as a piece of news! He advertised me but the other day of some pleasant green lanes which he had found out for me, *knowing me to be a great walker*, in my own immediate vicinity—who have haunted the identical spot any time these twenty years!—He has not much respect for that class of feelings which goes by the name of sentimental. He applies the definition of real evil to bodily sufferings exclusively—and rejecteth all others as imaginary. He is affected by the sight, or the bare supposition, of a creature in pain, to a degree which I have never witnessed out of womankind. A constitutional acuteness to this class of sufferings may in part account for this. The animal tribe in particular he taketh under his especial protection. A broken-winded or spur-galled horse is sure to find an advocate in him. An over-loaded ass is his client for ever. He is the apostle to the brute kind—the never-failing friend of those who have none to care for them. The contemplation of a lobster boiled, or eels skinned *alive*, will wring him so, that "all for pity he could die." It will take the savour from his palate, and the rest from his pillow, for days and nights. With the intense feeling of Thomas Clarkson, he wanted only the steadiness of pursuit, and unity of purpose, of that "true yoke-fellow with Time," to have effected as much for the *Animal* as he hath done for the *Negro Creation*. But my uncontrollable cousin is but imperfectly formed for purposes which demand co-operation. He cannot wait. His amelioration-plans must be ripened in a day. For this reason he has cut but an equivocal figure in benevolent societies, and combinations for the alleviation of human sufferings. His zeal constantly makes him to outrun, and put out, his coadjutors. He thinks of relieving,— while they think of debating. He was black-balled out of a society for the Relief of   *   *   *   * because the fervour of his humanity toiled beyond the formal apprehension and creeping processes of his associates. I shall always consider this distinction as a patent of nobility in the Elia family!

Do I mention these seeming inconsistencies to smile at, or upbraid, my unique cousin? Marry, heaven, and all good manners, and the understanding that should be between kinsfolk, forbid!—With all the strangenesses of this *strangest of the Elias*—I would not have him in one jot or tittle other than he is; neither would I barter or exchange my wild kinsman for the most exact, regular, and every way consistent kinsman breathing.

In my next, reader, I may perhaps give you some account of my cousin Bridget—if you are not already surfeited with cousins—and take you by the hand, if you are willing to go with us, on an excursion which we made a summer or two since, in search of *more cousins*—

Through the green plains of pleasant Hertfordshire.

MACKERY END, IN HERTFORDSHIRE.

BRIDGET ELIA has been my housekeeper for many a long year. I have obligations to Bridget, extending beyond the period of memory. We house together, old bachelor and maid, in a sort of double singleness; with such tolerable comfort, upon the whole, that I, for one, find in myself no sort of disposition to go out upon the mountains, with the rash king's offspring, to bewail my celibacy. We agree pretty well in our tastes and habits —yet so, as "with a difference." We are generally in harmony, with occasional bickerings—as it should be among near relations. Our sympathies are rather understood than expressed; and once, upon my dissembling a tone in my voice more kind than ordinary, my cousin burst into tears, and complained that I was altered. We are both great readers in different directions. While I am hanging over (for the thousandth time) some passage in old Burton, or one of his strange contemporaries, she is abstracted in some modern tale or adventure, whereof our common reading-table is daily fed with assiduously fresh supplies. Narrative teases me. I have little concern in the progress of events. She must have a story—well, ill, or indifferently told—so there be life stirring in it, and plenty of good or evil accidents. The fluctuations of fortune in fiction—and almost in real life—have ceased to interest, or operate but dully upon me. Out-of-the-way humours and opinions—heads with some diverting twist in them—the oddities of authorship, please me most. My cousin has a native disrelish of anything that sounds odd or bizarre. Nothing goes down with her that is quaint, irregular, or out of the road of common sympathy. She "holds Nature more clever." I can pardon her blindness to the beautiful obliquities of the Religio Medici; but she must apologize to me for certain disrespectful insinuations, which she has been pleased to throw out latterly, touching the intellectuals of a dear favourite of mine, of the last century but one—the thrice noble, chaste, and virtuous, but again somewhat fantastical and original brained, generous Margaret Newcastle.

It has been the lot of my cousin, oftener perhaps than I could have wished, to have had for her associates and mine, free-thinkers—leaders, and disciples, of novel philosophies and systems; but she neither wrangles with, nor accepts, their opinions. That which was good and venerable to her, when a child, retains its authority over her mind still. She never juggles or plays tricks with her understanding.

We are both of us inclined to be a little too positive; and I have observed the result of our disputes to be almost uniformly this—that in matters of fact, dates, and circumstances, it turns out that I was in the right, and my cousin in the wrong. But where we have differed upon moral points; upon something proper to be done, or let alone; whatever heat of opposition or steadiness of conviction I set out with, I am sure always, in the long-run, to be brought over to her way of thinking.

I must touch upon the foibles of my kinswoman with a gentle hand, for Bridget does not like to be told of her faults. She hath an awkward trick (to say no worse of it) of reading in company: at which times she will answer *yes* or *no* to a question, without fully understanding its purport—which is provoking, and derogatory in the highest degree to the dignity of the putter of the said question. Her presence of mind is equal to the most pressing trials of life, but will sometimes desert her upon trifling occasions. When the purpose requires it, and is a thing of moment, she can speak to it greatly; but in matters which are not stuff of the conscience, she hath been known sometimes to let slip a word less seasonably.

Her education in youth was not much attended to; and she happily missed all that train of female garniture which passeth by the name of accomplishments. She was tumbled early, by accident or design, into a spacious closet of good old English reading, without much selection or prohibition, and browsed at will upon that fair and wholesome pasturage. Had I twenty girls, they should be brought up exactly in this fashion. I know not whether their chance in wedlock might not be diminished by it, but I can answer for it that it makes (if the worst come to the worst) most incomparable old maids.

In a season of distress, she is the truest comforter; but in the teasing accidents and minor perplexities, which do not call out the *will* to meet them, she sometimes maketh matters worse by an excess of participation. If she does not always divide your trouble, upon the pleasanter occasions of life she is sure always to treble your satisfaction. She is excellent to be at a play with, or upon a visit; but best, when she goes a journey with you.

We made an excursion together a few summers since into Hertfordshire, to beat up the quarters of some of our less-known relations in that fine corn country.

The oldest thing I remember is Mackery End, or Mackarel End, as it is spelt, perhaps more properly, in some old maps of Hertfordshire: a farm-house,—delightfully situated within a gentle walk from Wheathampstead.

I can just remember having been there, on a visit to a great-aunt, when I was a child, under the care of Bridget; who, as I have said, is older than myself by some ten years. I wish that I could throw into a heap the remainder of our joint existences, that we might share them in equal division. But that is impossible. The house was at that time in the occupation of a substantial yeoman, who had married my grandmother's sister. His name was Gladman. My grandmother was a Bruton, married to a Field. The Gladmans and the Brutons are still flourishing in that part of the county, but the Fields are almost extinct. More than forty years had elapsed since the visit I speak of; and, for the greater portion of that period, we had lost sight of the other two branches also. Who or what sort of persons inherited Mackery End—kindred or strange folk—we were afraid almost to conjecture, but determined some day to explore.

By somewhat a circuitous route, taking the noble park at Luton in our way from St. Albans, we arrived at the spot of our anxious curiosity about noon. The sight of the old farm-house, though every trace of it was effaced from my recollections, affected me with a pleasure which I had not experienced for many a year. For though *I* had forgotten it, *we* had never forgotten being there together, and we had been talking about Mackery End all our lives, till memory on my part became mocked with a phantom of itself, and I thought I knew the aspect of a place which, when present, O how unlike it was to *that* which I had conjured up so many times instead of it!

Still the air breathed balmily about it: the season was in the "heart of June," and I could say with the poet,

> But thou, that didst appear so fair
> To fond imagination,
> Dost rival in the light of day
> Her delicate creation!

Bridget's was more a waking bliss than mine, for she

easily remembered her old acquaintance again—some altered features, of course, a little grudged at. At first, indeed, she was ready to disbelieve for joy; but the scene soon re-confirmed itself in her affections—and she traversed every outpost of the old mansion, to the wood-house, the orchard, the place where the pigeon-house had stood (house and birds were alike flown)—with a breathless impatience of recognition, which was more pardonable perhaps than decorous at the age of fifty odd. But Bridget in some things is behind her years.

The only thing left was to get into the house—and that was a difficulty which to me singly would have been insurmountable; for I am terribly shy in making myself known to strangers and out-of-date kinsfolk. Love, stronger than scruple, winged my cousin in without me; but she soon returned with a creature that might have sat to a sculptor for the image of Welcome. It was the youngest of the Gladmans; who, by marriage with a Bruton, had become mistress of the old mansion. A comely brood are the Brutons. Six of them, females, were noted as the handsomest young women in the county. But this adopted Bruton, in my mind, was better than they all—more comely. She was born too late to have remembered me. She just recollected in early life to have had her cousin Bridget once pointed out to her, climbing a stile. But the name of kindred and of cousinship was enough. Those slender ties, that prove slight as gossamer in the rending atmosphere of a metropolis, bind faster, as we found it, in hearty, homely, loving Hertfordshire. In five minutes we were as thoroughly acquainted as if we had been born and bred up together; were familiar, even to the calling each other by our Christian names. So Christians should call one another. To have seen Bridget and her— it was like the meeting of the two scriptural cousins! There was a grace and dignity, an amplitude of form and stature, answering to her mind, in this farmer's wife, which would have shined in a palace—or so we thought it. We were

made welcome by husband and wife equally— we, and
our friend that was with us. I had almost forgotten
him—but B. F. will not so soon forget that meeting, if
peradventure he shall read this on the far distant shores
where the kangaroo haunts. The fatted calf was made
ready, or rather was already so, as if in anticipation of
our coming; and, after an appropriate glass of native
wine, never let me forget with what honest pride this
hospitable cousin made us proceed to Wheathampstead,
to introduce us (as some new-found rarity) to her mother
and sister Gladmans, who did indeed know something
more of us, at a time when she almost knew nothing.—
With what corresponding kindness we were received by
them also—how Bridget's memory, exalted by the occasion, warmed into a thousand half-obliterated recollections
of things and persons, to my utter astonishment, and her
own—and to the astoundment of B. F. who sat by, almost
the only thing that was not a cousin there,—old effaced
images of more than half-forgotten names and circumstances still crowding back upon her, as words written in
lemon come out upon exposure to a friendly warmth,—
when I forget all this, then may my country cousins forget me; and Bridget no more remember, that in the days
of weakling infancy I was her tender charge—as I have
been her care in foolish manhood since—in those pretty
pastoral walks, long ago, about Mackery End, in Hertfordshire.

MY FIRST PLAY.

At the north end of Cross-court there yet stands a portal,
of some architectural pretensions, though reduced to humble use, serving at present for an entrance to a printing-office. This old door-way, if you are young, reader, you
may not know was the identical pit entrance to old Drury
—Garrick's Drury—all of it that is left. I never pass it
without shaking some forty years from off my shoulders,

recurring to the evening when I passed through it to see *my first play*. The afternoon had been wet, and the condition of our going (the elder folks and myself) was, that the rain should cease. With what a beating heart did I watch from the window the puddles, from the stillness of which I was taught to prognosticate the desired cessation! I seem to remember the last spurt, and the glee with which I ran to announce it.

We went with orders, which my godfather F. had sent us. He kept the oil shop (now Davies's) at the corner of Featherstone-buildings, in Holborn. F. was a tall grave person, lofty in speech, and had pretensions above his rank. He associated in those days with John Palmer, the comedian, whose gait and bearing he seemed to copy; if John (which is quite as likely) did not rather borrow somewhat of his manner from my godfather. He was also known to and visited by Sheridan. It was to his house in Holborn that young Brinsley brought his first wife on her elopement with him from a boarding-school at Bath—the beautiful Maria Linley. My parents were present (over a quadrille table) when he arrived in the evening with his harmonious charge. From either of these connections it may be inferred that my godfather could command an order for the then Drury-lane theatre at pleasure—and, indeed, a pretty liberal issue of those cheap billets, in Brinsley's easy autograph, I have heard him say was the sole remuneration which he had received for many years' nightly illumination of the orchestra and various avenues of that theatre—and he was content it should be so. The honour of Sheridan's familiarity—or supposed familiarity—was better to my godfather than money.

F. was the most gentlemanly of oilmen; grandiloquent, yet courteous. His delivery of the commonest matters of fact was Ciceronian. He had two Latin words almost constantly in his mouth (how odd sounds Latin from an oilman's lips!), which my better knowledge since has enabled me to correct. In strict pronunciation they should have been sounded *vice versâ*—but in those young years they impressed me with more awe than they would now do, read aright from Seneca or Varro—in his own peculiar pronunciation, monosyllabically elaborated, or Anglicised, into something like *verse verse*. By an imposing manner, and the help of these distorted syllables, he climbed (but that was little) to the highest parochial honours which St. Andrew's has to bestow.

He is dead—and thus much I thought due to his memory, both for my first orders (little wondrous talismans!—slight keys, and insignificant to outward sight, but opening to me more than Arabian paradises!) and, moreover, that by his testamentary beneficence I came into possession of the only landed property which I could ever call my own—situate near the road-way village of pleasant Puckeridge, in Hertfordshire. When I journeyed down to take possession, and planted foot on my own ground, the stately habits of the donor descended upon me, and I strode (shall I confess the vanity?) with larger paces over my allotment of three quarters of an acre, with its commodious mansion in the midst, with the feeling of an English freeholder that all betwixt sky and centre was my own. The estate has passed into more prudent hands, and nothing but an agrarian can restore it.

In those days were pit orders. Beshrew the uncomfortable manager who abolished them!—with one of these we went. I remember the waiting at the door—not that which is left—but between that and an inner door in shelter—O when shall I be such an expectant again!—with the cry of nonpareils, an indispensable play-house accompaniment in those days. As near as I can recollect, the fashionable pronunciation of the theatrical fruiteresses then was, "Chase some oranges, chase some nunparels, chase a bill of the play;"—chase *pro* chuse. But when we got in, and I beheld the green curtain that veiled a heaven to my imagination, which was soon to be disclosed—the breathless anticipations I endured! I had seen something like it in the plate prefixed to Troilus and

Cressida, in Rowe's Shakspeare—the tent scene with Diomede—and a sight of that plate can always bring back in a measure the feeling of that evening.—The boxes at that time, full of well-dressed women of quality, projected over the pit; and the pilasters reaching down were adorned with a glistening substance (I know not what) under glass (as it seemed), resembling—a homely fancy—but I judged it to be sugar-candy—yet to my raised imagination, divested of its homelier qualities, it appeared a glorified candy!—The orchestra lights at length rose, those "fair Auroras!" Once the bell sounded. It was to ring out yet once again—and, incapable of the anticipation, I reposed my shut eyes in a sort of resignation upon the maternal lap. It rang the second time. The curtain drew up—I was not past six years old, and the play was Artaxerxes!

I had dabbled a little in the Universal History—the ancient part of it—and here was the court of Persia.—It was being admitted to a sight of the past. I took no proper interest in the action going on, for I understood not its import—but I heard the word Darius, and I was in the midst of Daniel. All feeling was absorbed in vision. Gorgeous vests, gardens, palaces, princesses, passed before me. I knew not players. I was in Persepolis for the time, and the burning idol of their devotion almost converted me into a worshipper. I was awestruck, and believed those significations to be something more than elemental fires. It was all enchantment and a dream. No such pleasure has since visited me but in dreams.—Harlequin's invasion followed; where, I remember, the transformation of the magistrates into reverend beldams seemed to me a piece of grave historic justice, and the tailor carrying his own head to be as sober a verity as the legend of St. Denys.

The next play to which I was taken was the Lady of the Manor, of which, with the exception of some scenery, very faint traces are left in my memory. It was followed by a pantomime, called Lun's Ghost—a satiric touch, I apprehend, upon Rich, not long since dead—but to my apprehension (too sincere for satire), Lun was as remote a piece of antiquity as Lud—the father of a line of Harlequins—transmitting his dagger of lath (the wooden sceptre) through countless ages. I saw the primeval Motley come from his silent tomb in a ghastly vest of white patchwork, like the apparition of a dead rainbow. So Harlequins (thought I) look when they are dead.

My third play followed in quick succession. It was the Way of the World. I think I must have sat at it as grave as a judge; for I remember the hysteric affectations of good Lady Wishfort affected me like some solemn tragic passion. Robinson Crusoe followed; in which Crusoe, man Friday, and the parrot, were as good and authentic as in the story.—The clownery and pantaloonery of these pantomimes have clean passed out of my head. I believe, I no more laughed at them, than at the same age I should have been disposed to laugh at the grotesque Gothic heads (seeming to me then replete with devout meaning) that gape and grin, in stone around the inside of the old Round Church (my church) of the Templars.

I saw these plays in the season 1781-2, when I was from six to seven years old. After the intervention of six or seven other years (for at school all play-going was inhibited) I again entered the doors of a theatre. That old Artaxerxes evening had never done ringing in my fancy. I expected the same feelings to come again with the same occasion. But we differ from ourselves less at sixty and sixteen, than the latter does from six. In that interval what had I not lost! At the first period I knew nothing, understood nothing, discriminated nothing. I felt all, loved all, wondered all—

> Was nourished, I could not tell how—

I had left the temple a devotee, and was returned a rationalist. The same things were there materially; but the emblem, the reference, was gone! The green curtain was no longer a veil, drawn between two worlds, the unfolding of which was to bring back past ages, to present a "royal ghost," but a certain quantity of green baize, which was to separate the audience for a given time from certain of their fellow-men who were to come forward and pretend those parts. The lights—the orchestra lights—came up a clumsy machinery. The first ring, and the second ring, was now but a trick of the prompter's bell—which had been, like the note of the cuckoo, a phantom of a voice, no hand seen or guessed at which ministered to its warning. The actors were men and women painted. I thought the fault was in them; but it was in myself, and the alteration which those many centuries—of six short twelvemonths had wrought in me.—Perhaps it was fortunate for me that the play of the evening was but an indifferent comedy, as it gave me time to crop some unreasonable expectations, which might have interfered with the genuine emotions with which I was soon after enabled to enter upon the first appearance to me of Mrs. Siddons in Isabella. Comparison and retrospection soon yielded to the present attraction of the scene; and the theatre became to me, upon a new stock, the most delightful of recreations.

MODERN GALLANTRY.

In comparing modern with ancient manners, we are pleased to compliment ourselves upon the point of gallantry; a certain obsequiousness, or deferential respect, which we are supposed to pay to females, as females.

I shall believe that this principle actuates our conduct, when I can forget, that in the nineteenth century of the era from which we date our civility, we are but just beginning to leave off the very frequent practice of whipping females in public, in common with the coarsest male offenders.

I shall believe it to be influential, when I can shut

my eyes to the fact that in England women are still occasionally —hanged.

I shall believe in it, when actresses are no longer subject to be hissed off a stage by gentlemen.

I shall believe in it, when Dorimant hands a fish-wife across the kennel; or assists the apple-woman to pick up her wandering fruit, which some unlucky dray has just dissipated.

I shall believe in it, when the Dorimants in humbler life, who would be thought in their way notable adepts in this refinement, shall act upon it in places where they are not known, or think themselves not observed—when I shall see the traveller for some rich tradesman part with his admired box-coat, to spread it over the defenceless shoulders of the poor woman, who is passing to her parish on the roof of the same stage-coach with him, drenched in the rain—when I shall no longer see a woman standing up in the pit of a London theatre, till she is sick and faint with the exertion, with men about her, seated at their ease, and jeering at her distress; till one, that seems to have more manners or conscience than the rest, significantly declares "she should be welcome to his seat, if she were a little younger and handsomer." Place this dapper warehouseman, or that rider, in a circle of their own female acquaintance, and you shall confess you have not seen a politer-bred man in Lothbury.

Lastly, I shall begin to believe that there is some such principle influencing our conduct, when more than one-half of the drudgery and coarse servitude of the world shall cease to be performed by women.

Until that day comes I shall never believe this boasted point to be anything more than a conventional fiction; a pageant got up between the sexes, in a certain rank, and at a certain time of life, in which both find their account equally.

I shall be even disposed to rank it among the salutary fictions of life, when in polite circles I shall see the same attentions paid to age as to youth, to homely features as to handsome, to coarse complexions as to clear—to the woman, as she is a woman, not as she is a beauty, a fortune, or a title.

I shall believe it to be something more than a name, when a well-dressed gentleman in a well-dressed company can advert to the topic of *female old age* without exciting, and intending to excite, a sneer:—when the phrases "antiquated virginity," and such a one has "overstood her market," pronounced in good company, shall raise immediate offence in man, or woman, that shall hear them spoken.

Joseph Paice, of Bread-street-hill, merchant, and one of the Directors of the South Sea company—the same to whom Edwards, the Shakspeare commentator, has addressed a fine sonnet—was the only pattern of consistent gallantry I have met with. He took me under his shelter at an early age, and bestowed some pains upon me. I owe to his precepts and example whatever there is of the man of business (and that is not much) in my composition. It was not his fault that I did not profit more. Though bred a Presbyterian, and brought up a merchant, he was the finest gentleman of his time. He had not *one* system of attention to females in the drawing-room, and *another* in the shop, or at the stall. I do not mean that he made no distinction. But he never lost sight of sex, or overlooked it in the casualties of a disadvantageous situation. I have seen him stand bareheaded—smile if you please—to a poor servant-girl, while she has been inquiring of him the way to some street—in such a posture of unforced civility, as neither to embarrass her in the acceptance, nor himself in the offer, of it. He was no dangler, in the common acceptation of the word, after women; but he reverenced and upheld, in every form in which it came before him, *womanhood*. I have seen him

nay, smile not—tenderly escorting a market-woman, whom he had encountered in a shower, exalting his umbrella over her poor basket of fruit, that it might receive no damage, with as much carefulness as if she had been a countess. To the reverend form of Female Eld he would yield the wall (though it were to an ancient beggar-woman) with more ceremony than we can afford to show our grandams. He was the Preux Chevalier of Age; the Sir Calidore, or Sir Tristan, to those who have no Calidores or Tristans to defend them. The roses, that had long faded thence, still bloomed for him in those withered and yellow cheeks.

He was never married, but in his youth he paid his addresses to the beautiful Susan Winstanley—old Winstanley's daughter of Clapton—who dying in the early days of their courtship, confirmed in him the resolution of perpetual bachelorship. It was during their short courtship, he told me, that he had been one day treating his mistress with a profusion of civil speeches—the common gallantries—to which kind of thing she had hitherto manifested no repugnance—but in this instance with no effect. He could not obtain from her a decent acknowledgment in return. She rather seemed to resent his compliments. He could not set it down to caprice, for the lady had always shown herself above that littleness. When he ventured on the following day, finding her a little better humoured, to expostulate with her on her coldness of yesterday, she confessed, with her usual frankness, that she had no sort of dislike to his attentions; that she could even endure some high-flown compliments; that a young woman placed in her situation had a right to expect all sorts of civil things said to her; that she hoped she could digest a dose of adulation, short of insincerity, with as little injury to her humility as most young women; but that—a little before he had commenced his compliments—she had overheard him by accident, in rather rough language, rating a young woman, who had not brought home his cravats quite to the appointed time, and she thought to herself, "As I am Miss Susan Winstanley, and a young lady—a reputed beauty, and known to be a fortune—I can have my choice of the finest speeches from the mouth of this very fine gentleman who is courting me—but if I had been poor Mary Such-a-one (*naming the milliner*),—and had failed of bringing home the cravats to the appointed hour—though perhaps I had sat up half the night to forward them—what sort of compliments should I have received then?—And my woman's pride came to my assistance; and I thought, that if it were only to do *me* honour, a female, like myself, might have received handsomer usage; and I was determined not to accept any fine speeches to the compromise of that sex, the belonging to which was after all my strongest claim and title to them."

I think the lady discovered both generosity, and a just way of thinking, in this rebuke which she gave her lover; and I have sometimes imagined, that the uncommon strain of courtesy, which through life regulated the actions and behaviour of my friend towards all of womankind indiscriminately, owed its happy origin to this seasonable lesson from the lips of his lamented mistress.

I wish the whole female world would entertain the same notion of these things that Miss Winstanley showed. Then we should see something of the spirit of consistent gallantry; and no longer witness the anomaly of the same man—a pattern of true politeness to a wife—of cold contempt, or rudeness, to a sister—the idolater of his female mistress—the disparager and despiser of his no less female aunt, or unfortunate—still female—maiden cousin. Just so much respect as a woman derogates from her own sex, in whatever condition placed—her hand-maid, or dependent—she deserves to have diminished from herself on that score; and probably will feel the diminution, when youth, and beauty, and advantages, not inseparable from sex, shall lose of their attraction. What a woman should demand of a man in courtship, or after it, is first—respect for her as she is a woman;—and next to that—to be respected by him above all other women. But let her stand upon her female character as upon a foundation; and let the attentions, incident to individual preference, be so many pretty additaments and ornaments—as many,

and as fanciful, as you please—to that main structure.
Let her first lesson be with sweet Susan Winstanley—to
reverence her sex.

THE OLD BENCHERS OF THE INNER TEMPLE.

I WAS born, and passed the first seven years of my life,
in the Temple. Its church, its halls, its gardens, its
fountains, its river, I had almost said—for in those young
years, what was this king of rivers to me but a stream
that watered our pleasant places?—these are of my oldest
recollections. I repeat, to this day, no verses to myself
more frequently, or with kindlier emotion, than those of
Spenser, where he speaks of this spot :—

> There when they came, whereas those bricky towers,
> The which on Themmes brode aged back doth ride,
> Where now the studious lawyers have their bowers,
> There whylome wont the Templer knights to bide,
> Till they decayed through pride.

Indeed, it is the most elegant spot in the metropolis.
What a transition for a countryman visiting London for
the first time—the passing from the crowded Strand or
Fleet Street, by unexpected avenues, into its magnificent
ample squares, its classic green recesses! What a cheerful, liberal look hath that portion of it, which, from
three sides, overlooks the greater garden; that goodly pile

> Of building strong, albeit of Paper hight,

confronting with massy contrast, the lighter, older, more
fantastically-shrouded one, named of Harcourt, with the
cheerful Crown-Office-row (place of my kindly engendure),
right opposite the stately stream, which washes the garden-foot with her yet scarcely trade-polluted waters, and seems
but just weaned from her Twickenham Naïades! a man
would give something to have been born in such places.
What a collegiate aspect has that fine Elizabethan hall,

where the fountain plays, which I have made to rise and fall, how many times! to the astoundment of the young urchins, my contemporaries, who, not being able to guess at its recondite machinery, were almost tempted to hail the wondrous work as magic! What an antique air had the now almost effaced sun-dials, with their moral inscriptions, seeming coevals with that Time which they measured, and to take their revelations of its flight immediately from heaven, holding correspondence with the fountain of light! How would the dark line steal imperceptibly on, watched by the eye of childhood, eager to detect its movement, never catched, nice as an evanescent cloud, or the first arrests of sleep!

> Ah! yet doth beauty like a dial hand
> Steal from his figure, and no pace perceived!

What a dead thing is a clock, with its ponderous embowelments of lead and brass, its pert or solemn dulness of communication, compared with the simple altar-like structure and silent heart-language of the old dial! It stood as the garden god of Christian gardens. Why is it almost everywhere vanished? If its business-use be superseded by more elaborate inventions, its moral uses, its beauty, might have pleaded for its continuance. It spoke of moderate labours, of pleasures not protracted after sunset, of temperance, and good hours. It was the primitive clock, the horologe of the first world. Adam could scarce have missed it in Paradise. It was the measure appropriate for sweet plants and flowers to spring by, for the birds to apportion their silver warblings by, for flocks to pasture and be led to fold by. The shepherd "carved it out quaintly in the sun;" and, turning philosopher by the very occupation, provided it with mottoes more touching than tombstones. It was a pretty device of the gardener, recorded by Marvell, who, in the days of artificial gardening, made a dial out of herbs and flowers. I must quote his verses a little higher up, for they are full, as all his serious poetry was, of a witty delicacy.

They will not come in awkwardly, I hope, in a talk of fountains and sun-dials. He is speaking of sweet garden scenes :—

> What wondrous life is this I lead!
> Ripe apples drop about my head.
> The luscious clusters of the vine
> Upon my mouth do crush their wine.
> The nectarine, and curious peach,
> Into my hands themselves do reach.
> Stumbling on melons, as I pass,
> Insnared with flowers, I fall on grass.
> Meanwhile the mind from pleasure less
> Withdraws into its happiness.
> The mind, that ocean, where each kind
> Does straight its own resemblance find ;
> Yet it creates, transcending these,
> Far other worlds and other seas ;
> Annihilating all that's made
> To a green thought in a green shade.
> Here at the fountain's sliding foot
> Or at some fruit-tree's mossy root,
> Casting the body's vest aside,
> My soul into the boughs does glide ;
> There, like a bird, it sits and sings,
> Then whets and claps its silver wings,
> And, till prepared for longer flight,
> Waves in its plumes the various light
> How well the skilful gardener drew
> Of flowers and herbs, this dial new
> Where, from above, the milder sun
> Does through a fragrant zodiac run :
> And, as it works, the industrious bee
> Computes its time as well as we.
> How could such sweet and wholesome hours
> Be reckoned, but with herbs and flowers?[1]

The artificial fountains of the metropolis are, in like manner, fast vanishing. Most of them are dried up or bricked over. Yet, where one is left, as in that little green nook behind the South-Sea House, what a freshness it gives to the dreary pile! Four little winged marble boys used to play their virgin fancies, spouting out ever fresh streams from their innocent-wanton lips in the square

---

[1] From a copy of verses entitled "The Garden."

of Lincoln's Inn, when I was no bigger than they were
figured. They are gone, and the spring choked up. The
fashion, they tell me, is gone by, and these things are
esteemed childish. Why not, then, gratify children, by
letting them stand? Lawyers, I suppose, were children
once. They are awakening images to them at least. Why
must everything smack of man, and mannish? Is the
world all grown up? Is childhood dead? Or is there
not in the bosoms of the wisest and the best some of the
child's heart left, to respond to its earliest enchantments?
The figures were grotesque. Are the stiff-wigged living
figures, that still flitter and chatter about that area, less
Gothic in appearance? or is the splutter of their hot
rhetoric one-half so refreshing and innocent as the little
cool playful streams those exploded cherubs uttered?

They have lately gothicised the entrance to the Inner
Temple-hall, and the library front; to assimilate them, I
suppose, to the body of the hall, which they do not at all
resemble. What is become of the winged horse that stood
over the former? a stately arms! and who has removed
those frescoes of the Virtues, which Italianised the end
of the Paper-buildings?—my first hint of allegory! They
must account to me for these things, which I miss so
greatly.

The terrace is, indeed, left, which we used to call the
parade; but the traces are passed away of the footsteps
which made its pavement awful! It is become common
and profane. The old benchers had it almost sacred to
themselves, in the forepart of the day at least. They
might not be sided or jostled. Their air and dress
asserted the parade. You left wide spaces betwixt you
when you passed them. We walk on even terms with
their successors. The roguish eye of J———ll, ever ready
to be delivered of a jest, almost invites a stranger to vie
a repartee with it. But what insolent familiar durst
have mated Thomas Coventry?—whose person was a
quadrate, his step massy and elephantine, his face square
as the lion's, his gait peremptory and path-keeping, in-

divertible from his way as a moving column, the scarecrow of his inferiors, the browbeater of equals and superiors, who made a solitude of children wherever he came, for they fled his insufferable presence, as they would have shunned an Elisha bear. His growl was as thunder in their ears, whether he spake to them in mirth or in rebuke; his invitatory notes being, indeed, of all, the most repulsive and horrid. Clouds of snuff, aggravating the natural terrors of his speech, broke from each majestic nostril, darkening the air. He took it, not by pinches, but a palmful at once,—diving for it under the mighty flaps of his old-fashioned waistcoat pocket; his waistcoat red and angry, his coat dark rappee, tinctured by dye original, and by adjuncts, with buttons of obsolete gold. And so he paced the terrace.

By his side a milder form was sometimes to be seen; the pensive gentility of Samuel Salt. They were coevals, and had nothing but that and their benchership in common. In politics Salt was a whig, and Coventry a staunch tory. Many a sarcastic growl did the latter cast out—for Coventry had a rough spinous humour—at the political confederates of his associate, which rebounded from the gentle bosom of the latter like cannon-balls from wool. You could not ruffle Samuel Salt.

S. had the reputation of being a very clever man, and of excellent discernment in the chamber practice of the law. I suspect his knowledge did not amount to much. When a case of difficult disposition of money, testamentary or otherwise, came before him, he ordinarily handed it over, with a few instructions, to his man Lovel, who was a quick little fellow, and would despatch it out of hand by the light of natural understanding, of which he had an uncommon share. It was incredible what repute for talents S. enjoyed by the mere trick of gravity. He was a shy man; a child might pose him in a minute—indolent and procrastinating to the last degree. Yet men would give him credit for vast application, in spite of himself. He was not to be trusted with himself with impunity. He

never dressed for a dinner party but he forgot his sword
—they wore swords then—or some other necessary part of
his equipage. Lovel had his eye upon him on all these
occasions, and ordinarily gave him his cue. If there was
anything which he could speak unseasonably, he was
sure to do it.—He was to dine at a relative's of the
unfortunate Miss Blandy on the day of her execution;—
and L., who had a wary foresight of his probable hallucinations, before he set out schooled him, with great anxiety,
not in any possible manner to allude to her story that
day. S. promised faithfully to observe the injunction.
He had not been seated in the parlour, where the company was expecting the dinner summons, four minutes,
when, a pause in the conversation ensuing, he got up,
looked out of window, and pulling down his ruffles—an
ordinary motion with him—observed, "it was a gloomy
day," and added, "Miss Blandy must be hanged by this
time, I suppose." Instances of this sort were perpetual.
Yet S. was thought by some of the greatest men of his
time a fit person to be consulted, not alone in matters
pertaining to the law, but in the ordinary niceties and
embarrassments of conduct—from force of manner entirely.
He never laughed. He had the same good fortune among
the female world,—was a known toast with the ladies,
and one or two are said to have died for love of him- I
suppose, because he never trifled or talked gallantly with
them, or paid them, indeed, hardly common attentions.
He had a fine face and person, but wanted, methought,
the spirit that should have shown them off with advantage
to the women. His eye lacked lustre.—Not so, thought
Susan P—— —; who, at the advanced age of sixty, was
seen, in the cold evening time, unaccompanied, wetting
the pavement of B——d Row, with tears that fell in
drops which might be heard, because her friend had died
that day—he, whom she had pursued with a hopeless
passion for the last forty years— a passion which years
could not extinguish or abate; nor the long-resolved, yet
gently-enforced, puttings off of unrelenting bachelorhood

dissuade from its cherished purpose. Mild Susan P——, thou hast now thy friend in heaven!

Thomas Coventry was a cadet of the noble family of that name. He passed his youth in contracted circumstances, which gave him early those parsimonious habits which in after life never forsook him; so that with one windfall or another, about the time I knew him, he was master of four or five hundred thousand pounds; nor did he look or walk worth a moidore less. He lived in a gloomy house opposite the pump in Serjeant's-inn, Fleet-street. J., the counsel, is doing self-imposed penance in it, for what reason I divine not, at this day. C. had an agreeable seat at North Cray, where he seldom spent above a day or two at a time in the summer; but preferred, during the hot months, standing at his window in this damp, close, well-like mansion, to watch, as he said, "the maids drawing water all day long." I suspect he had his within-door reasons for the preference. *Hic currus et arma fuere.* He might think his treasures more safe. His house had the aspect of a strong box. C. was a close hunks—a hoarder rather than a miser—or, if a miser, none of the mad Elwes breed, who have brought discredit upon a character which cannot exist without certain admirable points of steadiness and unity of purpose. One may hate a true miser, but cannot, I suspect, so easily despise him. By taking care of the pence he is often enabled to part with the pounds, upon a scale that leaves us careless generous fellows halting at an immeasurable distance behind. C. gave away 30,000*l.* at once in his lifetime to a blind charity. His housekeeping was severely looked after, but he kept the table of a gentleman. He would know who came in and who went out of his house, but his kitchen chimney was never suffered to freeze.

Salt was his opposite in this, as in all—never knew what he was worth in the world; and having but a competency for his rank, which his indolent habits were little calculated to improve, might have suffered severely if he had not had honest people about him. Lovel took care of everything. He was at once his clerk, his good servant, his dresser, his friend, his "flapper," his guide, stop-watch, auditor, treasurer. He did nothing without consulting Lovel, or failed in anything without expecting and fearing his admonishing. He put himself almost too much in his hands, had they not been the purest in the world. He resigned his title almost to respect as a master, if L. could ever have forgotten for a moment that he was a servant.

I knew this Lovel. He was a man of an incorrigible and losing honesty. A good fellow withal, and "would strike." In the cause of the oppressed he never considered inequalities, or calculated the number of his opponents. He once wrested a sword out of the hand of a man of quality that had drawn upon him, and pommelled him severely with the hilt of it. The swordsman had offered insult to a female—an occasion upon which no odds against him could have prevented the interference of Lovel. He would stand next day bareheaded to the same person modestly to excuse his interference—for L. never forgot rank where something better was not concerned. L. was the liveliest little fellow breathing, had a face as gay as Garrick's, whom he was said greatly to resemble (I have a portrait of him which confirms it), possessed a fine turn for humorous poetry—next to Swift and Prior—moulded heads in clay or plaster of Paris to admiration, by the dint of natural genius merely; turned cribbage boards, and such small cabinet toys, to perfection; took a hand at quadrille or bowls with equal facility; made punch better than any man of his degree in England; had the merriest quips and conceits; and was altogether as brimful of rogueries and inventions as you could desire. He was a brother of the angle, moreover, and just such a free, hearty, honest companion as Mr. Izaak Walton would have chosen to go a-fishing with. I saw him in his old age and the decay of his faculties, palsy-smitten, in the last sad stage of human weakness—"a remnant most forlorn of what he was,"—yet even then his eye would light up upon the mention of his favourite Garrick. He was greatest, he would say, in Bayes—"was upon the stage nearly throughout the whole performance, and as busy as a bee." At intervals, too, he would speak of his former life, and how he came up a little boy from Lincoln, to go to service, and how his mother cried at parting with him, and how he returned, after some few years' absence, in his smart new livery, to see her, and she blest herself at the change, and could hardly be brought to believe that it was "her own bairn." And then, the excitement subsiding, he would weep, till I have wished that sad second-childhood might have a mother still to lay its head upon her lap. But the common mother of us all in no long time after received him gently into hers.

With Coventry and with Salt, in their walks upon the terrace, most commonly Peter Pierson would join to make up a third. They did not walk linked arm-in-arm in those days—"as now our stout triumvirs sweep the streets,"—but generally with both hands folded behind them for state, or with one at least behind, the other carrying a cane. P. was a benevolent, but not a prepossessing man. He had that in his face which you could not term unhappiness; it rather implied an incapacity of being happy. His cheeks were colourless, even to whiteness. His look was uninviting, resembling (but without his sourness) that of our great philanthropist. I know that he *did* good acts, but I could never make out what he *was*. Contemporary with these, but subordinate, was Daines Barrington—another oddity—he walked burly and square—in imitation, I think, of Coventry—howbeit he attained not to the dignity of his prototype. Nevertheless, he did pretty well, upon the strength of being a tolerable antiquarian, and having a brother a bishop. When the account of his year's treasurership came to be audited, the following singular charge was unanimously disallowed by the bench: "Item, disbursed

Mr. Allen, the gardener, twenty shillings for stuff to poison the sparrows, by my orders." Next to him was old Barton—a jolly negation, who took upon him the ordering of the bills of fare for the parliament chamber, where the benchers dine—answering to the combination rooms at College—much to the easement of his less epicurean brethren. I know nothing more of him.— Then Read, and Twopenny—Read, good-humoured and personable—Twopenny, good-humoured, but thin, and felicitous in jests upon his own figure. If T. was thin, Wharry was attenuated and fleeting. Many must remember him (for he was rather of later date) and his singular gait, which was performed by three steps and a jump regularly succeeding. The steps were little efforts, like that of a child beginning to walk; the jump comparatively vigorous, as a foot to an inch. Where he learned this figure, or what occasioned it, I could never discover. It was neither graceful in itself, nor seemed to answer the purpose any better than common walking. The extreme tenuity of his frame, I suspect, set him upon it. It was a trial of poising. Twopenny would often rally him upon his leanness, and hail him as Brother Lusty; but W. had no relish of a joke. His features were spiteful. I have heard that he would pinch his cat's ears extremely when anything had offended him. Jackson—the omniscient Jackson, he was called—was of this period. He had the reputation of possessing more multifarious knowledge than any man of his time. He was the Friar Bacon of the less literate portion of the Temple. I remember a pleasant passage of the cook applying to him, with much formality of apology, for instructions how to write down *edge* bone of beef in his bill of commons. He was supposed to know, if any man in the world did. He decided the orthography to be—as I have given it—fortifying his authority with such anatomical reasons as dismissed the maniciple (for the time) learned and happy. Some do spell it yet, perversely, *aitch* bone, from a fanciful resemblance between its shape and that of the aspirate so denominated I had almost forgotten Mingay with the iron hand—but he was somewhat later. He had lost his right hand by some accident, and supplied it with a grappling-hook, which he wielded with a tolerable adroitness. I detected the substitute before I was old enough to reason whether it were artificial or not. I remember the astonishment it raised in me. He was a blustering, loud-talking person; and I reconciled the phenomenon to my ideas as an emblem of power—somewhat like the horns in the forehead of Michael Angelo's Moses. Baron Maseres, who walks (or did till very lately) in the costume of the reign of George the Second, closes my imperfect recollections of the old benchers of the Inner Temple.

Fantastic forms, whither are ye fled? Or, if the like of you exist, why exist they no more for me? Ye inexplicable, half-understood appearances, why comes in reason to tear away the preternatural mist, bright or gloomy, that enshrouded you? Why make ye so sorry a figure in my relation, who made up to me—to my childish eyes—the mythology of the Temple? In those days I saw Gods, as "old men covered with a mantle," walking upon the earth. Let the dreams of classic idolatry perish,—extinct be the fairies and fairy trumpery of legendary fabling, in the heart of childhood there will, for ever, spring up a well of innocent or wholesome superstition—the seeds of exaggeration will be busy there, and vital—from every-day forms educing the unknown and the uncommon. In that little Goshen there will be light when the grown world flounders about in the darkness of sense and materiality. While childhood, and while dreams, reducing childhood, shall be left, imagination shall not have spread her holy wings totally to fly the earth.

P.S.—I have done injustice to the soft shade of Samuel Salt. See what it is to trust to imperfect memory, and the erring notices of childhood! Yet!

protest I always thought that he had been a bachelor! This gentleman, R. N. informs me, married young, and losing his lady in childbed, within the first year of their union, fell into a deep melancholy, from the effects of which, probably, he never thoroughly recovered. In what a new light does this place his rejection (O call it by a gentler name!) of mild Susan P——, unravelling into beauty certain peculiarities of this very shy and retiring character! Henceforth let no one receive the narratives of Elia for true records! They are, in truth, but shadows of fact—verisimilitudes, not verities—or sitting but upon the remote edges and outskirts of history. He is no such honest chronicler as R. N., and would have done better perhaps to have consulted that gentleman before he sent these incondite reminiscences to press. But the worthy sub-treasurer—who respects his old and his new masters—would but have been puzzled at the indecorous liberties of Elia. The good man wots not, peradventure, of the licence which *Magazines* have arrived at in this plain-speaking age, or hardly dreams of their existence beyond the *Gentleman's*—his furthest monthly excursions in this nature having been long confined to the holy ground of honest *Urban's* obituary. May it be long before his own name shall help to swell those columns of unenvied flattery!—Meantime, O ye New Benchers of the Inner Temple, cherish him kindly, for he is himself the kindliest of human creatures. Should infirmities overtake him—he is yet in green and vigorous senility—make allowances for them, remembering that "ye yourselves are old." So may the Winged Horse, your ancient badge and cognizance, still flourish! so may future Hookers and Seldens illustrate your church and chambers! so may the sparrows, in default of more melodious quiristers, unpoisoned hop about your walks! so may the fresh-coloured and cleanly nursery-maid, who, by leave, airs her playful charge in your stately gardens, drop her prettiest blushing courtesy as ye pass, reductive of juvenescent emotion! so may the younkers of this generation eye you, pacing your stately terrace, with the same superstitious veneration with which the child Elia gazed on the Old Worthies that solemnized the parade before ye!

GRACE BEFORE MEAT.

THE custom of saying grace at meals had, probably, its origin in the early times of the world, and the hunter-state of man, when dinners were precarious things, and a full meal was something more than a common blessing! when a belly-full was a wind-fall, and looked like a special providence. In the shouts and triumphal songs with which, after a season of sharp abstinence, a lucky booty of deer's or goat's flesh would naturally be ushered home, existed, perhaps, the germ of the modern grace. It is not otherwise easy to be understood, why the blessing of food—the act of eating—should have had a particular expression of thanksgiving annexed to it, distinct from that implied and silent gratitude with which we are expected to enter upon the enjoyment of the many other various gifts and good things of existence.

I own that I am disposed to say grace upon twenty other occasions in the course of the day besides my dinner. I want a form for setting out upon a pleasant walk, for a moonlight ramble, for a friendly meeting, or a solved problem. Why have we none for books, those spiritual repasts—a grace before Milton—a grace before Shakspeare a devotional exercise proper to be said before reading the Fairy Queen?—but the received ritual having prescribed these forms to the solitary ceremony of manducation, I shall confine my observations to the experience which I have had of the grace, properly so called; commending my new scheme for extension to a niche in the grand philosophical, poetical, and perchance in part heretical, liturgy, now compiling by my friend Homo

Humanus, for the use of a certain snug congregation of Utopian Rabelæsian Christians, no matter where assembled.

The form, then, of the benediction before eating has its beauty at a poor man's table, or at the simple and unprovocative repast of children. It is here that the grace becomes exceedingly graceful. The indigent man, who hardly knows whether he shall have a meal the next day or not, sits down to his fare with a present sense of the blessing, which can be but feebly acted by the rich, into whose minds the conception of wanting a dinner could never, but by some extreme theory, have entered. The proper end of food—the animal sustenance—is barely contemplated by them. The poor man's bread is his daily bread, literally his bread for the day. Their courses are perennial.

Again, the plainest diet seems the fittest to be preceded by the grace. That which is least stimulative to appetite, leaves the mind most free for foreign considerations. A man may feel thankful, heartily thankful, over a dish of plain mutton with turnips, and have leisure to reflect upon the ordinance and institution of eating; when he shall confess a perturbation of mind, inconsistent with the purposes of the grace, at the presence of venison or turtle. When I have sate (a *rarus hospes*) at rich men's tables, with the savoury soup and messes steaming up the nostrils, and moistening the lips of the guests with desire and a distracted choice, I have felt the introduction of that ceremony to be unseasonable. With the ravenous orgasm upon you, it seems impertinent to interpose a religious sentiment. It is a confusion of purpose to mutter out praises from a mouth that waters. The heats of epicurism put out the gentle flame of devotion. The incense which rises round is pagan, and the belly-god intercepts it for its own. The very excess of the provision beyond the needs, takes away all sense of proportion between the end and means. The giver is veiled by his gifts. You are startled at the injustice of returning thanks—for what?—for having too much while so many starve. It is to praise the Gods amiss.

I have observed this awkwardness felt, scarce consciously perhaps, by the good man who says the grace. I have seen it in clergymen and others—a sort of shame—a sense of the co-presence of circumstances which unhallow the blessing. After a devotional tone put on for a few seconds, how rapidly the speaker will fall into his common voice! helping himself or his neighbour, as if to get rid of some uneasy sensation of hypocrisy. Not that the good man was a hypocrite, or was not most conscientious in the discharge of the duty; but he felt in his inmost mind the incompatibility of the scene and the viands before him with the exercise of a calm and rational gratitude.

I hear somebody exclaim,—Would you have Christians sit down at table like hogs to their troughs, without remembering the Giver?—no—I would have them sit down as Christians, remembering the Giver, and less like hogs. Or, if their appetites must run riot, and they must pamper themselves with delicacies for which east and west are ransacked, I would have them postpone their benediction to a fitter season, when appetite is laid; when the still small voice can be heard, and the reason of the grace returns—with temperate diet and restricted dishes. Gluttony and surfeiting are no proper occasions for thanksgiving. When Jeshurun waxed fat, we read that he kicked. Virgil knew the harpy-nature better, when he put into the mouth of Celæno anything but a blessing. We may be gratefully sensible of the deliciousness of some kinds of food beyond others, though that is a meaner and inferior gratitude: but the proper object of the grace is sustenance, not relishes; daily bread, not delicacies; the means of life, and not the means of pampering the carcass. With what frame or composure, I wonder, can a city chaplain pronounce his benediction at some great Hall-feast, when he knows that his last concluding pious word—and that in all probability, the sacred name which he preaches—is but the signal for so many impatient harpies to commence their foul orgies, with as little sense of true thankfulness (which is temperance) as those Virgilian fowl! It is well if the good man himself does not feel his devotions a little clouded, those foggy sensuous steams mingling with and polluting the pure altar sacrifice.

The severest satire upon full tables and surfeits is the banquet which Satan, in the "Paradise Regained," provides for a temptation in the wilderness:

> A table richly spread in regal mode
> With dishes piled, and meats of noblest sort
> And savour; beasts of chase, or fowl of game,
> In pastry built, or from the spit, or boiled,
> Gris-amber-steamed; all fish from sea or shore,
> Freshet or purling brook, for which was drained
> Pontus, and Lucrine bay, and Afric coast.

The Tempter, I warrant you, thought these cates would go down without the recommendatory preface of a benediction. They are like to be short graces where the devil plays the host. I am afraid the poet wants his usual decorum in this place. Was he thinking of the old Roman luxury, or of a gaudy day at Cambridge? This was a temptation fitter for a Heliogabalus. The whole banquet is too civic and culinary, and the accompaniments altogether a profanation of that deep, abstracted, holy scene. The mighty artillery of sauces, which the cook-fiend conjures up, is out of proportion to the simple wants and plain hunger of the guest. He that disturbed him in his dreams, from his dreams might have been taught better. To the temperate fantasies of the famished Son of God, what sort of feasts presented themselves?— He dreamed indeed,

> ———As appetite is wont to dream,
> Of meats and drinks, nature's refreshment sweet.

But what meats?—

> Him thought he by the brook of Cherith stood,
> And saw the ravens with their horny beaks

> Food to Elijah bringing even and morn;
> Though ravenous, taught to abstain from what they brought.
> He saw the prophet also how he fled
> Into the desert, and how there he slept
> Under a juniper; then how awaked
> He found his supper on the coals prepared,
> And by the angel was bid rise and eat,
> And ate the second time after repose,
> The strength whereof sufficed him forty days:
> Sometimes, that with Elijah he partook,
> Or as a guest with Daniel at his pulse.

Nothing in Milton is finelier fancied than these temperate dreams of the divine Hungerer. To which of these two visionary banquets, think you, would the introduction of what is called the grace have been the most fitting and pertinent?

Theoretically I am no enemy to graces; but practically I own that (before meat especially) they seem to involve something awkward and unseasonable. Our appetites, of one or another kind, are excellent spurs to our reason, which might otherwise but feebly set about the great ends of preserving and continuing the species. They are fit blessings to be contemplated at a distance with a becoming gratitude; but the moment of appetite (the judicious reader will apprehend me) is, perhaps, the least fit season for that exercise. The Quakers, who go about their business of every description with more calmness than we, have more title to the use of these benedictory prefaces. I have always admired their silent grace, and the more because I have observed their applications to the meat and drink following to be less passionate and sensual than ours. They are neither gluttons nor wine-bibbers as a people. They eat, as a horse bolts his chopped hay, with indifference, calmness, and cleanly circumstances. They neither grease nor slop themselves. When I see a citizen in his bib and tucker, I cannot imagine it a surplice.

I am no Quaker at my food. I confess I am not indifferent to the kinds of it. Those unctuous morsels of deer's flesh were not made to be received with dispassionate services. I hate a man who swallows it, affecting not to know what he is eating. I suspect his taste in higher matters. I shrink instinctively from one who professes to like minced veal. There is a physiognomical character in the tastes for food. C—— holds that a man cannot have a pure mind who refuses apple-dumplings. I am not certain but he is right. With the decay of my first innocence, I confess a less and less relish daily for those innocuous cates. The whole vegetable tribe have lost their gust with me. Only I stick to asparagus, which still seems to inspire gentle thoughts. I am impatient and querulous under culinary disappointments, as to come home at the dinner hour, for instance, expecting some savoury mess, and to find one quite tasteless and sapidless. Butter ill melted—that commonest of kitchen failures—puts me beside my tenor.—The author of the Rambler used to make inarticulate animal noises over a favourite food. Was this the music quite proper to be preceded by the grace? or would the pious man have done better to postpone his devotions to a season when the blessing might be contemplated with less perturbation? I quarrel with no man's tastes, nor would set my thin face against those excellent things, in their way, jollity and feasting. But as these exercises, however laudable, have little in them of grace or gracefulness, a man should be sure, before he ventures so to grace them, that while he is pretending his devotions otherwhere, he is not secretly kissing his hand to some great fish—his Dagon—with a special consecration of no art but the fat tureen before him. Graces are the sweet preluding strains to the banquets of angels and children; to the roots and severer repasts of the Chartreuse; to the slender, but not slenderly acknowledged, refection of the poor and humble man: but at the heaped-up boards of the pampered and the luxurious they become of dissonant mood, less timed and tuned to the occasion, methinks, than the noise of those better befitting organs would be which children hear tales of, at Hog's Norton. We sit too long at our meals, or are too curious in the study of them, or too disordered in our application to them, or engross too great a portion of those good things (which should be common) to our share, to be able with any grace to say grace. To be thankful for what we grasp exceeding our proportion, is to add hypocrisy to injustice. A lurking sense of this truth is what makes the performance of this duty so cold and spiritless a service at most tables. In houses where the grace is as indispensable as the napkin, who has not seen that never-settled question arise, as to *who shall say it?* while the good man of the house and the visitor clergyman, or some other guest belike of next authority, from years or gravity, shall be bandying about the office between them as a matter of compliment, each of them not unwilling to shift the awkward burthen of an equivocal duty from his own shoulders?

I once drank tea in company with two Methodist divines of different persuasions, whom it was my fortune to introduce to each other for the first time that evening. Before the first cup was handed round, one of these reverend gentlemen put it to the other, with all due solemnity, whether he chose to *say anything*. It seems it is the custom with some sectaries to put up a short prayer before this meal also. His reverend brother did not at first quite apprehend him, but upon an explanation, with little less importance he made answer that it was not a custom known in his church: in which courteous evasion the other acquiescing for good manners' sake, or in compliance with a weak brother, the supplementary or tea grace was waived altogether. With what spirit might not Lucian have painted two priests, of *his* religion, playing into each other's hands the compliment of performing or omitting a sacrifice,—the hungry God meantime, doubtful of his incense, with expectant nostrils hovering over the two flamens, and (as between two stools) going away in the end without his supper.

A short form upon these occasions is felt to want reverence; a long one, I am afraid, cannot escape the charge of impertinence. I do not quite approve of the epigrammatic conciseness with which that equivocal wag (but my pleasant school-fellow) C. V. L., when importuned for a grace, used to inquire, first slyly leering down the table, "Is there no clergyman here?"—significantly adding, "Thank G- ." Nor do I think our old form at school quite pertinent, where we were used to preface our bald bread-and-cheese-suppers with a preamble, connecting with that humble blessing a recognition of benefits the most awful and overwhelming to the imagination which religion has to offer. *Non tunc illis erat locus.* I remember we were put to it to reconcile the phrase "good creatures," upon which the blessing rested, with the fare set before us, wilfully understanding that expression in a low and animal sense,—till some one recalled a legend, which told how, in the golden days of Christ's, the young Hospitallers were wont to have smoking joints of roast meat upon their nightly boards, till some pious benefactor, commiserating the decencies, rather than the palates, of the children, commuted our flesh for garments, and gave us—*horresco referens*—trousers instead of mutton.

DREAM CHILDREN: A REVERIE.

CHILDREN love to listen to stories about their elders, when *they* were children; to stretch their imagination to the conception of a traditionary great-uncle, or grandame, whom they never saw. It was in this spirit that my little ones crept about me the other evening to hear about their great-grandmother Field, who lived in a great house in Norfolk (a hundred times bigger than that in which they and papa lived) which had been the scene—so at least it was generally believed in that part of the country—of the tragic incidents which they had lately become familiar with from the ballad of the Children in the Wood. Certain it is that the whole story of the children and their cruel uncle was to be seen fairly carved out in wood upon the chimney-piece of the great hall, the whole story down to the Robin Redbreasts; till a foolish rich person pulled it down to set up a marble one of modern invention in its stead, with no story upon it. Here Alice put out one of her dear mother's looks, too tender to be called upbraiding. Then I went on to say, how religious and how good their great-grandmother Field was, how beloved and respected by everybody, though she was not indeed the mistress of this great house, but had only the charge of it (and yet in some respects she might be said to be the mistress of it too) committed to her by the owner, who preferred living in a newer and more fashionable mansion which he had purchased somewhere in the adjoining county; but still she lived in it in a manner as if it had been her own, and kept up the dignity of the great house in a sort while she lived, which afterwards came to decay, and was nearly pulled down, and all its old ornaments stripped and carried away to the owner's other house, where they were set up, and looked as awkward as if some one were to carry away the old tombs they had seen lately at the Abbey, and stick them up in Lady C.'s tawdry gilt drawing-room. Here John smiled, as much as to say, "that would be foolish indeed." And then I told how, when she came to die, her funeral was attended by a concourse of all the poor, and some of the gentry too, of the neighbourhood for many miles round, to show their respect for her memory, because she had been such a good and religious woman; so good indeed that she knew all the Psaltery by heart, ay, and a great part of the Testament besides. Here little Alice spread her hands. Then I told what a tall, upright, graceful person their great-grandmother Field once was; and how in her youth she was esteemed the best dancer— here Alice's little right foot played an involuntary movement, till, upon my looking grave, it desisted - the best dancer, I was saying, in the county, till a cruel disease, called a cancer, came, and bowed her

down with pain: but it could never bend her good
spirits, or make them stoop, but they were still upright,
because she was so good and religious. Then I told how
she was used to sleep by herself in a lone chamber of the
great lone house; and how she believed that an apparition
of two infants was to be seen at midnight gliding up and
down the great staircase near where she slept, but she
said "those innocents would do her no harm;" and
how frightened I used to be, though in those days I had
my maid to sleep with me, because I was never half so
good or religious as she—and yet I never saw the infants.
Here John expanded all his eyebrows and tried to look
courageous. Then I told how good she was to all her
grandchildren, having us to the great house in the holydays, where I in particular used to spend many hours by
myself, in gazing upon the old busts of the twelve
Cæsars, that had been Emperors of Rome, till the old
marble heads would seem to live again, or I to be turned
into marble with them; how I never could be tired with
roaming about that huge mansion, with its vast empty
rooms, with their worn-out hangings, fluttering tapestry,
and carved oaken panels, with the gilding almost rubbed
out—sometimes in the spacious old-fashioned gardens,
which I had almost to myself, unless when now and then
a solitary gardening man would cross me—and how the
nectarines and peaches hung upon the walls, without my
ever offering to pluck them, because they were forbidden
fruit, unless now and then,—and because I had more
pleasure in strolling about among the old melancholy-
looking yew-trees, or the firs, and picking up the red
berries, and the fir-apples, which were good for nothing
but to look at—or in lying about upon the fresh grass with
all the fine garden smells around me—or basking in the
orangery, till I could almost fancy myself ripening too
along with the oranges and the limes in that grateful
warmth—or in watching the dace that darted to and fro
in the fish-pond, at the bottom of the garden, with here
and there a great sulky pike hanging midway down the

water in silent state, as if it mocked at their impertinent friskings, — I had more pleasure in these busy-idle diversions than in all the sweet flavours of peaches, nectarines, oranges, and such-like common baits of children. Here John slyly deposited back upon the plate a bunch of grapes, which, not unobserved by Alice, he had meditated dividing with her, and both seemed willing to relinquish them for the present as irrelevant. Then, in somewhat a more heightened tone, I told how, though their great-grandmother Field loved all her grandchildren, yet in an especial manner she might be said to love their uncle, John L——, because he was so handsome and spirited a youth, and a king to the rest of us ; and, instead of moping about in solitary corners, like some of us, he would mount the most mettlesome horse he could get, when but an imp no bigger than themselves, and make it carry him half over the county in a morning, and join the hunters when there were any out—and yet he loved the old great house and gardens too, but had too much spirit to be always pent up within their boundaries — and how their uncle grew up to man's estate as brave as he was handsome, to the admiration of everybody, but of their great-grandmother Field most especially ; and how he used to carry me upon his back when I was a lame-footed boy—for he was a good bit older than me—many a mile when I could not walk for pain ; —and how in after life he became lame-footed too, and I did not always (I fear) make allowances enough for him when he was impatient and in pain, nor remember sufficiently how considerate he had been to me when I was lame-footed ; and how when he died, though he had not been dead an hour, it seemed as if he had died a great while ago, such a distance there is betwixt life and death ; and how I bore his death as I thought pretty well at first, but afterwards it haunted and haunted me ; and though I did not cry or take it to heart as some do, and as I think he would have done if I had died, yet I missed him all day long, and knew not till then how much I had loved him. I missed his kindness, and I missed his crossness, and wished him to be alive again, to be quarrelling with him (for we quarrelled sometimes), rather than not have him again, and was as uneasy without him, as he, their poor uncle, must have been when the doctor took off his limb.— Here the children fell a-crying, and asked if their little mourning which they had on was not for uncle John, and they looked up, and prayed me not to go on about their uncle, but to tell them some stories about their pretty dead mother. Then I told how for seven long years, in hope sometimes, sometimes in despair, yet persisting ever, I courted the fair Alice W——n; and as much as children could understand, I explained to them what coyness, and difficulty, and denial, meant in maidens—when suddenly turning to Alice, the soul of the first Alice looked out at her eyes with such a reality of re-presentment, that I became in doubt which of them stood there before me, or whose that bright hair was; and while I stood gazing, both the children gradually grew fainter to my view, receding, and still receding, till nothing at last but two mournful features were seen in the uttermost distance, which, without speech, strangely impressed upon me the effects of speech: "We are not of Alice, nor of thee, nor are we children at all. The children of Alice call Bartrum father. We are nothing; less than nothing, and dreams. We are only what might have been, and must wait upon the tedious shores of Lethe millions of ages before we have existence, and a name"——and immediately awaking, I found myself quietly seated in my bachelor armchair, where I had fallen asleep, with the faithful Bridget unchanged by my side—but John L. (or James Elia) was gone for ever.

DISTANT CORRESPONDENTS.

IN A LETTER TO B. F. ESQ., AT SYDNEY, NEW SOUTH WALES.

My dear F.—When I think how welcome the sight of a letter from the world where you were born must be to you in that strange one to which you have been transplanted, I feel some compunctious visitings at my long silence. But, indeed, it is no easy effort to set about a correspondence at our distance. The weary world of waters between us oppresses the imagination. It is difficult to conceive how a scrawl of mine should ever stretch across it. It is a sort of presumption to expect that one's thoughts should live so far. It is like writing for posterity; and reminds me of one of Mrs. Rowe's superscriptions, "Alcander to Strephon in the shades." Cowley's Post-Angel is no more than would be expedient in such an intercourse. One drops a packet at Lombard-street, and in twenty-four hours a friend in Cumberland gets it as fresh as if it came in ice. It is only like whispering through a long trumpet. But suppose a tube let down from the moon, with yourself at one end and *the man* at the other; it would be some balk to the spirit of conversation, if you knew that the dialogue exchanged with that interesting theosophist would take two or three revolutions of a higher luminary in its passage. Yet, for aught I know, you may be some parasangs nigher that primitive idea—Plato's man—than we in England here have the honour to reckon ourselves.

Epistolary matter usually compriseth three topics; news, sentiment, and puns. In the latter, I include all non-serious subjects; or subjects serious in themselves, but treated after my fashion, non-seriously.—And first, for news. In them the most desirable circumstance, I suppose, is that they shall be true. But what security can I have that what I now send you for truth shall not, before you get it, unaccountably turn into a lie? For instance, our mutual friend P. is at this present writing —*my Now*— in good health, and enjoys a fair share of worldly reputation. You are glad to hear it. This is natural and friendly. But at this present reading—*your Now*—he may possibly be in the Bench, or going to be hanged, which in reason ought to abate something of your transport (*i.e.*, at hearing he was well, etc.), or at least considerably to modify it. I am going to the play this evening, to have a laugh with Munden. You have no theatre, I think you told me, in your land of d——d realities. You naturally lick your lips, and envy me my felicity. Think but a moment, and you will correct the hateful emotion. Why, it is Sunday morning with you, and 1823. This confusion of tenses, this grand solecism of *two presents,* is in a degree common to all postage. But if I sent you word to Bath or Devizes, that I was expecting the aforesaid treat this evening, though at the moment you received the intelligence my full feast of fun would be over, yet there would be for a day or two after, as you would well know, a smack, a relish left upon my mental palate, which would give rational encouragement for you to foster a portion, at least, of the disagreeable passion, which it was in part my intention to produce. But ten months hence, your envy or your sympathy would be as useless as a passion spent upon the dead. Not only does truth, in these long intervals, unessence herself, but (what is harder) one cannot venture a crude fiction, for the fear that it may ripen into a truth upon the voyage. What a wild improbable banter I put upon you, some three years since,——of Will Weatherall having married a servant-maid! I remember gravely consulting you how we were to receive her—for Will's wife was in no case to be rejected; and your no less serious replication in the matter; how tenderly you advised an abstemious introduction of literary topics before the lady, with a caution not to be too forward in bringing on the carpet matters more within the sphere of her intelligence;

your deliberate judgment, or rather wise suspension of sentence, how far jacks, and spits, and mops, could, with propriety, be introduced as subjects; whether the conscious avoiding of all such matters in discourse would not have a worse look than the taking of them casually in our way; in what manner we should carry ourselves to our maid Becky, Mrs. William Weatherall being by; whether we should show more delicacy, and a truer sense of respect for Will's wife, by treating Becky with our customary chiding before her, or by an unusual deferential civility paid to Becky, as to a person of great worth, but thrown by the caprice of fate into a humble station. There were difficulties, I remember, on both sides, which you did me the favour to state with the precision of a lawyer, united to the tenderness of a friend. I laughed in my sleeve at your solemn pleadings, when lo! while I was valuing myself upon this flam put upon you in New South Wales, the devil in England, jealous possibly of any lie-children not his own, or working after my copy, has actually instigated our friend (not three days since) to the commission of a matrimony, which I had only conjured up for your diversion. William Weatherall has married Mrs. Cotterel's maid. But to take it in its truest sense, you will see, my dear F., that news from me must become history to you; which I neither profess to write, nor indeed care much for reading. No person, under a diviner, can, with any prospect of veracity, conduct a correspondence at such an arm's length. Two prophets, indeed, might thus interchange intelligence with effect; the epoch of the writer (Habakkuk) falling in with the true present time of the receiver (Daniel); but then we are no prophets.

Then as to sentiment. It fares little better with that. This kind of dish, above all, requires to be served up hot, or sent off in water-plates, that your friend may have it almost as warm as yourself. If it have time to cool, it is the most tasteless of all cold meats. I have often smiled at a conceit of the late Lord C. It seems that travelling somewhere about Geneva, he came to some pretty green spot, or nook, where a willow, or something, hung so fantastically and invitingly over a stream—was it?—or a rock?—no matter—but the stillness and the repose, after a weary journey, 'tis likely, in a languid moment of his Lordship's hot, restless life, so took his fancy that he could imagine no place so proper, in the event of his death, to lay his bones in. This was all very natural and excusable as a sentiment, and shows his character in a very pleasing light. But when from a passing sentiment it came to be an act; and when, by a positive testamentary disposal, his remains were actually carried all that way from England; who was there, some desperate sentimentalists excepted, that did not ask the question, Why could not his Lordship have found a spot as solitary, a nook as romantic, a tree as green and pendent, with a stream as emblematic to his purpose, in Surrey, in Dorset, or in Devon? Conceive the sentiment boarded up, freighted, entered at the Custom House (startling the tide-waiters with the novelty), hoisted into a ship. Conceive it pawed about and handled between the rude jests of tarpaulin ruffians—a thing of its delicate texture—the salt bilge wetting it till it became as vapid as a damaged lustring. Suppose it in material danger (mariners have some superstition about sentiments) of being tossed over in a fresh gale to some propitiatory shark (spirit of Saint Gothard, save us from a quietus so foreign to the deviser's purpose!) but it has happily evaded a fishy consummation. Trace it then to its lucky landing—at Lyons shall we say?

I have not the map before me—jostled upon four men's shoulders—baiting at this town—stopping to refresh at t'other village—waiting a passport here, a license there; the sanction of the magistracy in this district, the concurrence of the ecclesiastics in that canton; till at length it arrives at its destination, tired out and jaded, from a brisk sentiment into a feature of silly pride or tawdry senseless affectation. How few sentiments, my dear F., I am afraid we can set down, in the sailor's phrase, as quite seaworthy.

Lastly, as to the agreeable levities, which though contemptible in bulk, are the twinkling corpuscula which should irradiate a right friendly epistle—your puns and small jests are, I apprehend, extremely circumscribed in their sphere of action. They are so far from a capacity of being packed up and sent beyond sea, they will scarce endure to be transported by hand from this room to the next. Their vigour is as the instant of their birth. Their nutriment for their brief existence is the intellectual atmosphere of the bystanders: or this last is the fine slime of Nilus—the *melior lutus*—whose maternal recipiency is as necessary as the *sol pater* to their equivocal generation. A pun hath a hearty kind of present ear-kissing smack with it; you can no more transmit it in its pristine flavour than you can send a kiss.—Have you not tried in some instances to palm off a yesterday's pun upon a gentleman, and has it answered? Not but it was new to his hearing, but it did not seem to come new from you. It did not hitch in. It was like picking up at a village ale-house a two days'-old newspaper. You have not seen it before, but you resent the stale thing as an affront. This sort of merchandize above all requires a quick return. A pun, and its recognitory laugh, must be co-instantaneous. The one is the brisk lightning, the other the fierce thunder. A moment's interval, and the link is snapped. A pun is reflected from a friend's face as from a mirror. Who would consult his sweet visnomy, if the polished surface were two or three minutes (not to speak of twelve months, my dear F.) in giving back its copy?

I cannot image to myself whereabout you are. When I try to fix it, Peter Wilkins's island comes across me. Sometimes you seem to be in the *Hades* of *Thieves*. I see Diogenes prying among you with his perpetual fruitless lantern. What must you be willing by this time to give for the sight of an honest man! You must almost have forgotten how *we* look. And tell me what your Sydneyites do? are they th**v*ng all day long? Merciful Heaven! what property can stand against such a depredation! The kangaroos—your Aborigines—do they keep their primitive simplicity un-Europe-tainted, with those little short fore puds, looking like a lesson framed by nature to the pick-pocket! Marry, for diving into fobs they are rather lamely provided *à priori;* but if the hue and cry were once up, they would show as fair a pair of hind-shifters as the expertest loco-motor in the colony. We hear the most improbable tales at this distance. Pray is it true that the young Spartans among you are born with six fingers, which spoils their scanning?—It must look very odd; but use reconciles. For their scansion, it is less to be regretted; for if they take it into their heads to be poets, it is odds but they turn out, the greater part of them, vile plagiarists. Is there much difference to see, too, between the son of a th**f and the grandson? or where does the taint stop? Do you bleach in three or in four generations? I have many questions to put, but ten Delphic voyages can be made in a shorter time than it will take to satisfy my scruples. Do you grow your own hemp?—What is your staple trade,—exclusive of the national profession, I mean? Your locksmiths, I take it, are some of your great capitalists.

I am insensibly chatting to you as familiarly as when we used to exchange good-morrows out of our old contiguous windows, in pump-famed Hare Court in the Temple. Why did you ever leave that quiet corner?— Why did I?—with its complement of four poor elms, from whose smoke-dyed barks, the theme of jesting ruralists, I picked my first ladybirds! My heart is as dry as that spring sometimes proves in a thirsty August, when I revert to the space that is between us; a length of passage enough to render obsolete the phrases of our English letters before they can reach you. But while I talk I think you hear me,—thoughts dallying with vain surmise—

> Aye me! while thee the seas and sounding shores
> Hold far away.

Come back, before I am grown into a very old man, so as you shall hardly know me. Come, before Bridget walks on crutches. Girls whom you left children have become sage matrons while you are tarrying there. The blooming Miss W—r (you remember Sally W—r) called upon us yesterday, an aged crone. Folks whom you knew die off every year. Formerly, I thought that death was wearing out,—I stood ramparted about with so many healthy friends. The departure of J. W., two springs back, corrected my delusion. Since then the old divorcer has been busy. If you do not make haste to return, there will be little left to greet you, of me, or mine.

THE PRAISE OF CHIMNEY-SWEEPERS.

I LIKE to meet a sweep—understand me—not a grown sweeper—old chimney-sweepers are by no means attractive—but one of those tender novices, blooming through their first nigritude, the maternal washings not quite effaced from the cheek—such as come forth with the dawn, or somewhat earlier, with their little professional notes sounding like the *peep-peep* of a young sparrow; or liker to the matin lark should I pronounce them, in their aërial ascents not seldom anticipating the sunrise?

I have a kindly yearning towards these dim specks—poor blots—innocent blacknesses—

I reverence these young Africans of our own growth—these almost clergy imps, who sport their cloth without assumption; and from their little pulpits (the tops of chimneys), in the nipping air of a December morning, preach a lesson of patience to mankind.

When a child, what a mysterious pleasure it was to witness their operation! to see a chit no bigger than one's-self, enter, one knew not by what process, into what seemed the *fauces Averni*—to pursue him in imagination, as he went sounding on through so many dark stifling caverns, horrid shades! to shudder with the idea that "now, surely he must be lost for ever!"—to revive at hearing his feeble shout of discovered day-light—and then (O fulness of delight!) running out of doors, to come just in time to see the sable phenomenon emerge in safety, the brandished weapon of his art victorious like some flag waved over a conquered citadel! I seem to remember having been told, that a bad sweep was once left in a stack with his brush, to indicate which way the wind blew. It was an awful spectacle, certainly; not much unlike the old stage direction in Macbeth, where the "Apparition of a child crowned, with a tree in his hand, rises."

Reader, if thou meetest one of these small gentry in thy early rambles, it is good to give him a penny,—it is better to give him two-pence. If it be starving weather, and to the proper troubles of his hard occupation, a pair of kibed heels (no unusual accompaniment) be super-added, the demand on thy humanity will surely rise to a tester.

There is a composition, the ground-work of which I have understood to be the sweet wood 'yclept sassafras. This wood boiled down to a kind of tea, and tempered with an infusion of milk and sugar, hath to some tastes a delicacy beyond the China luxury. I know not how thy palate may relish it; for myself, with every deference to the judicious Mr. Read, who hath time out of mind kept open a shop (the only one he avers in London) for the vending of this "wholesome and pleasant beverage," on the south side of Fleet Street, as thou approachest Bridge Street—*the only Salopian house*—I have never yet adventured to dip my own particular lip in a basin of his commended ingredients—a cautious premonition to the olfactories constantly whispering to me, that my stomach must infallibly, with all due courtesy, decline it. Yet I have seen palates, otherwise not uninstructed in dietetical elegancies, sup it up with avidity.

I know not by what particular conformation of the organ it happens, but I have always found that this composition is surprisingly gratifying to the palate of a young chimney-sweeper—whether the oily particles (sassafras is slightly oleaginous) do attenuate and soften the fuliginous concretions, which are sometimes found (in dissections) to adhere to the roof of the mouth in these unfledged practitioners; or whether Nature, sensible that she had mingled too much of bitter wood in the lot of these raw victims, caused to grow out of the earth her sassafras for a sweet lenitive—but so it is, that no possible taste or odour to the senses of a young chimney-sweeper can convey a delicate excitement comparable to this mixture. Being penniless, they will yet hang their black heads over the ascending steam, to gratify one sense if possible, seemingly no less pleased than those domestic animals—cats—when they purr over a new-found sprig of valerian. There is something more in these sympathies than philosophy can inculcate.

Now albeit Mr. Read boasteth, not without reason, that his is the *only Salopian house;* yet be it known to thee, reader—if thou art one who keepest what are called good hours, thou art haply ignorant of the fact—he hath a race of industrious imitators, who from stalls, and under open sky, dispense the same savoury mess to humbler customers, at that dead time of the dawn, when (as extremes meet) the rake, reeling home from his midnight cups, and the hard-handed artizan leaving his bed to resume the premature labours of the day, jostle, not unfrequently to the manifest disconcerting of the former, for the honours of the pavement. It is the time when, in summer, between the expired and the not yet relumined kitchen-fires, the kennels of our fair metropolis give forth their least satisfactory odours. The rake, who wisheth to dissipate his o'ernight vapours in more grateful coffee, curses the ungenial fume, as he passeth; but the artizan stops to taste, and blesses the fragrant breakfast.

This is *saloop*—the precocious herb-woman's darling—the delight of the early gardener, who transports his smoking cabbages by break of day from Hammersmith to Covent Garden's famed piazzas—the delight, and oh! I fear, too often the envy, of the unpennied sweep. Him shouldst thou haply encounter, with his dim visage pendent over the grateful steam, regale him with a sumptuous basin (it will cost thee but three-halfpennies) and a slice of delicate bread and butter (an added halfpenny)—so may thy culinary fires, eased of the o'ercharged secretions from thy worse-placed hospitalities, curl up a lighter volume to the welkin—so may the descending soot never taint thy costly well-ingredienced soups—nor the odious cry, quick-reaching from street to street, of the *fired chimney*, invite the rattling engines from ten adjacent parishes, to disturb for a casual scintillation thy peace and pocket!

I am by nature extremely susceptible of street affronts; the jeers and taunts of the populace; the low-bred triumph they display over the casual trip, or splashed stocking, of a gentleman. Yet can I endure the jocularity of a young sweep with something more than forgiveness.—In the last winter but one, pacing along Cheapside with my accustomed precipitation when I walk westward, a treacherous slide brought me upon my back in an instant. I scrambled up with pain and shame enough—yet outwardly trying to face it down, as if nothing had happened—when the roguish grin of one of these young wits encountered me. There he stood, pointing me out with his dusky finger to the mob, and to a poor woman (I suppose his mother) in particular, till the tears for the exquisiteness of the fun (so he thought it) worked themselves out at the corners of his poor red eyes, red from many a previous weeping, and soot-inflamed, yet twinkling through all with such a joy, snatched out of desolation, that Hogarth —— but Hogarth has got him already (how could he miss him?)

in the March to Finchley, grinning at the pieman—there he stood, as he stands in the picture, irremovable, as if the jest was to last for ever—with such a maximum of glee, and minimum of mischief, in his mirth—for the grin of a genuine sweep hath absolutely no malice in it—that I could have been content, if the honour of a gentleman might endure it, to have remained his butt and his mockery till midnight.

I am by theory obdurate to the seductiveness of what are called a fine set of teeth. Every pair of rosy lips (the ladies must pardon me) is a casket presumably holding such jewels; but, methinks, they should take leave to "air" them as frugally as possible. The fine lady, or fine gentleman, who show me their teeth, show me bones. Yet must I confess, that from the mouth of a true sweep a display (even to ostentation) of those white and shiny ossifications, strikes me as an agreeable anomaly in manners, and an allowable piece of foppery. It is, as when

> A sable cloud
> Turns forth her silver lining on the night.

It is like some remnant of gentry not quite extinct: a badge of better days; a hint of nobility:—and, doubtless, under the obscuring darkness and double night of their forlorn disguisement, oftentimes lurketh good blood, and gentle conditions, derived from lost ancestry, and a lapsed pedigree. The premature apprenticements of these tender victims give but too much encouragement, I fear, to clandestine and almost infantile abductions; the seeds of civility and true courtesy, so often discernible in these young grafts (not otherwise to be accounted for) plainly hint at some forced adoptions; many noble Rachels mourning for their children, even in our days, countenance the fact; the tales of fairy spiriting may shadow a lamentable verity, and the recovery of the young Montagu be but a solitary instance of good fortune out of many irreparable and hopeless *defiliations*.

In one of the state-beds at Arundel Castle, a few years

since—under a ducal canopy—(that seat of the Howards is an object of curiosity to visitors, chiefly for its beds, in which the late duke was especially a connoisseur)—encircled with curtains of delicatest crimson, with starry coronets inwoven—folded between a pair of sheets whiter and softer than the lap where Venus lulled Ascanius—was discovered by chance, after all methods of search had failed, at noon-day, fast asleep, a lost chimney-sweeper. The little creature, having somehow confounded his passage among the intricacies of those lordly chimneys, by some unknown aperture had alighted upon this magnificent chamber; and, tired with his tedious explorations, was unable to resist the delicious invitement to repose, which he there saw exhibited; so creeping between the sheets very quietly, laid his black head upon the pillow, and slept like a young Howard.

Such is the account given to the visitors at the Castle.—But I cannot help seeming to perceive a confirmation of what I had just hinted at in this story. A high instinct was at work in the case, or I am mistaken. Is it probable that a poor child of that description, with whatever weariness he might be visited, would have ventured, under such a penalty as he would be taught to expect, to uncover the sheets of a Duke's bed, and deliberately to lay himself down between them, when the rug, or the carpet, presented an obvious couch, still far above his pretensions—is this probable, I would ask, if the great power of nature, which I contend for, had not been manifested within him, prompting to the adventure? Doubtless this young nobleman (for such my mind misgives me that he must be) was allured by some memory, not amounting to full consciousness, of his condition in infancy, when he was used to be lapped by his mother, or his nurse, in just such sheets as he there found, into which he was now but creeping back as into his proper *incunabula*, and resting-place.— By no other theory than by this sentiment of a pre-existent state (as I may call it), can I explain a deed so venturous, and, indeed, upon any other system, so indecorous, in this tender, but unseasonable, sleeper.

My pleasant friend Jem White was so impressed with a belief of metamorphoses like this frequently taking place, that in some sort to reverse the wrongs of fortune in these poor changelings, he instituted an annual feast of chimney-sweepers, at which it was his pleasure to officiate as host and waiter. It was a solemn supper held in Smithfield, upon the yearly return of the fair of St. Bartholomew. Cards were issued a week before to the master-sweeps in and about the metropolis, confining the invitation to their younger fry. Now and then an elderly stripling would get in among us, and be good-naturedly winked at; but our main body were infantry. One unfortunate wight, indeed, who, relying upon his dusky suit, had intruded himself into our party, but by tokens was providentially discovered in time to be no chimney-sweeper, (all is not soot which looks so,) was quoited out of the presence with universal indignation, as not having on the wedding garment; but in general the greatest harmony prevailed. The place chosen was a convenient spot among the pens, at the north side of the fair, not so far distant as to be impervious to the agreeable hubbub of that vanity, but remote enough not to be obvious to the interruption of every gaping spectator in it. The guests assembled about seven. In those little temporary parlours three tables were spread with napery, not so fine as substantial, and at every board a comely hostess presided with her pan of hissing sausages. The nostrils of the young rogues dilated at the savour. James White, as head waiter, had charge of the first table; and myself, with our trusty companion Bigod, ordinarily ministered to the other two. There was clambering and jostling, you may be sure, who should get at the first table, for Rochester in his maddest days could not have done the humours of the scene with more spirit than my friend. After some general expression of thanks for the honour the company had done him, his inaugural ceremony was to clasp the greasy waist of old dame Ursula (the fattest of the three), that stood frying and fretting, half-blessing, half-cursing "the gentleman," and imprint upon her chaste lips a tender salute, whereat the universal host would set up a shout that tore the concave, while hundreds of grinning teeth startled the night with their brightness. O it was a pleasure to see the sable younkers lick in the unctuous meat, with *his* more unctuous sayings—how he would fit the tit-bits to the puny mouths, reserving the lengthier links for the seniors—how he would intercept a morsel even in the jaws of some young desperado, declaring it "must to the pan again to be browned, for it was not fit for a gentleman's eating"—how he would recommend this slice of white bread, or that piece of kissing-crust, to a tender juvenile, advising them all to have a care of cracking their teeth, which were their best patrimony,—how genteelly he would deal about the small ale, as if it were wine, naming the brewer, and protesting, if it were not good, he should lose their custom; with a special recommendation to wipe the lip before drinking. Then we had our toasts—"the King,"—"the Cloth,"—which, whether they understood or not, was equally diverting and flattering; and for a crowning sentiment, which never failed, "May the Brush supersede the Laurel!" All these, and fifty other fancies, which were rather felt than comprehended by his guests, would he utter, standing upon tables, and prefacing every sentiment with a "Gentlemen, give me leave to propose so and so," which was a prodigious comfort to those young orphans; every now and then stuffing into his mouth (for it did not do to be squeamish on these occasions) indiscriminate pieces of those reeking sausages, which pleased them mightily, and was the savouriest part, you may believe, of the entertainment.

> Golden lads and lasses must,
> As chimney-sweepers, come to dust—

James White is extinct, and with him these suppers

have long ceased. He carried away with him half the fun of the world when he died—of my world at least. His old clients look for him among the pens; and, missing him, reproach the altered feast of St. Bartholomew, and the glory of Smithfield departed for ever.

A COMPLAINT OF THE DECAY OF BEGGARS,

IN THE METROPOLIS.

THE all-sweeping besom of societarian reformation—your only modern Alcides' club to rid the time of its abuses—is uplift with many-handed sway to extirpate the last fluttering tatters of the bugbear MENDICITY from the metropolis. Scrips, wallets, bags — staves, dogs, and crutches—the whole mendicant fraternity, with all their baggage, are fast posting out of the purlieus of this eleventh persecution. From the crowded crossing, from the corners of streets and turnings of alleys, the parting Genius of Beggary is "with sighing sent."

I do not approve of this wholesale going to work, this impertinent crusado, or *bellum ad exterminationem*, proclaimed against a species. Much good might be sucked from these Beggars.

They were the oldest and the honourablest form of pauperism. Their appeals were to our common nature; less revolting to an ingenuous mind than to be a suppliant to the particular humours or caprice of any fellow-creature, or set of fellow-creatures, parochial or societarian. Theirs were the only rates uninvidious in the levy, ungrudged in the assessment.

There was a dignity springing from the very depth of their desolation; as to be naked is to be so much nearer to the being a man, than to go in livery.

The greatest spirits have felt this in their reverses;

and when Dionysius from king turned schoolmaster, do we feel anything towards him but contempt? Could Vandyke have made a picture of him, swaying a ferula for a sceptre, which would have affected our minds with the same heroic pity, the same compassionate admiration, with which we regard his Belisarius begging for an *obolus?* Would the moral have been more graceful, more pathetic?

The Blind Beggar in the legend—the father of pretty Bessy—whose story doggrel rhymes and ale-house signs cannot so degrade or attenuate but that some sparks of a lustrous spirit will shine through the disguisements—this noble Earl of Cornwall (as indeed he was) and memorable sport of fortune, fleeing from the unjust sentence of his liege lord, stript of all, and seated on the flowering green of Bethnal, with his more fresh and springing daughter by his side, illumining his rags and his beggary—would the child and parent have cut a better figure doing the honours of a counter, or expiating their fallen condition upon the three-foot eminence of some sempstering shop-board?

In tale or history your Beggar is ever the just antipode to your King. The poets and romancical writers (as dear Margaret Newcastle would call them), when they would most sharply and feelingly paint a reverse of fortune, never stop till they have brought down their hero in good earnest to rags and the wallet. The depth of the descent illustrates the height he falls from. There is no medium which can be presented to the imagination without offence. There is no breaking the fall. Lear, thrown from his palace, must divest him of his garments, till he answer "mere nature;" and Cresseid, fallen from a prince's love, must extend her pale arms, pale with other whiteness than of beauty, supplicating lazar arms with bell and clap-dish.

The Lucian wits knew this very well; and, with a converse policy, when they would express scorn of greatness without the pity, they show us an Alexander in the shades cobbling shoes, or a Semiramis getting up foul linen.

How would it sound in song, that a great monarch had

declined his affections upon the daughter of a baker! yet do we feel the imagination at all violated when we read the "true ballad," where King Cophetua woos the beggar maid?

Pauperism, pauper, poor man, are expressions of pity, but pity alloyed with contempt. No one properly contemns a Beggar. Poverty is a comparative thing, and each degree of it is mocked by its "neighbour grice." Its poor rents and comings-in are soon summed up and told. Its pretences to property are almost ludicrous. Its pitiful attempts to save excite a smile. Every scornful companion can weigh his trifle-bigger purse against it. Poor man reproaches poor man in the streets with impolitic mention of his condition, his own being a shade better, while the rich pass by and jeer at both. No rascally comparative insults a Beggar, or thinks of weighing purses with him. He is not in the scale of comparison. He is not under the measure of property. He confessedly hath none, any more than a dog or a sheep. No one twitteth him with ostentation above his means. No one accuses him of pride, or upbraideth him with mock humility. None jostle with him for the wall, or pick quarrels for precedency. No wealthy neighbour seeketh to eject him from his tenement. No man sues him. No man goes to law with him. If I were not the independent gentleman that I am, rather than I would be a retainer to the great, a led captain, or a poor relation, I would choose, out of the delicacy and true greatness of my mind, to be a Beggar.

Rags, which are the reproach of poverty, are the Beggar's robes, and graceful *insignia* of his profession, his tenure, his full dress, the suit in which he is expected to show himself in public. He is never out of the fashion, or limpeth awkwardly behind it. He is not required to put on court mourning. He weareth all colours, fearing none. His costume hath undergone less change than the Quaker's. He is the only man in the universe who is not obliged to study appearances. The ups and downs of the world concern him no longer. He alone continueth in one stay. The price of stock or land affecteth him not. The fluctuations of agricultural or commercial prosperity touch him not, or at worst but change his customers. He is not expected to become bail or surety for any one. No man troubleth him with questioning his religion or politics. He is the only free man in the universe.

The Mendicants of this great city were so many of her sights, her lions. I can no more spare them than I could the Cries of London. No corner of a street is complete without them. They are as indispensable as the Ballad Singer; and in their picturesque attire as ornamental as the signs of old London. They were the standing morals, emblems, mementoes, dial-mottoes, the spital sermons, the books for children, the salutary checks and pauses to the high and rushing tide of greasy citizenry—

>   ———Look
> Upon that poor and broken bankrupt there.

Above all, those old blind Tobits that used to line the wall of Lincoln's-inn Garden, before modern fastidiousness had expelled them, casting up their ruined orbs to catch a ray of pity, and (if possible) of light, with their faithful Dog Guide at their feet,—whither are they fled? or into what corners, blind as themselves, have they been driven, out of the wholesome air and sun-warmth? immersed between four walls, in what withering poor-house do they endure the penalty of double darkness, where the chink of the dropt halfpenny no more consoles their forlorn bereavement, far from the sound of the cheerful and hope-stirring tread of the passenger? Where hang their useless staves? and who will farm their dogs?—Have the overseers of St. L— caused them to be shot? or were they tied up in sacks and dropt into the Thames, at the suggestion of B— the mild rector of ——?

Well fare the soul of unfastidious Vincent Bourne,—most classical, and, at the same time, most English of the Latinists! who has treated of this human and quadrupedal alliance, this dog and man friendship, in the sweetest of his poems, the *Epitaphium in Canem*, or, *Dog's Epitaph*. Reader, peruse it; and say, if customary sights, which could call up such gentle poetry as this, were of a nature to do more harm or good to the moral sense of the passengers through the daily thoroughfares of a vast and busy metropolis.

> Pauperis hic Iri requiesco Lyciscus, herilis,
> Dum vixi, tutela vigil columenque senectæ,
> Dux cæco fidus: nec, me ducente, solebat,
> Prætenso hinc atque hinc baculo, per iniqua locorum
> Incertam explorare viam; sed fila secutus,
> Quæ dubios regerent passûs, vestigia tuta
> Fixit inoffenso gressu; gelidumque sedile
> In nudo nactus saxo, quâ prætereuntium
> Unda frequens confluxit, ibi miserisque tenebras
> Lamentis, noctemque oculis ploravit obortam.
> Ploravit nec frustra; obolum dedit alter et alter,
> Queis corda et mentem indiderat natura benignam.
> Ad latus interea jacui sopitus herile,
> Vel mediis vigil in somnis; ad herilia jussa
> Auresque atque animum arrectus, seu frustula amicè
> Porrexit sociasque dapes, seu longa diei
> Tædia perpessus, reditum sub nocte parabat.
> Hi mores, hæc vita fuit, dum fata sinebant,
> Dum neque languebam morbis, nec inerte senectâ
> Quae tandem obrepsit, veterique satellite cæcum
> Orbavit dominum; prisci sed gratia facti
> Ne tota intereat, longos deleta per annos,
> Exiguum hunc Irus tumulum de cespite fecit,
> Etsi inopis, non ingratæ, munuscula dextræ;
> Carmine signavitque brevi, dominumque canemque,
> Quod memoret, fidumque Canem dominumque Benignum.

> Poor Irus' faithful wolf-dog here I lie,
> That wont to tend my old blind master's steps,
> His guide and guard; nor, while my service lasted,
> Had he occasion for that staff, with which
> He now goes picking out his path in fear
> Over the highways and crossings; but would plant,
> Safe in the conduct of my friendly string,
> A firm foot forward still, till he had reach'd
> His poor seat on some stone, nigh where the tide
> Of passers-by in thickest confluence flow'd:

> To whom with loud and passionate laments
> From morn to eve his dark estate he wail'd.
> Nor wail'd to all in vain: some here and there,
> The well-disposed and good, their pennies gave.
> I meantime at his feet obsequious slept;
> Not all-asleep in sleep, but heart and ear
> Prick'd up at his least motion; to receive
> At his kind hand my customary crumbs,
> And common portion in his feast of scraps;
> Or when night warn'd us homeward, tired and spent
> With our long day and tedious beggary.
>   These were my manners, this my way of life
> Till age and slow disease me overtook,
> And sever'd from my sightless master's side.
> But lest the grace of so good deeds should die,
> Through tract of years in mute oblivion lost,
> This slender tomb of turf hath Irus reared,
> Cheap monument of no ungrudging hand,
> And with short verse inscribed it, to attest,
> In long and lasting union to attest,
>   The virtues of the Beggar and his Dog.

These dim eyes have in vain explored for some months past a well-known figure, or part of the figure, of a man, who used to glide his comely upper half over the pavements of London, wheeling along with most ingenious celerity upon a machine of wood; a spectacle to natives, to foreigners, and to children. He was of a robust make, with a florid sailor-like complexion, and his head was bare to the storm and sunshine. He was a natural curiosity, a speculation to the scientific, a prodigy to the simple. The infant would stare at the mighty man brought down to his own level. The common cripple would despise his own pusillanimity, viewing the hale stoutness, and hearty heart, of this half-limbed giant. Few but must have noticed him; for the accident which brought him low took place during the riots of 1780, and he has been a groundling so long. He seemed earth-born, an Antæus, and to suck in fresh vigour from the soil which he neighboured. He was a grand fragment; as good as an Elgin marble. The nature, which should have recruited his reft legs and thighs, was not lost, but only retired into

M

his upper parts, and he was half a Hercules. I heard a tremendous voice thundering and growling, as before an earthquake, and casting down my eyes, it was this mandrake reviling a steed that had started at his portentous appearance. He seemed to want but his just stature to have rent the offending quadruped in shivers. He was as the man-part of a centaur, from which the horse-half had been cloven in some dire Lapithan controversy. He moved on, as if he could have made shift with yet half of the body-portion which was left him. The *os sublime* was not wanting; and he threw out yet a jolly countenance upon the heavens. Forty-and-two years had he driven this out-of-door trade, and now that his hair is grizzled in the service, but his good spirits no way impaired, because he is not content to exchange his free air and exercise for the restraints of a poor-house, he is expiating his contumacy in one of those houses (ironically christened) of Correction.

Was a daily spectacle like this to be deemed a nuisance, which called for legal interference to remove? or not rather a salutary and a touching object to the passers-by in a great city? Among her shows, her museums, and supplies for ever-gaping curiosity (and what else but an accumulation of sights—endless sights—*is* a great city; or for what else is it desirable?) was there not room for one *Lusus* (not *Naturæ*, indeed, but) *Accidentium?* What if in forty-and-two-years' going about, the man had scraped together enough to give a portion to his child (as the rumour ran) of a few hundreds—whom had he injured?

whom had he imposed upon? The contributors had enjoyed their *sight* for their pennies. What if after being exposed all day to the heats, the rains, and the frosts of heaven—shuffling his ungainly trunk along in an elaborate and painful motion—he was enabled to retire at night to enjoy himself at a club of his fellow cripples over a dish of hot meat and vegetables, as the charge was gravely brought against him by a clergyman deposing before a House of Commons' Committee—was *this*, or was his truly paternal consideration, which (if a fact) deserved a statue rather than a whipping-post, and is inconsistent, at least, with the exaggeration of nocturnal orgies which he has been slandered with—a reason that he should be deprived of his chosen, harmless, nay, edifying way of life, and be committed in hoary age for a sturdy vagabond?—

There was a Yorick once, whom it would not have shamed to have sate down at the cripples' feast, and to have thrown in his benediction, ay, and his mite too, for a companionable symbol. "Age, thou hast lost thy breed."—

✓ Half of these stories about the prodigious fortunes made by begging are (I verily believe) misers' calumnies. One was much talked of in the public papers some time since, and the usual charitable inferences deduced. A clerk in the Bank was surprised with the announcement of a five-hundred-pound legacy left him by a person whose name he was a stranger to. It seems that in his daily morning walks from Peckham (or some village thereabouts) where he lived, to his office, it had been his practice for the last twenty years to drop his halfpenny duly into the hat of some blind Bartimeus, that sate begging alms by the wayside in the Borough. The good old beggar recognised his daily benefactor by the voice only; and, when he died, left all the amassings of his alms (that had been half a century perhaps in the accumulating) to his old Bank friend. Was this a story to purse up people's hearts, and pennies, against giving an alms to the blind?—or not rather a beautiful moral of well-directed charity on the one part, and noble gratitude upon the other?

I sometimes wish I had been that Bank clerk.

I seem to remember a poor old grateful kind of creature, blinking and looking up with his no eyes in the sun

Is it possible I could have steeled my purse against him?

Perhaps I had no small change.

✓ Reader, do not be frightened at the hard words imposition, imposture—*give, and ask no questions.* Cast thy bread upon the waters. Some have unawares (like this Bank clerk) entertained angels.

Shut not thy purse-strings always against painted distress. Act a charity sometimes. When a poor creature (outwardly and visibly such) comes before thee, do not stay to inquire whether the "seven small children," in whose name he implores thy assistance, have a veritable existence. Rake not into the bowels of unwelcome truth to save a halfpenny. It is good to believe him. If he be not all that he pretendeth, *give*, and under a personate father of a family, think (if thou pleasest) that thou hast relieved an indigent bachelor. When they come with their counterfeit looks and mumping tones, think them players. You pay your money to see a comedian feign these things, which, concerning these poor people, thou canst not certainly tell whether they are feigned or not.

A DISSERTATION UPON ROAST PIG.

MANKIND, says a Chinese manuscript, which my friend M. was obliging enough to read and explain to me, for the first seventy thousand ages ate their meat raw, clawing or biting it from the living animal, just as they do in Abyssinia to this day. This period is not obscurely hinted at by their great Confucius in the second chapter of his Mundane Mutations, where he designates a kind of golden age by the term Cho-fang, literally the Cooks' Holiday. The manuscript goes on to say, that the art of roasting, or rather broiling (which I take to be the elder brother) was accidentally discovered in the manner following. The swine-herd, Ho-ti, having gone out into the woods one morning, as his manner was, to collect mast for his hogs, left his cottage in the care of his eldest son Bo-bo, a great lubberly boy, who being fond of playing with fire, as younkers of his age commonly are, let some sparks escape into a bundle of straw, which kindling quickly, spread the conflagration over every part of their poor mansion, till it was reduced to ashes. Together with the cottage (a sorry antediluvian make-shift of a building, you may think it), what was of much more importance, a fine litter of new-farrowed pigs, no less than nine in number, perished. China pigs have been esteemed a luxury all over the East, from the remotest periods that we read of. Bo-bo was in the utmost consternation, as you may think, not so much for the sake of the tenement, which his father and he could easily build up again with a few dry branches, and the labour of an hour or two, at any time, as for the loss of the pigs. While he was thinking what he should say to his father, and wringing his hands over the smoking remnants of one of those untimely sufferers, an odour assailed his nostrils, unlike any scent which he had before experienced. What could it proceed from?— not from the burnt cottage—he had smelt that smell before—indeed, this was by no means the first accident of the kind which had occurred through the negligence of this unlucky young firebrand. Much less did it resemble that of any known herb, weed, or flower. A premonitory moistening at the same time overflowed his nether lip. He knew not what to think. He next stooped down to feel the pig, if there were any signs of life in it. He burnt his fingers, and to cool them he applied them in his booby fashion to his mouth. Some of the crumbs of the scorched skin had come away with his fingers, and for the first time in his life (in the world's life indeed, for before him no man had known it) he tasted —*crackling!* Again he felt and fumbled at the pig. It did not burn him so much now, still he licked his fingers from a sort of habit. The truth at length broke into his slow understanding, that it was the pig that smelt so, and the pig that tasted so delicious; and surrendering himself up to the new-born pleasure, he fell to tearing up whole handfuls of the scorched skin with the flesh next it, and was cramming it down his throat in his beastly fashion, when his sire entered amid the smoking rafters, armed with retributory cudgel, and finding how affairs stood, began to rain blows upon the young rogue's shoulders, as thick as hail-stones, which Bo-bo heeded not any more than if they had been flies. The tickling pleasure, which he experienced in his lower regions, had rendered him quite callous to any inconveniences he might feel in those remote quarters. His father might lay on, but he could not beat him from his pig, till he had fairly made an end of it, when, becoming a little more sensible of his situation, something like the following dialogue ensued.

"You graceless whelp, what have you got there devouring? Is it not enough that you have burnt me down three houses with your dog's tricks, and be hanged to you! but you must be eating fire, and I know not what—what have you got there, I say?"

"O father, the pig, the pig! do come and taste how nice the burnt pig eats."

The ears of Ho-ti tingled with horror. He cursed his son, and he cursed himself that ever he should beget a son that should eat burnt pig.

Bo-bo, whose scent was wonderfully sharpened since morning, soon raked out another pig, and fairly rending it asunder, thrust the lesser half by main force into the fists of Ho-ti, still shouting out, "Eat, eat, eat the burnt pig, father, only taste—O Lord!"—with such-like barbarous ejaculations, cramming all the while as if he would choke.

Ho-ti trembled every joint while he grasped the abominable thing, wavering whether he should not put his son to death for an unnatural young monster, when the crackling scorching his fingers, as it had done his son's, and applying the same remedy to them, he in his turn tasted some of its flavour, which, make what sour mouths he would for a pretence, proved not altogether displeasing to him. In conclusion (for the manuscript here is a little tedious), both father and son fairly set down to the mess, and never left off till they had despatched all that remained of the litter.

Bo-bo was strictly enjoined not to let the secret escape, for the neighbours would certainly have stoned them for a couple of abominable wretches, who could think of improving upon the good meat which God had sent them. Nevertheless, strange stories got about. It was observed that Ho-ti's cottage was burnt down now more frequently than ever. Nothing but fires from this time forward. Some would break out in broad day, others in the nighttime. As often as the sow farrowed, so sure was the house of Ho-ti to be in a blaze; and Ho-ti himself, which was the more remarkable, instead of chastising his son, seemed to grow more indulgent to him than ever. At length they were watched, the terrible mystery discovered, and father and son summoned to take their trial at Pekin, then an inconsiderable assize town. Evidence was given, the obnoxious food itself produced in court, and verdict about to be pronounced, when the foreman of the jury begged that some of the burnt pig, of which the culprits stood accused, might be handed into the box. He handled it, and they all handled it; and burning their fingers, as Bo-bo and his father had done before them, and nature prompting to each of them the same remedy, against the face of all the facts, and the clearest charge which judge had ever given,—to the surprise of the whole court, townsfolk, strangers, reporters, and all present—without leaving the box, or any manner of consultation whatever, they brought in a simultaneous verdict of Not Guilty.

The judge, who was a shrewd fellow, winked at the manifest iniquity of the decision: and when the court was dismissed, went privily and bought up all the pigs that could be had for love or money. In a few days his lordship's town-house was observed to be on fire. The thing took wing, and now there was nothing to be seen but fires in every direction. Fuel and pigs grew enormously dear all over the district. The insurance-offices, one and all shut up shop. People built slighter and slighter every day, until it was feared that the very science of architecture would in no long time be lost to the world. Thus this custom of firing houses continued, till in process of time, says my manuscript, a sage arose, like our Locke, who made a discovery that the flesh of swine, or indeed of any other animal, might be cooked (*burnt*, as they called it) without the necessity of consuming a whole house to dress it. Then first began the rude form of a gridiron. Roasting by the string or spit came in a century or two later, I forget in whose dynasty. By such slow degrees, concludes the manuscript, do the most useful, and seemingly the most obvious, arts make their way among mankind——

Without placing too implicit faith in the account above given, it must be agreed that if a worthy pretext for so dangerous an experiment as setting houses on fire (especially in these days) could be assigned in favour of any culinary object, that pretext and excuse might be found in ROAST PIG.

Of all the delicacies in the whole *mundus edibilis*, I will maintain it to be the most delicate—*princeps obsoniorum*.

I speak not of your grown porkers—things between pig and pork—those hobbledehoys—but a young and tender suckling—under a moon old—guiltless as yet of the sty—with no original speck of the *amor immunditiæ*, the hereditary failing of the first parent, yet manifest his voice as yet not broken, but something between a childish treble and a grumble—the mild forerunner or *præludium* of a grunt.

He must be roasted. I am not ignorant that our ancestors ate them seethed, or boiled—but what a sacrifice of the exterior tegument!

There is no flavour comparable, I will contend, to that of the crisp, tawny, well-watched, not over-roasted, *crackling*, as it is well called—the very teeth are invited to their share of the pleasure at this banquet in overcoming the coy, brittle resistance—with the adhesive oleaginous—O call it not fat! but an indefinable sweetness growing up to it—the tender blossoming of fat—fat cropped in the bud—taken in the shoot—in the first innocence—the cream and quintessence of the child-pig's yet pure food—the lean, no lean, but a kind of animal manna—or, rather, fat and lean (if it must be so) so blended and running into each other, that both together make but one ambrosian result or common substance.

Behold him while he is "doing"—it seemeth rather a refreshing warmth, than a scorching heat, that he is so passive to. How equably he twirleth round the string! Now he is just done. To see the extreme sensibility of that tender age! he hath wept out his pretty eyes—radiant jellies—shooting stars.—

See him in the dish, his second cradle, how meek he lieth!—wouldst thou have had this innocent grow up to the grossness and indocility which too often accompany maturer swinehood? Ten to one he would have proved a glutton, a sloven, an obstinate, disagreeable animal—wallowing in all manner of filthy conversation—from these sins he is happily snatched away—

> Ere sin could blight or sorrow fade,
> Death came with timely care—

his memory is odoriferous—no clown curseth, while his stomach half rejecteth, the rank bacon—no coalheaver bolteth him in reeking sausages—he hath a fair sepulchre in the grateful stomach of the judicious epicure—and for such a tomb might be content to die.

He is the best of sapors. Pine-apple is great. She is indeed almost too transcendent—a delight, if not sinful, yet so like to sinning, that really a tender-conscienced person would do well to pause—too ravishing for mortal taste, she woundeth and excoriateth the lips that approach her—like lovers' kisses, she biteth—she is a pleasure bordering on pain from the fierceness and insanity of her relish—but she stoppeth at the palate—she meddleth not with the appetite—and the coarsest hunger might barter her consistently for a mutton-chop.

Pig—let me speak his praise—is no less provocative

of the appetite than he is satisfactory to the criticalness of the censorious palate. The strong man may batten on him, and the weakling refuseth not his mild juices.

Unlike to mankind's mixed characters, a bundle of virtues and vices, inexplicably intertwisted, and not to be unravelled without hazard, he is—good throughout. No part of him is better or worse than another. He helpeth, as far as his little means extend, all around. He is the least envious of banquets. He is all neighbours' fare.

I am one of those who freely and ungrudgingly impart a share of the good things of this life which fall to their lot (few as mine are in this kind) to a friend. I protest I take as great an interest in my friend's pleasures, his relishes, and proper satisfactions, as in mine own. "Presents," I often say, "endear Absents." Hares, pheasants, partridges, snipes, barn-door chickens (those "tame villatic fowl"), capons, plovers, brawn, barrels of oysters, I dispense as freely as I receive them. I love to taste them, as it were, upon the tongue of my friend. But a stop must be put somewhere. One would not, like Lear, "give everything." I make my stand upon pig. Methinks it is an ingratitude to the Giver of all good flavours to extra-domiciliate, or send out of the house slightingly (under pretext of friendship, or I know not what) a blessing so particularly adapted, predestined, I may say, to my individual palate.—It argues an insensibility.

I remember a touch of conscience in this kind at school. My good old aunt, who never parted from me at the end of a holiday without stuffing a sweetmeat, or some nice thing, into my pocket, had dismissed me one evening with a smoking plum-cake, fresh from the oven. In my way to school (it was over London Bridge) a grey-headed old beggar saluted me (I have no doubt, at this time of day, that he was a counterfeit). I had no pence to console him with, and in the vanity of self-denial, and the very coxcombry of charity, school-boy like, I made him a present of — the whole cake! I walked on a little, buoyed up, as one is on such occasions, with a sweet soothing of self-satisfaction; but, before I had got to the end of the bridge, my better feelings returned, and I burst into tears, thinking how ungrateful I had been to my good aunt, to go and give her good gift away to a stranger that I had never seen before, and who might be a bad man for aught I knew; and then I thought of the pleasure my aunt would be taking in thinking that I—I myself, and not another—would eat her nice cake—and what should I say to her the next time I saw her—how naughty I was to part with her pretty present!—and the odour of that spicy cake came back upon my recollection, and the pleasure and the curiosity I had taken in seeing her make it, and her joy when she sent it to the oven, and how disappointed she would feel that I had never had a bit of it in my mouth at last—and I blamed my impertinent spirit of alms-giving, and out-of-place hypocrisy of goodness; and above all I wished never to see the face again of that insidious, good-for-nothing, old grey impostor.

Our ancestors were nice in their method of sacrificing these tender victims. We read of pigs whipt to death with something of a shock, as we hear of any other obsolete custom. The age of discipline is gone by, or it would be curious to inquire (in a philosophical light merely) what effect this process might have towards intenerating and dulcifying a substance, naturally so mild and dulcet as the flesh of young pigs. It looks like refining a violet. Yet we should be cautious, while we condemn the inhumanity, how we censure the wisdom of the practice. It might impart a gusto.—

I remember an hypothesis, argued upon by the young students, when I was at St. Omer's, and maintained with much learning and pleasantry on both sides, "Whether, supposing that the flavour of a pig who obtained his death by whipping (*per flagellationem extremam*) superadded a pleasure upon the palate of a man more intense than any possible suffering we can conceive in the animal, is man justified in using that method of putting the animal to death?" I forget the decision.

His sauce should be considered. Decidedly, a few bread crumbs, done up with his liver and brains, and a dash of mild sage. But banish, dear Mrs. Cook, I beseech you, the whole onion tribe. Barbecue your whole hogs to your palate, steep them in shalots, stuff them out with plantations of the rank and guilty garlic; you cannot poison them, or make them stronger than they are—but consider, he is a weakling—a flower.

A BACHELOR'S COMPLAINT OF THE BEHAVIOUR OF MARRIED PEOPLE.

As a single man, I have spent a good deal of my time in noting down the infirmities of Married People, to console myself for those superior pleasures, which they tell me I have lost by remaining as I am.

I cannot say that the quarrels of men and their wives ever made any great impression upon me, or had much tendency to strengthen me in those anti-social resolutions which I took up long ago upon more substantial considerations. What oftenest offends me at the houses of married persons where I visit, is an error of quite a different description;—it is that they are too loving.

Not too loving neither: that does not explain my meaning. Besides, why should that offend me? The very act of separating themselves from the rest of the world, to have the fuller enjoyment of each other's society, implies that they prefer one another to all the world.

But what I complain of is, that they carry this preference so undisguisedly, they perk it up in the faces of us single people so shamelessly, you cannot be in their company a moment without being made to feel, by some indirect hint or open avowal, that *you* are not the object of this preference. Now there are some things which give no offence, while implied or taken for granted merely; but expressed, there is much offence in them. If a man were to accost the first homely-featured or plain-dressed young woman of his acquaintance, and tell her bluntly, that she was not handsome or rich enough for him, and he could not marry her, he would deserve to be kicked for his ill-manners ; yet no less is implied in the fact, that having access and opportunity of putting the question to her, he has never yet thought fit to do it. The young woman understands this as clearly as if it were put into words; but no reasonable young woman would think of making this the ground of a quarrel. Just as little right have a married couple to tell me by speeches, and looks that are scarce less plain than speeches, that I am not the happy man,—the lady's choice. It is enough that I know I am not: I do not want this perpetual reminding.

The display of superior knowledge or riches may be made sufficiently mortifying, but these admit of a palliative. The knowledge which is brought out to insult me, may accidentally improve me; and in the rich man's houses and pictures,—his parks and gardens, I have a temporary usufruct at least. But the display of married happiness has none of these palliatives: it is throughout pure, unrecompensed, unqualified insult.

Marriage by its best title is a monopoly, and not of the least invidious sort. It is the cunning of most possessors of any exclusive privilege to keep their advantage as much out of sight as possible, that their less favoured neighbours, seeing little of the benefit, may the less be disposed to question the right. But these married monopolists thrust the most obnoxious part of their patent into our faces.

Nothing is to me more distasteful than that entire complacency and satisfaction which beam in the countenances of a new-married couple,—in that of the lady particularly: it tells you, that her lot is disposed of in this world: that *you* can have no hopes of her. It is true, I have none; nor wishes either, perhaps: but this is one of those truths which ought, as I said before, to be taken for granted, not expressed.

The excessive airs which those people give themselves, founded on the ignorance of us unmarried people, would be more offensive if they were less irrational. We will allow them to understand the mysteries belonging to their own craft better than we, who have not had the happiness to be made free of the company: but their arrogance is not content within these limits. If a single person presume to offer his opinion in their presence, though upon the most indifferent subject, he is immediately silenced as an incompetent person. Nay, a young married lady of my acquaintance, who, the best of the jest was, had not changed her condition above a fortnight before, in a question on which I had the misfortune to differ from her, respecting the properest mode of breeding oysters for the London market, had the assurance to ask with a sneer, how such an old Bachelor as I could pretend to know anything about such matters!

But what I have spoken of hitherto is nothing to the airs which these creatures give themselves when they come, as they generally do, to have children. When I consider how little of a rarity children are,—that every street and blind alley swarms with them,—that the poorest people commonly have them in most abundance,—that there are few marriages that are not blest with at least one of these bargains,—how often they turn out ill, and defeat the fond hopes of their parents, taking to vicious courses, which end in poverty, disgrace, the gallows, etc.—I cannot for my life tell what cause for pride there can possibly be in having them. If they were young phœnixes, indeed, that were born but one in a year, there might be a pretext. But when they are so common——

I do not advert to the insolent merit which they assume with their husbands on these occasions. Let *them* look to that. But why *we*, who are not their natural-born subjects, should be expected to bring our spices, myrrh, and incense,—our tribute and homage of admiration,—I do not see.

"Like as the arrows in the hand of the giant, even so are the young children;" so says the excellent office in our Prayer-book appointed for the churching of women. "Happy is the man that hath his quiver full of them." So say I; but then don't let him discharge his quiver upon us that are weaponless;—let them be arrows, but not to gall and stick us. I have generally observed that these arrows are double-headed: they have two forks, to be sure to hit with one or the other. As for instance, where you come into a house which is full of children, if you happen to take no notice of them (you are thinking of something else, perhaps, and turn a deaf ear to their innocent caresses), you are set down as untractable, morose, a hater of children. On the other hand, if you find them more than usually engaging,—if you are taken with their pretty manners, and set about in earnest to romp and play with them,—some pretext or other is sure to be found for sending them out of the room; they are too noisy or boisterous, or Mr. —— does not like children. With one or other of these forks the arrow is sure to hit you.

I could forgive their jealousy, and dispense with toying with their brats, if it gives them any pain; but I think it unreasonable to be called upon to *love* them, where I see no occasion,—to love a whole family, perhaps eight, nine, or ten, indiscriminately,—to love all the pretty dears, because children are so engaging!

I know there is a proverb, "Love me, love my dog:" that is not always so very practicable, particularly if the dog be set upon you to tease you or snap at you in sport. But a dog, or a lesser thing—any inanimate substance, as a keepsake, a watch or a ring, a tree, or the place where we last parted when my friend went away upon a long absence, I can make shift to love, because I love him, and anything that reminds me of him; provided it be in its nature indifferent, and apt to receive whatever hue fancy can give it. But children have a real character, and an essential being of themselves: they are amiable or unamiable *per se;* I must love or hate them as I see cause for either in their qualities. A child's nature is too serious a thing to admit of its being regarded as a mere appendage to another being, and to be loved or hated accordingly; they stand with me upon their own stock, as much as men and women do. Oh! but you will say, sure it is an attractive age,—there is something in the tender years of infancy that of itself charms us? That is the very reason why I am more nice about them. I know that a sweet child is the sweetest thing in nature, not even excepting the delicate creatures which bear them; but the prettier the kind of a thing is, the more desirable it is that it should be pretty of its kind. One daisy differs not much from another in glory; but a violet should look and smell the daintiest.—I was always rather squeamish in my women and children.

But this is not the worst: one must be admitted into their familiarity at least, before they can complain of inattention. It implies visits, and some kind of intercourse. But if the husband be a man with whom you have lived on a friendly footing before marriage—if you did not come in on the wife's side—if you did not sneak into the house in her train, but were an old friend in fast habits of intimacy before their courtship was so much as thought on, look about you—your tenure is precarious before a twelvemonth shall roll over your head, you shall find your old friend gradually grow cool and altered towards you, and at last seek opportunities of breaking with you. I have scarce a married friend of my acquaintance, upon whose firm faith I can rely, whose friendship did not commence *after the period of his marriage.* With some limitations, they can endure that; but that the good man should have dared to enter into a solemn league of friendship in which they were not consulted, though it happened before they knew him,— before they that are now man and wife ever met,—this is intolerable to them. Every long friendship, every old authentic intimacy, must be brought into their office to be new stamped with their currency, as a sovereign prince calls in the good old money that was coined in some reign before he was born or thought of, to be new marked and minted with the stamp of his authority, before he will let it pass current in the world. You may guess what luck generally befalls such a rusty piece of metal as I am in these *new mintings*.

Innumerable are the ways which they take to insult and worm you out of their husband's confidence. Laughing at all you say with a kind of wonder, as if you were a queer kind of fellow that said good things, *but an oddity*, is one of the ways;—they have a particular kind of stare for the purpose;—till at last the husband, who used to defer to your judgment, and would pass over some excrescences of understanding and manner for the sake of a general vein of observation (not quite vulgar) which he perceived in you, begins to suspect whether you are not altogether a humorist,—a fellow well enough to have consorted with in his bachelor days, but not quite so proper to be introduced to ladies. This may be called the staring way; and is that which has oftenest been put in practice against me.

Then there is the exaggerating way, or the way of irony; that is, where they find you an object of especial regard with their husband, who is not so easily to be shaken from the lasting attachment founded on esteem which he has conceived towards you, by never qualified exaggerations to cry up all that you say or do, till the good man, who understands well enough that it is all done in compliment to him, grows weary of the debt of gratitude which is due to so much candour, and by relaxing a little on his part, and taking down a peg or two in his enthusiasm, sinks at length to the kindly level of moderate esteem—that "decent affection and complacent kindness" towards you, where she herself can join in sympathy with him without much stretch and violence to her sincerity.

Another way (for the ways they have to accomplish so desirable a purpose are infinite) is, with a kind of innocent simplicity, continually to mistake what it was which first made their husband fond of you. If an esteem for something excellent in your moral character was that which riveted the chain which she is to break, upon any imaginary discovery of a want of poignancy in your conversation, she will cry, "I thought, my dear, you described your friend, Mr. ———, as a great wit?" If, on the other hand, it was for some supposed charm in your conversation that he first grew to like you, and was content for this to overlook some trifling irregularities in your moral deportment, upon the first notice of any of these she as readily exclaims, "This, my dear, is your good Mr. ———!" One good lady whom I took the liberty of expostulating with for not showing me quite so much respect as I thought due to her husband's old friend, had the candour to confess to me that she had often heard Mr. ——— speak of me before marriage, and that she had conceived a great desire to be acquainted with me, but that the sight of me had very much disappointed her expectations; for, from her husband's representations of me, she had formed a notion that she was to see a fine, tall, officer-like looking man (I use her very words), the very reverse of which proved to be the truth. This was candid; and I had the civility not to ask her in return, how she came to pitch upon a standard of personal accomplishments for her husband's friends which differed so much from his own; for my friend's dimensions as near as possible approximate to mine; he standing five feet five in his shoes, in which I have the advantage of him by about half an inch; and he no more than myself exhibiting any indications of a martial character in his air or countenance.

These are some of the mortifications which I have encountered in the absurd attempt to visit at their houses. To enumerate them all would be a vain endeavour; I shall therefore just glance at the very common impropriety of which married ladies are guilty,— of treating us as if we were their husbands, and *vice versâ*. I mean, when they use us with familiarity, and their husbands with ceremony. *Testacea*, for instance, kept me the other night two or three hours beyond my usual time of supping, while she was fretting because Mr. ——— did not come home, till the oysters were all spoiled, rather than she would be guilty of the impoliteness of touching one in his absence. This was reversing the point of good manners: for ceremony is an invention to take off the uneasy feeling which we derive from knowing ourselves to be less the object of love and esteem with a fellow-creature than some other person is. It endeavours to make up, by superior attentions in little points, for that invidious preference which it is forced to deny in the greater. Had *Testacea* kept the oysters back for me, and withstood her husband's importunities to go to supper, she would have acted according to the strict rules of propriety. I know no ceremony that ladies are bound to observe to their husbands, beyond the point of a modest behaviour and decorum: therefore I must protest against the vicarious gluttony of *Cerasia*, who at her own table sent away a dish of Morellas, which I was applying to with great good-will, to her husband at the other end of the table, and recommended a plate of less extraordinary gooseberries to my unwedded palate in their stead. Neither can I excuse the wanton affront of ———

But I am weary of stringing up all my married acquaintance by Roman denominations. Let them amend and change their manners, or I promise to record the full-length English of their names, to the terror of all such desperate offenders in future.

ON SOME OF THE OLD ACTORS.

The casual sight of an old Play Bill, which I picked up the other day—I know not by what chance it was preserved so long—tempts me to call to mind a few of the Players, who make the principal figure in it. It presents the cast of parts in the Twelfth-Night, at the old Drury-lane Theatre two-and-thirty years ago. There is something very touching in these old remembrances. They make us think how we *once* used to read a Play Bill—not, as now peradventure, singling out a favourite performer, and casting a negligent eye over the rest; but spelling out every name, down to the very mutes and servants of the scene; when it was a matter of no small moment to us whether Whitfield, or Packer, took the part of Fabian; when Benson, and Burton, and Phillimore—names of small account—had an importance, beyond what we can be content to attribute now to the time's best actors.—" Orsino, by Mr. Barrymore."—What a full Shaksperian sound it carries! how fresh to memory arise the image and the manner of the gentle actor! Those who have only seen Mrs. Jordan within the last ten or fifteen years, can have no adequate notion of her performance of such parts as Ophelia; Helena, in All's Well that Ends Well; and Viola, in this play. Her voice had latterly acquired a coarseness, which suited well enough with her Nells and Hoydens, but in those days it sank, with her steady, melting eye, into the heart. Her joyous parts—in which her memory now chiefly lives—in her youth were outdone by her plaintive ones. There is no giving an account how she delivered the disguised story of her love for Orsino. It was no set speech, that she had foreseen, so as to weave it into an harmonious period, line necessarily following line, to make up the music—yet I have heard it so spoken, or rather *read*, not without its grace and beauty—but, when she had declared her sister's history to be a "blank," and that she "never told her love," there was a pause, as if the story had ended—and then the image of the "worm in the bud" came up as a new suggestion—and the heightened image of "Patience" still followed after that as by some growing (and not mechanical) process, thought springing up after thought, I would almost say, as they were watered by her tears. So in those fine lines—

> Write loyal cantons of contemned love—
> Halloo your name to the reverberate hills—

there was no preparation made in the foregoing image for that which was to follow. She used no rhetoric in her passion; or it was nature's own rhetoric, most legitimate then, when it seemed altogether without rule or law.

Mrs. Powel (now Mrs. Renard), then in the pride of her beauty, made an admirable Olivia. She was particularly excellent in her unbending scenes in conversation with the Clown. I have seen some Olivias—and those very sensible actresses too—who in these interlocutions have seemed to set their wits at the jester, and to vie conceits with him in downright emulation. But she used him for her sport, like what he was, to trifle a leisure sentence or two with, and then to be dismissed, and she to be the Great Lady still. She touched the imperious fantastic humour of the character with nicety. Her fine spacious person filled the scene.

The part of Malvolio has, in my judgment, been so often misunderstood, and the *general merits* of the actor, who then played it, so unduly appreciated, that I shall hope for pardon, if I am a little prolix upon these points.

Of all the actors who flourished in my time—a melancholy phrase if taken aright, reader—Bensley had most of the swell of soul, was greatest in the delivery of heroic conceptions, the emotions consequent upon the presentment of a great idea to the fancy. He had the true poetical enthusiasm—the rarest faculty among players.

None that I remember possessed even a portion of that fine madness which he threw out in Hotspur's famous rant about glory, or the transports of the Venetian incendiary at the vision of the fired city. His voice had the dissonance, and at times the inspiriting effect, of the trumpet. His gait was uncouth and stiff, but no way embarrassed by affectation; and the thorough-bred gentleman was uppermost in every movement. He seized the moment of passion with greatest truth; like a faithful clock, never striking before the time; never anticipating or leading you to anticipate. He was totally destitute of trick and artifice. He seemed come upon the stage to do the poet's message simply, and he did it with as genuine fidelity as the nuncios in Homer deliver the errands of the gods. He let the passion or the sentiment do its own work without prop or bolstering. He would have scorned to mountebank it; and betrayed none of that *cleverness* which is the bane of serious acting. For this reason, his Iago was the only endurable one which I remember to have seen. No spectator, from his action, could divine more of his artifice than Othello was supposed to do. His confessions in soliloquy alone put you in possession of the mystery. There were no by-intimations to make the audience fancy their own discernment so much greater than that of the Moor—who commonly stands like a great helpless mark, set up for mine Ancient, and a quantity of barren spectators, to shoot their bolts at. The Iago of Bensley did not go to work so grossly. There was a triumphant tone about the character, natural to a general consciousness of power; but none of that petty vanity which chuckles and cannot contain itself upon any little successful stroke of its knavery—as is common with your small villains, and green probationers in mischief. It did not clap or crow before its time. It was not a man setting his wits at a child, and winking all the while at other children, who are mightily pleased at being let into the secret; but a consummate villain entrapping a noble nature into toils against which no discernment was available, where the manner was as fathomless as the purpose seemed dark, and without motive. The part of Malvolio, in the Twelfth Night, was performed by Bensley with a richness and a dignity, of which (to judge from some recent castings of that character) the very tradition must be worn out from the stage. No manager in those days would have dreamed of giving it to Mr. Baddely, or Mr. Parsons; when Bensley was occasionally absent from the theatre, John Kemble thought it no derogation to succeed to the part. Malvolio is not essentially ludicrous. He becomes comic but by accident. He is cold, austere, repelling; but dignified, consistent, and, for what appears, rather of an over-stretched morality. Maria describes him as a sort of Puritan; and he might have worn his gold chain with honour in one of our old roundhead families, in the service of a Lambert, or a Lady Fairfax. But his morality and his manners are misplaced in Illyria. He is opposed to the proper *levities* of the piece, and falls in the unequal contest. Still his pride, or his gravity (call it which you will), is inherent, and native to the man, not mock or affected, which latter only are the fit objects to excite laughter. His quality is at the best unlovely, but neither buffoon nor contemptible. His bearing is lofty, a little above his station, but probably not much above his deserts. We see no reason why he should not have been brave, honourable, accomplished. His careless committal of the ring to the ground (which he was commissioned to restore to Cesario), bespeaks a generosity of birth and feeling. His dialect on all occasions is that of a gentleman and a man of education. We must not confound him with the eternal old, low steward of comedy. He is master of the household to a great princess; a dignity probably conferred upon him for other respects than age or length of service. Olivia, at the first indication of his supposed madness, declares that she "would not have him miscarry for half of her dowry." Does this look as if the character was meant to appear little or insignificant? Once, indeed, she accuses him to his face of what?—of being "sick of self-love,"—but with a gentleness and considerateness, which could not have been, if she had not thought that this particular infirmity shaded some virtues. His rebuke to the knight and his sottish revellers, is sensible and spirited; and when we take into consideration the unprotected condition of his mistress, and the strict regard with which her state of real or dissembled mourning would draw the eyes of the world upon her house-affairs, Malvolio might feel the honour of the family in some sort in his keeping; as it appears not that Olivia had any more brothers, or kinsmen, to look to it—for Sir Toby had dropped all such nice respects at the buttery-hatch. That Malvolio was meant to be represented as possessing estimable qualities, the expression of the Duke, in his anxiety to have him reconciled, almost infers: "Pursue him, and entreat him to a peace." Even in his abused state of chains and darkness, a sort of greatness seems never to desert him. He argues highly and well with the supposed Sir Topas, and philosophizes gallantly upon his straw.[1] There must have been some shadow of worth about the man; he must have been something more than a mere vapour—a thing of straw, or Jack in office—before Fabian and Maria could have ventured sending him upon a courting-errand to Olivia. There was some consonancy (as he would say) in the undertaking, or the jest would have been too bold even for that house of misrule.

Bensley, accordingly, threw over the part an air of Spanish loftiness. He looked, spake, and moved like an old Castilian. He was starch, spruce, opinionated, but his superstructure of pride seemed bottomed upon a sense of worth. There was something in it beyond the cox-

---

[1] *Clown.* What is the opinion of Pythagoras concerning wild fowl?
Mal. That the soul of our grandam might haply inhabit a bird.
Clown. What thinkest thou of his opinion?
Mal. I think nobly of the soul, and no way approve of his opinion.

comb. It was big and swelling, but you could not be sure that it was hollow. You might wish to see it taken down, but you felt that it was upon an elevation. He was magnificent from the outset; but when the decent sobrieties of the character began to give way, and the poison of self-love, in his conceit of the Countess's affection, gradually to work, you would have thought that the hero of La Mancha in person stood before you. How he went smiling to himself! with what ineffable carelessness would he twirl his gold chain! what a dream it was! you were infected with the illusion, and did not wish that it should be removed! you had no room for laughter! if an unseasonable reflection of morality obtruded itself, it was a deep sense of the pitiable infirmity of man's nature, that can lay him open to such frenzies—but, in truth, you rather admired than pitied the lunacy while it lasted —you felt that an hour of such mistake was worth an age with the eyes open. Who would not wish to live but for a day in the conceit of such a lady's love as Olivia? Why, the Duke would have given his principality but for a quarter of a minute, sleeping or waking, to have been so deluded. The man seemed to tread upon air, to taste manna, to walk with his head in the clouds, to mate Hyperion. O! shake not the castles of his pride—endure yet for a season, bright moments of confidence—" stand still, ye watches of the element," that Malvolio may be still in fancy fair Olivia's lord!—but fate and retribution say no—I hear the mischievous titter of Maria—the witty taunts of Sir Toby—the still more insupportable triumph of the foolish knight—the counterfeit Sir Topas is unmasked and "thus the whirligig of time," as the true clown hath it, " brings in his revenges." I confess that I never saw the catastrophe of this character, while Bensley played it, without a kind of tragic interest. There was good foolery too. Few now remember Dodd. What an Aguecheek the stage lost in him! Lovegrove, who came nearest to the old actors, revived the character some few seasons ago, and made it sufficiently grotesque; but Dodd was *it*, as it came out of nature's hands. It might be said to remain *in puris naturalibus*. In expressing slowness of apprehension, this actor surpassed all others. You could see the first dawn of an idea stealing slowly over his countenance, climbing up by little and little, with a painful process, till it cleared up at last to the fulness of a twilight conception—its highest meridian. He seemed to keep back his intellect, as some have had the power to retard their pulsation. The balloon takes less time in filling than it took to cover the expansion of his broad moony face over all its quarters with expression. A glimmer of understanding would appear in a corner of his eye, and for lack of fuel go out again. A part of his forehead would catch a little intelligence, and be a long time in communicating it to the remainder.

I am ill at dates, but I think it is now better than five-and-twenty years ago, that walking in the gardens of Gray's Inn—they were then far finer than they are now—the accursed Verulam Buildings had not encroached upon all the east side of them, cutting out delicate green crankles, and shouldering away one or two of the stately alcoves of the terrace—the survivor stands gaping and relationless as if it remembered its brother—they are still the best gardens of any of the Inns of Court, my beloved Temple not forgotten—have the gravest character; their aspect being altogether reverend and law-breathing—Bacon has left the impress of his foot upon their gravel walks——taking my afternoon solace on a summer day upon the aforesaid terrace, a comely sad personage came towards me, whom, from his grave air and deportment, I judged to be one of the old Benchers of the Inn. He had a serious, thoughtful forehead, and seemed to be in meditations of mortality. As I have an instinctive awe of old Benchers, I was passing him with that sort of sub-indicative token of respect which one is apt to demonstrate towards a venerable stranger, and which rather denotes an inclination to greet him, than any positive

motion of the body to that effect — a species of humility
and will-worship which I observe, nine times out of ten,
rather puzzles than pleases the person it is offered to—
when the face turning full upon me strangely identified
itself with that of Dodd. Upon close inspection I was not
mistaken. But could this sad thoughtful countenance be
the same vacant face of folly which I had hailed so often
under circumstances of gaiety; which I had never seen
without a smile, or recognised but as the usher of mirth;
that looked out so formally flat in Foppington, so frothily
pert in Tattle, so impotently busy in Backbite; so blankly
divested of all meaning, or resolutely expressive of none,
in Acres, in Fribble, and a thousand agreeable impertinences? Was this the face—full of thought and carefulness—that had so often divested itself at will of every
trace of either to give me diversion, to clear my cloudy
face for two or three hours at least of its furrows! Was
this the face—manly, sober, intelligent—which I had so
often despised, made mocks at, made merry with! The
remembrance of the freedoms which I had taken with it
came upon me with a reproach of insult. I could have
asked it pardon. I thought it looked upon me with a
sense of injury. There is something strange as well as
sad in seeing actors—your pleasant fellows particularly—
subjected to and suffering the common lot;—their fortunes, their casualties, their deaths, seem to belong to the
scene, their actions to be amenable to poetic justice only.
We can hardly connect them with more awful responsi-
bilities. The death of this fine actor took place shortly
after this meeting. He had quitted the stage some
months; and, as I learned afterwards, had been in the
habit of resorting daily to these gardens, almost to the
day of his decease. In these serious walks, probably, he
was divesting himself of many scenic and some real
vanities—weaning himself from the frivolities of the lesser
and the greater theatre—doing gentle penance for a life
of no very reprehensible fooleries—taking off by degrees
the buffoon mask which he might feel he had worn too

long—and rehearsing for a more solemn cast of part. Dying, he "put on the weeds of Dominic."[1]

If few can remember Dodd, many yet living will not easily forget the pleasant creature, who in those days enacted the part of the Clown to Dodd's Sir Andrew.— Richard, or rather Dicky Suett—for so in his life-time he delighted to be called, and time hath ratified the appellation—lieth buried on the north side of the cemetery of Holy Paul, to whose service his nonage and tender years were dedicated. There are who do yet remember him at that period—his pipe clear and harmonious. He would often speak of his chorister days, when he was "cherub Dicky."

What clipped his wings, or made it expedient that he should exchange the holy for the profane state; whether he had lost his good voice (his best recommendation to that office), like Sir John, "with hallooing and singing of anthems;" or whether he was adjudged to lack something, even in those early years, of the gravity indispensable to an occupation which professeth to "commerce with the skies,"—I could never rightly learn; but we find him, after the probation of a twelvemonth or so, reverting to a secular condition and become one of us.

I think he was not altogether of that timber out of which cathedral seats and sounding-boards are hewed. But if a glad heart—kind, and therefore glad—be any part of sanctity, then might the robe of Motley, with which he invested himself with so much humility after his deprivation, and which he wore so long with so much

---

[1] Dodd was a man of reading, and left at his death a choice collection of old English literature. I should judge him to have been a man of wit. I know one instance of an impromptu which no length of study could have bettered. My merry friend, Jem White, had seen him one evening in Aguecheek, and recognising Dodd the next day in Fleet Street, was irresistibly impelled to take off his hat and salute him as the identical Knight of the preceding evening with a "Save you, *Sir Andrew*." Dodd, not at all disconcerted at this unusual address from a stranger, with a courteous half-rebuking wave of the hand, put him off with an "Away, *Fool*."

blameless satisfaction to himself and to the public, be accepted for a surplice—his white stole, and *albe*.

The first fruits of his secularization was an engagement upon the boards of Old Drury, at which theatre he commenced, as I have been told, with adopting the manner of Parsons in old men's characters. At the period in which most of us knew him, he was no more an imitator than he was in any true sense himself imitable.

He was the Robin Goodfellow of the stage. He came in to trouble all things with a welcome perplexity, himself no whit troubled for the matter. He was known, like Puck, by his note—*Ha! Ha! Ha!*—sometimes deepening to *Ho! Ho! Ho!* with an irresistible accession, derived, perhaps, remotely from his ecclesiastical education, foreign to his prototype of—*O La!* Thousands of hearts yet respond to the chuckling *O La!* of Dicky Suett, brought back to their remembrance by the faithful transcript of his friend Mathews's mimicry. The "force of nature could no further go." He drolled upon the stock of these two syllables richer than the cuckoo.

Care, that troubles all the world, was forgotten in his composition. Had he had but two grains (nay, half a grain) of it, he could never have supported himself upon those two spider's strings, which served him (in the latter part of his unmixed existence) as legs. A doubt or a scruple must have made him totter, a sigh have puffed him down; the weight of a frown had staggered him, a wrinkle made him lose his balance. But on he went, scrambling upon those airy stilts of his, with Robin Goodfellow, "thorough brake, thorough briar," reckless of a scratched face or a torn doublet.

Shakspeare foresaw him, when he framed his fools and jesters. They have all the true Suett stamp, a loose and shambling gait, a slippery tongue, this last the ready midwife to a without-pain-delivered jest; in words, light as air, venting truths deep as the centre; with idlest rhymes tagging conceit when busiest, singing with Lear in the tempest, or Sir Toby at the buttery-hatch.

Jack Bannister and he had the fortune to be more of personal favourites with the town than any actors before or after. The difference, I take it, was this :—Jack was more *beloved* for his sweet, good-natured, moral pretensions. Dicky was more *liked* for his sweet, good-natured, no pretensions at all. Your whole conscience stirred with Bannister's performance of Walter in the Children in the Wood—but Dicky seemed like a thing, as Shakspeare says of Love, too young to know what conscience is. He put us into Vesta's days. Evil fled before him—not as from Jack, as from an antagonist,—but because it could not touch him, any more than a cannon-ball a fly. He was delivered from the burthen of that death ; and, when Death came himself, not in metaphor, to fetch Dicky, it is recorded of him by Robert Palmer, who kindly watched his exit, that he received the last stroke, neither varying his accustomed tranquillity, nor tune, with the simple exclamation, worthy to have been recorded in his epitaph— *O La ! O La ! Bobby !*

The elder Palmer (of stage-trading celebrity) commonly played Sir Toby in those days ; but there is a solidity of wit in the jests of that half-Falstaff which he did not quite fill out. He was as much too showy as Moody (who sometimes took the part) was dry and sottish. In sock or buskin there was an air of swaggering gentility about Jack Palmer. He was a *gentleman* with a slight infusion of *the footman*. His brother Bob (of recenter memory), who was his shadow in everything while he lived, and dwindled into less than a shadow afterwards— was a *gentleman* with a little stronger infusion of the *latter ingredient ;* that was all. It is amazing how a little of the more or less makes a difference in these things. When you saw Bobby in the "Duke's Servant,"[1] you said, "What a pity such a pretty fellow was only a servant !" When you saw Jack figuring in Captain Absolute, you thought you could trace his promotion to some lady of quality who fancied the handsome fellow in his topknot,

[1] High Life Below Stairs.

and had bought him a commission. Therefore Jack in Dick Amlet was insuperable.

Jack had two voices, both plausible, hypocritical, and insinuating; but his secondary or supplemental voice still more decisively histrionic than his common one. It was reserved for the spectator; and the *dramatis personæ* were supposed to know nothing at all about it. The *lies* of Young Wilding, and the *sentiments* in Joseph Surface, were thus marked out in a sort of italics to the audience. This secret correspondence with the company before the curtain (which is the bane and death of tragedy) has an extremely happy effect in some kinds of comedy, in the more highly artificial comedy of Congreve or of Sheridan especially, where the absolute sense of reality (so indispensable to scenes of interest) is not required, or would rather interfere to diminish your pleasure. The fact is, you do not believe in such characters as Surface—the villain of artificial comedy—even while you read or see them. If you did, they would shock and not divert you. When Ben, in Love for Love, returns from sea, the following exquisite dialogue occurs at his first meeting with his father:—

Sir Sampson. Thou hast been many a weary league, Ben, since I saw thee.

Ben. Ey, ey, been. Been far enough, an that be all.—Well, father, and how do all at home? how does brother Dick and brother Val?

Sir Sampson. Dick! body o' me, Dick has been dead these two years. I writ you word when you were at Leghorn.

Ben. Mess, that's true; Marry, I had forgot. Dick's dead, as you say—well, and how?—I have a many questions to ask you.

Here is an instance of insensibility which in real life would be revolting, or rather in real life could not have co-existed with the warm-hearted temperament of the character. But when you read it in the spirit with which such playful selections and specious combinations rather than strict *metaphrases* of nature should be taken, or when you saw Bannister play it, it neither did, nor does, wound the moral sense at all. For what is Ben—the pleasant sailor which Bannister gives us—but a piece of satire—a creation of Congreve's fancy—a dreamy combination of all the accidents of a sailor's character—his contempt of money—his credulity to women—with that necessary estrangement from home which it is just within the verge of credibility to suppose *might* produce such an hallucination as is here described. We never think the worse of Ben for it, or feel it as a stain upon his character. But when an actor comes, and instead of the delightful phantom—the creature dear to half-belief—which Bannister exhibited—displays before our eyes a downright concretion of a Wapping sailor—a jolly warm-hearted Jack Tar—and nothing else—when instead of investing it with a delicious confusedness of the head, and a veering undirected goodness of purpose—he gives to it a downright daylight understanding, and a full consciousness of its actions; thrusting forward the sensibilities of the character with a pretence as if it stood upon nothing else, and was to be judged by them alone—we feel the discord of the thing; the scene is disturbed; a real man has got in among the *dramatis personæ*, and puts them out. We want the sailor turned out. We feel that his true place is not behind the curtain, but in the first or second gallery.

ON THE ARTIFICIAL COMEDY OF THE LAST CENTURY.

THE artificial Comedy, or Comedy of manners, is quite extinct on our stage. Congreve and Farquhar show their heads once in seven years only, to be exploded and put down instantly. The times cannot bear them. Is it for a few wild speeches, an occasional license of dialogue? I think not altogether. The business of their dramatic characters will not stand the moral test. We screw everything up to that. Idle gallantry in a fiction, a dream, the passing pageant of an evening, startles us in the same way as the alarming indications of profligacy in a son or ward in real life should startle a parent or guardian. We have no such middle emotions as dramatic interests left. We see a stage libertine playing his loose pranks of two hours' duration, and of no after consequence, with the severe eyes which inspect real vices with their bearings upon two worlds. We are spectators to a plot or intrigue (not reducible in life to the point of strict morality), and take it all for truth. We substitute a real for a dramatic person, and judge him accordingly. We try him in our courts, from which there is no appeal to the *dramatis personæ*, his peers. We have been spoiled with—not sentimental comedy—but a tyrant far more pernicious to our pleasures which has succeeded to it, the exclusive and all-devouring drama of common life; where the moral point is everything; where, instead of the fictitious half-believed personages of the stage (the phantoms of old comedy), we recognise ourselves, our brothers, aunts, kinsfolk, allies, patrons, enemies,—the same as in life,—with an interest in what is going on so hearty and substantial, that we cannot afford our moral judgment, in its deepest and most vital results, to compromise or slumber for a moment. What is *there* transacting, by no modification is made to affect us in any other manner than the same events or characters would do in our relationships of life. We carry our fire-side concerns to the theatre with us. We do not go thither like our ancestors, to escape from the pressure of reality, so much as to confirm our experience of it; to make assurance double, and take a bond of fate. We must live our toilsome lives twice over, as it was the mournful privilege of Ulysses to descend twice to the shades. All that neutral ground of character, which stood between vice and virtue; or which in fact was indifferent to neither, where neither properly was called in question; that happy breathing-place from the burthen of a perpetual moral questioning—the sanctuary and quiet Alsatia of hunted casuistry—is broken up and disfranchised, as injurious to the interests of society. The privileges of the place are taken away by law. We dare not dally with images, or names, of wrong. We bark like foolish dogs at shadows. We dread infection from the scenic representation of disorder, and fear a painted pustule. In our anxiety that our morality should not take cold, we wrap it up in a great blanket surtout of precaution against the breeze and sunshine.

I confess for myself that (with no great delinquencies to answer for) I am glad for a season to take an airing beyond the diocese of the strict conscience,—not to live always in the precincts of the law courts,—but now and then, for a dream-while or so, to imagine a world with no meddling restrictions—to get into recesses, whither the hunter cannot follow me—

———— Secret shades
Of woody Ida's inmost grove,
While yet there was no fear of Jove.

I come back to my cage and my restraint the fresher and more healthy for it. I wear my shackles more contentedly for having respired the breath of an imaginary freedom. I do not know how it is with others, but I feel the better always for the perusal of one of Congreve's—nay, why should I not add even of Wycherley's—comedies. I am the gayer at least for it ; and I could never connect those sports of a witty fancy in any shape with any result to be drawn from them to imitation in real life. They are a world of themselves almost as much as fairy land. Take one of their characters, male or female (with few exceptions they are alike), and place it in a modern play, and my virtuous indignation shall rise against the profligate wretch as warmly as the Catos of the pit could desire ; because in a modern play I am to judge of the right and the wrong. The standard of *police* is the measure of *political justice*. The atmosphere will blight it ; it cannot live here. It has got into a moral world, where it has no business, from which it must needs fall headlong; as dizzy, and incapable of making a stand, as a Swedenborgian bad spirit that has wandered unawares into the sphere of one of his Good Men, or Angels. But in its own world do we feel the creature is so very bad?—The Fainalls and the Mirabels, the Dorimants and the Lady Touchwoods, in their own sphere, do not offend my moral sense; in fact, they do not appeal to it at all. They seem engaged in their proper element. They break through no laws or conscientious restraints. They know of none. They have got out of Christendom into the land—what shall I call it?—of cuckoldry—the Utopia of gallantry, where pleasure is duty, and the manners perfect freedom. It is altogether a speculative scene of things, which has no reference whatever to the world that is. No good person can be justly offended as a spectator, because no good person suffers on the stage. Judged morally, every character in these plays—the few exceptions only are *mistakes*—is alike essentially vain and worthless. The great art of Congreve is especially shown in this, that he has entirely excluded from his scenes—some little generosities in the part of Angelica perhaps excepted—not only anything like a faultless character, but any pretensions to goodness or good feelings whatsoever. Whether he did this designedly, or instinctively, the effect is as happy as the design (if design) was bold. I used to wonder at the strange power which his Way of the World in particular possesses of interesting you all along in the pursuits of characters, for whom you absolutely care nothing—for you neither hate nor love his personages—and I think it is owing to this very indifference for any, that you endure the whole. He has spread a privation of moral light, I will call it, rather than by the ugly name of palpable darkness, over his creations; and his shadows flit before you without distinction or preference. Had he introduced a good character, a single gush of moral feeling, a revulsion of the judgment to actual life and actual duties, the impertinent Goshen would have only lighted to the discovery of deformities, which now are none, because we think them none.

Translated into real life, the characters of his, and his friend Wycherley's dramas, are profligates and strumpets, —the business of their brief existence, the undivided pursuit of lawless gallantry. No other spring of action, or possible motive of conduct, is recognised; principles which, universally acted upon, must reduce this frame of things to a chaos. But we do them wrong in so translating them. No such effects are produced, in *their* world. When we are among them, we are amongst a chaotic people. We are not to judge them by our usages. No reverend institutions are insulted by their proceedings—for they have none among them. No peace of families is violated—for no family ties exist among them. No purity of the marriage bed is stained—for none is supposed to have a being. No deep affections are disquieted, no holy wedlock bands are snapped asunder—for affection's depth and wedded faith are not of the growth of that soil. There is neither right nor wrong,—gratitude or its opposite,—claim or duty,—paternity or sonship. Of what consequence is it to Virtue, or how is she at all concerned about it, whether Sir Simon or Dapperwit steal away Miss Martha; or who is the father of Lord Froth's or Sir Paul Pliant's children?

The whole is a passing pageant, where we should sit as unconcerned at the issues, for life or death, as at the battle of the frogs and mice. But, like Don Quixote, we take part against the puppets, and quite as impertinently. We dare not contemplate an Atlantis, a scheme, out of which our coxcombical moral sense is for a little transitory ease excluded. We have not the courage to imagine a state of things for which there is neither reward nor punishment. We cling to the painful necessities of shame and blame. We would indict our very dreams.

Amidst the mortifying circumstances attendant upon growing old, it is something to have seen the School for

Scandal in its glory. This comedy grew out of Congreve and Wycherley, but gathered some allays of the sentimental comedy which followed theirs. It is impossible that it should be now *acted*, though it continues, at long intervals, to be announced in the bills. Its hero, when Palmer played it at least, was Joseph Surface. When I remember the gay boldness, the graceful solemn plausibility, the measured step, the insinuating voice—to express it in a word—the downright *acted* villany of the part, so different from the pressure of conscious actual wickedness,—the hypocritical assumption of hypocrisy,—which made Jack so deservedly a favourite in that character, I must needs conclude the present generation of playgoers more virtuous than myself, or more dense. I freely confess that he divided the palm with me with his better brother; that, in fact, I liked him quite as well. Not but there are passages,—like that, for instance, where Joseph is made to refuse a pittance to a poor relation,—incongruities which Sheridan was forced upon by the attempt to join the artificial with the sentimental comedy, either of which must destroy the other—but over these obstructions Jack's manner floated him so lightly, that a refusal from him no more shocked you, than the easy compliance of Charles gave you in reality any pleasure; you got over the paltry question as quickly as you could, to get back into the regions of pure comedy, where no cold moral reigns. The highly artificial manner of Palmer in this character counteracted every disagreeable impression which you might have received from the contrast, supposing them real, between the two brothers. You did not believe in Joseph with the same faith with which you believed in Charles. The latter was a pleasant reality, the former a no less pleasant poetical foil to it. The comedy, I have said, is incongruous: a mixture of Congreve with sentimental incompatibilities: the gaiety upon the whole is buoyant; but it required the consummate art of Palmer to reconcile the discordant elements.

A player with Jack's talents, if we had one now would not dare to do the part in the same manner. He would instinctively avoid every turn which might tend to unrealise, and so to make the character fascinating. He must take his cue from his spectators, who would expect a bad man and a good man as rigidly opposed to each other as the deathbeds of those geniuses are contrasted in the prints, which I am sorry to say have disappeared from the windows of my old friend Carrington Bowles, of St. Paul's Churchyard memory — (an exhibition as venerable as the adjacent cathedral, and almost coeval) of the bad and good man at the hour of death; where the ghastly apprehensions of the former,—and truly the grim phantom with his reality of a toasting-fork is not to be despised,—so finely contrast with the meek complacent kissing of the rod,—taking it in like honey and butter,—with which the latter submits to the scythe of the gentle bleeder, Time, who wields his lancet with the apprehensive finger of a popular young ladies' surgeon. What flesh, like loving grass, would not covet to meet halfway the stroke of such a delicate mower?— John Palmer was twice an actor in this exquisite part. He was playing to you all the while that he was playing upon Sir Peter and his lady. You had the first intimation of a sentiment before it was on his lips. His altered voice was meant to you, and you were to suppose that his fictitious co-flutterers on the stage perceived nothing at all of it. What was it to you if that half reality, the husband, was overreached by the puppetry—or the thin thing (Lady Teazle's reputation) was persuaded it was dying of a plethory? The fortunes of Othello and Desdemona were not concerned in it. Poor Jack has passed from the stage in good time, that he did not live to this our age of seriousness. The pleasant old Teazle *King*, too, is gone in good time. His manner would scarce have passed current in our day. We must love or hate—acquit or condemn—censure or pity—exert our detestable coxcombry of moral judgment upon everything. Joseph

Surface, to go down now, must be a downright revolting villain—no compromise—his first appearance must shock and give horror—his specious plausibilities, which the pleasurable faculties of our fathers welcomed with such hearty greetings, knowing that no harm (dramatic harm even) could come, or was meant to come, of them, must inspire a cold and killing aversion. Charles (the real canting person of the scene—for the hypocrisy of Joseph has its ulterior legitimate ends, but his brother's professions of a good heart centre in downright self-satisfaction) must be *loved*, and Joseph *hated*. To balance one disagreeable reality with another, Sir Peter Teazle must be no longer the comic idea of a fretful old bachelor bridegroom, whose teasings (while King acted it) were evidently as much played off at you, as they were meant to concern anybody on the stage,—he must be a real person, capable in law of sustaining an injury—a person towards whom duties are to be acknowledged—the genuine crim. con. antagonist of the villanous seducer Joseph. To realise him more, his sufferings under his unfortunate match must have the downright pungency of life—must (or should) make you not mirthful but uncomfortable, just as the same predicament would move you in a neighbour or old friend.

The delicious scenes which give the play its name and zest, must affect you in the same serious manner as if you heard the reputation of a dear female friend attacked in your real presence. Crabtree and Sir Benjamin—those poor snakes that live but in the sunshine of your mirth—must be ripened by this hot-bed process of realization into asps or amphisbaenas; and Mrs. Candour—O! frightful!—become a hooded serpent. O! who that remembers Parsons and Dodd—the wasp and butterfly of the School for Scandal—in those two characters; and charming natural Miss Pope, the perfect gentlewoman as distinguished from the fine lady of comedy, in this latter part—would forego the true scenic delight—the escape from life—the oblivion of consequences—the holiday barring out of the pedant Reflection—those Saturnalia of two or three brief hours, well won from the world - to sit instead at one of our modern plays—to have his coward conscience (that forsooth must not be left for a moment) stimulated with perpetual appeals - dulled rather, and blunted, as a faculty without repose must be —and his moral vanity pampered with images of notional justice, notional beneficence, lives saved without the spectator's risk, and fortunes given away that cost the author nothing?

No piece was, perhaps, ever so completely cast in all its parts as this *manager's comedy*. Miss Farren had succeeded to Mrs. Abington in Lady Teazle; and Smith, the original Charles, had retired when I first saw it. The rest of the characters, with very slight exceptions, remained. I remember it was then the fashion to cry down John Kemble, who took the part of Charles after Smith; but, I thought, very unjustly. Smith, I fancy, was more airy, and took the eye with a certain gaiety of person. He brought with him no sombre recollections of tragedy. He had not to expiate the fault of having pleased beforehand in lofty declamation. He had no sins of Hamlet or of Richard to atone for. His failure in these parts was a passport to success in one of so opposite a tendency. But, as far as I could judge, the weighty sense of Kemble made up for more personal incapacity than he had to answer for. His harshest tones in this part came steeped and dulcified in good humour. He made his defects a grace. His exact declamatory manner, as he managed it, only served to convey the points of his dialogue with more precision. It seemed to head the shafts to carry them deeper. Not one of his sparkling sentences was lost. I remember minutely how he delivered each in succession, and cannot by any effort imagine how any of them could be altered for the better. No man could deliver brilliant dialogue—the dialogue of Congreve or of Wycherley because none understood it - half so well as John Kemble. His Valentine, in Love

for Love, was, to my recollection, faultless. He flagged
sometimes in the intervals of tragic passion. He would
slumber over the level parts of an heroic character. His
Macbeth has been known to nod. But he always seemed
to me to be particularly alive to pointed and witty
dialogue. The relaxing levities of tragedy have not been
touched by any since him—the playful court-bred spirit
in which he condescended to the players in Hamlet—the
sportive relief which he threw into the darker shades of
Richard—disappeared with him. He had his sluggish
moods, his torpors—but they were the halting-stones and
resting-place of his tragedy — politic savings, and fetches
of the breath—husbandry of the lungs, where nature
pointed him to be an economist—rather, I think than
errors of the judgment. They were, at worst, less painful than the eternal tormenting unappeasable vigilance,—
the "lidless dragon eyes," of present fashionable tragedy.

ON THE ACTING OF MUNDEN.

Not many nights ago I had come home from seeing this
extraordinary performer in Cockletop; and when I retired
to my pillow, his whimsical image still stuck by me, in a
manner as to threaten sleep. In vain I tried to divest
myself of it, by conjuring up the most opposite associations. I resolved to be serious. I raised up the gravest
topics of life; private misery, public calamity. All would
not do:

> - There the antic sate
> Mocking our state

his queer visnomy—his bewildering costume—all the
strange things which he had raked together—his serpen-
tine rod swagging about in his pocket—Cleopatra's tear,
and the rest of his relics—O'Keefe's wild farce, and *his*
wilder commentary— till the passion of laughter, like

grief in excess, relieved itself by its own weight, inviting the sleep which in the first instance it had driven away.

But I was not to escape so easily. No sooner did I fall into slumbers, than the same image, only more perplexing, assailed me in the shape of dreams. Not one Munden, but five hundred, were dancing before me, like the faces which, whether you will or no, come when you have been taking opium—all the strange combinations, which this strangest of all strange mortals ever shot his proper countenance into, from the day he came commissioned to dry up the tears of the town for the loss of the now almost forgotten Edwin. O for the power of the pencil to have fixed them when I awoke! A season or two since, there was exhibited a Hogarth gallery. I do not see why there should not be a Munden gallery. In richness and variety, the latter would not fall far short of the former.

There is one face of Farley, one face of Knight, one (but what a one it is!) of Liston; but Munden has none that you can properly pin down, and call *his*. When you think he has exhausted his battery of looks, in unaccountable warfare with your gravity, suddenly he sprouts out an entirely new set of features, like Hydra. He is not one, but legion; not so much a comedian, as a company. If his name could be multiplied like his countenance, it might fill a play-bill. He, and he alone, literally *makes faces:* applied to any other person, the phrase is a mere figure, denoting certain modifications of the human countenance. Out of some invisible wardrobe he dips for faces, as his friend Suett used for wigs, and fetches them out as easily. I should not be surprised to see him some day put out the head of a river-horse: or come forth a pewitt, or lapwing, some feathered metamorphosis.

I have seen this gifted actor in Sir Christopher Curry —in old Dornton—diffuse a glow of sentiment which has made the pulse of a crowded theatre beat like that of one man; when he has come in aid of the pulpit, doing good to the moral heart of a people. I have seen some faint approaches to this sort of excellence in other players. But in the grand grotesque of farce, Munden stands out as single and unaccompanied as Hogarth. Hogarth, strange to tell, had no followers. The school of Munden began, and must end, with himself.

Can any man *wonder*, like him? can any man *see ghosts*, like him? or *fight with his own shadow*—"SESSA"—as he does in that strangely-neglected thing, the Cobbler of Preston—where his alternations from the Cobbler to the Magnifico, and from the Magnifico to the Cobbler, keep the brain of the spectator in as wild a ferment, as if some Arabian Night were being acted before him. Who like him can throw, or ever attempted to throw, a preternatural interest over the commonest daily-life objects? A table or a joint-stool, in his conception, rises into a dignity equivalent to Cassiopeia's chair. It is invested with constellatory importance. You could not speak of it with more deference, if it were mounted into the firmament. A beggar in the hands of Michael Angelo, says Fuseli, rose the Patriarch of Poverty. So the gusto of Munden antiquates and ennobles what it touches. His pots and his ladles are as grand and primal as the seething-pots and hooks seen in old prophetic vision. A tub of butter, contemplated by him, amounts to a Platonic idea. He understands a leg of mutton in its quiddity. He stands wondering, amid the commonplace materials of life, like primaeval man with the sun and stars about him.

THE LAST ESSAYS OF ELIA.

BLAKESMOOR IN H——SHIRE.

I do not know a pleasure more affecting than to range at will over the deserted apartments of some fine old family mansion. The traces of extinct grandeur admit of a better passion than envy: and contemplations on the great and good, whom we fancy in succession to have been its inhabitants, weave for us illusions, incompatible with the bustle of modern occupancy, and vanities of foolish present aristocracy. The same difference of feeling, I think, attends us between entering an empty and a crowded church. In the latter it is chance but some present human frailty —an act of inattention on the part of some of the auditory—or a trait of affectation, or worse, vain-glory, on that of the preacher, puts us by our best thoughts, disharmonising the place and the occasion. But wouldst thou know the beauty of holiness?—go alone on some week-day, borrowing the keys of good Master Sexton, traverse the cool aisles of some country church: think of the piety that has kneeled there—the congregations, old and young, that have found consolation there—the meek pastor—the docile parishioner. With no disturbing emotions, no cross conflicting comparisons, drink in the tranquillity of the place, till thou thyself become as fixed and motionless as the marble effigies that kneel and weep around thee.

Journeying northward lately, I could not resist going some few miles out of my road to look upon the remains of an old great house with which I had been impressed in this way in infancy. I was apprised that the owner of it had lately pulled it down; still I had a vague notion that it could not all have perished,—that so much solidity with magnificence could not have been crushed all at once into the mere dust and rubbish which I found it.

The work of ruin had proceeded with a swift hand indeed, and the demolition of a few weeks had reduced it to—an antiquity.

I was astonished at the indistinction of everything. Where had stood the great gates? What bounded the court-yard? Whereabout did the out-houses commence? A few bricks only lay as representatives of that which was so stately and so spacious.

Death does not shrink up his human victim at this rate. The burnt ashes of a man weigh more in their proportion.

Had I seen these brick-and-mortar knaves at their process of destruction, at the plucking of every panel I should have felt the varlets at my heart. I should have cried out to them to spare a plank at least out of the cheerful storeroom, in whose hot window-seat I used to sit and read Cowley, with the grass-plot before, and the hum and flappings of that one solitary wasp that ever haunted it about me—it is in mine ears now, as oft as summer returns; or a panel of the yellow-room.

Why, every plank and panel of that house for me had magic in it. The tapestried bedrooms—tapestry so much better than painting—not adorning merely, but peopling the wainscots—at which childhood ever and anon would steal a look, shifting its coverlid (replaced as quickly) to exercise its tender courage in a momentary eye-encounter with those stern bright visages, staring reciprocally—all Ovid on the walls, in colours vivider than his description. Actæon in mid sprout, with the unappeasable prudery of Diana; and the still more provoking and almost culinary coolness of Dan Phœbus, eel-fashion, deliberately divesting of Marsyas.

Then, that haunted room—in which old Mrs. Battle died—whereinto I have crept, but always in the daytime, with a passion of fear; and a sneaking curiosity, terror-tainted, to hold communication with the past.—*How shall they build it up again?*

It was an old deserted place, yet not so long deserted that the traces of the splendour of past inmates were everywhere apparent. Its furniture was still standing—even to the tarnished gilt leather battledores, and crumbling feathers of shuttlecocks in the nursery, which told that children had once played there. But I was a lonely child, and had the range at will of every apartment, knew every nook and corner, wondered and worshipped everywhere.

The solitude of childhood is not so much the mother of thought as it is the feeder of love, of silence, and admiration. So strange a passion for the place possessed me in those years, that, though there lay—I shame to say how few roods distant from the mansion—half hid by trees, what I judged some romantic lake, such was the spell which bound me to the house, and such my carefulness not to pass its strict and proper precincts, that the idle waters lay unexplored for me; and not till late in life, curiosity prevailing over elder devotion, I found, to my astonishment, a pretty brawling brook had been the Lacus Incognitus of my infancy. Variegated views, extensive prospects—and those at no great distance from the house—I was told of such—what were they to me, being out of the boundaries of my Eden? So far from a wish to roam, I would have drawn, methought, still closer the fences of my chosen prison, and have been hemmed in by a yet securer cincture of those excluding garden walls. I could have exclaimed with the garden-loving poet—

> Bind me, ye woodbines, in your twines;
> Curl me about, ye gadding vines;
> And oh so close your circles lace,
> That I may never leave this place;
> But, lest your fetters prove too weak,
> Ere I your silken bondage break,

> Do you, O brambles, chain me too,
> And, courteous briars, nail me through.[1]

I was here as in a lonely temple. Snug fire-sides—the low-built roof—parlours ten feet by ten—frugal boards, and all the homeliness of home—these were the condition of my birth—the wholesome soil which I was planted in. Yet, without impeachment to their tenderest lessons, I am not sorry to have had glances of something beyond, and to have taken, if but a peep, in childhood, at the contrasting accidents of a great fortune.

To have the feeling of gentility, it is not necessary to have been born gentle. The pride of ancestry may be had on cheaper terms than to be obliged to an importunate race of ancestors; and the coatless antiquary in his un-emblazoned cell, revolving the long line of a Mowbray's or De Clifford's pedigree, at those sounding names may warm himself into as gay a vanity as those who do inherit them. The claims of birth are ideal merely, and what herald shall go about to strip me of an idea? Is it trenchant to their swords? can it be hacked off as a spur can? or torn away like a tarnished garter?

What, else, were the families of the great to us? what pleasure should we take in their tedious genealogies, or their capitulatory brass monuments? What to us the uninterrupted current of their bloods, if our own did not answer within us to a cognate and corresponding elevation?

Or wherefore, else, O tattered and diminished 'Scutcheon that hung upon the time-worn walls of thy princely stairs, BLAKESMOOR! have I in childhood so oft stood poring upon thy mystic characters—thy emblematic supporters, with their prophetic "Resurgam"—till, every dreg of peasantry purging off, I received into myself Very Gentility? Thou wert first in my morning eyes; and of nights hast detained my steps from bedward, till it was but a step from gazing at thee to dreaming on thee.

---

[1] [Marvell, on Appleton House, to the Lord Fairfax.]

This is the only true gentry by adoption; the veritable change of blood, and not as empirics have fabled, by transfusion.

Who it was by dying that had earned the splendid trophy, I know not, I inquired not: but its fading rags, and colours cobweb-stained, told that its subject was of two centuries back.

And what if my ancestor at that date was some Damœtas,—feeding flocks, not his own, upon the hills of Lincoln—did I in less earnest vindicate to myself the family trappings of this once proud Ægon? repaying by a backward triumph the insults he might possibly have heaped in his life-time upon my poor pastoral progenitor.

If it were presumption so to speculate, the present owners of the mansion had least reason to complain. They had long forsaken the old house of their fathers for a newer trifle; and I was left to appropriate to myself what images I could pick up, to raise my fancy, or to soothe my vanity.

I was the true descendant of those old W——s, and not the present family of that name, who had fled the old waste places.

Mine was that gallery of good old family portraits, which as I have gone over, giving them in fancy my own family name, one—and then another—would seem to smile, reaching forward from the canvas, to recognise the new relationship; while the rest looked grave, as it seemed, at the vacancy in their dwelling, and thoughts of fled posterity.

The Beauty with the cool blue pastoral drapery, and a lamb—that hung next the great bay window—with the bright yellow H——shire hair, and eye of watchet hue—so like my Alice!—I am persuaded she was a true Elia—Mildred Elia, I take it.

Mine, too, BLAKESMOOR, was thy noble Marble Hall, with its mosaic pavements, and its Twelve Cæsars—stately busts in marble, ranged round: of whose countenances, young reader of faces as I was, the frowning beauty of

Nero, I remember, had most of my wonder : but the mild Galba had my love. There they stood in the coldness of death, yet freshness of immortality.

Mine, too, thy lofty Justice Hall, with its one chair of authority, high-backed and wickered, once the terror of luckless poacher, or self-forgetful maiden—so common since, that bats have roosted in it.

Mine, too,—whose else?—thy costly fruit-garden, with its sun-baked southern wall; the ampler pleasure-garden, rising backwards from the house in triple terraces, with flower-pots now of palest lead, save that a speck here and there, saved from the elements, bespake their pristine state to have been gilt and glittering; the verdant quarters backwarder still; and, stretching still beyond, in old formality, thy firry wilderness, the haunt of the squirrel, and the day-long murmuring wood-pigeon, with that antique image in the centre, God or Goddess I wist not ; but child of Athens or old Rome paid never a sincerer worship to Pan or to Sylvanus in their native groves, than I to that fragmental mystery.

Was it for this, that I kissed my childish hands too fervently in your idol-worship, walks and windings of BLAKESMOOR! for this, or what sin of mine, has the plough passed over your pleasant places? I sometimes think that as men, when they die, do not die all, so of their extinguished habitations there may be a hope—a germ to be revivified.

POOR RELATIONS.

A POOR Relation—is the most irrelevant thing in nature, a piece of impertinent correspondency,—an odious approximation,—a haunting conscience,—a preposterous shadow, lengthening in the noon-tide of our prosperity,—an unwelcome remembrancer,—a perpetually recurring mortification,—a drain on your purse,—a more intolerable dun upon your pride,—a drawback upon success,—a rebuke to your rising,—a stain in your blood,—a blot on your 'scutcheon,—a rent in your garment,—a death's head at your banquet,—Agathocles' pot,—a Mordecai in your gate,—a Lazarus at your door,—a lion in your path,—a frog in your chamber,—a fly in your ointment,—a mote in your eye,—a triumph to your enemy,—an apology to your friends,—the one thing not needful,—the hail in harvest,—the ounce of sour in a pound of sweet.

He is known by his knock. Your heart telleth you "That is Mr. ———." A rap, between familiarity and respect; that demands, and at the same time seems to despair of, entertainment. He entereth smiling and—embarrassed. He holdeth out his hand to you to shake, and—draweth it back again. He casually looketh in about dinner-time—when the table is full. He offereth to go away, seeing you have company—but is induced to stay. He filleth a chair, and your visitor's two children are accommodated at a side-table. He never cometh upon open days, when your wife says, with some complacency, "My dear, perhaps Mr. ——— will drop in to-day." He remembereth birth-days—and professeth he is fortunate to have stumbled upon one. He declareth against fish, the turbot being small—yet suffereth himself to be importuned into a slice, against his first resolution. He sticketh by the port—yet will be prevailed upon to empty the remainder glass of claret, if a stranger press it upon him. He is a puzzle to the servants, who are fearful of being too obsequious, or not civil enough, to him. The guests think "they have seen him before." Every one speculateth upon his condition: and the most part take him to be a—tide-waiter. He calleth you by your Christian name, to imply that his other is the same with your own. He is too familiar by half, yet you wish he had less diffidence. With half the familiarity, he might pass for a casual dependant; with more boldness, he would be in no danger of being taken for what he is. He is too humble for a friend; yet taketh on him more state than

befits a client. He is a worse guest than a country
tenant, inasmuch as he bringeth up no rent—yet 'tis odds,
from his garb and demeanour, that your guests take him
for one. He is asked to make one at the whist table;
refuseth on the score of poverty, and—resents being left
out. When the company break up, he proffereth to go
for a coach—and lets the servant go. He recollects your
grandfather; and will thrust in some mean and quite un-
important anecdote—of the family. He knew it when it
was not quite so flourishing as " he is blest in seeing it
now." He reviveth past situations, to institute what he
calleth—favourable comparisons. With a reflecting sort
of congratulation, he will inquire the price of your furniture: and insults you with a special commendation of
your window-curtains. He is of opinion that the urn is
the more elegant shape; but, after all, there was something more comfortable about the old tea-kettle—which
you must remember. He dare say you must find a great
convenience in having a carriage of your own, and
appealeth to your lady if it is not so. Inquireth if you
have had your arms done on vellum yet; and did not
know, till lately, that such-and-such had been the crest
of the family. His memory is unseasonable; his compliments perverse; his talk a trouble; his stay pertina-
cious; and when he goeth away, you dismiss his chair
into a corner as precipitately as possible, and feel fairly
rid of two nuisances.

There is a worse evil under the sun, and that is—a
female Poor Relation. You may do something with the
other; you may pass him off tolerably well; but your
indigent she-relative is hopeless. " He is an old humorist," you may say, " and affects to go threadbare. His
circumstances are better than folks would take them to
be. You are fond of having a Character at your table,
and truly he is one." But in the indications of female
poverty there can be no disguise. No woman dresses below herself from caprice. The truth must out without
shuffling. "She is plainly related to the L——'s; or

what does she at their house?" She is, in all probability, your wife's cousin. Nine times out of ten, at least, this is the case.—Her garb is something between a gentlewoman and a beggar, yet the former evidently predominates. She is most provokingly humble, and ostentatiously sensible to her inferiority. He may require to be repressed sometimes—*aliquando sufflaminandus erat*—but there is no raising her. You send her soup at dinner, and she begs to be helped—after the gentlemen. Mr. —— requests the honour of taking wine with her; she hesitates between Port and Madeira, and chooses the former—because he does. She calls the servant *Sir;* and insists on not troubling him to hold her plate. The housekeeper patronises her. The children's governess takes upon her to correct her, when she has mistaken the piano for a harpsichord.

Richard Amlet, Esq., in the play, is a notable instance of the disadvantages to which this chimerical notion of *affinity constituting a claim to acquaintance,* may subject the spirit of a gentleman. A little foolish blood is all that is betwixt him and a lady with a great estate. His stars are perpetually crossed by the malignant maternity of an old woman, who persists in calling him "her son Dick." But she has wherewithal in the end to recompense his indignities, and float him again upon the brilliant surface, under which it had been her seeming business and pleasure all along to sink him. All men, besides, are not of Dick's temperament. I knew an Amlet in real life, who, wanting Dick's buoyancy, sank indeed. Poor W—— was of my own standing at Christ's, a fine classic, and a youth of promise. If he had a blemish, it was too much pride; but its quality was inoffensive; it was not of that sort which hardens the heart, and serves to keep inferiors at a distance; it only sought to ward off derogation from itself. It was the principle of self-respect carried as far as it could go, without infringing upon that respect, which he would have every one else equally maintain for himself. He would have you to think alike with him on this topic. Many a quarrel have I had with him, when we were rather older boys, and our tallness made us more obnoxious to observation in the blue clothes, because I would not thread the alleys and blind ways of the town with him to elude notice, when we have been out together on a holiday in the streets of this sneering and prying metropolis. W—— went, sore with these notions, to Oxford, where the dignity and sweetness of a scholar's life, meeting with the alloy of a humble introduction, wrought in him a passionate devotion to the place, with a profound aversion from the society. The servitor's gown (worse than his school array) clung to him with Nessian venom. He thought himself ridiculous in a garb, under which Latimer must have walked erect, and in which Hooker, in his young days, possibly flaunted in a vein of no discommendable vanity. In the depth of college shades, or in his lonely chamber, the poor student shrunk from observation. He found shelter among books, which insult not; and studies, that ask no questions of a youth's finances. He was lord of his library, and seldom cared for looking out beyond his domains. The healing influence of studious pursuits was upon him to soothe and to abstract. He was almost a healthy man, when the waywardness of his fate broke out against him with a second and worse malignity. The father of W—— had hitherto exercised the humble profession of house-painter, at N——, near Oxford. A supposed interest with some of the heads of colleges had now induced him to take up his abode in that city, with the hope of being employed upon some public works which were talked of. From that moment I read in the countenance of the young man the determination which at length tore him from academical pursuits for ever. To a person unacquainted with our universities, the distance between the gownsmen and the townsmen, as they are called—the trading part of the latter especially—is carried to an excess that would appear harsh and incredible. The temperament of W——'s father was diametrically the reverse

of his own. Old W—— was a little, busy, cringing
tradesman, who, with his son upon his arm, would stand
bowing and scraping, cap in hand, to anything that wore
the semblance of a gown—insensible to the winks and
opener remonstrances of the young man, to whose chamber-
fellow, or equal in standing, perhaps, he was thus obse-
quiously and gratuitously ducking. Such a state of things
could not last. W—— must change the air of Oxford,
or be suffocated. He chose the former; and let the
sturdy moralist, who strains the point of the filial duties
as high as they can bear, censure the dereliction; he cannot estimate the struggle. I stood with W——, the last
afternoon I ever saw him, under the eaves of his paternal
dwelling. It was in the fine lane leading from the High
Street to the back of * * * * college, where W—— kept
his rooms. He seemed thoughtful and more reconciled.
I ventured to rally him—finding him in a better mood—
upon a representation of the Artist Evangelist, which the
old man, whose affairs were beginning to flourish, had
caused to be set up in a splendid sort of frame over his
really handsome shop, either as a token of prosperity or
badge of gratitude to his saint. W—— looked up at
the Luke, and, like Satan, "knew his mounted sign—
and fled." A letter on his father's table, the next morning, announced that he had accepted a commission in a
regiment about to embark for Portugal. He was among
the first who perished before the walls of St. Sebastian.

I do not know how, upon a subject which I began with
treating half seriously, I should have fallen upon a recital
so eminently painful; but this theme of poor relationship
is replete with so much matter for tragic as well as comic
associations, that it is difficult to keep the account distinct without blending. The earliest impressions which
I received on this matter are certainly not attended with
anything painful, or very humiliating, in the recalling.
At my father's table (no very splendid one) was to be
found, every Saturday, the mysterious figure of an aged
gentleman, clothed in neat black, of a sad yet comely

appearance. His deportment was of the essence of
gravity ; his words few or none ; and I was not to make
a noise in his presence. I had little inclination to have
done so — for my cue was to admire in silence. A particular elbow-chair was appropriated to him, which was in
no case to be violated. A peculiar sort of sweet pudding,
which appeared on no other occasion, distinguished the
days of his coming. I used to think him a prodigiously
rich man. All I could make out of him was, that he
and my father had been schoolfellows, a world ago, at
Lincoln, and that he came from the Mint. The Mint I
knew to be a place where all the money was coined — and
I thought he was the owner of all that money. Awful
ideas of the Tower twined themselves about his presence.
He seemed above human infirmities and passions. A
sort of melancholy grandeur invested him. From some
inexplicable doom I fancied him obliged to go about in
an eternal suit of mourning ; a captive — a stately being
let out of the Tower on Saturdays. Often have I
wondered at the temerity of my father, who, in spite of
an habitual general respect which we all in common
manifested towards him, would venture now and then to
stand up against him in some argument touching their
youthful days. The houses of the ancient city of Lincoln
are divided (as most of my readers know) between the
dwellers on the hill and in the valley. This marked
distinction formed an obvious division between the boys
who lived above (however brought together in a common
school) and the boys whose paternal residence was on the
plain ; a sufficient cause of hostility in the code of these
young Grotiuses. My father had been a leading Moun-
taineer ; and would still maintain the general superiority
in skill and hardihood of the *Above Boys* (his own
faction), over the *Below Boys* (so were they called), of
which party his contemporary had been a chieftain.
Many and hot were the skirmishes on this topic — the
only one upon which the old gentleman was ever brought
out — and bad blood bred ; even sometimes almost to the

recommencement (so I expected) of actual hostilities.
But my father, who scorned to insist upon advantages,
generally contrived to turn the conversation upon some
adroit by-commendation of the old Minster; in the
general preference of which, before all other cathedrals in
the island, the dweller on the hill, and the plain-born,
could meet on a conciliating level, and lay down their
less important differences. Once only I saw the old
gentleman really ruffled, and I remember with anguish
the thought that came over me: "Perhaps he will never
come here again." He had been pressed to take another
plate of the viand, which I have already mentioned as
the indispensable concomitant of his visits. He had
refused with a resistance amounting to rigour, when my
aunt, an old Lincolnian, but who had something of this,
in common with my cousin Bridget, that she would
sometimes press civility out of season—uttered the
following memorable application—"Do take another
slice, Mr. Billet, for you do not get pudding every day."
The old gentleman said nothing at the time—but he took
occasion in the course of the evening, when some argument had intervened between them, to utter with an
emphasis which chilled the company, and which chills
me now as I write it "Woman, you are superannuated!"
John Billet did not survive long, after the digesting of
this affront; but he survived long enough to assure me
that peace was actually restored! and if I remember
aright, another pudding was discreetly substituted in the
place of that which had occasioned the offence. He
died at the Mint (anno 1781) where he had long held,
what he accounted, a comfortable independence; and
with five pounds, fourteen shillings, and a penny, which
were found in his escritoir after his decease, left the
world, blessing God that he had enough to bury him,
and that he had never been obliged to any man for a
sixpence. This was—a Poor Relation.

DETACHED THOUGHTS ON BOOKS AND READING.

To mind the inside of a book is to entertain one's self with the forced product of another man's brain. Now I think a man of quality and breeding may be much amused with the natural sprouts of his own.—*Lord Foppington, in "The Relapse."*

AN ingenious acquaintance of my own was so much struck with this bright sally of his Lordship, that he has left off reading altogether, to the great improvement of his originality. At the hazard of losing some credit on this head, I must confess that I dedicate no inconsiderable portion of my time to other people's thoughts. I dream away my life in others' speculations. I love to lose myself in other men's minds. When I am not walking, I am reading; I cannot sit and think. Books think for me.

I have no repugnances. Shaftesbury is not too genteel for me, nor Jonathan Wild too low. I can read anything which I call *a book*. There are things in that shape which I cannot allow for such.

In this catalogue of *books which are no books—biblia a-biblia*—I reckon Court Calendars, Directories, Pocket Books, Draught Boards, bound and lettered on the back, Scientific Treatises, Almanacs, Statutes at Large: the works of Hume, Gibbon, Robertson, Beattie, Soame Jenyns, and generally, all those volumes which "no gentleman's library should be without:" the Histories of Flavius Josephus (that learned Jew), and Paley's Moral Philosophy. With these exceptions, I can read almost anything. I bless my stars for a taste so catholic, so unexcluding.

I confess that it moves my spleen to see these *things*

in books' clothing perched upon shelves, like false saints, usurpers of true shrines, intruders into the sanctuary, thrusting out the legitimate occupants. To reach down a well-bound semblance of a volume, and hope it some kind-hearted play-book, then, opening what "seem its leaves," to come bolt upon a withering Population Essay. To expect a Steele or a Farquhar, and find—Adam Smith. To view a well-arranged assortment of block-headed Encyclopædias (Anglicanas or Metropolitanas) set out in an array of russia, or morocco, when a tithe of that good leather would comfortably re-clothe my shivering folios, would renovate Paracelsus himself, and enable old Raymund Lully to look like himself again in the world. I never see these impostors, but I long to strip them, to warm my ragged veterans in their spoils.

To be strong-backed and neat-bound is the desideratum of a volume. Magnificence comes after. This, when it can be afforded, is not to be lavished upon all kinds of books indiscriminately. I would not dress a set of magazines, for instance, in full suit. The dishabille, or half-binding (with russia backs ever) is *our* costume. A Shakspeare or a Milton (unless the first editions), it were mere foppery to trick out in gay apparel. The possession of them confers no distinction. The exterior of them (the things themselves being so common), strange to say, raises no sweet emotions, no tickling sense of property in the owner. Thomson's Seasons, again, looks best (I maintain it) a little torn and dog's-eared. How beautiful to a genuine lover of reading are the sullied leaves, and worn-out appearance, nay, the very odour (beyond russia) if we would not forget kind feelings in fastidiousness, of an old "Circulating Library" Tom Jones, or Vicar of Wakefield! How they speak of the thousand thumbs that have turned over their pages with delight!—of the lone sempstress, whom they may have cheered (milliner, or hard-working mantua-maker) after her long day's needle-toil, running far into midnight, when she has snatched an hour, ill spared from sleep, to steep her cares, as in some Lethean cup, in spelling out their enchanting contents! Who would have them a whit less soiled? What better condition could we desire to see them in?

In some respects the better a book is, the less it demands from binding. Fielding, Smollett, Sterne, and all that class of perpetually self-reproductive volumes— Great Nature's Stereotypes—we see them individually perish with less regret, because we know the copies of them to be "eterne." But where a book is at once both good and rare—where the individual is almost the species, and when *that* perishes,

> We know not where is that Promethean torch
> That can its light relumine,—

such a book, for instance, as the Life of the Duke of Newcastle, by his Duchess—no casket is rich enough, no casing sufficiently durable, to honour and keep safe such a jewel.

Not only rare volumes of this description, which seem hopeless ever to be reprinted, but old editions of writers, such as Sir Philip Sydney, Bishop Taylor, Milton in his prose works, Fuller—of whom we *have* reprints, yet the books themselves, though they go about, and are talked of here and there, we know have not endenizened themselves (nor possibly ever will) in the national heart, so as to become stock books—it is good to possess these in durable and costly covers. I do not care for a First Folio of Shakspeare. [You cannot make a *pet* book of an author whom everybody reads.] I rather prefer the common editions of Rowe and Tonson, without notes, and with *plates*, which, being so execrably bad, serve as maps or modest remembrancers, to the text; and, without pretending to any supposable emulation with it, are so much better than the Shakspeare gallery *engravings*, which *did*. I have a community of feeling with my countrymen about his Plays, and I like those editions of him best which have been oftenest tumbled about and handled.—On the contrary, I cannot read Beaumont and Fletcher but in Folio. The Octavo editions are painful to look at. I have no sympathy with them. If they were as much read as the current editions of the other poet, I should prefer them in that shape to the older one. I do not know a more heartless sight than the reprint of the Anatomy of Melancholy. What need was there of unearthing the bones of that fantastic old great man, to expose them in a winding-sheet of the newest fashion to modern censure? what hapless stationer could dream of Burton ever becoming popular?—The wretched Malone could not do worse, when he bribed the sexton of Stratford church to let him whitewash the painted effigy of old Shakspeare, which stood there, in rude but lively fashion depicted, to the very colour of the cheek, the eye, the eyebrow, hair, the very dress he used to wear—the only authentic testimony we had, however imperfect, of these curious parts and parcels of him. They covered him over with a coat of white paint. By ——, if I had been a justice of peace for Warwickshire, I would have clapped both commentator and sexton fast in the stocks, for a pair of meddling sacrilegious varlets.

I think I see them at their work—these sapient trouble-tombs.

Shall I be thought fantastical if I confess that the names of some of our poets sound sweeter, and have a finer relish to the ear—to mine, at least—than that of Milton or of Shakspeare? It may be that the latter are more staled and rung upon in common discourse. The sweetest names, and which carry a perfume in the mention, are, Kit Marlowe, Drayton, Drummond of Hawthornden, and Cowley.

Much depends upon *when* and *where* you read a book. In the five or six impatient minutes, before the dinner is quite ready, who would think of taking up the Fairy Queen for a stop-gap or a volume of Bishop Andrewes' sermons?

Milton almost requires a solemn service of music to be played before you enter upon him. But he brings his music, to which, who listens, had need bring docile thoughts, and purged ears.

Winter evenings—the world shut out—with less of ceremony the gentle Shakspeare enters. At such a season the Tempest, or his own Winter's Tale—

These two poets you cannot avoid reading aloud—to yourself, or (as it chances) to some single person listening. More than one—and it degenerates into an audience.

Books of quick interest, that hurry on for incidents, are for the eye to glide over only. It will not do to read them out. I could never listen to even the better kind of modern novels without extreme irksomeness.

A newspaper, read out, is intolerable. In some of the Bank offices it is the custom (to save so much individual time) for one of the clerks—who is the best scholar—to commence upon the *Times* or the *Chronicle* and recite its entire contents aloud, *pro bono publico*. With every advantage of lungs and elocution, the effect is singularly vapid. In barbers' shops and public-houses a fellow will get up and spell out a paragraph, which he communicates as some discovery. Another follows with *his* selection. So the entire journal transpires at length by piecemeal. Seldom-readers are slow readers, and, without this expedient, no one in the company would probably ever travel through the contents of a whole paper.

Newspapers always excite curiosity. No one ever lays one down without a feeling of disappointment.

What an eternal time that gentleman in black, at Nando's, keeps the paper! I am sick of hearing the waiter bawling out incessantly, "The *Chronicle* is in hand, Sir."

Coming into an inn at night—having ordered your supper—what can be more delightful than to find lying in the window-seat, left there time out of mind by the carelessness of some former guest—two or three numbers of the old Town and Country Magazine, with its amusing *tête-à-tête* pictures—" The Royal Lover and Lady G——;" " The Melting Platonic and the old Beau,"—and suchlike antiquated scandal? Would you exchange it—at that time, and in that place—for a better book?

Poor Tobin, who latterly fell blind, did not regret it so much for the weightier kinds of reading— the Paradise Lost, or Comus, he could have *read* to him—but he missed the pleasure of skimming over with his own eye a magazine, or a light pamphlet.

I should not care to be caught in the serious avenues of some cathedral alone, and reading *Candide*.

I do not remember a more whimsical surprise than having been once detected—by a familiar damsel—reclined at my ease upon the grass, on Primrose Hill (her Cythera) reading—*Pamela*. There was nothing in the book to make a man seriously ashamed at the exposure; but as she seated herself down by me, and seemed determined to read in company, I could have wished it had been—any other book. We read on very sociably for a few pages; and, not finding the author much to her taste, she got up, and - went away. Gentle casuist, I leave it to thee to conjecture, whether the blush (for there was one between us) was the property of the nymph or the swain in this dilemma. From me you shall never get the secret.

I am not much a friend to out-of-doors reading. I cannot settle my spirits to it. I knew a Unitarian minister, who was generally to be seen upon Snow Hill (as yet Skinner's Street *was not*), between the hours of ten and eleven in the morning, studying a volume of Lardner. I own this to have been a strain of abstraction beyond my reach. I used to admire how he sidled along, keeping clear of secular contacts. An illiterate encounter with a porter's knot, or a bread basket, would have quickly put to flight all the theology I am master of, and have left me worse than indifferent to the five points.

There is a class of street readers, whom I can never contemplate without affection—the poor gentry, who, not having wherewithal to buy or hire a book, filch a little learning at the open stalls—the owner, with his hard eye, casting envious looks at them all the while, and thinking when they will have done. Venturing tenderly, page after page, expecting every moment when he shall interpose his interdict, and yet unable to deny themselves the gratification, they "snatch a fearful joy." Martin B——, in this way, by daily fragments, got through two volumes of Clarissa, when the stall-keeper damped his laudable ambition, by asking him (it was in his younger days) whether he meant to purchase the work. M. declares, that under no circumstance in his life did he ever peruse a book with half the satisfaction which he took in those uneasy snatches. A quaint poetess of our day has moralised upon this subject in two very touching but homely stanzas:

> I saw a boy with eager eye
> Open a book upon a stall,
> And read, as he'd devour it all;
> Which, when the stall-man did espy,
> Soon to the boy I heard him call,
> "You Sir, you never buy a book,
> Therefore in one you shall not look."
> The boy pass'd slowly on, and with a sigh
> He wish'd he never had been taught to read,
> Then of the old churl's books he should have had no need.
>
> Of sufferings the poor have many,
> Which never can the rich annoy.
> I soon perceived another boy,
> Who look'd as if he had not any
> Food, for that day at least—enjoy
> The sight of cold meat in a tavern larder.
> This boy's case, then thought I, is surely harder,
> Thus hungry, longing, thus without a penny,
> Beholding choice of dainty-dressèd meat:
> No wonder if he wished he ne'er had learn'd to eat.

STAGE ILLUSION.

A play is said to be well or ill acted, in proportion to the scenical illusion produced. Whether such illusion can in any case be perfect, is not the question. The nearest approach to it, we are told, is when the actor appears wholly unconscious of the presence of spectators. In tragedy—in all which is to affect the feelings—this undivided attention to his stage business seems indispensable. Yet it is, in fact, dispensed with every day by our cleverest tragedians; and while these references to an audience, in the shape of rant or sentiment, are not too frequent or palpable, a sufficient quantity of illusion for the purposes of dramatic interest may be said to be produced in spite of them. But, tragedy apart, it may be inquired whether, in certain characters in comedy, especially those which are a little extravagant, or which involve some notion repugnant to the moral sense, it is not a proof of the highest skill in the comedian when, without absolutely appealing to an audience, he keeps up a tacit understanding with them; and makes them, unconsciously to themselves, a party in the scene. The utmost nicety is required in the mode of doing this; but we speak only of the great artists in the profession.

The most mortifying infirmity in human nature, to feel in ourselves, or to contemplate in another, is, perhaps, cowardice. To see a coward *done to the life* upon a stage would produce anything but mirth. Yet we most of us remember Jack Bannister's cowards. Could anything be more agreeable, more pleasant? We loved the rogues. How was this effected but by the exquisite art of the actor in a perpetual sub-insinuation to us, the spectators, even in the extremity of the shaking fit, that he was not half such a coward as we took him for? We saw all the common symptoms of the malady upon him; the quivering lip, the cowering knees, the teeth chattering; and could have sworn "that man was frightened." But we forgot all the while—or kept it almost a secret to ourselves—that he never once lost his self-possession; that he let out, by a thousand droll looks and gestures—meant at *us*, and not at all supposed to be visible to his fellows in the scene, that his confidence in his own resources had never once deserted him. Was this a genuine picture of a coward; or not rather a likeness, which the clever artist contrived to palm upon us instead of an original; while we secretly connived at the delusion for the purpose of greater pleasure, than a more genuine counterfeiting of the imbecility, helplessness, and utter self-desertion, which we know to be concomitants of cowardice in real life, could have given us?

Why are misers so hateful in the world, and so endurable on the stage, but because the skilful actor, by a sort of subreference, rather than direct appeal to us, disarms the character of a great deal of its odiousness, by seeming to engage *our* compassion for the insecure tenure by which he holds his money-bags and parchments? By this subtle vent half of the hatefulness of the character—the self-closeness with which in real life it coils itself up from the sympathies of men—evaporates. The miser becomes sympathetic; *i.e.*, is no genuine miser. Here again a diverting likeness is substituted for a very disagreeable reality.

Spleen, irritability—the pitiable infirmities of old men, which produce only pain to behold in the realities, counterfeited upon a stage, divert not altogether for the comic appendages to them, but in part from an inner conviction that they are *being acted* before us; that a likeness only is going on, and not the thing itself. They please by being done under the life, or beside it; not *to the life*. When Gattie acts an old man, is he angry indeed? or only a pleasant counterfeit, just enough of a likeness to recognise, without pressing upon us the uneasy sense of a reality?

Comedians, paradoxical as it may seem, may be too natural. It was the case with a late actor. Nothing could be more earnest or true than the manner of Mr. Emery; this told excellently in his Tyke, and characters of a tragic cast. But when he carried the same rigid exclusiveness of attention to the stage business, and wilful blindness and oblivion of everything before the curtain into his comedy, it produced a harsh and dissonant effect. He was out of keeping with the rest of the *dramatis personæ*. There was as little link between him and them, as betwixt himself and the audience. He was a third estate—dry, repulsive, and unsocial to all. Individually considered, his execution was masterly. But comedy is not this unbending thing: for this reason, that the same degree of credibility is not required of it as to serious scenes. The degrees of credibility demanded to the two things may be illustrated by the different sort of truth which we expect when a man tells us a mournful or a merry story. If we suspect the former of falsehood in any one tittle, we reject it altogether. Our tears refuse to flow at a suspected imposition. But the teller of a mirthful tale has latitude allowed him. We are content with less than absolute truth. 'Tis the same with dramatic illusion. We confess we love in comedy to see an audience naturalised behind the scenes—taken into the interest of the drama, welcomed as bystanders, however. There is something ungracious in a comic actor holding himself aloof from all participation or concern with those who are come to be diverted by him. Macbeth must see the dagger, and no ear but his own be told of it; but an old fool in farce may think he *sees something*, and by conscious words and looks express it, as plainly as he can speak, to pit, box, and gallery. When an impertinent in tragedy, an Osric, for instance, breaks in upon the serious passions of the scene, we approve of the contempt with which he is treated. But when the pleasant impertinent of comedy, in a piece purely meant to give delight, and raise mirth out of whimsical perplexities, worries the studious man with taking up his leisure, or making his house his home, the same sort of contempt expressed (however *natural*) would destroy the balance of delight in the spectators. To make the intrusion comic, the actor who plays the annoyed man must a little desert nature; he must, in short, be thinking of the audience, and express only so much dissatisfaction and peevishness as is consistent with the pleasure of comedy. In other words, his perplexity must seem half put on. If he repel the intruder with the sober set face of a man in earnest, and more especially if he deliver his expostulations in a tone which in the world must necessarily provoke a duel, his real-life manner will destroy the whimsical and purely dramatic existence of the other character (which to render it comic demands an antagonist comicality on the part of the character opposed to it), and convert what was meant for mirth, rather than belief, into a downright piece of impertinence indeed, which would raise no diversion in us, but rather stir pain, to see inflicted in earnest upon any worthy person. A very judicious actor (in most of his parts) seems to have fallen into an error of this sort in his playing with Mr. Wrench in the farce of Free and Easy.

Many instances would be tedious: these may suffice to show that comic acting at least does not always demand from the performer that strict abstraction from all reference to an audience which is exacted of it; but that in some cases a sort of compromise may take place, and all the purposes of dramatic delight be attained by a judicious understanding, not too openly announced, between the ladies and gentlemen—on both sides of the curtain.

TO THE SHADE OF ELLISTON.

Joyousest of once embodied spirits, whither at length hast thou flown? to what genial region are we permitted to conjecture that thou hast flitted?

Art thou sowing thy WILD OATS yet (the harvest-time was still to come with thee) upon casual sands of Avernus? or art thou enacting ROVER (as we would gladlier think) by wandering Elysian streams?

This mortal frame, while thou didst play thy brief antics amongst us, was in truth anything but a prison to thee, as the vain Platonist dreams of this *body* to be no better than a county gaol, forsooth, or some house of durance vile, whereof the five senses are the fetters. Thou knewest better than to be in a hurry to cast off these gyves; and had notice to quit, I fear, before thou wert quite ready to abandon this fleshy tenement. It was thy Pleasure-House, thy Palace of Dainty Devices: thy Louvre, or thy White-Hall.

What new mysterious lodgings dost thou tenant now? or when may we expect thy aërial house-warming?

Tartarus we know, and we have read of the Blessed Shades; now cannot I intelligibly fancy thee in either.

Is it too much to hazard a conjecture, that (as the school-men admitted a receptacle apart for Patriarchs and unchrisom babes) there may exist — not far perchance from that store-house of all vanities, which Milton saw in visions,—a LIMBO somewhere for PLAYERS? and that

> Up thither like aërial vapours fly
> Both all Stage things, and all that in Stage things
> Built their fond hopes of glory, or lasting fame?
> All the unaccomplished works of Authors' hands,
> Abortive, monstrous, or unkindly mixed,
> Damn'd upon earth, fleet thither —
> Play, Opera, Farce, with all their trumpery. -

There, by the neighbouring moon (by some not improperly supposed thy Regent Planet upon earth), mayst thou not still be acting thy managerial pranks, great disembodied Lessee? but Lessee still, and still a manager.

In Green Rooms, impervious to mortal eye, the muse beholds thee wielding posthumous empire.

Thin ghosts of Figurantes (never plump on earth) circle thee in endlessly, and still their song is *Fie on sinful Phantasy!*

Magnificent were thy capriccios on this globe of earth, ROBERT WILLIAM ELLISTON! for as yet we know not thy new name in heaven.

It irks me to think, that, stript of thy regalities, thou shouldst ferry over, a poor forked shade, in crazy Stygian wherry. Methinks I hear the old boatman, paddling by the weedy wharf, with rancid voice, bawling "SCULLS, SCULLS!" to which, with waving hand, and majestic action, thou deignest no reply, other than in two curt monosyllables, "No: Oars."

But the laws of Pluto's kingdom know small difference between king and cobbler; manager and call-boy; and, if haply your dates of life were conterminant, you are quietly taking your passage, cheek by cheek (O ignoble levelling of Death) with the shade of some recently departed candle-snuffer.

But mercy! what strippings, what tearing off of histrionic robes, and private vanities! what denudations to the bone, before the surly Ferryman will admit you to set a foot within his battered lighter.

Crowns, sceptres; shield, sword, and truncheon; thy own coronation robes (for thou hast brought the whole property-man's wardrobe with thee, enough to sink a navy); the judge's ermine; the coxcomb's wig; the snuff-box *à la Foppington* —all must overboard, he positively swears —and that Ancient Mariner brooks no denial; for, since the tiresome monodrame of the old Thracian Harper, Charon, it is to be believed, hath shown small taste for theatricals.

Ay, now 'tis done. You are just boat-weight; *pura et puta anima.*

But, bless me, how *little* you look!

So shall we all look—kings and keysars—stripped for the last voyage.

But the murky rogue pushes off. Adieu pleasant, and thrice pleasant shade! with my parting thanks for many a heavy hour of life lightened by thy harmless extravaganzas, public or domestic.

Rhadamanthus, who tries the lighter causes below, leaving to his two brethren the heavy calendars—honest Rhadamanth, always partial to players, weighing their particoloured existence here upon earth,—making account of the few foibles, that may have shaded thy *real life*, as we call it (though, substantially, scarcely less a vapour than thy idlest vagaries upon the boards of the Drury), as but of so many echoes, natural re-percussions, and results to be expected from the assumed extravagancies of thy *secondary* or *mock life*, nightly upon a stage—after a lenient castigation with rods lighter than of those Medusean ringlets, but just enough to "whip the offending Adam out of thee," shall courteously dismiss thee at the right hand gate—the o. p. side of Hades—that conducts to masques and merry-makings in the Theatre Royal of Proserpine.

PLAUDITO, ET VALETO.

ELLISTONIANA.

My acquaintance with the pleasant creature, whose loss we all deplore, was but slight.

My first introduction to E., which afterwards ripened into an acquaintance a little on this side of intimacy, was over a counter in the Leamington Spa Library, then newly entered upon by a branch of his family. E., whom nothing misbecame—to auspicate, I suppose, the filial concern, and set it a-going with a lustre —was serving in person two damsels fair, who had come into the shop ostensibly to inquire for some new publication, but in reality to have a sight of the illustrious shopman, hoping some conference. With what an air did he reach down the volume, dispassionately giving his opinion of the worth of the work in question, and launching out into a dissertation on its comparative merits with those of certain publications of a similar stamp, its rivals! his enchanted customers fairly hanging on his lips, subdued to their authoritative sentence. So have I seen a gentleman in comedy *acting* the shopman. So Lovelace sold his gloves in King Street. I admired the histrionic art, by which he contrived to carry clean away every notion of disgrace, from the occupation he had so generously submitted to; and from that hour I judged him, with no after repentance, to be a person with whom it would be a felicity to be more acquainted.

To descant upon his merits as a Comedian would be superfluous. With his blended private and professional habits alone I have to do; that harmonious fusion of the manners of the player into those of every-day life, which brought the stage boards into streets and dining-parlours, and kept up the play when the play was ended.—"I like Wrench," a friend was saying to him one day, "because he is the same natural, easy creature, *on* the stage, that he is *off*." "My case exactly," retorted Elliston—with a charming forgetfulness, that the converse of a proposition does not always lead to the same conclusion—"I am the same person *off* the stage that I am *on*." The inference, at first sight, seems identical; but examine it a little, and it confesses only, that the one performer was never, and the other always, *acting*.

And in truth this was the charm of Elliston's private deportment. You had spirited performance always going on before your eyes, with nothing to pay. As where a monarch takes up his casual abode for the night, the poorest hovel which he honours by his sleeping in it, becomes *ipso facto* for that time a palace; so wherever Elliston walked, sate, or stood still, there was the theatre. He carried about with him his pit, boxes, and galleries, and set up his portable play-house at corners of streets, and in the market-places. Upon flintiest pavements he trod the boards still; and if his theme chanced to be passionate, the green baize carpet of tragedy spontaneously rose beneath his feet. Now this was hearty, and showed a love for his art. So Apelles *always* painted— in thought. So G. D. *always* poetises. I hate a lukewarm artist. I have known actors—and some of them of Elliston's own stamp—who shall have agreeably been amusing you in the part of a rake or a coxcomb, through the two or three hours of their dramatic existence; but no sooner does the curtain fall with its leaden clatter, but a spirit of lead seems to seize on all their faculties. They emerge sour, morose persons, intolerable to their families, servants, etc. Another shall have been expanding your heart with generous deeds and sentiments, till it even beats with yearnings of universal sympathy; you absolutely long to go home and do some good action. The play seems tedious, till you can get fairly out of the house, and realise your laudable intentions. At length the final bell rings, and this cordial representative of all that is amiable in human breasts steps forth—a miser. Elliston was more of a piece. Did he *play* Ranger? and did Ranger fill the general bosom of the town with satisfaction? why should *he* not be Ranger, and diffuse the same cordial satisfaction among his private circles? with *his* temperament, *his* animal spirits, *his* good nature, *his* follies perchance, could he do better than identify himself with his impersonation? Are we to like a pleasant rake, or coxcomb, on the stage, and give ourselves airs of aversion for the identical character, presented to us in actual life? or what would the performer have gained by divesting himself of the impersonation? Could the man Elliston have been essentially different from his part, even if he had avoided to reflect to us studiously, in private circles, the airy briskness, the forwardness, the 'scape-goat trickeries of the prototype?

"But there is something not natural in this everlasting *acting;* we want the real man."

Are you quite sure that it is not the man himself, whom you cannot, or will not see, under some adventitious trappings which, nevertheless, sit not at all inconsistently upon him? What if it is the nature of some men to be highly artificial? The fault is least reprehensible in *players.* Cibber was his own Foppington, with almost as much wit as Vanbrugh could add to it.

"My conceit of his person,"—it is Ben Jonson speaking of Lord Bacon,—"was never increased towards him by his *place* or *honours.* But I have, and do reverence him for the *greatness,* that was only proper to himself: in that he seemed to me ever one of the *greatest* men, that had been in many ages. In his adversity I ever prayed that Heaven would give him strength: for *greatness* he could not want."

The quality here commended was scarcely less conspicuous in the subject of these idle reminiscences than in my Lord Verulam. Those who have imagined that an unexpected elevation to the direction of a great London Theatre affected the consequence of Elliston, or at all changed his nature, knew not the essential *greatness* of the man whom they disparage. It was my fortune to encounter him near St. Dunstan's Church (which, with its punctual giants, is now no more than dust and a shadow), on the morning of his election to that high office. Grasping my hand with a look of significance, he only uttered,—"Have you heard the news?"—then, with another look following up the blow, he subjoined, "I am the future manager of Drury Lane Theatre."--Breathless as he saw me, he stayed not for congratulation or reply, but mutely stalked away, leaving me to chew upon his new-blown dignities at leisure. In fact, nothing could be said to it. Expressive silence alone could muse his praise. This was in his *great* style.

But was he less *great* (be witness, O ye powers of Equanimity, that supported in the ruins of Carthage the consular exile, and more recently transmuted, for a more illustrious exile, the barren constableship of Elba into an image of Imperial France), when, in melancholy afteryears, again, much near the same spot, I met him, when that sceptre had been wrested from his hand, and his dominion was curtailed to the petty managership, and part proprietorship, of the small Olympic, *his Elba!* He still played nightly upon the boards of Drury, but in parts, alas! allotted to him, not magnificently distributed by him. Waiving his great loss as nothing, and magnificently sinking the sense of fallen *material* grandeur in the more liberal resentment of depreciations done to his more lofty *intellectual* pretensions, "Have you heard" (his customary exordium)—"have you heard," said he, "how they treat me? they put me in *comedy*." Thought I—but his finger on his lips forbade any verbal interruption—"where could they have put you better?" Then, after a pause—"Where I formerly played Romeo, I now play Mercutio," and so again he stalked away, neither staying, nor caring for, responses.

O, it was a rich scene,—but Sir A—— C——, the best of story-tellers and surgeons, who mends a lame narrative almost as well as he sets a fracture, alone could do justice to it, that I was a witness to, in the tarnished room (that had once been green) of that same little Olympic. There, after his deposition from Imperial Drury, he substituted a throne. That Olympic Hill was his "highest heaven;" himself "Jove in his chair." There he sat in state, while before him, on complaint of prompter, was brought for judgment—how shall I describe her?—one of those little tawdry things that flirt at the tails of choruses—a probationer for the town, in either of its senses—the pertest little drab—a dirty fringe and appendage of the lamp's smoke—who, it seems, on some disapprobation expressed by a "highly respectable" audience had precipitately quitted her station on the boards, and withdrawn her small talents in disgust.

"And how dare you," said her manager,—assuming a censorial severity, which would have crushed the confidence of a Vestris, and disarmed that beautiful Rebel herself of her professional caprices—I verily believe, he thought *her* standing before him —"how dare you, Madam, withdraw yourself, without a notice, from your theatrical duties?" "I was hissed, Sir." "And you have the presumption to decide upon the taste of the town?" "I don't know that, Sir, but I will never stand to be hissed," was the subjoinder of young Confidence —when gathering up his features into one significant mass of wonder, pity, and expostulatory indignation—in a lesson never to have been lost upon a creature less forward than she who stood before him —his words were these: "They have hissed *me*."

'Twas the identical argument *à fortiori*, which the son of Peleus uses to Lycaon trembling under his lance, to persuade him to take his destiny with a good grace. "I too am mortal." And it is to be believed that in both cases the rhetoric missed of its application, for want of a proper understanding with the faculties of the respective recipients.

"Quite an Opera pit," he said to me, as he was courteously conducting me over the benches of his Surrey Theatre, the last retreat, and recess, of his every-day waning grandeur.

Those who knew Elliston, will know the *manner* in which he pronounced the latter sentence of the few words I am about to record. One proud day to me he took his roast mutton with us in the Temple, to which I had superadded a preliminary haddock. After a rather plentiful partaking of the meagre banquet, not unrefreshed with the humbler sort of liquors, I made a sort of apology for the humility of the fare, observing that for my own part I never ate but of one dish at dinner. "I too never eat but one thing at dinner,"—was his reply—then after a pause—"reckoning fish as nothing." The manner was all. It was as if by one peremptory sentence he had decreed the annihilation of all the savoury esculents, which the pleasant and nutritious-food-giving Ocean pours forth upon poor humans from her watery bosom. This was *greatness*, tempered with considerate *tenderness* to the feelings of his scanty but welcoming entertainer,

Great wert thou in thy life, Robert William Elliston! and *not lessened* in thy death, if report speak truly, which says that thou didst direct that thy mortal remains should repose under no inscription but one of pure *Latinity*. Classical was thy bringing up! and beautiful was the feeling on thy last bed, which, connecting the man with the boy, took thee back to thy latest exercise of imagination, to the days when, undreaming of Theatres and Managerships, thou wert a scholar, and an early ripe one, under the roofs builded by the munificent and pious Colet. For thee the Pauline Muses weep. In elegies, that shall silence this crude prose, they shall celebrate thy praise.

THE OLD MARGATE HOY.

I AM fond of passing my vacations (I believe I have said so before) at one or other of the Universities. Next to these my choice would fix me at some woody spot, such as the neighbourhood of Henley affords in abundance, on the banks of my beloved Thames. But somehow or other my cousin contrives to wheedle me, once in three or four seasons, to a watering-place. Old attachments cling to her in spite of experience. We have been dull at Worthing one summer, duller at Brighton another, dullest at Eastbourn a third, and are at this moment doing dreary penance at – Hastings!– and all because we were happy many years ago for a brief week at Margate. That was our first sea-side experiment, and many circumstances combined to make it the most agreeable holiday of my life. We had neither of us seen the sea, and we had never been from home so long together in company.

Can I forget thee, thou old Margate Hoy, with thy weather-beaten, sun-burnt captain, and his rough accommodations—ill exchanged for the foppery and fresh-water niceness of the modern steam-packet? To the winds and waves thou committedst thy goodly freightage, and didst ask no aid of magic fumes, and spells, and boiling caldrons. With the gales of heaven thou wentest swimmingly; or, when it was their pleasure, stoodest still with sailor-like patience. Thy course was natural, not forced, as in a hotbed; nor didst thou go poisoning the breath of ocean with sulphureous smoke—a great sea chimera, chimneying and furnacing the deep; or liker to that fire-god parching up Scamander.

Can I forget thy honest, yet slender crew, with their coy reluctant responses (yet to the suppression of anything like contempt) to the raw questions, which we of the great city would be ever and anon putting to them, as to the uses of this or that strange naval implement? 'Specially can I forget thee, thou happy medium, thou shade of refuge between us and them, conciliating interpreter of their skill to our simplicity, comfortable ambassador between sea and land!—whose sailor-trousers did not more convincingly assure thee to be an adopted denizen of the former, than thy white cap, and whiter apron over them, with thy neat-fingered practice in thy culinary vocation, bespoke thee to have been of inland nurture heretofore—a master cook of Eastcheap? How busily didst thou ply thy multifarious occupation, cook, mariner, attendant, chamberlain; here, there, like another Ariel, flaming at once about all parts of the deck, yet with kindlier ministrations—not to assist the tempest, but, as if touched with a kindred sense of our infirmities, to soothe the qualms which that untried motion might haply raise in our crude land-fancies. And when the o'erwashing billows drove us below deck (for it was far gone in October, and we had still and blowing weather), how did thy officious ministerings, still catering for our comfort, with cards, and cordials, and thy more cordial conversation, alleviate the closeness and the confinement of thy else (truth to say) not very savoury, nor very inviting, little cabin!

With these additaments to boot, we had on board a fellow-passenger, whose discourse in verity might have beguiled a longer voyage than we meditated, and have made mirth and wonder abound as far as the Azores. He was a dark, Spanish-complexioned young man, remarkably handsome, with an officer-like assurance, and an insuppressible volubility of assertion. He was, in fact, the greatest liar I had met with then, or since. He was none of your hesitating, half story-tellers (a most painful description of mortals) who go on sounding your belief, and only giving you as much as they see you can swallow at a time—the nibbling pickpockets of your patience—but one who committed downright, daylight depredations upon his neighbour's faith. He did not stand shivering upon the brink, but was a hearty, thorough-paced liar, and plunged at once into the depths of your credulity. I partly believe, he made pretty sure of his company. Not many rich, not many wise, or learned, composed at that time the common stowage of a Margate packet. We were, I am afraid, a set of as unseasoned Londoners (let our enemies give it a worse name) as Aldermanbury, or Watling Street, at that time of day could have supplied. There might be an exception or two among us, but I scorn to make any invidious distinctions among such a jolly, companionable ship's company as those were whom I sailed with. Something too must be conceded to the *Genius Loci*. Had the confident fellow told us half the legends on land which he favoured us with on the other element, I flatter myself the good sense of most of us would have revolted. But we were in a new world, with everything unfamiliar about us, and the time and place disposed us to the reception of any prodigious marvel whatsoever. Time

has obliterated from my memory much of his wild
fablings; and the rest would appear but dull, as written,
and to be read on shore. He had been Aide-de-camp
(among other rare accidents and fortunes) to a Persian
Prince, and at one blow had stricken off the head of the
King of Carimania on horseback. He, of course, married
the Prince's daughter. I forget what unlucky turn in
the politics of that court, combining with the loss of his
consort, was the reason of his quitting Persia; but, with
the rapidity of a magician, he transported himself, along
with his hearers, back to England, where we still found
him in the confidence of great ladies. There was some
story of a princess—Elizabeth, if I remember—having
intrusted to his care an extraordinary casket of jewels,
upon some extraordinary occasion—but, as I am not
certain of the name or circumstance at this distance of
time, I must leave it to the Royal daughters of England
to settle the honour among themselves in private. I
cannot call to mind half his pleasant wonders; but I
perfectly remember that, in the course of his travels, he
had seen a phœnix; and he obligingly undeceived us of
the vulgar error, that there is but one of that species at
a time, assuring us that they were not uncommon in
some parts of Upper Egypt. Hitherto he had found the
most implicit listeners. His dreaming fancies had transported us beyond the "ignorant present." But when
(still hardying more and more in his triumphs over our
simplicity) he went on to affirm that he had actually
sailed through the legs of the Colossus at Rhodes, it
really became necessary to make a stand. And here I
must do justice to the good sense and intrepidity of one
of our party, a youth, that had hitherto been one of his
most deferential auditors, who, from his recent reading,
made bold to assure the gentleman, that there must be
some mistake, as "the Colossus in question had been
destroyed long since;" to whose opinion, delivered with
all modesty, our hero was obliging enough to concede
thus much, that "the figure was indeed a little damaged."

This was the only opposition he met with, and it did not at all seem to stagger him, for he proceeded with his fables, which the same youth appeared to swallow with still more complacency than ever,—confirmed, as it were, by the extreme candour of that concession. With these prodigies he wheedled us on till we came in sight of the Reculvers, which one of our own company (having been the voyage before) immediately recognizing, and pointing out to us, was considered by us as no ordinary seaman.

All this time sat upon the edge of the deck quite a different character. It was a lad, apparently very poor, very infirm, and very patient. His eye was ever on the sea, with a smile; and, if he caught now and then some snatches of these wild legends, it was by accident, and they seemed not to concern him. The waves to him whispered more pleasant stories. He was as one being with us, but not of us. He heard the bell of dinner ring without stirring; and when some of us pulled out our private stores—our cold meat and our salads—he produced none, and seemed to want none. Only a solitary biscuit he had laid in; provision for the one or two days and nights, to which these vessels then were oftentimes obliged to prolong their voyage. Upon a nearer acquaintance with him, which he seemed neither to court nor decline, we learned that he was going to Margate, with the hope of being admitted into the Infirmary there for sea-bathing. His disease was a scrofula, which appeared to have eaten all over him. He expressed great hopes of a cure; and when we asked him whether he had any friends where he was going, he replied, "he *had* no friends."

These pleasant, and some mournful passages, with the first sight of the sea, co-operating with youth, and a sense of holidays, and out-of-door adventure, to me that had been pent up in populous cities for many months before,—have left upon my mind the fragrance as of summer days gone by, bequeathing nothing but their remembrance for cold and wintry hours to chew upon.

Will it be thought a digression (it may spare some

unwelcome comparisons) if I endeavour to account for the *dissatisfaction* which I have heard so many persons confess to have felt (as I did myself feel in part on this occasion), *at the sight of the sea for the first time?* I think the reason usually given—referring to the incapacity of actual objects for satisfying our preconceptions of them—scarcely goes deep enough into the question. Let the same person see a lion, an elephant, a mountain for the first time in his life, and he shall perhaps feel himself a little mortified. The things do not fill up that space which the idea of them seemed to take up in his mind. But they have still a correspondency to his first notion, and in time grow up to it, so as to produce a very similar impression: enlarging themselves (if I may say so) upon familiarity. But the sea remains a disappointment. Is it not, that in *the latter* we had expected to behold (absurdly, I grant, but, I am afraid, by the law of imagination, unavoidably) not a definite object, as those wild beasts, or that mountain compassable by the eye, but *all the sea at once*, THE COMMENSURATE ANTAGONIST OF THE EARTH? I do not say we tell ourselves so much, but the craving of the mind is to be satisfied with nothing less. I will suppose the case of a young person of fifteen (as I then was) knowing nothing of the sea, but from description. He comes to it for the first time—all that he has been reading of it all his life, and *that* the most enthusiastic part of life,—all he has gathered from narratives of wandering seamen,—what he has gained from true voyages, and what he cherishes as credulously from romance and poetry,—crowding their images, and exacting strange tributes from expectation.—He thinks of the great deep, and of those who go down unto it; of its thousand isles, and of the vast continents it washes; of its receiving the mighty Plata, or Orellana, into its bosom, without disturbance, or sense of augmentation; of Biscay swells, and the mariner

> For many a day, and many a dreadful night,
> Incessant labouring round the stormy Cape;

of fatal rocks, and the "still-vexed Bermoothes;" of great whirlpools, and the water-spout; of sunken ships, and sunless treasures swallowed up in the unrestoring depths; of fishes and quaint monsters, to which all that is terrible on earth—

> Be but as buggs to frighten babes withal,
> Compared with the creatures in the sea's entral;

of naked savages, and Juan Fernandez; of pearls, and shells; of coral beds, and of enchanted isles; of mermaids' grots—

I do not assert that in sober earnest he expects to be shown all these wonders at once, but he is under the tyranny of a mighty faculty, which haunts him with confused hints and shadows of all these; and when the actual object opens first upon him, seen (in tame weather, too, most likely) from our unromantic coasts—a speck, a slip of sea-water, as it shows to him—what can it prove but a very unsatisfying and even diminutive entertainment? Or if he has come to it from the mouth of a river, was it much more than the river widening? and, even out of sight of land, what had he but a flat watery horizon about him, nothing comparable to the vast o'er-curtaining sky, his familiar object, seen daily without dread or amazement?—Who, in similar circumstances, has not been tempted to exclaim with Charoba, in the poem of Gebir,

> Is this the mighty ocean? is this *all*?

I love town or country; but this detestable Cinque Port is neither. I hate these scrubbed shoots, thrusting out their starved foliage from between the horrid fissures of dusty innutritious rocks; which the amateur calls "verdure to the edge of the sea." I require woods, and they show me stunted coppices. I cry out for the water-brooks, and pant for fresh streams, and inland murmurs. I cannot stand all day on the naked beach, watching the capricious hues of the sea, shifting like the colours of a dying mullet. I am tired of looking out at the windows of this island-prison. I would fain retire into the interior of my cage. While I gaze upon the sea, I want to be on it, over it, across it. It binds me in with chains, as of iron. My thoughts are abroad. I should not so feel in Staffordshire. There is no home for me here. There is no sense of home at Hastings. It is a place of fugitive resort, an heterogeneous assemblage of sea-mews and stock-brokers, Amphitrites of the town, and misses that coquet with the Ocean. If it were what it was in its primitive shape, and what it ought to have remained, a fair, honest fishing-town, and no more, it were something—with a few straggling fishermen's huts scattered about, artless as its cliffs, and with their materials filched from them, it were something. I could abide to dwell with Meshech; to assort with fisher-swains, and smugglers. There are, or I dream there are, many of this latter occupation here. Their faces become the place. I like a smuggler. He is the only honest thief. He robs nothing but the revenue—an abstraction I never greatly cared about. I could go out with them in their mackerel boats, or about their less ostensible business, with some satisfaction. I can even tolerate those poor victims to monotony, who from day to day pace along the beach, in endless progress and recurrence, to watch their illicit countrymen—townsfolk or brethren, perchance—whistling to the sheathing and unsheathing of their cutlasses (their only solace), who, under the mild name of preventive service, keep up a legitimated civil warfare in the deplorable absence of a foreign one, to show their detestation of rum hollands, and zeal for Old England. But it is the visitants from town, that come here to *say* that they have been here, with no more relish of the sea than a pond-perch or a dace might be supposed to have, that are my aversion. I feel like a foolish dace in these regions, and have as little toleration for myself here as for them. What can they want here? If they had a true relish of the ocean, why have they brought all this land luggage with them? or why pitch their civilized tents in the desert? What mean these scanty book-rooms—marine libraries as they entitle them—if the sea were, as they would have us believe, a book "to read strange matter in"? what are their foolish concert-rooms, if they come, as they would fain be thought to do, to listen to the music of the waves? All is false and hollow pretension. They come because it is the fashion, and to spoil the nature of the place. They are, mostly, as I have said, stock-brokers; but I have watched the better sort of them —now and then, an honest citizen (of the old stamp), in the simplicity of his heart, shall bring down his wife and daughters to taste the sea breezes. I always know the date of their arrival. It is easy to see it in their countenance. A day or two they go wandering on the shingles, picking up cockle-shells, and thinking them great things; but, in a poor week, imagination slackens: they begin to discover that cockles produce no pearls, and then O then!—if I could interpret for the pretty creatures (I know they have not the courage to confess it themselves), how gladly would they exchange their sea-side rambles for a Sunday walk on the green sward of their accustomed Twickenham meadows!

I would ask one of these sea-charmed emigrants, who think they truly love the sea, with its wild usages, what would their feelings be if some of the unsophisticated aborigines of this place, encouraged by their courteous questionings here, should venture, on the faith of such assured sympathy between them, to return the visit, and come up to see—London. I must imagine them with their fishing-tackle on their back, as we carry our town necessaries. What a sensation would it cause in Lothbury! What vehement laughter would it not excite among

The daughters of Cheapside, and wives of Lombard-street!

I am sure that no town-bred or inland-born subjects can feel their true and natural nourishment at these sea-places. Nature, where she does not mean us for mariners and vagabonds, bids us stay at home. The salt foam seems to nourish a spleen. I am not half so good-natured as by the milder waters of my natural river. I would exchange these sea-gulls for swans, and send a swallow for ever about the banks of Thamesis.

THE CONVALESCENT.

A PRETTY severe fit of indisposition which, under the name of a nervous fever, has made a prisoner of me for some weeks past, and is but slowly leaving me, has reduced me to an incapacity of reflecting upon any topic foreign to itself. Expect no healthy conclusions from me this month, reader; I can offer you only sick men's dreams.

And truly the whole state of sickness is such; for what else is it but a magnificent dream for a man to lie a-bed, and draw daylight curtains about him; and, shutting out the sun, to induce a total oblivion of all the works which are going on under it? To become insensible to all the operations of life, except the beatings of one feeble pulse!

If there be a regal solitude, it is a sick-bed. How the patient lords it there; what caprices he acts without control! how king-like he sways his pillow—tumbling, and tossing, and shifting, and lowering, and thumping, and flatting, and moulding it, to the ever-varying requisitions of his throbbing temples.

He changes *sides* oftener than a politician. Now he lies full length, then half length, obliquely, transversely, head and feet quite across the bed; and none accuses him of tergiversation. Within the four curtains he is absolute. They are his Mare Clausum.

How sickness enlarges the dimensions of a man's self to himself! he is his own exclusive object. Supreme selfishness is inculcated upon him as his only duty. 'Tis the Two Tables of the Law to him. He has nothing to think of but how to get well. What passes out of doors, or within them, so he hear not the jarring of them, affects him not.

A little while ago he was greatly concerned in the event of a lawsuit, which was to be the making or the marring of his dearest friend. He was to be seen trudging about upon this man's errand to fifty quarters of the town at once, jogging this witness, refreshing that solicitor. The cause was to come on yesterday. He is absolutely as indifferent to the decision as if it were a question to be tried at Pekin. Peradventure from some whispering, going on about the house, not intended for his hearing, he picks up enough to make him understand that things went cross-grained in the court yesterday, and his friend is ruined. But the word "friend," and the word "ruin," disturb him no more than so much jargon. He is not to think of anything but how to get better.

What a world of foreign cares are merged in that absorbing consideration!

He has put on the strong armour of sickness, he is wrapped in the callous hide of suffering; he keeps his sympathy, like some curious vintage, under trusty lock and key, for his own use only.

He lies pitying himself, honing and moaning to himself; he yearneth over himself; his bowels are even melted within him, to think what he suffers; he is not ashamed to weep over himself.

He is for ever plotting how to do some good to himself; studying little stratagems and artificial alleviations.

He makes the most of himself; dividing himself, by an allowable fiction, into as many distinct individuals as he hath sore and sorrowing members. Sometimes he meditates—as of a thing apart from him—upon his poor aching head, and that dull pain which, dozing or waking, lay in it all the past night like a log, or palpable substance of pain, not to be removed without opening the very skull, as it seemed, to take it thence. Or he pities his long, clammy, attenuated fingers. He compassionates himself all over; and his bed is a very discipline of humanity, and tender heart.

He is his own sympathizer; and instinctively feels that none can so well perform that office for him. He cares for few spectators to his tragedy. Only that punctual face of the old nurse pleases him, that announces his broths and his cordials. He likes it because it is so unmoved, and because he can pour forth his feverish ejaculations before it as unreservedly as to his bed-post.

To the world's business he is dead. He understands not what the callings and occupations of mortals are; only he has a glimmering conceit of some such thing, when the doctor makes his daily call; and even in the lines on that busy face he reads no multiplicity of patients, but solely conceives of himself as *the sick man*. To what other uneasy couch the good man is hastening, when he slips out of his chamber, folding up his thin douceur so carefully, for fear of rustling—is no speculation which he can at present entertain. He thinks only of the regular return of the same phenomenon at the same hour to-morrow.

Household rumours touch him not. Some faint murmur, indicative of life going on within the house, soothes him, while he knows not distinctly what it is. He is not to know anything, not to think of anything. Servants gliding up or down the distant staircase, treading as upon velvet, gently keep his ear awake, so long as he troubles not himself further than with some feeble guess at their errands. Exacter knowledge would be a burthen to him: he can just endure the pressure of conjecture. He opens his eye faintly at the dull stroke of the muffled knocker, and closes it again without asking "Who was it?" He is flattered by a general notion that inquiries are making after him, but he cares not to know the name of the inquirer. In the general stillness, and awful hush of the house, he lies in state, and feels his sovereignty.

To be sick is to enjoy monarchal prerogatives. Compare the silent tread and quiet ministry, almost by the eye only, with which he is served—with the careless demeanour, the unceremonious goings in and out (slapping of doors, or leaving them open) of the very same attendants, when he is getting a little better—and you will confess, that from the bed of sickness (throne let me rather call it) to the elbow-chair of convalescence, is a fall from dignity, amounting to a deposition.

How convalescence shrinks a man back to his pristine stature! Where is now the space, which he occupied so lately, in his own, in the family's eye?

The scene of his regalities, his sick room, which was his presence-chamber, where he lay and acted his despotic fancies—how is it reduced to a common bedroom! The trimness of the very bed has something petty and unmeaning about it. It is *made* every day. How unlike to that wavy, many-furrowed, oceanic surface, which it presented so short a time since, when to *make* it was a service not to be thought of at oftener than three or four day revolutions, when the patient was with pain and grief to be lifted for a little while out of it, to submit to the encroachments of unwelcome neatness, and decencies which his shaken frame deprecated; then to be lifted into it again, for another three or four days' respite, to flounder it out of shape again, while every fresh furrow was an historical record of some shifting posture, some uneasy turning, some seeking for a little ease; and the shrunken skin scarce told a truer story than the crumpled coverlid.

Hushed are those mysterious sighs—those groans—so much more awful, while we knew not from what caverns of vast hidden suffering they proceeded. The Lernean pangs are quenched. The riddle of sickness is solved; and Philoctetes is become an ordinary personage.

Perhaps some relic of the sick man's dream of greatness survives in the still lingering visitations of the medical attendant. But how is he, too, changed with everything else? Can this be he—this man of news—of chat—of anecdote—of everything but physic—can this be he, who so lately came between the patient and his cruel enemy, as on some solemn embassy from Nature, erecting herself into a high mediating party?—Pshaw! 'tis some old woman.

Farewell with him all that made sickness pompous—the spell that hushed the household—the desert-like stillness, felt throughout its inmost chambers—the mute attendance—the inquiry by looks—the still softer delicacies of self-attention—the sole and single eye of distemper alonely fixed upon itself—world-thoughts excluded—the man a world unto himself—his own theatre—

What a speck is he dwindled into!

In this flat swamp of convalescence, left by the ebb of sickness, yet far enough from the terra-firma of established health, your note, dear Editor, reached me, requesting—an article. In Articulo Mortis, thought I; but it is something hard—and the quibble, wretched as it was, relieved me. The summons, unseasonable as it appeared, seemed to link me on again to the petty businesses of life, which I had lost sight of; a gentle call to activity, however trivial; a wholesome weaning from that preposterous dream of self-absorption—the puffy state of sickness—in which I confess to have lain so long, insensible to the magazines and monarchies of the world alike; to its laws, and to its literature. The hypochondriac flatus is subsiding; the acres, which in imagination I had spread over—for the sick man swells in the sole contemplation of his single sufferings, till he becomes a Tityus to himself—are wasting to a span; and for the giant of self-importance, which I was so lately, you have me once again in my natural pretensions—the lean and meagre figure of your insignificant Essayist.

SANITY OF TRUE GENIUS.

So far from the position holding true, that great wit (or genius, in our modern way of speaking) has a necessary alliance with insanity, the greatest wits, on the contrary, will ever be found to be the sanest writers. It is impossible for the mind to conceive of a mad Shakspeare. The greatness of wit, by which the poetic talent is here chiefly to be understood, manifests itself in the admirable balance of all the faculties. Madness is the disproportionate straining or excess of any one of them. "So strong a wit," says Cowley, speaking of a poetical friend,

> "- —did Nature to him frame,
> As all things but his judgment overcame;
> His judgment like the heavenly moon did show,
> Tempering that mighty sea below."

The ground of the mistake is, that men, finding in the raptures of the higher poetry a condition of exaltation, to which they have no parallel in their own experience, besides the spurious resemblance of it in dreams and fevers, impute a state of dreaminess and fever to the poet. But the true poet dreams being awake. He is not possessed by his subject, but has dominion over it. In the groves of Eden he walks familiar as in his native paths. He ascends the empyrean heaven, and is not intoxicated. He treads the burning marl without dismay; he wins his flight without self-loss through realms of chaos " and old night." Or if, abandoning himself to that severer chaos of a "human mind untuned," he is content awhile to be mad with Lear, or to hate mankind (a sort of madness) with Timon, neither is that madness, nor this misanthropy, so unchecked, but that,—never letting the reins of reason wholly go, while most he seems to do so,—he has his better genius still whispering at his ear, with the good servant Kent suggesting saner counsels, or with the honest steward Flavius recommending kindlier resolutions. Where he seems most to recede from humanity, he will be found the truest to it. From beyond the scope of Nature if he summon possible existences, he subjugates them to the law of her consistency. He is beautifully loyal to that sovereign directress, even when he appears most to betray and desert her. His ideal tribes submit to policy; his very monsters are tamed to his hand, even as that wild sea-brood, shepherded by Proteus. He tames, and he clothes them with attributes of flesh and blood, till they wonder at themselves, like Indian Islanders forced to submit to European vesture. Caliban, the Witches, are as true to the laws of their own nature (ours with a difference), as Othello, Hamlet, and Macbeth. Herein the great and the little wits are differenced; that if the latter wander ever so little from nature or actual existence, they lose themselves and their readers. Their phantoms are lawless; their visions nightmares. They do not create, which implies shaping and consistency. Their imaginations are not active—for to be active is to call something into act and form—but passive, as men in sick dreams. For the super-natural, or something super-added to what we know of nature, they give you the plainly non-natural. And if this were all, and that these mental hallucinations were discoverable only in the treatment of subjects out of nature, or transcending it, the judgment might with some plea be pardoned if it ran riot, and a little wantonized: but even in the describing of real and every-day life, that which is before their eyes, one of these lesser wits shall more deviate from nature—show more of that inconsequence, which has a natural alliance with frenzy,—than a great genius in his "maddest fits," as Wither somewhere calls them. We appeal to any one that is acquainted with the common run of Lane's novels, as they existed some twenty or thirty years back,—those scanty intellectual viands of the whole female reading public, till a happier genius arose, and expelled for ever the innutritious phantoms,—whether he has not found his brain more "betossed," his memory more puzzled, his sense of when and where more confounded, among the improbable events, the incoherent incidents, the inconsistent characters, or no characters, of some third-rate love-intrigue—where the persons shall be a Lord Glendamour and a Miss Rivers, and the scene only alternate between Bath and Bond Street—a more bewildering dreaminess induced upon him than he has felt wandering over all the fairy-grounds of Spenser. In the productions we refer to, nothing but names and places is familiar; the persons are neither of this world nor of any other conceivable one; an endless stream of activities without purpose, of purposes destitute of motive:—we meet phantoms in our known walks; *fantasques* only christened. In the poet we have names which announce fiction; and we have absolutely no place at all, for the things and persons of the Fairy Queen prate not of their "whereabout." But in their inner nature, and the law of their speech and actions, we are at home, and upon acquainted ground. The one turns life into a dream; the other to the wildest dreams gives the sobrieties of everyday occurrences. By what subtle art of tracing the mental processes it is effected, we are not philosophers enough to explain, but in that wonderful episode of the cave of Mammon, in which the Money God appears first in the lowest form of a miser, is then a worker of metals, and becomes the god of all the treasures of the world; and has a daughter, Ambition, before whom all the world kneels for favours—with the Hesperian fruit, the waters of Tantalus, with Pilate washing his hands vainly, but not impertinently, in the same stream—that we should be at one moment in the cave of an old hoarder of treasures, at the next at the forge of the Cyclops, in a palace and yet in hell, all at once, with the shifting mutations of the most rambling dream, and our judgment yet all the time awake, and neither able nor willing to detect the fallacy,—is a proof of that hidden sanity which still guides the poet in the wildest seeming-aberrations.

It is not enough to say that the whole episode is a copy of the mind's conceptions in sleep; it is, in some sort —but what a copy! Let the most romantic of us, that has been entertained all night with the spectacle of some wild and magnificent vision, recombine it in the morning, and try it by his waking judgment. That which appeared so shifting, and yet so coherent, while that faculty was passive, when it comes under cool examination shall appear so reasonless and so unlinked, that we are ashamed to have been so deluded; and to have taken, though but in sleep, a monster for a god. But the transitions in this episode are every whit as violent as in the most extravagant dream, and yet the waking judgment ratifies them.

CAPTAIN JACKSON.

AMONG the deaths in our obituary for this month, I observe with concern "At his cottage on the Bath Road, Captain Jackson." The name and attribution are common enough; but a feeling like reproach persuades me that this could have been no other in fact than my dear old friend, who some five-and-twenty years ago rented a tenement, which he was pleased to dignify with the appellation here used, about a mile from Westbourn Green. Alack, how good men, and the good turns they do us, slide out of memory, and are recalled but by the surprise of some such sad memento as that which now lies before us!

He whom I mean was a retired half-pay officer, with a wife and two grown-up daughters, whom he maintained with the port and notions of gentlewomen upon that slender professional allowance. Comely girls they were, too.

And was I in danger of forgetting this man?--his cheerful suppers—the noble tone of hospitality, when first you set your foot in *the cottage*—the anxious ministerings about you, where little or nothing (God knows) was to be ministered.—Althea's horn in a poor platter—the power of self-enchantment, by which, in his magnificent wishes to entertain you, he multiplied his means to bounties.

You saw with your bodily eyes indeed what seemed a bare scrag—cold savings from the foregone meal—remnant hardly sufficient to send a mendicant from the door contented. But in the copious will—the revelling imagination of your host—the "mind, the mind, Master Shallow," whole beeves were spread before you—hecatombs—no end appeared to the profusion.

It was the widow's cruse—the loaves and fishes; carving could not lessen, nor helping diminish it—the stamina were left—the elemental bones still flourished, divested of its accidents.

"Let us live while we can," methinks I hear the openhanded creature exclaim; "while we have, let us not want," "here is plenty left;" "want for nothing"—with many more such hospitable sayings, the spurs of appetite, and old concomitants of smoking boards and feast-oppressed chargers. Then sliding a slender ratio of Single Gloucester upon his wife's plate, or the daughters', he would convey the remanent rind into his own, with a merry quirk of "the nearer the bone," etc., and declaring that he universally preferred the outside. For we had our table distinctions, you are to know, and some of us in a manner sate above the salt. None but his guest or guests dreamed of tasting flesh luxuries at night, the fragments were *veré hospitibus sacra*. But of one thing or another there was always enough, and leavings: only he would sometimes finish the remainder crust, to show that he wished no savings.

Wine we had none; nor, except on very rare occasions, spirits; but the sensation of wine was there. Some thin kind of ale I remember—"British beverage," he would say! "Push about, my boys;" "Drink to your sweethearts, girls." At every meagre draught a toast must ensue, or a song. All the forms of good liquor were there, with none of the effects wanting. Shut your eyes, and you would swear a capacious bowl of punch was foaming in the centre, with beams of generous Port or Madeira radiating to it from each of the table corners. You got flustered, without knowing whence; tipsy upon words; and reeled under the potency of his unperforming Bacchanalian encouragements.

We had our songs—" Why, Soldiers, why,"—and the " British Grenadiers "—in which last we were all obliged to bear chorus. Both the daughters sang. Their proficiency was a nightly theme—the masters he had given them—the " no-expense" which he spared to accomplish them in a science " so necessary to young women." But then—they could not sing " without the instrument."

Sacred, and, by me, never-to-be-violated, secrets of Poverty! Should I disclose your honest aims at grandeur, your makeshift efforts of magnificence? Sleep, sleep, with all thy broken keys, if one of the bunch be extant; thrummed by a thousand ancestral thumbs; dear, cracked spinnet of dearer Louisa! Without mention of mine, be dumb, thou thin accompanier of her thinner warble! A veil be spread over the dear delighted face of the well-deluded father, who now haply listening to cherubic notes, scarce feels sincerer pleasure than when she awakened thy time-shaken chords responsive to the twitterings of that slender image of a voice.

We were not without our literary talk either. It did not extend far, but as far as it went it was good. It was bottomed well; had good grounds to go upon. In *the cottage* was a room, which tradition authenticated to have been the same in which Glover, in his occasional retirements, had penned the greater part of his Leonidas. This circumstance was nightly quoted, though none of the present inmates, that I could discover, appeared ever to have met with the poem in question. But that was no matter. Glover had written there, and the anecdote was pressed into the account of the family importance. It diffused a learned air through the apartment, the little side casement of which (the poet's study window), opening upon a superb view as far as the pretty spire of Harrow, over domains and patrimonial acres, not a rood nor square yard whereof our host could call his own, yet gave occasion to an immoderate expansion of — vanity shall I call it? — in his bosom, as he showed them in a glowing summer evening. It was all his, he took it all in, and communicated rich portions of it to his guests. It was a part of his largess, his hospitality; it was going over his grounds; he was lord for the time of showing them, and you the implicit lookers-up to his magnificence.

He was a juggler, who threw mists before your eyes — you had no time to detect his fallacies. He would say, "Hand me the *silver* sugar-tongs;" and before you could discover it was a single spoon, and that *plated*, he would disturb and captivate your imagination by a misnomer of "the urn" for a tea-kettle; or by calling a homely bench a sofa. Rich men direct you to their furniture, poor ones divert you from it; he neither did one nor the other, but by simply assuming that everything was handsome about him, you were positively at a demur what you did, or did not see, at *the cottage*. With nothing to live on, he seemed to live on everything. He had a stock of wealth in his mind; not that which is properly termed *Content*, for in truth he was not to be *contained* at all, but overflowed all bounds by the force of a magnificent self-delusion.

Enthusiasm is catching; and even his wife, a sober native of North Britain, who generally saw things more as they were, was not proof against the continual collision of his credulity. Her daughters were rational and discreet young women; in the main, perhaps, not insensible to their true circumstances. I have seen them assume a thoughtful air at times. But such was the preponderating opulence of his fancy, that I am persuaded not for my half hour together did they ever look their own prospects fairly in the face. There was no resisting the vortex of his temperament. His riotous imagination

s

conjured up handsome settlements before their eyes, which kept them up in the eye of the world too, and seem at last to have realized themselves; for they both have married since, I am told, more than respectably.

It is long since, and my memory waxes dim on some subjects, or I should wish to convey some notion of the manner in which the pleasant creature described the circumstances of his own wedding-day. I faintly remember something of a chaise-and-four, in which he made his entry into Glasgow on that morning to fetch the bride home, or carry her thither, I forget which. It so completely made out the stanza of the old ballad —

> When we came down through Glasgow town,
>   We were a comely sight to see;
> My love was clad in black velvet,
>   And I myself in cramasie.

I suppose it was the only occasion upon which his own actual splendour at all corresponded with the world's notions on that subject. In homely cart, or travelling caravan, by whatever humble vehicle they chanced to be transported in less prosperous days, the ride through Glasgow came back upon his fancy, not as a humiliating contrast, but as a fair occasion for reverting to that one day's state. It seemed an "equipage etern" from which no power of fate or fortune, once mounted, had power thereafter to dislodge him.

There is some merit in putting a handsome face upon indigent circumstances. To bully and swagger away the sense of them before strangers, may not be always discommendable. Tibbs, and Bobadil, even when detected, have more of our admiration than contempt. But for a man to put the cheat upon himself; to play the Bobadil at home; and, steeped in poverty up to the lips, to fancy himself all the while chin-deep in riches, is a strain of constitutional philosophy, and a mastery over fortune, which was reserved for my old friend Captain Jackson.

THE SUPERANNUATED MAN.

> Sera tamen respexit
> Libertas.   VIRGIL.
> A Clerk I was in London gay.—O'KEEFE.

IF peradventure, Reader, it has been thy lot to waste the golden years of thy life—thy shining youth—in the irksome confinement of an office; to have thy prison days prolonged through middle age down to decrepitude and silver hairs, without hope of release or respite; to have lived to forget that there are such things as holidays, or to remember them but as the prerogatives of childhood; then, and then only, will you be able to appreciate my deliverance.

It is now six-and-thirty years since I took my seat at the desk in Mincing Lane. Melancholy was the transition at fourteen from the abundant playtime, and the frequently-intervening vacations of school days, to the eight, nine, and sometimes ten hours' a-day attendance at the counting-house. But time partially reconciles us to anything. I gradually became content—doggedly contented, as wild animals in cages.

It is true I had my Sundays to myself; but Sundays, admirable as the institution of them is for purposes of worship, are for that very reason the very worst adapted for days of unbending and recreation. In particular, there is a gloom for me attendant upon a city Sunday, a weight in the air. I miss the cheerful cries of London, the music, and the ballad-singers—the buzz and stirring murmur of the streets. Those eternal bells depress me. The closed shops repel me. Prints, pictures, all the glittering and endless succession of knacks and gewgaws, and ostentatiously displayed wares of tradesmen, which make a weekday saunter through the

less busy parts of the metropolis so delightful—are shut
out. No book-stalls deliciously to idle over—no busy
faces to recreate the idle man who contemplates them
ever passing by—the very face of business a charm by
contrast to his temporary relaxation from it. Nothing to
be seen but unhappy countenances—or half-happy at best
—of emancipated 'prentices and little tradesfolks, with
here and there a servant-maid that has got leave to go
out, who, slaving all the week, with the habit has lost
almost the capacity of enjoying a free hour; and livelily
expressing the hollowness of a day's pleasuring. The
very strollers in the fields on that day look anything but
comfortable.

But besides Sundays, I had a day at Easter, and a
day at Christmas, with a full week in the summer to go
and air myself in my native fields of Hertfordshire.
This last was a great indulgence; and the prospect of its
recurrence, I believe, alone kept me up through the year,
and made my durance tolerable. But when the week
came round, did the glittering phantom of the distance
keep touch with me, or rather was it not a series of
seven uneasy days, spent in restless pursuit of pleasure,
and a wearisome anxiety to find out how to make the
most of them? Where was the quiet, where the promised
rest? Before I had a taste of it, it was vanished. I
was at the desk again, counting upon the fifty-one tedious
weeks that must intervene before such another snatch
would come. Still the prospect of its coming threw
something of an illumination upon the darker side of my
captivity. Without it, as I have said, I could scarcely
have sustained my thraldom.

Independently of the rigours of attendance, I have ever
been haunted with a sense (perhaps a mere caprice) of
incapacity for business. This, during my latter years,
had increased to such a degree, that it was visible in all
the lines of my countenance. My health and my good
spirits flagged. I had perpetually a dread of some
crisis, to which I should be found unequal. Besides

my daylight servitude, I served over again all night
in my sleep, and would awake with terrors of imaginary
false entries, errors in my accounts, and the like. I
was fifty years of age, and no prospect of emancipation
presented itself. I had grown to my desk, as it were;
and the wood had entered into my soul.

My fellows in the office would sometimes rally me
upon the trouble legible in my countenance; but I did
not know that it had raised the suspicions of any of my
employers, when, on the fifth of last month, a day ever
to be remembered by me, L——, the junior partner in
the firm, calling me on one side, directly taxed me with
my bad looks, and frankly inquired the cause of them.
So taxed, I honestly made confession of my infirmity,
and added that I was afraid I should eventually be
obliged to resign his service. He spoke some words of
course to hearten me, and there the matter rested. A
whole week I remained labouring under the impression
that I had acted imprudently in my disclosure; that I
had foolishly given a handle against myself, and had been
anticipating my own dismissal. A week passed in this
manner--the most anxious one, I verily believe, in my
whole life—when on the evening of the 12th of April,
just as I was about quitting my desk to go home (it
might be about eight o'clock), I received an awful summons to attend the presence of the whole assembled firm
in the formidable back parlour. I thought now my time
is surely come, I have done for myself, I am going to be
told that they have no longer occasion for me. L——,
I could see, smiled at the terror I was in, which was
a little relief to me,—when to my utter astonishment
B——, the eldest partner, began a formal harangue to
me on the length of my services, my very meritorious
conduct during the whole of the time (the deuce, thought
I, how did he find out that? I protest I never had the
confidence to think as much). He went on to descant
on the expediency of retiring at a certain time of life,
(how my heart panted!) and asking me a few questions as

to the amount of my own property, of which I have a little, ended with a proposal, to which his three partners nodded a grave assent, that I should accept from the house, which I had served so well, a pension for life to the amount of two-thirds of my accustomed salary—a magnificent offer! I do not know what I answered between surprise and gratitude, but it was understood that I accepted their proposal, and I was told that I was free from that hour to leave their service. I stammered out a bow, and at just ten minutes after eight I went home —for ever. This noble benefit—gratitude forbids me to conceal their names—I owe to the kindness of the most munificent firm in the world—the house of Boldero, Merryweather, Bosanquet, and Lacy.

Esto perpetua!

For the first day or two I felt stunned—overwhelmed. I could only apprehend my felicity; I was too confused to taste it sincerely. I wandered about, thinking I was happy, and knowing that I was not. I was in the condition of a prisoner in the old Bastile, suddenly let loose after a forty years' confinement. I could scarce trust myself with myself. It was like passing out of Time into Eternity—for it is a sort of Eternity for a man to have all his Time to himself. It seemed to me that I had more time on my hands than I could ever manage. From a poor man, poor in Time, I was suddenly lifted up into a vast revenue; I could see no end of my possessions; I wanted some steward, or judicious bailiff, to manage my estates in Time for me. And here let me caution persons grown old in active business, not lightly, nor without weighing their own resources, to forego their customary employment all at once, for there may be danger in it. I feel it by myself, but I know that my resources are sufficient; and now that those first giddy raptures have subsided, I have a quiet home-feeling of the blessedness of my condition. I am in no hurry. Having all holidays, I am as though I had none. If Time hung heavy upon me, I could walk it away; but I do *not* walk all day long, as I used to do in those old transient holidays, thirty miles a day, to make the most of them. If Time were troublesome, I could read it away; but I do *not* read in that violent measure, with which, having no Time my own but candlelight Time, I used to weary out my head and eyesight in bygone winters. I walk, read, or scribble (as now) just when the fit seizes me. I no longer hunt after pleasure; I let it come to me. I am like the man

——————— that's born, and has his years come to him,
In some green desert.

"Years!" you will say: "what is this superannuated simpleton calculating upon? He has already told us he is past fifty."

I have indeed lived nominally fifty years, but deduct out of them the hours which I have lived to other people, and not to myself, and you will find me still a young fellow. For *that* is the only true Time, which a man can properly call his own—that which he has all to himself; the rest, though in some sense he may be said to live it, is other people's Time, not his. The remnant of my poor days, long or short, is at least multiplied for me threefold. My ten next years, if I stretch so far, will be as long as any preceding thirty. 'Tis a fair rule-of-three sum.

Among the strange fantasies which beset me at the commencement of my freedom, and of which all traces are not yet gone, one was, that a vast tract of time had intervened since I quitted the Counting House. I could not conceive of it as an affair of yesterday. The partners, and the clerks with whom I had for so many years, and for so many hours in each day of the year, been closely associated—being suddenly removed from them—they seemed as dead to me. There is a fine passage, which may serve to illustrate this fancy, in a Tragedy by Sir Robert Howard, speaking of a friend's death :—

>   ——— - 'Twas but just now he went away;
>   I have not since had time to shed a tear;
>   And yet the distance does the same appear
>   As if he had been a thousand years from me.
>   Time takes no measure in Eternity.

To dissipate this awkward feeling, I have been fain to go among them once or twice since; to visit my old desk-fellows—my co-brethren of the quill—that I had left below in the state militant. Not all the kindness with which they received me could quite restore to me that pleasant familiarity, which I had heretofore enjoyed among them. We cracked some of our old jokes, but methought they went off but faintly. My old desk; the peg where I hung my hat, were appropriated to another. I knew it must be, but I could not take it kindly. D——l take me, if I did not feel some remorse—beast, if I had not—at quitting my old compeers, the faithful partners of my toils for six-and-thirty years, that soothed for me with their jokes and conundrums the ruggedness of my professional road. Had it been so rugged then, after all? or was I a coward simply? Well, it is too late to repent; and I also know that these suggestions are a common fallacy of the mind on such occasions. But my heart smote me. I had violently broken the bands betwixt us. It was at least not courteous. I shall be some time before I get quite reconciled to the separation. Farewell, old cronies, yet not for long, for again and again I will come among ye, if I shall have your leave. Farewell, Ch——, dry, sarcastic, and friendly! Do——, mild, slow to move, and gentlemanly! Pl——, officious to do, and to volunteer, good services!—and thou, thou dreary pile, fit mansion for a Gresham or a Whittington of old, stately house of Merchants; with thy labyrinthine passages, and light-excluding, pent-up offices, where candles for one-half the year supplied the place of the sun's light; unhealthy contributor to my weal, stern fosterer of my living, farewell! In thee remain, and not in the obscure collection of some wandering bookseller, my "works!" There let them rest, as I do from my labours, piled on thy massy shelves, more MSS. in folio than ever Aquinas left, and full as useful! My mantle I bequeath among ye.

A fortnight has passed since the date of my first communication. At that period I was approaching to tranquillity, but had not reached it. I boasted of a calm indeed, but it was comparative only. Something of the first flutter was left; an unsettling sense of novelty; the dazzle to weak eyes of unaccustomed light. I missed my old chains, forsooth, as if they had been some necessary part of my apparel. I was a poor Carthusian, from strict cellular discipline suddenly by some revolution returned upon the world. I am now as if I had never been other than my own master. It is natural for me to go where I please, to do what I please. I find myself at 11 o'clock in the day in Bond Street, and it seems to me that I have been sauntering there at that very hour for years past. I digress into Soho, to explore a bookstall. Methinks I have been thirty years a collector. There is nothing strange nor new in it. I find myself before a fine picture in the morning. Was it ever otherwise? What is become of Fish Street Hill? Where is Fenchurch Street? Stones of old Mincing Lane, which I have worn with my daily pilgrimage for six-and-thirty years, to the footsteps of what toil-worn clerk are your everlasting flints now vocal? I indent the gayer flags of Pall Mall. It is 'Change time, and I am strangely among the Elgin marbles. It was no hyperbole when I ventured to compare the change in my condition to passing into another world. Time stands still in a manner to me. I have lost all distinction of season. I do not know the day of the week or of the month. Each day used to be individually felt by me in its reference to the foreign post days; in its distance from, or propinquity to, the next Sunday. I had my Wednesday feelings, my Saturday nights' sensations. The genius of each day was upon me distinctly during the whole of it, affecting my appetite, spirits, etc. The phantom of the next day, with the dreary five to follow, sate as a load upon my poor Sabbath recreations. What charm has washed that Ethiop white? What is gone of Black Monday? All days are the same. Sunday itself—that unfortunate failure of a holiday, as it too often proved, what with my sense of its fugitiveness, and over-care to get the greatest quantity of pleasure out of it—is melted down into a week-day. I can spare to go to church now, without grudging the huge cantle which it used to seem to cut out of the holiday. I have time for everything. I can visit a sick friend. I can interrupt the man of much occupation when he is busiest. I can insult over him with an invitation to take a day's pleasure with me to Windsor this fine May-morning. It is Lucretian pleasure to behold the poor drudges, whom I have left behind in the world, carking and caring; like horses in a mill, drudging on in the same eternal round—and what is it all for? A man can never have too much Time to himself, nor too little to do. Had I a little son, I would christen him NOTHING-TO-DO; he should do nothing. Man, I verily believe, is out of his element as long as he is operative. I am altogether for the life contemplative. Will no kindly earthquake come and swallow up those accursed cotton-mills? Take me that lumber of a desk there, and bowl it down

As low as to the fiends.

I am no longer ******, clerk to the Firm of, etc. I am Retired Leisure. I am to be met with in trim gardens. I am already come to be known by my vacant face and careless gesture, perambulating at no fixed pace, nor with any settled purpose. I walk about; not to and from. They tell me, a certain *cum dignitate* air, that has been buried so long with my other good parts, has begun to shoot forth in my person. I grow into gentility perceptibly. When I take up a newspaper, it is to read the state of the opera. *Opus operatum est.* I have done all that I came into this world to do. I have worked task-work, and have the rest of the day to myself.

THE GENTEEL STYLE IN WRITING.

It is an ordinary criticism, that my Lord Shaftesbury and Sir William Temple are models of the genteel style in writing. We should prefer saying—of the lordly, and the gentlemanly. Nothing can be more unlike, than the inflated finical rhapsodies of Shaftesbury and the plain natural chit-chat of Temple. The man of rank is discernible in both writers; but in the one it is only insinuated gracefully, in the other it stands out offensively. The peer seems to have written with his coronet on, and his Earl's mantle before him; the commoner in his elbow-chair and undress.—What can be more pleasant than the way in which the retired statesman peeps out in his essays, penned by the latter in his delightful retreat at Shene? They scent of Nimeguen and the Hague. Scarce an authority is quoted under an ambassador. Don Francisco de Melo, a "Portugal Envoy in England," tells him it was frequent in his country for men, spent with age and other decays, so as they could not hope for above a year or two of life, to ship themselves away in a Brazil fleet, and after their arrival there to go on a great length, sometimes of twenty or thirty years, or more, by the force of that vigour they recovered with that remove. "Whether such an effect (Temple beautifully adds) might grow from the air, or the fruits of that climate, or by approaching nearer the sun, which is the fountain of light and heat, when their natural heat was so far decayed; or whether the piecing out of an old man's life were worth the pains; I cannot tell: perhaps the play is not worth the candle." Monsieur

Pompone, " French Ambassador in his (Sir William's) time at the Hague," certifies him, that in his life he had never heard of any man in France that arrived at a hundred years of age ; a limitation of life which the old gentleman imputes to the excellence of their climate, giving them such a liveliness of temper and humour, as disposes them to more pleasures of all kinds than in other countries ; and moralizes upon the matter very sensibly. The " late Robert Earl of Leicester " furnishes him with a story of a Countess of Desmond, married out of England in Edward the Fourth's time, and who lived far in King James's reign. The " same noble person " gives him an account, how such a year, in the same reign, there went about the country a set of morrice-dancers, composed of ten men who danced, a Maid Marian, and a tabor and pipe ; and how these twelve, one with another, made up twelve hundred years. " It was not so much (says Temple) that so many in one small county (Hertfordshire) should live to that age, as that they should be in vigour and in humour to travel and to dance." Monsieur Zulichem, one of his " colleagues at the Hague," informs him of a cure for the gout ; which is confirmed by another " Envoy," Monsieur Serinchamps, in that town, who had tried it. Old Prince Maurice of Nassau recommends to him the use of hammocks in that complaint ; having been allured to sleep, while suffering under it himself, by the " constant motion or swinging of those airy beds." Count Egmont, and the Rhinegrave who " was killed last summer before Maestricht," impart to him their experiences.

But the rank of the writer is never more innocently disclosed, than where he takes for granted the compliments paid by foreigners to his fruit-trees. For the taste and perfection of what we esteem the best, he can truly say, that the French, who have eaten his peaches and grapes at Shene in no very ill year, have generally concluded that the last are as good as any they have eaten in France on this side Fontainebleau ; and the first as good as any they have eat in Gascony. Italians have agreed his white figs to be as good as any of that sort in Italy, which is the earlier kind of white fig there; for in the latter kind and the blue, we cannot come near the warm climates, no more than in the Frontignac or Muscat grape. His orange-trees, too, are as large as any he saw when he was young in France, except those of Fontainebleau; or what he had seen since in the Low Countries, except some very old ones of the Prince of Orange's. Of grapes he had the honour of bringing over four sorts into England, which he enumerates, and supposes that they are all by this time pretty common among some gardeners in his neighbourhood, as well as several persons of quality: for he ever thought all things of this kind "the commoner they are made the better." The garden pedantry with which he asserts that 'tis to little purpose to plant any of the best fruits, as peaches or grapes, hardly, he doubts, beyond Northamptonshire at the farthest northwards; and praises the "Bishop of Munster at Cosevelt," for attempting nothing beyond cherries in that cold climate; is equally pleasant and in character. "I may perhaps" (he thus ends his sweet Garden Essay with a passage worthy of Cowley) " be allowed to know something of this trade, since I have so long allowed myself to be good for nothing else, which few men will do, or enjoy their gardens, without often looking abroad to see how other matters play, what motions in the state, and what invitations they may hope for into other scenes. For my own part, as the country life, and this part of it more particularly, were the inclination of my youth itself, so they are the pleasures of my age; and I can truly say that, among many great employments that have fallen to my share, I have never asked or sought for any of them, but have often endeavoured to escape from them, into the ease and freedom of a private scene, where a man may go his own way and his own pace in the common paths and circles of life. The measure of choosing well is whether a man likes what he has chosen, which, I thank God, has befallen me; and though among the follies of my life, building and planting have not been the least, and have cost me more than I have the confidence to own; yet they have been fully recompensed by the sweetness and satisfaction of this retreat, where, since my resolution taken of never entering again into any public employments, I have passed five years without ever once going to town, though I am almost in sight of it, and have a house there always ready to receive me. Nor has this been any sort of affectation, as some have thought it, but a mere want of desire or humour to make so small a remove; for when I am in this corner I can truly say with Horace, *Me quoties reficit*, etc.

> ' Me, when the cold Digentian stream revives,
> What does my friend believe I think or ask?
> Let me yet less possess, so I may live,
> Whate'er of life remains, unto myself.
> May I have books enough; and one year's store,
> Not to depend upon each doubtful hour:
> This is enough of mighty Jove to pray,
> Who, as he pleases, gives and takes away.' "

The writings of Temple are, in general, after this easy copy. On one occasion, indeed, his wit, which was mostly subordinate to nature and tenderness, has seduced him into a string of felicitous antitheses; which, it is obvious to remark, have been a model to Addison and succeeding essayists. "Who would not be covetous, and with reason," he says, "if health could be purchased with gold? who not ambitious, if it were at the command of power, or restored by honour? but, alas! a white staff will not help gouty feet to walk better than a common cane; nor a blue ribband bind up a wound so well as a fillet. The glitter of gold, or of diamonds, will but hurt sore eyes instead of curing them; and an aching head will be no more eased by wearing a crown than a common nightcap." In a far better style, and more accordant with his own humour of plainness, are the concluding sentences of his "Discourse upon Poetry." Temple took a part in the controversy about the ancient and the modern learning; and, with that partiality so natural and so graceful in an old man, whose state engagements had left him little leisure to look into modern productions, while his retirement gave him occasion to look back upon the classic studies of his youth—decided in favour of the latter. "Certain it is," he says, "that, whether the fierceness of the Gothic humours, or noise of their perpetual wars, frighted it away, or that the unequal mixture of the modern languages would not bear it—the great heights and excellency both of poetry and music fell with the Roman learning and empire, and have never since recovered the admiration and applauses that before attended them. Yet, such as they are amongst us, they must be confessed to be the softest and the sweetest, the most general and most innocent amusements of common time and life. They still find room in the courts of princes, and the cottages of shepherds. They serve to revive and animate the dead calm of poor and idle lives, and to allay or divert the violent passions and perturbations of the greatest and the busiest men. And both these effects are of equal use to human life; for the mind of man is like the sea, which is neither agreeable to the beholder nor the voyager, in a calm or in a storm, but is so to both when a little agitated by gentle gales; and so the mind, when moved by soft and easy passions or affections. I know very well that many who pretend to be wise by the forms of being grave, are apt to despise both poetry and music, as toys and trifles too light for the use or entertainment of serious men. But whoever find themselves wholly insensible to their charms, would, I think, do well to keep their own counsel, for fear of reproaching their own temper, and bringing the goodness of their natures, if not of their understandings, into question. While this world lasts, I doubt not but the pleasure and request of these two entertainments will do so too; and happy those that content themselves with these, or any other so easy and so innocent, and do not trouble the world or other men, because they cannot be quiet themselves, though nobody hurts them." "When all is done (he concludes), human life is at the greatest and the best but like a froward child, that must be played with, and humoured a little, to keep it quiet, till it falls asleep, and then the care is over."

BARBARA S——.

ON the noon of the 14th of November, 1743 or 4, I forget which it was, just as the clock had struck one, Barbara S——, with her accustomed punctuality, ascended the long rambling staircase, with awkward interposed landing-places, which led to the office, or rather a sort of box with a desk in it, whereat sat the then treasurer of (what few of our readers may remember) the old Bath Theatre. All over the island it was the custom, and remains so I believe to this day, for the players to receive their weekly stipend on the Saturday. It was not much that Barbara had to claim.

The little maid had just entered her eleventh year; but her important station at the theatre, as it seemed to her, with the benefits which she felt to accrue from her pious application of her small earnings, had given an air of womanhood to her steps and to her behaviour. You would have taken her to have been at least five years older.

Till latterly she had merely been employed in choruses, or where children were wanted to fill up the scene. But the manager, observing a diligence and adroitness in her above her age, had for some few months past intrusted to her the performance of whole parts. You may guess the self-consequence of the promoted Barbara. She had already drawn tears in young Arthur; had rallied Richard with infantine petulance in the Duke of York; and in her turn had rebuked that petulance when she was Prince of Wales. She would have done the elder child in Morton's pathetic afterpiece to the life; but as yet the "Children in the Wood" was not.

Long after this little girl was grown an aged woman, I have seen some of these small parts, each making two or three pages at most, copied out in the rudest hand of the then prompter, who doubtless transcribed a little more carefully and fairly for the grown-up tragedy ladies of the establishment. But such as they were, blotted and scrawled, as for a child's use, she kept them all; and in the zenith of her after reputation it was a delightful sight to behold them bound up in costliest morocco, each single —each small part making a *book*—with fine clasps, gilt-splashed, etc. She had conscientiously kept them as they had been delivered to her; not a blot had been effaced or tampered with. They were precious to her for their affecting remembrancings. They were her principia, her rudiments; the elementary atoms; the little steps by which she pressed forward to perfection. "What," she would say, "could India-rubber, or a pumice-stone, have done for these darlings?"

I am in no hurry to begin my story—indeed, I have little or none to tell—so I will just mention an observation of hers connected with that interesting time.

Not long before she died I had been discoursing with her on the quantity of real present emotion which a great tragic performer experiences during acting. I ventured to think, that though in the first instance such players must have possessed the feelings which they so powerfully called up in others, yet by frequent repetition those feelings must become deadened in great measure, and the performer trust to the memory of past emotion, rather than express a present one. She indignantly repelled the notion, that with a truly great tragedian the operation, by which such effects were produced upon an audience, could ever degrade itself into what was purely mechanical. With much delicacy, avoiding to instance in her *self*-ex-

T

perience, she told me, that so long ago as when she used to play the part of the Little Son to Mrs. Porter's Isabella (I think it was), when that impressive actress has been bending over her in some heart-rending colloquy, she has felt real hot tears come trickling from her, which (to use her powerful expression) have perfectly scalded her back.

I am not quite so sure that it was Mrs. Porter; but it was some great actress of that day. The name is indifferent; but the fact of the scalding tears I most distinctly remember.

I was always fond of the society of players, and am not sure that an impediment in my speech (which certainly kept me out of the pulpit), even more than certain personal disqualifications, which are often got over in that profession, did not prevent me at one time of life from adopting it. I have had the honour (I must ever call it) once to have been admitted to the tea-table of Miss Kelly. I have played at serious whist with Mr. Liston. I have chatted with ever good-humoured Mrs. Charles Kemble. I have conversed as friend to friend with her accomplished husband. I have been indulged with a classical conference with Macready; and with a sight of the Player-picture gallery, at Mr. Mathews's, when the kind owner, to remunerate me for my love of the old actors (whom he loves so much), went over it with me, supplying to his capital collection, what alone the artist could not give them—voice; and their living motion. Old tones, half-faded, of Dodd, and Parsons, and Baddeley, have lived again for me at his bidding. Only Edwin he could not restore to me. I have supped with ——; but I am growing a coxcomb.

As I was about to say—at the desk of the then treasurer of the old Bath Theatre— not Diamond's—presented herself the little Barbara S--   .

The parents of Barbara had been in reputable circumstances. The father had practised, I believe, as an apothecary in the town. But his practice, from causes which I feel my own infirmity too sensibly that way to arraign—or perhaps from that pure infelicity which accompanies some people in their walk through life, and which it is impossible to lay at the door of imprudence—was now reduced to nothing. They were, in fact, in the very teeth of starvation, when the manager, who knew and respected them in better days, took the little Barbara into his company.

At the period I commenced with, her slender earnings were the sole support of the family, including two younger sisters. I must throw a veil over some mortifying circumstances. Enough to say, that her Saturday's pittance was the only chance of a Sunday's (generally their only) meal of meat.

One thing I will only mention, that in some child's part, where in her theatrical character she was to sup off a roast fowl (O joy to Barbara!) some comic actor, who was for the night caterer for this dainty—in the misguided humour of his part, threw over the dish such a quantity of salt (O grief and pain of heart to Barbara!) that when he crammed a portion of it into her mouth, she was obliged sputteringly to reject it; and what with shame of her ill-acted part, and pain of real appetite at missing such a dainty, her little heart sobbed almost to breaking, till a flood of tears, which the well-fed spectators were totally unable to comprehend, mercifully relieved her.

This was the little starved, meritorious maid, who stood before old Ravenscroft, the treasurer, for her Saturday's payment.

Ravenscroft was a man, I have heard many old theatrical people besides herself say, of all men least calculated for a treasurer. He had no head for accounts, paid away at random, kept scarce any books, and summing up at the week's end, if he found himself a pound or so deficient, blest himself that it was no worse.

Now Barbara's weekly stipend was a bare half-guinea. By mistake he popped into her hand—a whole one.

Barbara tripped away.

She was entirely unconscious at first of the mistake—
God knows, Ravenscroft would never have discovered it.

But when she had got down to the first of those uncouth landing-places, she became sensible of an unusual weight of metal pressing in her little hand.

Now mark the dilemma.

She was by nature a good child. From her parents and those about her, she had imbibed no contrary influence. But then they had taught her nothing. Poor men's smoky cabins are not always porticoes of moral philosophy. This little maid had no instinct to evil, but then she might be said to have no fixed principle. She had heard honesty commended, but never dreamed of its application to herself. She thought of it as something which concerned grown-up people, men and women. She had never known temptation, or thought of preparing resistance against it.

Her first impulse was to go back to the old treasurer, and explain to him his blunder. He was already so confused with age, besides a natural want of punctuality, that she would have had some difficulty in making him understand it. She saw *that* in an instant. And then it was such a bit of money! and then the image of a larger allowance of butcher's meat on their table the next day came across her, till her little eyes glistened, and her mouth moistened. But then Mr. Ravenscroft had always been so good-natured, had stood her friend behind the scenes, and even recommended her promotion to some of her little parts. But again the old man was reputed to be worth a world of money. He was supposed to have fifty pounds a-year clear of the theatre. And then came staring upon her the figures of her little stockingless and shoeless sisters. And when she looked at her own neat white cotton stockings, which her situation at the theatre had made it indispensable for her mother to provide for her, with hard straining and pinching from the family stock, and thought how glad she should be to cover their poor feet with the same—and how then they could accompany her to rehearsals, which they had hitherto been precluded from doing, by reason of their unfashionable attire,—in these thoughts she reached the second landing-place—the second, I mean, from the top—for there was still another left to traverse.

Now virtue support Barbara!

And that never-failing friend *did* step in—for at that moment a strength not her own, I have heard her say, was revealed to her—a reason above reasoning—and without her own agency, as it seemed (for she never felt her feet to move), she found herself transported back to the individual desk she had just quitted, and her hand in the old hand of Ravenscroft, who in silence took back the refunded treasure, and who had been sitting (good man) insensible to the lapse of minutes, which to her were anxious ages, and from that moment a deep peace fell upon her heart, and she knew the quality of honesty.

A year or two's unrepining application to her profession brightened up the feet and the prospects of her little sisters, set the whole family upon their legs again, and released her from the difficulty of discussing moral dogmas upon a landing-place.

I have heard her say that it was a surprise, not much short of mortification to her, to see the coolness with which the old man pocketed the difference, which had caused her such mortal throes.

This anecdote of herself I had in the year 1800, from the mouth of the late Mrs. Crawford,[1] then sixty-seven years of age (she died soon after); and to her struggles upon this childish occasion I have sometimes ventured to think her indebted for that power of rending the heart in the representation of conflicting emotions, for which in after years she was considered as little inferior (if at all so in the part of Lady Randolph) even to Mrs. Siddons.

---

[1] The maiden name of this lady was Street, which she changed, by successive marriages, for those of Dancer, Barry, and Crawford. She was Mrs. Crawford, a third time a widow, when I knew her.

THE TOMBS IN THE ABBEY.

IN A LETTER TO R—— S——, ESQ.

THOUGH in some points of doctrine, and perhaps of discipline, I am diffident of lending a perfect assent to that church which you have so worthily *historified*, yet may the ill time never come to me, when with a chilled heart or a portion of irreverent sentiment, I shall enter her beautiful and time-hallowed Edifices. Judge, then, of my mortification when, after attending the choral anthems of last Wednesday at Westminster, and being desirous of renewing my acquaintance, after lapsed years, with the tombs and antiquities there, I found myself excluded; turned out, like a dog, or some profane person, into the common street, with feelings not very congenial to the place, or to the solemn service which I had been listening to. It was a jar after that music.

You had your education at Westminster; and doubtless among those dim aisles and cloisters, you must have gathered much of that devotional feeling in those young years, on which your purest mind feeds still—and may it feed! The antiquarian spirit, strong in you, and gracefully blending ever with the religious, may have been sown in you among those wrecks of splendid mortality. You owe it to the place of your education; you owe it to your learned fondness for the architecture of your ancestors; you owe it to the venerableness of your ecclesiastical establishment, which is daily lessened and called in question through these practices—to speak aloud your sense of them; never to desist raising your voice against them, till they be totally done away with and abolished; till the doors of Westminster Abbey be no longer closed against the decent, though low-in-purse, enthusiast, or blameless devotee, who must commit an injury against his family economy, if he would be indulged with a bare admission within its walls. You owe it to the decencies which you wish to see maintained in its impressive services, that our cathedral be no longer an object of inspection to the poor at those times only, in which they must rob from their attendance on the worship every minute which they can bestow upon the fabric. In vain the public prints have taken up this subject,—in vain such poor, nameless writers as myself express their indignation. A word from you, sir,—a hint in your Journal—would be sufficient to fling open the doors of the Beautiful Temple again, as we can remember them when we were boys. At that time of life, what would the imaginative faculty (such as it is) in both of us, have suffered, if the entrance to so much reflection had been obstructed by the demand of so much silver! -If we had scraped it up to gain an occasional admission (as we certainly should have done), would the sight of those old tombs have been as impressive to us (while we have been weighing anxiously prudence against sentiment) as when the gates stood open as those of the adjacent park; when we could walk in at any time, as the mood brought us, for a shorter or longer time, as that lasted? Is the being shown over a place the same as silently for ourselves detecting the genius of it? In no part of our beloved Abbey now can a person find entrance (out of service-time) under the sum of *two shillings*. The rich and the great will smile at the anti-climax, presumed to lie in these two short words. But you can tell them, sir, how much quiet worth, how much capacity for enlarged feeling, how much taste and genius, may coexist, especially in youth, with a purse incompetent to this demand. A respected friend of ours, during his late visit to the metropolis, presented himself for admission to St. Paul's. At the same time a decently-clothed man, with as decent a wife and child, were bargaining for the same indulgence. The price was only two-pence each person. The poor but decent man hesitated, desirous to go in; but there were three of them, and he turned away reluctantly.

Perhaps he wished to have seen the tomb of Nelson. Perhaps the Interior of the Cathedral was his object. But in the state of his finances, even sixpence might reasonably seem too much. Tell the Aristocracy of the country (no man can do it more impressively); instruct them of what value these insignificant pieces of money, these minims to their sight, may be to their humbler brethren. Shame these Sellers out of the Temple. Stifle not the suggestions of your better nature with the pretext, that an indiscriminate admission would expose the Tombs to violation. Remember your boy-days. Did you ever see, or hear, of a mob in the Abbey, while it was free to all? Do the rabble come there, or trouble their heads about such speculations? It is all that you can do to drive them into your churches; they do not voluntarily offer themselves. They have, alas! no passion for antiquities; for tomb of king or prelate, sage or poet. If they had, they would be no longer the rabble.

For forty years that I have known the Fabric, the only well-attested charge of violation adduced has been—a ridiculous dismemberment committed upon the effigy of that amiable spy, Major André. And is it for this—the wanton mischief of some school-boy, fired perhaps with raw notions of Transatlantic Freedom—or the remote possibility of such a mischief occurring again, so easily to be prevented by stationing a constable within the walls, if the vergers are incompetent to the duty—is it upon such wretched pretences that the people of England are made to pay a new Peter's Pence, so long abrogated; or must content themselves with contemplating the ragged Exterior of their Cathedral? The mischief was done about the time that you were a scholar there. Do you know anything about the unfortunate relic?—

AMICUS REDIVIVUS.

Where were ye, Nymphs, when the remorseless deep
Closed o'er the head of your loved Lycidas?

I DO not know when I have experienced a stranger sensation than on seeing my old friend, G. D., who had been paying me a morning visit, a few Sundays back, at my cottage at Islington, upon taking leave, instead of turning down the right-hand path by which he had entered— with staff in hand, and at noonday, deliberately march right forwards into the midst of the stream that runs by us, and totally disappear.

A spectacle like this at dusk would have been appalling enough; but in the broad, open daylight, to witness such an unreserved motion towards self-destruction in a valued friend, took from me all power of speculation.

How I found my feet I know not. Consciousness was quite gone. Some spirit, not my own, whirled me to the spot. I remember nothing but the silvery apparition of a good white head emerging; nigh which a staff (the hand unseen that wielded it) pointed upwards, as feeling for the skies. In a moment (if time was in that time) he was on my shoulders, and I—freighted with a load more precious than his who bore Anchises.

And here I cannot but do justice to the officious zeal of sundry passers-by, who, albeit arriving a little too late to participate in the honours of the rescue, in philanthropic shoals came thronging to communicate their advice as to the recovery; prescribing variously the application, or non-application, of salt, etc., to the person of the patient. Life, meantime, was ebbing fast away, amidst the stifle of conflicting judgments, when one, more sagacious than the rest, by a bright thought, proposed sending for the Doctor. Trite as the counsel was, and impossible, as one should think, to be missed on,—

shall I confess?—in this emergency it was to me as if an
Angel had spoken. Great previous exertions—and mine
had not been inconsiderable—are commonly followed by a
debility of purpose. This was a moment of irresolution.

MONOCULUS—for so, in default of catching his true
name, I choose to designate the medical gentleman who
now appeared—is a grave, middle-aged person, who,
without having studied at the college, or truckled to the
pedantry of a diploma, hath employed a great portion of
his valuable time in experimental processes upon the
bodies of unfortunate fellow-creatures, in whom the vital
spark, to mere vulgar thinking, would seem extinct and
lost for ever. He omitteth no occasion of obtruding his
services, from a case of common surfeit suffocation to the
ignobler obstructions, sometimes induced by a too wilful
application of the plant *cannabis* outwardly. But though
he declineth not altogether these drier extinctions, his
occupation tendeth, for the most part, to water-practice;
for the convenience of which, he hath judiciously fixed
his quarters near the grand repository of the stream
mentioned, where day and night, from his little watch-
tower, at the Middleton's Head, he listeneth to detect
the wrecks of drowned mortality—partly, as he saith, to
be upon the spot—and partly, because the liquids which
he useth to prescribe to himself and his patients, on these
distressing occasions, are ordinarily more conveniently to
be found at these common hostelries than in the shops
and phials of the apothecaries. His ear hath arrived to
such finesse by practice, that it is reported he can distinguish a plunge, at half a furlong distance; and can
tell if it be casual or deliberate. He weareth a medal,
suspended over a suit, originally of a sad brown, but
which, by time and frequency of nightly divings, has
been dinged into a true professional sable. He passeth
by the name of Doctor, and is remarkable for wanting
his left eye. His remedy—after a sufficient application
of warm blankets, friction, etc., is a simple tumbler, or
more, of the purest Cognac, with water, made as hot as

the convalescent can bear it. Where he findeth, as in the case of my friend, a squeamish subject, he condescendeth to be the taster; and showeth, by his own example, the innocuous nature of the prescription. Nothing can be more kind or encouraging than this procedure. It addeth confidence to the patient, to see his medical adviser go hand in hand with himself in the remedy. When the doctor swalloweth his own draught, what peevish invalid can refuse to pledge him in the potion? In fine, MONOCULUS is a humane, sensible man, who, for a slender pittance, scarce enough to sustain life, is content to wear it out in the endeavour to save the lives of others—his pretensions so moderate, that with difficulty I could press a crown upon him, for the price of restoring the existence of such an invaluable creature to society as G. D.

It was pleasant to observe the effect of the subsiding alarm upon the nerves of the dear absentee. It seemed to have given a shake to memory, calling up notice after notice, of all the providential deliverances he had experienced in the course of his long and innocent life. Sitting up on my couch—my couch which, naked and void of furniture hitherto, for the salutary repose which it administered, shall be honoured with costly valance, at some price, and henceforth be a state-bed at Colebrook, —he discoursed of marvellous escapes—by carelessness of nurses—by pails of gelid, and kettles of the boiling element, in infancy—by orchard pranks, and snapping twigs, in schoolboy frolics—by descent of tiles at Trumpington, and of heavier tomes at Pembroke—by studious watchings, inducing frightful vigilance—by want, and the fear of want, and all the sore throbbings of the learned head. Anon, he would burst out into little fragments of chanting—of songs long ago—ends of deliverance hymns, not remembered before since childhood, but coming up now, when his heart was made tender as a child's—for the *tremor cordis*, in the retrospect of a recent deliverance, as in a case of impending danger, acting upon an innocent heart, will produce a self-tenderness, which we should do ill to christen cowardice; and Shakspeare, in the latter crisis, has made his good Sir Hugh to remember the sitting by Babylon, and to mutter of shallow rivers.

Waters of Sir Hugh Middleton—what a spark you were like to have extinguished for ever! Your salubrious streams to this City, for now near two centuries, would hardly have atoned for what you were in a moment washing away. Mockery of a river—liquid artifice—wretched conduit! henceforth rank with canals and sluggish aqueducts. Was it for this that, smit in boyhood with the explorations of that Abyssinian traveller, I paced the vales of Amwell to explore your tributary springs, to trace your salutary waters sparkling through green Hertfordshire, and cultured Enfield parks?—Ye have no swans—no Naïads—no river God—or did the benevolent hoary aspect of my friend tempt ye to suck him in, that ye also might have the tutelary genius of your waters?

Had he been drowned in Cam, there would have been some consonancy in it; but what willows had ye to wave and rustle over his moist sepulture?—or, having no *name*, besides that unmeaning assumption of *eternal novity*, did ye think to get one by the noble prize, and henceforth to be termed the STREAM DYERIAN?

> And could such spacious virtue find a grave
> Beneath the imposthumed bubble of a wave?

I protest, George, you shall not venture out again—no, not by daylight—without a sufficient pair of spectacles—in your musing moods especially. Your absence of mind we have borne, till your presence of body came to be called in question by it. You shall not go wandering into Euripus with Aristotle, if we can help it. Fie, man, to turn dipper at your years, after your many tracts in favour of sprinkling only!

I have nothing but water in my head o'nights since this frightful accident. Sometimes I am with Clarence in his dream. At others, I behold Christian beginning to sink, and crying out to his good brother Hopeful (that is, to me), "I sink in deep waters; the billows go over my head, all the waves go over me. Selah." Then I have before me Palinurus, just letting go the steerage. I cry out too late to save. Next follow—a mournful procession—*suicidal faces*, saved against their will from drowning; dolefully trailing a length of reluctant gratefulness, with ropy weeds pendent from locks of watchet hue—constrained Lazari—Pluto's half-subjects—stolen fees from the grave—bilking Charon of his fare. At their head Arion—or is it G. D.?—in his singing garments marcheth singly, with harp in hand, and votive garland, which Machaon (or Dr. Hawes) snatcheth straight, intending to suspend it to the stern God of Sea. Then follow dismal streams of Lethe, in which the half-drenched on earth are constrained to drown downright, by wharfs where Ophelia twice acts her muddy death.

And, doubtless, there is some notice in that invisible world when one of us approacheth (as my friend did so lately) to their inexorable precincts. When a soul knocks once, twice, at Death's door, the sensation aroused within the palace must be considerable; and the grim Feature, by modern science so often dispossessed of his prey, must have learned by this time to pity Tantalus.

A pulse assuredly was felt along the line of the Elysian shades, when the near arrival of G. D. was announced by no equivocal indications. From their seats of Asphodel arose the gentler and the graver ghosts—poet, or historian —of Grecian or of Roman lore—to crown with unfading chaplets the half-finished love-labours of their unwearied scholiast. Him Markland expected—him Tyrwhitt hoped to encounter—him the sweet lyrist of Peter House, whom he had barely seen upon earth,[1] with newest airs prepared to greet ——; and patron of the gentle Christ's boy, who should have been his patron through life—the mild Askew, with longing aspirations leaned foremost from his

[1] GRAIUM *tantum vidit.*

venerable Æsculapian chair, to welcome into that happy company the matured virtues of the man, whose tender scions in the boy he himself upon earth had so prophetically fed and watered.

SOME SONNETS OF SIR PHILIP SYDNEY.

SYDNEY'S SONNETS—I speak of the best of them—are among the very best of their sort. They fall below the plain moral dignity, the sanctity, and high yet modest spirit of self-approval, of Milton, in his compositions of a similar structure. They are in truth what Milton, censuring the Arcadia, says of that work (to which they are a sort of after-tune or application), "vain and amatorious" enough, yet the things in their kind (as he confesses to be true of the romance) may be "full of worth and wit." They savour of the Courtier, it must be allowed, and not of the Commonwealthsman. But Milton was a Courtier when he wrote the Masque at Ludlow Castle, and still more a Courtier when he composed the Arcades. When the national struggle was to begin, he becomingly cast these vanities behind him; and if the order of time had thrown Sir Philip upon the crisis which preceded the revolution, there is no reason why he should not have acted the same part in that emergency, which has glorified the name of a later Sydney. He did not want for plainness or boldness of spirit. His letter on the French match may testify he could speak his mind freely to Princes. The times did not call him to the scaffold.

The Sonnets which we oftenest call to mind of Milton were the compositions of his maturest years. Those of Sydney, which I am about to produce, were written in the very heyday of his blood. They are stuck full of amorous fancies—far-fetched conceits, befitting his occupation; for True Love thinks no labour to send out

Thoughts upon the vast and more than Indian voyages, to bring home rich pearls, outlandish wealth, gums, jewels, spicery, to sacrifice in self-depreciating similitudes, as shadows of true amiabilities in the Beloved. We must be Lovers—or at least the cooling touch of time, the *circum præcordia frigus*, must not have so damped our faculties, as to take away our recollection that we were once so—before we can duly appreciate the glorious vanities and graceful hyperboles of the passion. The images which lie before our feet (though by some accounted the only natural) are least natural for the high Sydnean love to express its fancies by. They may serve for the loves of Tibullus, or the dear Author of the Schoolmistress; for passions that creep and whine in Elegies and Pastoral Ballads. I am sure Milton never loved at this rate. I am afraid some of his addresses (*ad Leonoram* I mean) have rather erred on the farther side; and that the poet came not much short of a religious indecorum, when he could thus apostrophize a singing-girl:—

> Angelus unicuique suus (sic credite gentes)
>   Obtigit æthereis ales ab ordinibus.
> Quid mirum, Leonora, tibi si gloria major,
>   Nam tua præsentem vox sonat ipsa Deum?
> Aut Deus, aut vacui certè mens tertia cœli
>   Per tua secretò guttura serpit agens;
> Serpit agens, facilisque docet mortalia corda
>   Sensim immortali assuescere posse sono.
> QUOD SI CUNCTA QUIDEM DEUS EST, PER CUNCTAQUE FUSUS,
> IN TE UNA LOQUITUR, CÆTERA MUTUS HABET.

This is loving in a strange fashion; and it requires some candour of construction (besides the slight darkening of a dead language) to cast a veil over the ugly appearance of something very like blasphemy in the last two verses. I think the Lover would have been staggered if he had gone about to express the same thought in English. I am sure Sydney has no flights like this. His extravaganzas do not strike at the sky, though he takes leave to adopt the pale Dian into a fellowship with his mortal passions.

I.

> With how sad steps, O Moon, thou climb'st the skies
> How silently; and with how wan a face!
> What! may it be, that even in heavenly place
> That busy Archer his sharp arrow tries?
> Sure, if that long-with-love-acquainted eyes
> Can judge of love, thou feel'st a lover's case;
> I read it in thy looks; thy languisht grace
> To me, that feel the like, thy state descries.
> Then, even of fellowship, O Moon, tell me,
> Is constant love deem'd there but want of wit?
> Are beauties there as proud as here they be?
> Do they above love to be loved, and yet
> Those lovers scorn, whom that love doth possess?
> Do they call *virtue* there—*ungratefulness!*

The last line of this poem is a little obscured by transposition. He means, Do they call ungratefulness there a virtue?

II.

> Come, Sleep, O Sleep, the certain knot of peace,
> The baiting-place of wit, the balm of woe,
> The poor man's wealth, the prisoner's release,
> The indifferent judge between the high and low;
> With shield of proof shield me from out the prease[1]
> Of those fierce darts despair at me doth throw;
> O make in me those civil wars to cease:
> I will good tribute pay if thou do so.
> Take thou of me sweet pillows, sweetest bed;
> A chamber deaf to noise, and blind to light;
> A rosy garland, and a weary head.
> And if these things, as being thine by right,
> Move not thy heavy grace, thou shalt in me,
> Livelier than elsewhere, STELLA's image see.

III.

> The curious wits, seeing dull pensiveness
> Bewray itself in my long-settled eyes,

---

[1] Press.

Whence those same fumes of melancholy rise,
With idle pains, and missing aim, do guess.
Some, that know how my spring I did address,
Deem that my Muse some fruit of knowledge plies.
Others, because the Prince my service tries,
Think, that I think state errors to redress ;
But harder judges judge, ambition's rage,
Scourge of itself, still climbing slippery place,
Holds my young brain captiv'd in golden cage.
O fools, or over-wise ! alas, the race
Of all my thoughts hath neither stop nor start,
But only STELLA's eyes, and STELLA's heart.

IV.

Because I oft in dark abstracted guise
Seem most alone in greatest company,
With dearth of words, or answers quite awry,
To them that would make speech of speech arise ;
They deem, and of their doom the rumour flies,
That poison foul of bubbling *Pride* doth lie
So in my swelling breast, that only I
Fawn on myself, and others do despise ;
Yet *Pride*, I think, doth not my soul possess,
Which looks too oft in his unflattering glass ;
But one worse fault—*Ambition*—I confess,
That makes me oft my best friends overpass,
Unseen, unheard—while Thought to highest place
Bends all his powers, even unto STELLA's grace.

V.

Having this day, my horse, my hand, my lance,
Guided so well that I obtained the prize,
Both by the judgment of the English eyes,
And of some sent from that *sweet enemy*,—France ;
Horsemen my skill in horsemanship advance ;
Townsfolk my strength ; a daintier judge applies
His praise to sleight, which from good use doth rise ;
Some lucky wits impute it but to chance ;
Others, because of both sides I do take
My blood from them, who did excel in this,
Think Nature me a man of arms did make.
How far they shot awry ! the true cause is,
STELLA look'd on, and from her heavenly face
Sent forth the beams which made so fair my race.

VI.

In martial sports I had my cunning tried,
And yet to break more staves did me address,
While with the people's shouts (I must confess)
Youth, luck, and praise, even fill'd my veins with pride—
When Cupid having me (his slave) descried
In Mars' livery, prancing in the press,
"What now, Sir Fool!" said he; "I would no less:
Look here, I say." I look'd, and STELLA spied,
Who hard by made a window send forth light.
My heart then quaked, then dazzled were mine eyes;
One hand forgot to rule, th' other to fight;
Nor trumpet's sound I heard, nor friendly cries.
My foe came on, and beat the air for me—
Till that her blush made me my shame to see.

VII.

No more, my dear, no more these counsels try;
O give my passions leave to run their race;
Let Fortune lay on me her worst disgrace;
Let folk o'ercharged with brain against me cry;
Let clouds bedim my face, break in mine eye;
Let me no steps, but of lost labour, trace;
Let all the earth with scorn recount my case—
But do not will me from my love to fly.
I do not envy Aristotle's wit,
Nor do aspire to Cæsar's bleeding fame;
Nor aught do care, though some above me sit;
Nor hope, nor wish, another course to frame,
But that which once may win thy cruel heart:
Thou art my wit, and thou my virtue art.

VIII.

LOVE still a boy, and oft a wanton, is,
School'd only by his mother's tender eye:
What wonder, then, if he his lesson miss,
When for so soft a rod dear play he try?
And yet my STAR, because a sugar'd kiss
In sport I suck'd, while she asleep did lie,
Doth lour, nay chide, nay threat, for only this.
Sweet, it was saucy LOVE, not humble I.
But no 'scuse serves; she makes her wrath appear
In Beauty's throne—see now who dares come near

Those scarlet judges, threat'ning bloody pain?
O heav'nly Fool, thy most kiss-worthy face
Anger invests with such a lovely grace,
That anger's self I needs must kiss again.

IX.

I never drank of Aganippe well,
Nor ever did in shade of Tempe sit,
And Muses scorn with vulgar brains to dwell;
Poor lay-man I, for sacred rites unfit.
Some do I hear of Poet's fury tell,
But (God wot) wot not what they mean by it;
And this I swear by blackest brook of hell,
I am no pick-purse of another's wit.
How falls it then, that with so smooth an ease
My thoughts I speak, and what I speak doth flow
In verse, and that my verse best wits doth please?
Guess me the cause—what is it thus?—fye, no!
Or so?—much less. How then? sure thus it is,
My lips are sweet, inspir'd with STELLA's kiss.

X.

Of all the kings that ever here did reign,
Edward, named Fourth, as first in praise I name.
Not for his fair outside, nor well-lined brain—
Although less gifts imp feathers oft on Fame.
Nor that he could, young-wise, wise-valiant, frame
His sire's revenge, join'd with a kingdom's gain;
And, gain'd by Mars could yet mad Mars so tame,
That Balance weigh'd what Sword did late obtain
Nor that he made the Floure-de-luce so 'fraid,
Though strongly hedged of bloody Lions' paws,
That witty Lewis to him a tribute paid.
Nor this, nor that, nor any such small cause—
But only, for this worthy knight durst prove
To lose his crown rather than fail his love.

XI.

O happy Thames, that didst my STELLA bear,
I saw thyself, with many a smiling line
Upon thy cheerful face, Joy's livery wear,
While those fair planets on thy streams did shine.

>The boat for joy could not to dance forbear,
>While wanton winds, with beauty so divine
>Ravish'd, stay'd not, till in her golden hair
>They did themselves (O sweetest prison) twine.
>And fain those Æol's youth there would their stay
>Have made ; but, forced by nature still to fly,
>First did with puffing kiss those locks display.
>She, so dishevell'd, blush'd ; from window I
>With sight thereof cried out, O fair disgrace,
>Let Honour's self to thee grant highest place !

XII.

>Highway, since you my chief Parnassus be ;
>And that my Muse, to some ears not unsweet,
>Tempers her words to trampling horses' feet,
>More soft than to a chamber melody ;
>Now blessed You bear onward blessed Me
>To Her, where I my heart safe left shall meet,
>My Muse and I must you of duty greet
>With thanks and wishes, wishing thankfully.
>Be you still fair, honour'd by public heed,
>By no encroachment wrong'd, nor time forgot ;
>Nor blamed for blood, nor shamed for sinful deed.
>And that you know, I envy you no lot
>Of highest wish, I wish you so much bliss,
>Hundreds of years you STELLA's feet may kiss.

Of the foregoing, the first, the second, and the last sonnet, are my favourites. But the general beauty of them all is, that they are so perfectly characteristical. The spirit of "learning and of chivalry,"—of which union, Spenser has entitled Sydney to have been the "president,"—shines through them. I confess I can see nothing of the "jejune" or "frigid" in them ; much less of the "stiff" and "cumbrous"—which I have sometimes heard objected to the Arcadia. The verse runs off swiftly and gallantly. It might have been tuned to the trumpet ; or tempered (as himself expresses it) to "trampling horses' feet." They abound in felicitous phrases—

>O heav'nly Fool, thy most kiss-worthy face
>>*8th Sonnet.*

———— Sweet pillows, sweetest bed ;
A chamber deaf to noise, and blind to light ;
A rosy garland, and a weary head.
                                    2d *Sonnet.*

———— That sweet enemy,—France—
                                    5th *Sonnet.*

But they are not rich in words only, in vague and unlocalised feelings—the failing too much of some poetry of the present day—they are full, material, and circumstantiated. Time and place appropriates every one of them. It is not a fever of passion wasting itself upon a thin diet of dainty words, but a transcendent passion pervading and illuminating action, pursuits, studies, feats of arms, the opinions of contemporaries, and his judgment of them. An historical thread runs through them, which almost affixes a date to them; marks the *when* and *where* they were written.

I have dwelt the longer upon what I conceive the merit of these poems, because I have been hurt by the wantonness (I wish I could treat it by a gentler name) with which W. H. takes every occasion of insulting the memory of Sir Philip Sydney. But the decisions of the Author of Table Talk, etc. (most profound and subtle where they are, as for the most part, just), are more safely to be relied upon, on subjects and authors he has a partiality for, than on such as he has conceived an accidental prejudice against. Milton wrote sonnets, and was a king-hater; and it was congenial perhaps to sacrifice a courtier to a patriot. But I was unwilling to lose a *fine idea* from my mind. The noble images, passions, sentiments, and poetical delicacies of character, scattered all over the Arcadia (spite of some stiffness and encumberment), justify to me the character which his contemporaries have left us of the writer. I cannot think with the *Critic*, that Sir Philip Sydney was that *opprobrious thing* which a foolish nobleman in his insolent hostility chose to term him. I call to mind the epitaph made on him, to guide me to juster thoughts of him; and I repose upon the beautiful lines in the "Friend's Passion for his Astrophel," printed with the Elegies of Spenser and others.

> You knew—who knew not Astrophel?
> (That I should live to say I knew,
> And have not in possession still!)—
> Things known permit me to renew—
>   Of him you know his merit such,
>   I cannot say—you hear—too much.
>
> Within these woods of Arcady
> He chief delight and pleasure took;
> And on the mountain Partheny,
> Upon the crystal liquid brook,
>   The Muses met him every day,
>   That taught him sing, to write, and say.
>
> When he descended down the mount,
> His personage seemed most divine:
> A thousand graces one might count
> Upon his lovely cheerful eyne.
>   To hear him speak, and sweetly smile,
>   You were in Paradise the while.
>
> *A sweet attractive kind of grace;*
> *A full assurance given by looks;*
> *Continual comfort in a face,*
> *The lineaments of Gospel books—*
>   I trow that count'nance cannot lye,
>   Whose thoughts are legible in the eye.
>
>   *   *   *   *   *
>
> Above all others this is he,
> Which erst approved in his song,
> That love and honour might agree,
> And that pure love will do no wrong.
>   Sweet saints, it is no sin or blame
>   To love a man of virtuous name.
>
> Did never love so sweetly breathe
> In any mortal breast before;
> Did never Muse inspire beneath
> A Poet's brain with finer store!
>   He wrote of Love with high conceit,
>   And Beauty rear'd above her height.

Or let any one read the deeper sorrows (grief running

into rage) in the Poem,—the last in the collection accompanying the above,—which from internal testimony I believe to be Lord Brooke's—beginning with "Silence augmenteth grief," and then seriously ask himself, whether the subject of such absorbing and confounding regrets could have been *that thing* which Lord Oxford termed him.

NEWSPAPERS THIRTY-FIVE YEARS AGO.

DAN STUART once told us, that he did not remember that he ever deliberately walked into the Exhibition at Somerset House in his life. He might occasionally have escorted a party of ladies across the way that were going in, but he never went in of his own head. Yet the office of the *Morning Post* newspaper stood then just where it does now—we are carrying you back, reader, some thirty years or more—with its gilt-globe-topt front facing that emporium of our artists' grand Annual Exposure. We sometimes wish that we had observed the same abstinence with Daniel.

A word or two of D. S. He ever appeared to us one of the finest-tempered of Editors. Perry, of the *Morning Chronicle*, was equally pleasant, with a dash, no slight one either, of the courtier. S. was frank, plain, and English all over. We have worked for both these gentlemen.

It is soothing to contemplate the head of the Ganges; to trace the first little bubblings of a mighty river,

> With holy reverence to approach the rocks,
> Whence glide the streams renowned in ancient song.

Fired with a perusal of the Abyssinian Pilgrim's exploratory ramblings after the cradle of the infant Nilus, we well remember on one fine summer holyday (a "whole day's leave" we called it at Christ's hospital) sallying forth at rise of sun, not very well provisioned either for such an undertaking, to trace the current of the New River—Middletonian stream!—to its scaturient source, as we had read, in meadows by fair Amwell. Gallantly did we commence our solitary quest—for it was essential to the dignity of a DISCOVERY, that no eye of schoolboy, save our own, should beam on the detection. By flowery spots, and verdant lanes skirting Hornsey, Hope trained us on in many a baffling turn; endless, hopeless meanders, as it seemed; or as if the jealous waters had *dodged* us, reluctant to have the humble spot of their nativity revealed: till spent, and nigh famished, before set of the same sun, we sate down somewhere by Bowes Farm near Tottenham, with a tithe of our proposed labours only yet accomplished; sorely convinced in spirit, that that Brucian enterprise was as yet too arduous for our young shoulders.

Not more refreshing to the thirsty curiosity of the traveller is the tracing of some mighty waters up to their shallow fontlet, than it is to a pleased and candid reader to go back to the inexperienced essays, the first callow flights in authorship, of some established name in literature; from the Gnat which preluded to the Æneid, to the Duck which Samuel Johnson trod on.

In those days, every Morning Paper, as an essential retainer to its establishment, kept an author, who was bound to furnish daily a quantum of witty paragraphs. Sixpence a joke—and it was thought pretty high too—was Dan Stuart's settled remuneration in these cases. The chat of the day—scandal, but, above all, *dress*—furnished the material. The length of no paragraph was to exceed seven lines. Shorter they might be, but they must be poignant.

A fashion of *flesh*, or rather *pink*-coloured hose for the ladies, luckily coming up at the juncture when we were on our probation for the place of Chief Jester to S.'s Paper, established our reputation in that line. We were pronounced a "capital hand." O the conceits which we varied upon *red* in all its prismatic differences! from the trite and obvious flower of Cytherea, to the flaming costume of the lady that has her sitting upon "many waters." Then there was the collateral topic of ankles. What an occasion to a truly chaste writer, like ourself, of touching that nice brink, and yet never tumbling over it, of a seemingly ever approximating something "not quite proper;" while, like a skilful posture-master, balancing betwixt decorums and their opposites, he keeps the line, from which a hair's-breadth deviation is destruction; hovering in the confines of light and darkness, or where "both seem either;" a hazy uncertain delicacy: Autolycus-like in the Play, still putting off his expectant auditory with "Whoop, do me no harm, good man!" But above all, that conceit arrided us most at that time, and still tickles our midriff to remember, where, allusively to the flight of Astræa—*ultima Cœlestûm terras reliquit*—we pronounced—in reference to the stockings still—that MODESTY, TAKING HER FINAL LEAVE OF MORTALS, HER LAST BLUSH WAS VISIBLE IN HER ASCENT TO THE HEAVENS BY THE TRACT OF THE GLOWING INSTEP. This might be called the crowning conceit: and was esteemed tolerable writing in those days.

But the fashion of jokes, with all other things, passes away; as did the transient mode which had so favoured us. The ankles of our fair friends in a few weeks began to reassume their whiteness, and left us scarce a leg to stand upon. Other female whims followed, but none, methought, so pregnant, so invitatory of shrewd conceits, and more than single meanings.

Somebody has said, that to swallow six cross-buns daily consecutively for a fortnight, would surfeit the stoutest digestion. But to have to furnish as many jokes daily, and that not for a fortnight, but for a long twelvemonth, as we were constrained to do, was a little harder exaction. "Man goeth forth to his work until the evening"—from a reasonable hour in the morning, we presume it was meant. Now, as our main occupation took us up from eight till five every day in the city; and as our evening hours, at that time of life, had generally to do with anything rather than business, it follows, that the only time we could spare for this manufactory of jokes—our supplementary livelihood, that supplied us in every want beyond mere bread and cheese—was exactly that part of the day which (as we have heard of No Man's Land) may be fitly denominated No Man's Time; that is, no time in which a man ought to be up, and awake, in. To speak more plainly, it is that time of an hour, or an hour and a half's duration, in which a man, whose occasions call him up so preposterously, has to wait for his breakfast.

O those head-aches at dawn of day, when at five, or half-past five in summer, and not much later in the dark seasons, we were compelled to rise, having been perhaps not above four hours in bed—(for we were no go-to-beds with the lamb, though we anticipated the lark ofttimes in her rising—we like a parting cup at midnight, as all young men did before these effeminate times, and to have our friends about us—we were not constellated under Aquarius that watery sign, and therefore incapable of Bacchus, cold, washy, bloodless—we were none of your Basilian watersponges, nor had taken our degrees at Mount Ague—we were right toping Capulets, jolly companions, we and they)—but to have to get up, as we said before, curtailed of half our fair sleep, fasting, with only a dim vista of refreshing bohea in the distance—to be necessitated to rouse ourselves at the detestable rap of an old hag of a domestic, who seemed to take a diabolical pleasure in her announcement that it was "time to rise;" and whose chappy knuckles we have often yearned to amputate, and string them up at our chamber door, to be a terror to all such unseasonable rest-breakers in future—

"Facil" and sweet, as Virgil sings, had been the "descending" of the over-night, balmy the first sinking of the heavy head upon the pillow; but to get up, as he goes on to say,

—revocare gradus, superasque evadere ad auras—

and to get up, moreover, to make jokes with malice prepended—there was the "labour," there the "work."

No Egyptian taskmaster ever devised a slavery like to that, our slavery. No fractious operants ever turned out for half the tyranny which this necessity exercised upon us. Half a dozen jests in a day (bating Sundays too), why, it seems nothing! We make twice the number every day in our lives as a matter of course, and claim no Sabbatical exemptions. But then they come into our head. But when the head has to go out to them—when the mountain must go to Mahomet—

Reader, try it for once, only for a short twelvemonth. It was not every week that a fashion of pink stockings came up; but mostly, instead of it, some rugged untractable subject; some topic impossible to be contorted into the risible; some feature, upon which no smile could play; some flint, from which no process of ingenuity could procure a scintillation. There they lay: there your appointed tale of brick-making was set before you, which you must finish, with or without straw, as it happened. The craving dragon—*the Public*—like him in Bel's Temple—must be fed, it expected its daily rations; and Daniel, and ourselves, to do us justice, did the best we could on this side bursting him.

While we were wringing out coy sprightlinesses for the *Post*, and writhing under the toil of what is called "easy writing," Bob Allen, our *quondam* schoolfellow, was tapping his impracticable brains in a like service for the *Oracle*. Not that Robert troubled himself much about wit. If his paragraphs had a sprightly air about them, it was sufficient. He carried this nonchalance so far at last, that a matter of intelligence, and that no very important one, was not seldom palmed upon his employers for a good jest; for example sake —" *Walking* yesterday morning casually down Snow Hill, who should we meet but Mr. Deputy Humphreys! we rejoice to add, that the worthy Deputy appeared to enjoy a good state of health. We do not remember ever to have seen him look better." This gentleman so surprisingly met upon Snow Hill, from some peculiarities in gait or gesture, was a constant butt for mirth to the small paragraph-mongers of the day; and our friend thought that he might have his fling at him with the rest. We met A. in Holborn shortly after this extraordinary rencounter, which he told with tears of satisfaction in his eyes, and chuckling at the anticipated effects of its announcement next day in the paper.

We did not quite comprehend where the wit of it lay at the time; nor was it easy to be detected, when the thing came out advantaged by type and letterpress. He had better have met anything that morning than a Common Council Man. His services were shortly after dispensed with, on the plea that his paragraphs of late had been deficient in point. The one in question, it must be owned, had an air, in the opening especially, proper to awaken curiosity; and the sentiment, or moral, wears the aspect of humanity and good neighbourly feeling. But somehow the conclusion was not judged altogether to answer to the magnificent promise of the premises. We traced our friend's pen afterwards in the *True Briton*, the *Star*, the *Traveller*,—from all which he was successively dismissed, the Proprietors having "no further occasion for his services." Nothing was easier than to detect him. When wit failed, or topics ran low, there constantly appeared the following:—"*It is not generally known that the three Blue Balls at the Pawnbrokers' shops are the ancient arms of Lombardy. The Lombards were the first money-brokers in Europe.*" Bob has done more to set the public right on this important point of blazonry, than the whole College of Heralds.

The appointment of a regular wit has long ceased to be a part of the economy of a Morning Paper. Editors find their own jokes, or do as well without them. Parson Este, and Topham, brought up the set custom of "witty paragraphs" first in the *World*. Boaden was a reigning paragraphist in his day, and succeeded poor Allen in the *Oracle*. But, as we said, the fashion of jokes passes away; and it would be difficult to discover in the biographer of Mrs. Siddons, any traces of that vivacity and fancy which charmed the whole town at the commencement of the present century. Even the prelusive delicacies of the present writer—the curt "Astræan allusion"—would be thought pedantic and out of date, in these days.

From the office of the *Morning Post* (for we may as well exhaust our Newspaper Reminiscences at once) by change of property in the paper, we were transferred, mortifying exchange! to the office of the *Albion* Newspaper, late Rackstrow's Museum, in Fleet street. What a transition—from a handsome apartment, from rosewood desks and silver inkstands, to an office—no office, but a *den* rather, but just redeemed from the occupation of dead monsters, of which it seemed redolent—from the centre of loyalty and fashion, to a focus of vulgarity and sedition! Here in murky closet, inadequate from its square contents to the receipt of the two bodies of Editor and humble paragraph-maker, together at one time, sat in the discharge of his new editorial functions (the "Bigod" of Elia) the redoubted John Fenwick.

F., without a guinea in his pocket, and having left not many in the pockets of his friends whom he might command, had purchased (on tick, doubtless) the whole and sole Editorship, Proprietorship, with all the rights and titles (such as they were worth) of the *Albion* from one Lovell; of whom we know nothing, save that he had stood in the pillory for a libel on the Prince of Wales. With this hopeless concern—for it had been sinking ever since its commencement, and could now reckon upon not more than a hundred subscribers—F. resolutely determined upon pulling down the Government in the first instance, and making both our fortunes by way of corollary. For seven weeks and more did this infatuated democrat go about borrowing seven-shilling pieces, and lesser coin, to meet the daily demands of the Stamp Office, which allowed no credit to publications of that side in politics. An outcast from politer bread, we attached our small talents to the forlorn fortunes of our friend. Our occupation now was to write treason.

Recollections of feelings—which were all that now remained from our first boyish heats kindled by the French Revolution, when, if we were misled, we erred in the company of some who are accounted very good men now—rather than any tendency at this time to Republican doctrines—assisted us in assuming a style of writing, while the paper lasted, consonant in no very under tone to the right earnest fanaticism of F. Our cue was now to insinuate, rather than recommend, possible abdications. Blocks, axes, Whitehall tribunals, were covered with flowers of so cunning a periphrasis—as Mr. Bayes says, never naming the *thing* directly—that the keen eye of an Attorney-General was insufficient to detect the lurking snake among them. There were times, indeed, when we sighed for our more gentleman-like occupation under Stuart. But with change of masters it is ever change of service. Already one paragraph, and another, as we learned afterwards from a gentleman at the Treasury, had begun to be marked at that office, with a view of its being submitted at least to the attention of the proper Law Officers—when an unlucky, or rather lucky epigram from our pen, aimed at Sir J——s M——h, who was on the eve of departing for India to reap the fruits of his apostasy, as F. pronounced it (it is hardly worth particularizing), happening to offend the nice sense of Lord (or, as he then delighted to be called Citizen) Stanhope, deprived F. at once of the last hopes of a guinea from the last patron that had stuck by us; and breaking up our establishment, left us to the safe, but somewhat mortifying, neglect of the Crown Lawyers. It was about this time, or a little earlier, that Dan Stuart made that curious confession to us, that he had " never deliberately walked into an Exhibition at Somerset House in his life."

BARRENNESS OF THE IMAGINATIVE FACULTY IN THE PRODUCTIONS OF MODERN ART.

HOGARTH excepted, can we produce any one painter within the last fifty years, or since the humour of exhibiting began, that has treated a story *imaginatively?* By this we mean, upon whom his subject has so acted, that it has seemed to direct *him*—not to be arranged by him? Any upon whom its leading or collateral points have impressed themselves so tyrannically, that he dared not treat it otherwise, lest he should falsify a revelation? Any that has imparted to his compositions, not merely so much truth as is enough to convey a story with clearness, but that individualizing property, which should keep the subject so treated distinct in feature from every other subject, however similar, and to common apprehensions almost identical; so that we might say, this and this part could have found an appropriate place in no other picture in the world but this? Is there anything in modern art—we will not demand that it should be equal — but in any way analogous to what Titian has effected, in that wonderful bringing together of two times in the "Ariadne," in the National Gallery? Precipitous, with his reeling satyr rout about him, repeopling and re-illuming suddenly the waste places, drunk with a new fury beyond the grape, Bacchus, born in fire, fire-like flings himself at the Cretan. This is the time present. With this telling of the story, an artist, and no ordinary one,— might remain richly proud. Guido, in his harmonious version of it, saw no farther. But from the depths of the imaginative spirit Titian has recalled past time, and laid it contributory with the present to one simultaneous effect. With the desert all ringing with the mad cymbals of his followers, made lucid with the presence and new offers of a god,—as if unconscious of Bacchus, or but idly casting her eyes as upon some unconcerning pageant—her soul undistracted from Theseus—Ariadne is still pacing the solitary shore in as much heart-silence, and in almost the same local solitude, with which she awoke at daybreak to catch the forlorn last glances of the sail that bore away the Athenian.

Here are two points miraculously co-uniting; fierce society, with the feeling of solitude still absolute; noon-day revelations, with the accidents of the dull gray dawn unquenched and lingering; the *present* Bacchus, with the *past* Ariadne: two stories, with double Time; separate, and harmonizing. Had the artist made the woman one shade less indifferent to the God; still more, had she expressed a rapture at his advent, where would have been the story of the mighty desolation of the heart previous? merged in the insipid accident of a flattering offer met with a welcome acceptance. The broken heart for Theseus was not likely to be pieced up by a God.

We have before us a fine rough print, from a picture by Raphael in the Vatican. It is the Presentation of the new-born Eve to Adam by the Almighty. A fairer mother of mankind we might imagine, and a goodlier sire perhaps of men since born. But these are matters subordinate to the conception of the *situation*, displayed in this extraordinary production. A tolerable modern artist would have been satisfied with tempering certain raptures of connubial anticipation, with a suitable acknowledgment to the Giver of the blessing, in the countenance of the first bridegroom: something like the divided attention of the child (Adam was here a child-man) between the given toy, and the mother who had just blest it with the bauble. This is the obvious, the first-sight view, the superficial. An artist of a higher grade, considering the awful presence they were in, would have taken care to subtract something from the expression of the more human passion, and to heighten the more spiritual one. This would be as much as an exhibition-goer, from the opening of Somerset House to last year's show, has been encouraged to look for. It is obvious to hint at a lower expression yet, in a picture that, for respects of drawing and colouring, might be deemed not wholly inadmissible within these art-fostering walls, in which the raptures should be as ninety-nine, the gratitude as one, or perhaps zero! By neither the one passion nor the other has Raphael expounded the situation of Adam. Singly upon his brow sits the absorbing sense of wonder at the created miracle. The *moment* is seized by the intuitive artist, perhaps not self-conscious of his art, in which neither of the conflicting emotions—a moment how abstracted!—have had time to spring up, or to battle for indecorous mastery.— We have seen a landscape of a justly-admired neoteric, in which he aimed at delineating a fiction, one of the most severely beautiful in antiquity—the gardens of the Hesperides. To do Mr. —— justice, he had painted a laudable orchard, with fitting seclusion, and a veritable dragon (of which a Polypheme, by Poussin, is somehow a fac-simile for the situation), looking over into the world shut out backwards, so that none but a "still-climbing Hercules" could hope to catch a peep at the admired Ternary of Recluses. No conventual porter could keep his keys better than this custos with the "lidless eyes." He not only sees that none *do* intrude into that privacy, but, as clear as daylight, that none but *Hercules aut Diabolus* by any manner of means *can*. So far all is well. We have absolute solitude here or nowhere. *Ab extra*, the damsels are snug enough. But here the artist's courage seems to have failed him. He began to pity his pretty charge, and, to comfort the irksomeness, has peopled their solitude with a bevy of fair attendants, maids of honour, or ladies of the bed-chamber, according to the approved etiquette at a court of the nineteenth century; giving to the whole scene the air of a *fête-champêtre*, if we will but excuse the absence of the gentlemen. This is well, and Watteauish. But what is become of the solitary mystery—the

> Daughters three,
> That sing around the golden tree?

This is not the way in which Poussin would have treated this subject.

The paintings, or rather the stupendous architectural designs, of a modern artist, have been urged as objections to the theory of our motto. They are of a character, we confess, to stagger it. His towered structures are of the highest order of the material sublime. Whether they were dreams, or transcripts of some elder workmanship—Assyrian ruins old—restored by this mighty artist, they satisfy our most stretched and craving conceptions of the glories of the antique world. It is a pity that they were ever peopled. On that side, the imagination of the artist halts, and appears defective. Let us examine the point of the story in the "Belshazzar's Feast." We will introduce it by an apposite anecdote.

The court historians of the day record, that at the first dinner given by the late King (then Prince Regent) at the Pavilion, the following characteristic frolic was played off. The guests were select and admiring; the banquet profuse and admirable; the lights lustrous and oriental; the eye was perfectly dazzled with the display of plate, among which the great gold salt-cellar, brought from the regalia in the Tower for this especial purpose, itself a tower! stood conspicuous for its magnitude. And now the Rev. * * *, the then admired court Chaplain, was proceeding with the grace, when, at a signal given, the lights were suddenly overcast, and a huge transparency was discovered, in which glittered in gold letters—

"BRIGHTON—EARTHQUAKE—SWALLOW-UP-ALIVE!"

Imagine the confusion of the guests; the Georges and

garters, jewels, bracelets, moulted upon the occasion! The fans dropped, and picked up the next morning by the sly court-pages! Mrs. Fitz-what's-her-name fainting, and the Countess of * * * holding the smelling-bottle, till the good-humoured Prince caused harmony to be restored, by calling in fresh candles, and declaring that the whole was nothing but a pantomime *hoax*, got up by the ingenious Mr. Farley, of Covent Garden, from hints which his Royal Highness himself had furnished! Then imagine the infinite applause that followed, the mutual rallyings, the declarations that " they were not much frightened," of the assembled galaxy.

The point of time in the picture exactly answers to the appearance of the transparency in the anecdote. The huddle, the flutter, the bustle, the escape, the alarm, and the mock alarm ; the prettinesses heightened by consternation ; the courtier's fear which was flattery ; and the lady's which was affectation : all that we may conceive to have taken place in a mob of Brighton courtiers, sympathizing with the well-acted surprise of their sovereign ; all this, and no more, is exhibited by the well-dressed lords and ladies in the Hall of Belus. Just this sort of consternation we have seen among a flock of disquieted wild geese at the report only of a gun having gone off!

But is this vulgar fright, this mere animal anxiety for the preservation of their persons—such as we have witnessed at a theatre, when a slight alarm of fire has been given—an adequate exponent of a supernatural terror? the way in which the finger of God, writing judgments, would have been met by the withered conscience? There is a human fear, and a divine fear. The one is disturbed, restless, and bent upon escape; the other is bowed down, effortless, passive. When the spirit appeared before Eliphaz in the visions of the night, and the hair of his flesh stood up, was it in the thoughts of the Temanite to ring the bell of his chamber, or to call up the servants? But let us see in the text what there is to justify all this huddle of vulgar consternation.

From the words of Daniel it appears that Belshazzar had made a great feast to a thousand of his lords, and drank wine before the thousand. The golden and silver vessels are gorgeously enumerated, with the princes, the king's concubines, and his wives. Then follows—

"In the same hour came forth fingers of a man's hand, and wrote over against the candlestick upon the plaster of the wall of the king's palace; and the *king* saw the part of the hand that wrote. Then the *king's* countenance was changed, and his thoughts troubled him, so that the joints of his loins were loosened, and his knees smote one against another."

This is the plain text. By no hint can it be otherwise inferred, but that the appearance was solely confined to the fancy of Belshazzar, that his single brain was troubled. Not a word is spoken of its being seen by any else there present, not even by the queen herself, who merely undertakes for the interpretation of the phenomenon, as related to her, doubtless, by her husband. The lords are simply said to be astonished; *i.e.* at the trouble and the change of countenance in their sovereign. Even the prophet does not appear to have seen the scroll, which the king saw. He recalls it only, as Joseph did the Dream to the King of Egypt. "Then was the part of the hand sent from him [the Lord], and this writing was written." He speaks of the phantasm as past.

Then what becomes of this needless multiplication of the miracle? this message to a royal conscience, singly expressed—for it was said, "Thy kingdom is divided,"—simultaneously impressed upon the fancies of a thousand courtiers, who were implied in it neither directly nor grammatically?

But, admitting the artist's own version of the story, and that the sight was seen also by the thousand courtiers—let it have been visible to all Babylon—as the knees of Belshazzar were shaken, and his countenance troubled, even so would the knees of every man in Babylon, and their countenances, as of an individual man, have been troubled; bowed, bent down, so would they have remained, stupor-fixed, with no thought of struggling with that inevitable judgment.

Not all that is optically possible to be seen, is to be shown in every picture. The eye delightedly dwells upon the brilliant individualities in a "Marriage at Cana," by Veronese, or Titian, to the very texture and colour of the wedding garments, the ring glittering upon the bride's finger, the metal and fashion of the wine-pots; for at such seasons there is leisure and luxury to be curious. But in a "day of judgment," or in a "day of lesser horrors, yet divine," as at the impious feast of Belshazzar, the eye should see, as the actual eye of an agent or patient in the immediate scene would see, only in masses and indistinction. Not only the female attire and jewelry exposed to the critical eye of the fashion, as minutely as the dresses in a Lady's Magazine, in the criticised picture—but perhaps the curiosities of anatomical science, and studied diversities of posture, in the falling angels and sinners of Michael Angelo,—have no business in their great subjects. There was no leisure for them.

By a wise falsification, the great masters of painting got at their true conclusions; by not showing the actual appearances, that is, all that was to be seen at any given moment by an indifferent eye, but only what the eye might be supposed to see in the doing or suffering of some portentous action. Suppose the moment of the swallowing up of Pompeii. There they were to be seen — houses, columns, architectural proportions, differences of public and private buildings, men and women at their standing occupations, the diversified thousand postures, attitudes, dresses, in some confusion truly, but physically they were visible. But what eye saw them at that eclipsing moment, which reduces confusion to a kind of unity, and when the senses are upturned from their proprieties, when sight and hearing are a feeling only? A thousand years have passed, and we are at leisure to contemplate the weaver fixed standing at his shuttle, the baker at his oven, and to turn over with antiquarian coolness the pots and pans of Pompeii.

"Sun, stand thou still upon Gibeon, and thou, Moon, in the valley of Ajalon." Who, in reading this magnificent Hebraism, in his conception, sees aught but the heroic son of Nun, with the outstretched arm, and the greater and lesser light obsequious? Doubtless there were to be seen hill and dale, and chariots and horsemen, on open plain, or winding by secret defiles, and all the circumstances and stratagems of war. But whose eyes would have been conscious of this array at the interposition of the synchronic miracle? Yet in the picture of this subject by the artist of the "Belshazzar's Feast"—no ignoble work, either—the marshalling and landscape of the war is everything, the miracle sinks into an anecdote of the day; and the eye may "dart through rank and file traverse" for some minutes, before it shall discover, among his armed followers, *which is Joshua!* Not modern art alone, but ancient, where only it is to be found if anywhere, can be detected erring, from defect of this imaginative faculty. The world has nothing to show of the preternatural in painting, transcending the figure of Lazarus bursting his grave-clothes, in the great picture at Angerstein's. It seems a thing between two beings. A ghastly horror at itself struggles with newly-apprehending gratitude at second life bestowed. It cannot forget that it was a ghost. It has hardly felt that it is a body. It has to tell of the world of spirits.—Was it from a feeling, that the crowd of half-impassioned bystanders, and the still more irrelevant herd of passers-by at a distance, who have not heard, or but faintly have been told of the passing miracle, admirable as they are in design and hue—for it is a glorified work—do not respond adequately to the action—that the single figure of the Lazarus has been attributed to Michael Angelo, and the mighty Sebastian unfairly robbed of the fame of the greater half of the interest? Now that there were not indifferent passers-by within actual scope of the eyes of those present at the miracle, to whom the sound of it had but faintly, or not at all, reached, it would be hardihood to deny; but would they see them? or can the mind in the conception of it admit of such unconcerning objects; can it think of them at all? or what associating league to the imagination can there be between the seers and the seers not, of a presential miracle?

Were an artist to paint upon demand a picture of a Dryad, we will ask whether, in the present low state of expectation, the patron would not, or ought not be fully satisfied with a beautiful naked figure recumbent under wide-stretched oaks? Dis-seat those woods, and place the same figure among fountains, and falls of pellucid water, and you have a—Naïad! Not so in a rough print we have seen after Julio Romano, we think—for it is long since—*there*, by no process, with mere change of scene, could the figure have reciprocated characters. Long, grotesque, fantastic, yet with a grace of her own, beautiful in convolution and distortion, linked to her connatural tree, co-twisting with its limbs her own, till both seemed either—these, animated branches; those, disanimated members—yet the animal and vegetable lives sufficiently kept distinct—*his* Dryad lay—an approximation of two natures, which to conceive, it must be seen; analogous to, not the same with, the delicacies of Ovidian transformations.

To the lowest subjects, and, to a superficial comprehension, the most barren, the Great Masters gave loftiness and fruitfulness. The large eye of genius saw in the meanness of present objects their capabilities of treatment from their relations to some grand Past or Future. How has Raphael—we must still linger about the Vatican—treated the humble craft of the ship-builder, in *his* "Building of the Ark"? It is in that scriptural series, to which we have referred, and which, judging from some fine rough old graphic sketches of them which we possess, seem to be of a higher and more poetic grade than even the Cartoons. The dim of sight are the timid and the shrinking. There is a cowardice in modern art. As the Frenchman, of whom Coleridge's friend made the prophetic guess at Rome, from the beard and horns of the Moses of Michael Angelo collected no inferences beyond that of a He Goat and a Cornuto ; so from this subject, of mere mechanic promise, it would instinctively turn away, as from one incapable of investiture with any grandeur. The dock-yards at Woolwich would object derogatory associations. The depôt at Chatham would be the mote and the beam in its intellectual eye. But not to the nautical preparations in the ship-yards of Civita Vecchia did Raphael look for instructions, when he imagined the building of the Vessel that was to be conservatory of the wrecks of the species of drowned mankind. In the intensity of the action he keeps ever out of sight the meanness of the operation. There is the Patriarch, in calm forethought, and with holy prescience, giving directions. And there are his agents—the solitary but sufficient Three—hewing, sawing, every one with the might and earnestness of a Demiurgus ; under some instinctive rather than technical guidance ! giant-muscled ; every one a Hercules ; or liker to those Vulcanian Three, that in sounding caverns under Mongibello wrought in fire—Brontes, and black Steropes, and Pyracmon. So work the workmen that should repair a world !

Artists again err in the confounding of *poetic* with *pictorial subjects*. In the latter, the exterior accidents are nearly everything, the unseen qualities as nothing. Othello's colour—the infirmities and corpulence of a Sir John Falstaff—do they haunt us perpetually in the reading ? or are they obtruded upon our conceptions one time for ninety-nine that we are lost in admiration at the respective moral or intellectual attributes of the character ? But in a picture Othello is *always* a Blackamoor ; and the other only Plump Jack. Deeply corporealized, and enchained hopelessly in the grovelling fetters of externality, must be the mind, to which, in its better moments, the image of the high-souled, high-intelligenced Quixote—the errant Star of Knighthood, made more tender by eclipse—has never presented itself divested from the unhallowed accompaniment of a Sancho, or a rabblement at the heels of Rosinante. That man has read his book by halves ; he has laughed, mistaking his author's purport, which was—tears. The artist that pictures Quixote (and it is in this degrading point that he is every season held up at our Exhibitions) in the shallow hope of exciting mirth, would have joined the rabble at the heels of his starved steed. We wish not to see *that* counterfeited, which we would not have wished to see in the reality. Conscious of the heroic inside of the noble Quixote, who, on hearing that his withered person was passing, would have stepped over his threshold to gaze upon his forlorn habiliments, and the "strange bed-fellows which misery brings a man acquainted with"? Shade of Cervantes! who in thy Second Part could put into the mouth of thy Quixote those high aspirations of a super-chivalrous gallantry, where he replies to one of the shepherdesses, apprehensive that he would spoil their pretty net-works, and inviting him to be a guest with them, in accents like these: "Truly, fairest Lady, Actæon was not more astonished when he saw Diana bathing herself at the fountain, than I have been in beholding your beauty: I commend the manner of your pastime, and thank you for your kind offers ; and, if I may serve you, so I may be sure you will be obeyed, you may command me : for my profession is this, To show myself thankful, and a doer of good to all sorts of people, especially of the rank that your person shows you to be ; and if those nets, as they take up but a little piece of ground, should take up the whole world, I would seek out new worlds to pass through, rather than break them : and (he adds) that you may give credit to this my exaggeration, behold at least he that promiseth you this, is Don Quixote de la Mancha, if haply this name hath come to your hearing." Illustrious Romancer! were the "fine frenzies," which possessed the brain of thy own Quixote, a fit subject, as in this Second Part, to be exposed to the jeers of Duennas and Serving-men? to be monstered, and shown up at the heartless banquets of great men? Was that pitiable infirmity, which in thy First Part misleads him, *always from within*, into half-ludicrous, but more than half-compassionable and admirable errors, not infliction enough from heaven, that men by studied artifices must devise and practise upon the humour, to inflame where they should soothe it? Why, Goneril would have blushed to practise upon the abdicated king at this rate, and the she-wolf Regan not have endured to play the pranks upon his fled wits, which thou first made thy Quixote suffer in Duchesses' halls, and at the hands of that unworthy nobleman.[1]

In the First Adventures, even, it needed all the art of the most consummate artist in the Book way that the world hath yet seen, to keep up in the mind of the reader the heroic attributes of the character without relaxing; so as absolutely that they shall suffer no alloy from the debasing fellowship of the clown. If it ever obtrudes itself as a disharmony, are we inclined to laugh; or not, rather, to indulge a contrary emotion?—Cervantes, stung, perchance, by the relish with which *his* Reading Public had received the fooleries of the man, more to their palates than the generosities of the master, in the sequel let his pen run riot, lost the harmony and the balance, and sacrificed a great idea to the taste of his contemporaries. We know that in the present day the Knight has fewer admirers than the Squire. Anticipating, what did actually happen to him—as afterwards it did to his scarce inferior follower, the Author of "Guzman de Alfarache"—that some less knowing hand would prevent him by a spurious Second Part; and judging that it would be easier for his competitor to outbid him

---

[1] Yet from this Second Part, our cried-up pictures are mostly selected; the waiting-women with beards, etc.

in the comicalities, than in the *romance*, of his work, he abandoned his Knight, and has fairly set up the Squire for his Hero. For what else has he unsealed the eyes of Sancho? and instead of that twilight state of semi-insanity—the madness at second-hand—the contagion, caught from a stronger mind infected—that war between native cunning, and hereditary deference, with which he has hitherto accompanied his master—two for a pair almost—does he substitute a downright Knave, with open eyes, for his own ends only following a confessed Madman; and offering at one time to lay, if not actually laying, hands upon him! From the moment that Sancho loses his reverence, Don Quixote is become—a treatable lunatic. Our artists handle him accordingly.

THE WEDDING.

I DO not know when I have been better pleased than at being invited last week to be present at the wedding of a friend's daughter. I like to make one at these ceremonies, which to us old people give back our youth in a manner, and restore our gayest season, in the remembrance of our own success, or the regrets, scarcely less tender, of our own youthful disappointments, in this point of a settlement. On these occasions I am sure to be in good humour for a week or two after, and enjoy a reflected honeymoon. Being without a family, I am flattered with these temporary adoptions into a friend's family; I feel a sort of cousinhood, or uncleship, for the season; I am inducted into degrees of affinity; and, in the participated socialities of the little community, I lay down for a brief while my solitary bachelorship. I carry this humour so far, that I take it unkindly to be left out, even when a funeral is going on in the house of a dear friend. But to my subject.——

The union itself had been long settled, but its celebration had been hitherto deferred, to an almost unreasonable state of suspense in the lovers, by some invincible prejudices which the bride's father had unhappily contracted upon the subject of the too early marriages of females. He has been lecturing any time these five years—for to that length the courtship had been protracted—upon the propriety of putting off the solemnity, till the lady should have completed her five-and-twentieth year. We all began to be afraid that a suit, which as yet had abated of none of its ardours, might at last be lingered on, till passion had time to cool, and love go out in the experiment. But a little wheedling on the part of his wife, who was by no means a party to these overstrained notions, joined to some serious expostulations on that of his friends, who, from the growing infirmities of the old gentleman, could not promise ourselves many years' enjoyment of his company, and were anxious to bring matters to a conclusion during his lifetime, at length prevailed; and on Monday last the daughter of my old friend, Admiral ———, having attained the *womanly* age of nineteen, was conducted to the church by her pleasant cousin J———, who told some few years older.

Before the youthful part of my female readers express their indignation at the abominable loss of time occasioned to the lovers by the preposterous notions of my old friend, they will do well to consider the reluctance which a fond parent naturally feels at parting with his child. To this unwillingness, I believe, in most cases may be traced the difference of opinion on this point between child and parent, whatever pretences of interest or prudence may be held out to cover it. The hard-heartedness of fathers is a fine theme for romance writers, a sure and moving topic; but is there not something untender, to say no more of it, in the hurry which a beloved child is sometimes in to tear herself from the paternal stock, and commit herself to strange graftings? The case is heightened where the lady, as in the present instance, happens to be an only child. I do not understand these matters experimentally, but I can make a shrewd guess at the wounded pride of a parent upon these occasions. It is no new observation, I believe, that a lover in most cases has no rival so much to be feared as the father. Certainly there is a jealousy in *unparallel subjects*, which is little less heartrending than the passion which we more strictly christen by that name. Mothers' scruples are more easily got over; for this reason, I suppose, that the protection transferred to a husband is less a derogation and a loss to their authority than to the paternal. Mothers, besides, have a trembling foresight, which paints the inconveniences (impossible to be conceived in the same degree by the other parent) of a life of forlorn celibacy, which the refusal of a tolerable match may entail upon their child. Mothers' instinct is a surer guide here than the cold reasonings of a father on such a topic. To this instinct may be imputed, and by it alone may be excused, the unbeseeming artifices, by which some wives push on the matrimonial projects of their daughters, which the husband, however approving, shall entertain with comparative indifference. A little shamelessness on this head is pardonable. With this explanation, forwardness becomes a grace, and maternal importunity receives the name of a virtue.—But the parson stays, while I preposterously assume his office; I am preaching, while the bride is on the threshold.

Nor let any of my female readers suppose that the sage reflections which have just escaped me have the obliquest tendency of application to the young lady, who, it will be seen, is about to venture upon a change in her condition, at a *mature and competent age*, and not without the fullest approbation of all parties. I only deprecate *very hasty marriages*.

It had been fixed that the ceremony should be gone through at an early hour, to give time for a little *déjeûne* afterwards, to which a select party of friends had been invited. We were in church a little before the clock struck eight.

Nothing could be more judicious or graceful than the dress of the bride-maids—the three charming Miss Foresters—on this morning. To give the bride an opportunity of shining singly, they had come habited all in green. I am ill at describing female apparel; but while *she* stood at the altar in vestments white and candid as her thoughts, a sacrificial whiteness, *they* assisted in robes such as might become Diana's nymphs—Foresters indeed—as such who had not yet come to the resolution of putting off cold virginity. These young maids, not being so blest as to have a mother living, I am told, keep single for their father's sake, and live altogether so happy with their remaining parent, that the hearts of their lovers are ever broken with the prospect (so inauspicious to their hopes) of such uninterrupted and provoking home-comfort. Gallant girls! each a victim worthy of Iphigenia!

I do not know what business I have to be present in solemn places. I cannot divest me of an unseasonable disposition to levity upon the most awful occasions. I was never cut out for a public functionary. Ceremony and I have long shaken hands; but I could not resist the importunities of the young lady's father, whose gout unhappily confined him at home, to act as parent on this occasion, and *give away the bride*. Something ludicrous occurred to me at this most serious of all moments—a sense of my unfitness to have the disposal, even in imagination, of the sweet young creature beside me. I fear I was betrayed to some lightness, for the awful eye of the parson—and the rector's eye of St. Mildred's in the Poultry is no trifle of a rebuke—was upon me in an instant, souring my incipient jest to the tristful severities of a funeral.

This was the only misbehaviour which I can plead to upon this solemn occasion, unless what was objected to me after the ceremony, by one of the handsome Miss T——s, be accounted a solecism. She was pleased to say that she had never seen a gentleman before me give away a bride, in black. Now black has been my ordinary apparel so long—indeed, I take it to be the proper costume of an author—the stage sanctions it—that to have appeared in some lighter colour would have raised more mirth at my expense than the anomaly had created censure. But I could perceive that the bride's mother, and some elderly ladies present (God bless them!) would have been well content, if I had come in any other colour than that. But I got over the omen by a lucky apologue, which I remembered out of Pilpay, or some Indian author, of all the birds being invited to the linnet's wedding, at which, when all the rest came in their gayest feathers, the raven alone apologised for his cloak because "he had no other." This tolerably reconciled the elders. But with the young people all was merriment, and shaking of hands, and congratulations, and kissing away the bride's tears, and kissing from her in return, till a young lady, who assumed some experience in these matters, having worn the nuptial bands some four or five weeks longer than her friend, rescued her, archly observing, with half an eye upon the bridegroom, that at this rate she would have "none left."

My friend the Admiral was in fine wig and buckle on this occasion—a striking contrast to his usual neglect of personal appearance. He did not once shove up his borrowed locks (his custom ever at his morning studies) to betray the few gray stragglers of his own beneath them. He wore an aspect of thoughtful satisfaction. I trembled for the hour, which at length approached, when after a protracted *breakfast* of three hours—if stores of cold fowls, tongues, hams, botargoes, dried fruits, wines, cordials, etc., can deserve so meagre an appellation—the coach was announced, which was come to carry off the bride and bridegroom for a season, as custom has sensibly ordained, into the country; upon which design, wishing them a felicitous journey, let us return to the assembled guests.

> As when a well-graced actor leaves the stage,
> The eyes of men
> Are idly bent on him that enters next,

so idly did we bend our eyes upon one another, when the chief performers in the morning's pageant had vanished. None told his tale. None sipped her glass. The poor Admiral made an effort—it was not much. I had anticipated so far. Even the infinity of full satisfaction, that had betrayed itself through the prim looks and quiet deportment of his lady, began to wane into something of misgiving. No one knew whether to take their leave or stay. We seemed assembled upon a silly occasion. In this crisis, betwixt tarrying and departure, I must do justice to a foolish talent of mine, which had otherwise like to have brought me into disgrace in the fore-part of the day; I mean a power, in any emergency, of thinking and giving vent to all manner of strange nonsense. In this awkward dilemma I found it sovereign. I rattled off some of my most excellent absurdities. All were willing to be relieved, at any expense of reason, from the pressure of the intolerable vacuum which had succeeded to the morning bustle. By this means I was fortunate in keeping together the better part of the company to a late hour; and a rubber of whist (the Admiral's favourite game) with some rare strokes of chance as well as skill, which came opportunely on his side—lengthened out till midnight—dismissed the old gentleman at last to his bed with comparatively easy spirits.

I have been at my old friend's various times since. I do not know a visiting place where every guest is so perfectly at his ease; nowhere, where harmony is so strangely the result of confusion. Everybody is at cross purposes, yet the effect is so much better than uniformity. Contradictory orders; servants pulling one way; master and mistress driving some other, yet both diverse; visitors huddled up in corners; chairs unsymmetrized; candles disposed by chance; meals at odd hours, tea and supper at once, or the latter preceding the former; the host and the guest conferring, yet each upon a different topic, each understanding himself, neither trying to understand or hear the other; draughts and politics, chess and political economy, cards and conversation on nautical matters, going on at once, without the hope, or indeed the wish, of distinguishing them, make it altogether the most perfect *concordia discors* you shall meet with. Yet somehow the old house is not quite what it should be. The Admiral still enjoys his pipe, but he has no Miss Emily to fill it for him. The instrument stands where it stood, but she is gone, whose delicate touch could sometimes for a short minute appease the warring elements. He has learnt, as Marvel expresses it, to " make his destiny his choice." He bears bravely up, but he does not come out with his flashes of wild wit so thick as formerly. His sea-songs seldomer escape him. His wife, too, looks as if she wanted some younger body to scold and set to rights. We all miss a junior presence. It is wonderful how one young maiden freshens up, and keeps green, the paternal roof. Old and young seem to have an interest in her, so long as she is not absolutely disposed of. The youthfulness of the house is flown. Emily is married.

REJOICINGS UPON THE NEW YEAR'S COMING OF AGE.

THE *Old Year* being dead, and the *New Year* coming of age, which he does, by Calendar Law, as soon as the breath is out of the old gentleman's body, nothing would serve the young spark but he must give a dinner upon the occasion, to which all the *Days* in the year were invited. The *Festivals*, whom he deputed as his stewards, were mightily taken with the notion. They had been engaged time out of mind, they said, in providing mirth and good cheer for mortals below; and it was time they should have a taste of their own bounty. It was stiffly debated among them whether the *Fasts* should be admitted. Some said the appearance of such lean, starved guests, with their mortified faces, would pervert the ends of the meeting. But the objection was overruled by *Christmas Day*, who had a design upon *Ash Wednesday* (as you shall hear), and a mighty desire to see how the old Domine would behave himself in his cups. Only the *Vigils* were requested to come with their lanterns, to light the gentlefolks home at night.

All the *Days* came to their day. Covers were provided for three hundred and sixty-five guests at the principal table; with an occasional knife and fork at the side-board for the *Twenty-Ninth of February*.

I should have told you that cards of invitation had been issued. The carriers were the *Hours;* twelve little, merry, whirligig foot-pages, as you should desire to see, that went all round, and found out the persons invited well enough, with the exception of *Easter Day, Shrove Tuesday*, and a few such *Moveables*, who had lately shifted their quarters.

Well, they all met at last—foul *Days*, fine *Days*, all sorts of *Days*, and a rare din they made of it. There was nothing but, Hail! fellow *Day*, well met—brother *Day*—sister *Day*—only *Lady Day* kept a little on the aloof, and seemed somewhat scornful. Yet some said *Twelfth Day* cut her out and out, for she came in a tiffany suit, white and gold, like a queen on a frost-cake, all royal, glittering, and *Epiphanous*. The rest came, some in green, some in white—but old *Lent and his family* were not yet out of mourning. Rainy *Days* came in, dripping; and sunshiny *Days* helped them to change their stockings. *Wedding Day* was there in his marriage finery, a little the worse for wear. *Pay Day* came late, as he always does; and *Doomsday* sent word—he might be expected.

April Fool (as my young lord's jester) took upon himself to marshal the guests, and wild work he made with it. It would have posed old Erra Pater to have found out any given *Day* in the year to erect a scheme upon—

good *Days*, bad *Days*, were so shuffled together, to the confounding of all sober horoscopy.

He had stuck the *Twenty-First of June* next to the *Twenty-Second of December*, and the former looked like a Maypole siding a marrow-bone. *Ash Wednesday* got wedged in (as was concerted) betwixt *Christmas* and *Lord Mayor's Days*. Lord! how he laid about him! Nothing but barons of beef and turkeys would go down with him —to the great greasing and detriment of his new sackcloth bib and tucker. And still *Christmas Day* was at his elbow, plying him with the wassail-bowl, till he roared, and hiccupp'd, and protested there was no faith in dried ling, but commended it to the devil for a sour, windy, acrimonious, censorious, hy-po-crit-crit-critical mess, and no dish for a gentleman. Then he dipt his fist into the middle of the great custard that stood before his *left-hand neighbour*, and daubed his hungry beard all over with it, till you would have taken him for the *Last Day in December*, it so hung in icicles.

At another part of the table, *Shrove Tuesday* was helping the *Second of September* to some cock broth,— which courtesy the latter returned with the delicate thigh of a hen pheasant—so that there was no love lost for that matter. The *Last of Lent* was spunging upon *Shrove-tide's* pancakes; which *April Fool* perceiving, told him that e did well, for pancakes were proper to a *good fryday*.

In another part, a hubbub arose about the *Thirtieth f January*, who, it seems, being a sour, puritanic character, that thought nobody's meat good or sanctified nough for him, had smuggled into the room a calf's head, hich he had had cooked at home for that purpose, thinking to feast thereon incontinently; but as it lay in the ish, *March Manyweathers*, who is a very fine lady, and bject to the meagrims, screamed out there was a "human ead in the platter," and raved about Herodias' daughter that degree, that the obnoxious viand was obliged to removed; nor did she recover her stomach till she had gulped down a *Restorative*, confected of *Oak Apple*, which the merry *Twenty-Ninth of May* always carries about with him for that purpose.

The King's health[1] being called for after this, a notable dispute arose between the *Twelfth of August* (a zealous old Whig gentlewoman) and the *Twenty-Third of April* (a new-fangled lady of the Tory stamp), as to which of them should have the honour to propose it. *August* grew hot upon the matter, affirming time out of mind the prescriptive right to have lain with her, till her rival had basely supplanted her; whom she represented as little better than a *kept* mistress, who went about in *fine clothes*, while she (the legitimate BIRTHDAY) had scarcely a rag, etc.

April Fool, being made mediator, confirmed the right, in the strongest form of words, to the appellant, but decided for peace' sake, that the exercise of it should remain with the present possessor. At the same time, he slyly rounded the first lady in the ear, that an action might lie against the Crown for *bi-geny*.

It beginning to grow a little duskish, *Candlemas* lustily bawled out for lights, which was opposed by all the *Days*, who protested against burning daylight. Then fair water was handed round in silver ewers, and the *same lady* was observed to take an unusual time in *Washing* herself.

May Day, with that sweetness which is peculiar to her, in a neat speech proposing the health of the founder, crowned her goblet (and by her example the rest of the company) with garlands. This being done, the lordly *New Year*, from the upper end of the table, in a cordial but somewhat lofty tone, returned thanks. He felt proud, on an occasion of meeting so many of his worthy father's late tenants, promised to improve their farms, and at the same time to abate (if anything was found unreasonable) in their rents.

At the mention of this, the four *Quarter Days* involuntarily looked at each other, and smiled; *April Fool*

---

[1] King George IV.

whistled to an old tune of "New Brooms;" and a surly old rebel at the farther end of the table (who was discovered to be no other than the *Fifth of November*) muttered out, distinctly enough to be heard by the whole company, words to this effect—that "when the old one is gone, he is a fool that looks for a better." Which rudeness of his, the guests resenting, unanimously voted his expulsion; and the malcontent was thrust out neck and heels into the cellar, as the properest place for such a *boutefeu* and firebrand as he had shown himself to be.

Order being restored—the young lord (who, to say truth, had been a little ruffled, and put beside his oratory) in as few and yet as obliging words as possible, assured them of entire welcome; and, with a graceful turn, singling out poor *Twenty-Ninth of February*, that had sate all this while munchance at the side-board, begged to couple his health with that of the good company before him—which he drank accordingly: observing that he had not seen his honest face any time these four years—with a number of endearing expressions besides. At the same time removing the solitary *Day* from the forlorn seat which had been assigned him, he stationed him at his own board, somewhere between the *Greek Calends* and *Latter Lammas*.

Ash Wednesday being now called upon for a song, with his eyes fast stuck in his head, and as well as the canary he had swallowed would give him leave, struck up a Carol, which *Christmas Day* had taught him for the nonce; and was followed by the latter, who gave "Miserere" in fine style, hitting off the mumping notes and lengthened drawl of *Old Mortification* with infinite humour. *April Fool* swore they had exchanged conditions; but *Good Friday* was observed to look extremely grave; and *Sunday* held her fan before her face that she might not be seen to smile.

Shrove-tide, *Lord Mayor's Day*, and *April Fool*, next joined in a glee

Which is the properest day to drink?

in which all the *Days* chiming in, made a merry burden.

They next fell to quibbles and conundrums. The question being proposed, who had the greatest number of followers—the *Quarter Days* said, there could be no question as to that; for they had all the creditors in the world dogging their heels. But *April Fool* gave it in favour of the *Forty Days before Easter;* because the debtors in all cases outnumbered the creditors, and they kept *Lent* all the year.

All this while *Valentine's Day* kept courting pretty *May*, who sate next him, slipping amorous *billets-doux* under the table, till the *Dog Days* (who are naturally of a warm constitution) began to be jealous, and to bark and rage exceedingly. *April Fool*, who likes a bit of sport above measure, and had some pretensions to the lady besides, as being but a cousin once removed,—clapped and halloo'd them on; and as fast as their indignation cooled, those mad wags, the *Ember Days*, were at it with their bellows, to blow it into a flame: and all was in a ferment, till old Madam *Septuagesima* (who boasts herself the *Mother of the Days*) wisely diverted the conversation with a tedious tale of the lovers which she could reckon when she was young, and of one Master *Rogation Day* in particular, who was for ever putting the *question* to her; but she kept him at a distance, as the chronicle would tell—by which I apprehend she meant the Almanack. Then she rambled on to the *Days that were gone*, the *good old Days*, and so to the *Days before the Flood*—which plainly showed her old head to be little better than crazed and doited.

Day being ended, the *Days* called for their cloaks and greatcoats, and took their leave. *Lord Mayor's Day* went off in a Mist, as usual; *Shortest Day* in a deep black Fog, that wrapt the little gentleman all round like a hedge-hog. Two *Vigils*—so watchmen are called in heaven—saw *Christmas Day* safe home—they had been used to the business before. Another *Vigil*—a stout, sturdy patrole, called the *Eve of St. Christopher*—seeing *Ash Wednesday* in a condition little better than he should be— e'en whipt him over his shoulders, pick-a-back fashion, and *Old Mortification* went floating home singing—

On the bat's back I do fly,

and a number of old snatches besides, between drunk and sober; but very few Aves or Penitentiaries (you may believe me) were among them. *Longest Day* set off westward in beautiful crimson and gold—the rest, some in one fashion, some in another; but *Valentine* and pretty *May* took their departure together in one of the prettiest silvery twilights a Lover's Day could wish to set in.

OLD CHINA.

I HAVE an almost feminine partiality for old china. When I go to see any great house, I inquire for the china-closet, and next for the picture-gallery. I cannot defend the order of preference, but by saying that we have all some taste or other, of too ancient a date to admit of our remembering distinctly that it was an acquired one. I can call to mind the first play, and the first exhibition, that I was taken to; but I am not conscious of a time when china jars and saucers were introduced into my imagination.

I had no repugnance then—why should I now have? —to those little, lawless, azure-tinctured grotesques, that, under the notion of men and women, float about, uncircumscribed by any element, in that world before perspective—a china tea-cup.

I like to see my old friends—whom distance cannot diminish—figuring up in the air (so they appear to our optics), yet on *terra firma* still—for so we must in courtesy interpret that speck of deeper blue, which the decorous artist, to prevent absurdity, had made to spring up beneath their sandals.

I love the men with women's faces, and the women, if possible, with still more womanish expressions.

Here is a young and courtly Mandarin, handing tea to a lady from a salver—two miles off. See how distance seems to set off respect! And here the same lady, or another—for likeness is identity on tea-cups—is stepping into a little fairy boat, moored on the hither side of this calm garden river, with a dainty mincing foot, which in a right angle of incidence (as angles go in our world) must infallibly land her in the midst of a flowery mead—a furlong off on the other side of the same strange stream!

Farther on—if far or near can be predicated of their world—see horses, trees, pagodas, dancing the hays.

Here—a cow and rabbit couchant, and coextensive—so objects show, seen through the lucid atmosphere of fine Cathay.

I was pointing out to my cousin last evening, over our Hyson (which we are old-fashioned enough to drink unmixed still of an afternoon), some of these *speciosa miracula* upon a set of extraordinary old blue china (a recent purchase) which we were now for the first time using; and could not help remarking, how favourable circumstances had been to us of late years, that we could afford to please the eye sometimes with trifles of this sort—when a passing sentiment seemed to overshade the brows of my companion. I am quick at detecting these summer clouds in Bridget.

"I wish the good old times would come again," she said, "when we were not quite so rich. I do not mean that I want to be poor: but there was a middle state"—so she was pleased to ramble on,—"in which I am sure we were a great deal happier. A purchase is but a purchase, now that you have money enough and to spare. Formerly it used to be a triumph. When we coveted a cheap luxury (and, O! how much ado I had to get you to consent in those times!)—we were used to have a debate two or three days before, and to weigh the *for* and *against*, and think what we might spare it out of, and what saving we could hit upon, that should be an equivalent. A thing was worth buying then, when we felt the money that we paid for it.

"Do you remember the brown suit, which you made to hang upon you, till all your friends cried shame upon you, it grew so threadbare—and all because of that folio Beaumont and Fletcher, which you dragged home late at night from Barker's in Covent Garden? Do you remember how we eyed it for weeks before we could make up our minds to the purchase, and had not come to a determination till it was near ten o'clock of the Saturday night, when you set off from Islington, fearing you should be too late—and when the old bookseller with some grumbling opened his shop, and by the twinkling taper (for he was setting bedwards) lighted out the relic from his dusty treasures—and when you lugged it home, wishing it were twice as cumbersome—and when you presented it to me—and when we were exploring the perfectness of it (*collating*, you called it)—and while I was repairing some of the loose leaves with paste, which your impatience would not suffer to be left till day-break—was there no pleasure in being a poor man? or can those neat black clothes which you wear now, and are so careful to keep brushed, since we have become rich and finical—give you half the honest vanity with which you flaunted it about in that overworn suit—your old corbeau—for four or five weeks longer than you should have done, to pacify your conscience for the mighty sum of fifteen—or sixteen shillings was it?—a great affair we thought it then—which you had lavished on the old folio. Now you can afford to buy any book that pleases you, but I do not see that you ever bring me home any nice old purchases now.

"When you came home with twenty apologies for laying out a less number of shillings upon that print after Lionardo, which we christened the 'Lady Blanch;'

when you looked at the purchase, and thought of the money—and thought of the money, and looked again at the picture—was there no pleasure in being a poor man? Now, you have nothing to do but to walk into Colnaghi's, and buy a wilderness of Lionardos. Yet do you?

"Then, do you remember our pleasant walks to Enfield, and Potter's bar, and Waltham, when we had a holyday—holydays and all other fun are gone now we are rich—and the little hand-basket in which I used to deposit our day's fare of savoury cold lamb and salad—and how you would pry about at noon-tide for some decent house, where we might go in and produce our store—only paying for the ale that you must call for—and speculate upon the looks of the landlady, and whether she was likely to allow us a tablecloth—and wish for such another honest hostess as Izaak Walton has described many a one on the pleasant banks of the Lea, when he went a-fishing—and sometimes they would prove obliging enough, and sometimes they would look grudgingly upon us—but we had cheerful looks still for one another, and would eat our plain food savourily, scarcely grudging Piscator his Trout Hall? Now—when we go out a day's pleasuring, which is seldom, moreover, we *ride* part of the way, and go into a fine inn, and order the best of dinners, never debating the expense—which, after all, never has half the relish of those chance country snaps, when we were at the mercy of uncertain usage, and a precarious welcome.

"You are too proud to see a play anywhere now but in the pit. Do you remember where it was we used to sit, when we saw the battle of Hexham, and the Surrender of Calais, and Bannister and Mrs. Bland in the Children in the Wood—when we squeezed out our shillings apiece to sit three or four times in a season in the one-shilling gallery—where you felt all the time that you ought not to have brought me—and more strongly I felt obligation to you for having brought me—and the pleasure was the better for a little shame—and when the curtain drew up, what cared we for our place in the house, or what mattered it where we were sitting, when our thoughts were with Rosalind in Arden, or with Viola at the Court of Illyria? You used to say that the Gallery was the best place of all for enjoying a play socially— that the relish of such exhibitions must be in proportion to the infrequency of going—that the company we met there, not being in general readers of plays, were obliged to attend the more, and did attend, to what was going on, on the stage—because a word lost would have been a chasm, which it was impossible for them to fill up. With such reflections we consoled our pride then—and I appeal to you whether, as a woman, I met generally with less attention and accommodation than I have done since in more expensive situations in the house? The getting in, indeed, and the crowding up those inconvenient staircases, was bad enough—but there was still a law of civility to woman recognized to quite as great an extent as we ever found in the other passages—and how a little difficulty overcome heightened the snug seat and the play, afterwards! Now we can only pay our money and walk in. You cannot see, you say, in the galleries now. I am sure we saw, and heard too, well enough then—but sight, and all, I think, is gone with our poverty.

"There was pleasure in eating strawberries, before they became quite common—in the first dish of peas, while they were yet dear—to have them for a nice supper, a treat. What treat can we have now? If we were to treat ourselves now—that is, to have dainties a little above our means, it would be selfish and wicked. It is the very little more that we allow ourselves beyond what the actual poor can get at, that makes what I call a treat—when two people, living together as we have done, now and then indulge themselves in a cheap luxury, which both like; while each apologizes, and is willing to take both halves of the blame to his single share. I see no harm in people making much of themselves, in that sense of the word. It may give them a hint how to make much of others. But now—what I mean by the word—we never *do* make much of ourselves. None but the poor can do it. I do not mean the veriest poor of all, but persons as we were, just above poverty.

"I know what you were going to say, that it is mighty pleasant at the end of the year to make all meet,—and much ado we used to have every Thirty-first Night of December to account for our exceedings—many a long face did you make over your puzzled accounts, and in contriving to make it out how we had spent so much—or that we had not spent so much—or that it was impossible we should spend so much next year—and still we found our slender capital decreasing—but then,—betwixt ways, and projects, and compromises of one sort or another, and talk of curtailing this charge, and doing without that for the future—and the hope that youth brings, and laughing spirits (in which you were never poor till now), we pocketed up our loss, and in conclusion, with 'lusty brimmers' (as you used to quote it out of *hearty cheerful Mr. Cotton*, as you called him), we used to welcome in the 'coming guest.' Now we have no reckoning at all at the end of the old year—no flattering promises about the new year doing better for us."

Bridget is so sparing of her speech on most occasions, that when she gets into a rhetorical vein, I am careful how I interrupt it. I could not help, however, smiling at the phantom of wealth which her dear imagination had conjured up out of a clear income of poor —— hundred pounds a year. "It is true we were happier when we were poorer, but we were also younger, my cousin. I am afraid we must put up with the excess, for if we were to shake the superflux into the sea, we should not much mend ourselves. That we had much to struggle with, as we grew up together, we have reason to be most thankful. It strengthened and knit our compact closer. We could never have been what we have been to each other, if we had always had the sufficiency which you now complain of. The resisting power—those natural dilations of the youthful spirit, which circumstances cannot straiten — with us are long since passed away. Competence to age is supplementary youth, a sorry supplement indeed, but I fear the best that is to be had. We must ride where we formerly walked: live better and lie softer — and shall be wise to do so — than we had means to do in those good old days you speak of. Yet could those days return — could you and I once more walk our thirty miles a day — could Bannister and Mrs. Bland again be young, and you and I be young to see them — could the good old one-shilling gallery days return — they are dreams, my cousin, now — but could you and I at this moment, instead of this quiet argument, by our well-carpeted fireside, sitting on this luxurious sofa — be once more struggling up those inconvenient staircases, pushed about and squeezed, and elbowed by the poorest rabble of poor gallery scramblers — could I once more hear those anxious shrieks of yours — and the delicious *Thank God, we are safe*, which always followed when the topmost stair, conquered, let in the first light of the whole cheerful theatre down beneath us — I know not the fathom line that ever touched a descent so deep as I would be willing to bury more wealth in than Crœsus had, or the great Jew R—— is supposed to have, to purchase it. And now do just look at that merry little Chinese waiter holding an umbrella, big enough for a bed-tester, over the head of that pretty insipid half Madonna-ish chit of a lady in that very blue summerhouse."

THE CHILD ANGEL; A DREAM.

I CHANCED upon the prettiest, oddest, fantastical thing of a dream the other night, that you shall hear of. I had been reading the "Loves of the Angels," and went to bed with my head full of speculations, suggested by that extraordinary legend. It had given birth to innumerable conjectures; and, I remember the last waking thought, which I gave expression to on my pillow, was a sort of wonder, "what could come of it."

I was suddenly transported, how or whither I could scarcely make out—but to some celestial region. It was not the real heavens neither—not the downright Bible heaven—but a kind of fairyland heaven, about which a poor human fancy may have leave to sport and air itself, I will hope, without presumption.

Methought—what wild things dreams are!—I was present—at what would you imagine?—at an angel's gossiping.

Whence it came, or how it came, or who bid it come, or whether it came purely of its own head, neither you nor I know—but there lay, sure enough, wrapt in its little cloudy swaddling-bands—a Child Angel.

Sun-threads—filmy beams—ran through the celestial napery of what seemed its princely cradle. All the winged orders hovered round, watching when the new born should open its yet closed eyes; which, when it did, first one, and then the other—with a solicitude and apprehension, yet not such as, stained with fear, dim the expanding eyelids of mortal infants, but as if to explore its path in those its unhereditary palaces—what an inextinguishable titter that time spared not celestial visages! Nor wanted there to my seeming—O, the inexplicable simpleness of dreams!—bowls of that cheering nectar,

which mortals *caudle* call below.

Nor were wanting faces of female ministrants,—stricken in years, as it might seem,—so dexterous were those heavenly attendants to counterfeit kindly similitudes of earth, to greet with terrestrial child-rites the young *present*, which earth had made to heaven.

Then were celestial harpings heard, not in full symphony, as those by which the spheres are tutored; but, as loudest instruments on earth speak oftentimes, muffled;

so to accommodate their sound the better to the weak ears of the imperfect-born. And, with the noise of these subdued soundings, the Angelet sprang forth, fluttering its rudiments of pinions—but forthwith flagged and was recovered into the arms of those full-winged angels. And a wonder it was to see how, as years went round in heaven—a year in dreams is as a day—continually its white shoulders put forth buds of wings, but wanting the perfect angelic nutriment, anon was shorn of its aspiring, and fell fluttering—still caught by angel hands, for ever to put forth shoots, and to fall fluttering, because its birth was not of the unmixed vigour of heaven.

And a name was given to the Babe Angel, and it was to be called *Ge-Urania*, because its production was of earth and heaven.

And it could not taste of death, by reason of its adoption into immortal palaces; but it was to know weakness, and reliance, and the shadow of human imbecility; and it went with a lame gait; but in its goings it exceeded all mortal children in grace and swiftness. Then pity first sprang up in angelic bosoms; and yearnings (like the human) touched them at the sight of the immortal lame one.

And with pain did then first those Intuitive Essences, with pain and strife to their natures (not grief), put back their bright intelligences, and reduce their ethereal minds, schooling them to degrees and slower processes, so to adapt their lessons to the gradual illumination (as must needs be) of the half-earth-born: and what intuitive notices they could not repel (by reason that their nature is, to know all things at once) the half-heavenly novice, by the better part of its nature, aspired to receive into its understanding; so that Humility and Aspiration went on even-paced in the instruction of the glorious Amphibium.

But, by reason that Mature Humanity is too gross to breathe the air of that super-subtile region, its portion was, and is, to be a child for ever.

And because the human part of it might not press into

the heart and inwards of the palace of its adoption, those full-natured angels tended it by turns in the purlieus of the palace, where were shady groves and rivulets, like this green earth from which it came ; so Love, with Voluntary Humility, waited upon the entertainment of the new-adopted.

And myriads of years rolled round (in dreams Time is nothing), and still it kept, and is to keep, perpetual childhood, and is the Tutelar Genius of Childhood upon earth, and still goes lame and lovely.

By the banks of the river Pison is seen, lone sitting by the grave of the terrestrial Adah, whom the angel Nadir loved, a Child ; but not the same which I saw in heaven. A mournful hue overcasts its lineaments ; nevertheless, a correspondency is between the child by the grave, and that celestial orphan, whom I saw above ; and the dimness of the grief upon the heavenly, is a shadow or emblem of that which stains the beauty of the terrestrial. And this correspondency is not to be understood but by dreams.

And in the archives of heaven I had grace to read, how that once the angel Nadir, being exiled from his place for mortal passion, upspringing on the wings of parental love (such power had parental love for a moment to suspend the else-irrevocable law) appeared for a brief instant in his station, and, depositing a wondrous Birth, straightway disappeared, and the palaces knew him no more. And this charge was the self-same Babe, who goeth lame and lovely—but Adah sleepeth by the river Pison.

CONFESSIONS OF A DRUNKARD.

DEHORTATIONS from the use of strong liquors have been the favourite topic of sober declaimers in all ages, and have been received with abundance of applause by water-drinking critics. But with the patient himself, the man that is to be cured, unfortunately their sound has seldom prevailed. Yet the evil is acknowledged, the remedy simple. Abstain. No force can oblige a man to raise the glass to his head against his will. 'Tis as easy as not to steal, not to tell lies.

Alas! the hand to pilfer, and the tongue to bear false witness, have no constitutional tendency. These are actions indifferent to them. At the first instance of the reformed will, they can be brought off without a murmur. The itching finger is but a figure in speech, and the tongue of the liar can with the same natural delight give forth useful truths with which it has been accustomed to scatter their pernicious contraries. But when a man has commenced sot——

O pause, thou sturdy moralist, thou person of stout nerves and a strong head, whose liver is happily untouched, and ere thy gorge riseth at the *name* which I had written, first learn what the *thing* is; how much of compassion, how much of human allowance, thou mayest virtuously mingle with thy disapprobation. Trample not on the ruins of a man. Exact not, under so terrible a penalty as infamy, a resuscitation from a state of death almost as real as that from which Lazarus rose not but by a miracle.

Begin a reformation, and custom will make it easy. But what if the beginning be dreadful, the first steps not like climbing a mountain but going through fire? what if the whole system must undergo a change violent as that which we conceive of the mutation of form in some insects? what if a process comparable to flaying alive be to be gone through? is the weakness that sinks under such struggles to be confounded with the pertinacity which clings to other vices, which have induced no constitutional necessity, no engagement of the whole victim, body and soul?

I have known one in that state, when he has tried to abstain but for one evening,—though the poisonous potion had long ceased to bring back its first enchantments, though he was sure it would rather deepen his gloom than brighten it,—in the violence of the struggle, and the necessity he had felt of getting rid of the present sensation at any rate, I have known him to scream out, to cry aloud, for the anguish and pain of the strife within him.

Why should I hesitate to declare, that the man of whom I speak is myself? I have no puling apology to make to mankind. I see them all in one way or another deviating from the pure reason. It is to my own nature alone I am accountable for the woe that I have brought upon it.

I believe that there are constitutions, robust heads and iron insides, whom scarce any excesses can hurt; whom brandy (I have seen them drink it like wine), at all events whom wine, taken in ever so plentiful a measure, can do no worse injury to than just to muddle their faculties, perhaps never very pellucid. On them this discourse is wasted. They would but laugh at a weak brother, who, trying his strength with them, and coming off foiled from the contest, would fain persuade them that such agonistic exercises are dangerous. It is to a very different description of persons I speak. It is to the weak—the nervous; to those who feel the want of some artificial aid to raise their spirits in society to what is no more than the ordinary pitch of all around them without it. This is the secret of our drinking. Such must fly the convivial board in the first instance, if they do not mean to sell themselves for term of life.

Twelve years ago I had completed my six-and-twentieth year. I had lived from the period of leaving school to that time pretty much in solitude. My companions were chiefly books, or at most one or two living ones of my own book-loving and sober stamp. I rose early, went to bed betimes, and the faculties which God had given me, I have reason to think, did not rust in me unused.

About that time I fell in with some companions of a

different order. They were men of boisterous spirits, sitters up a-nights, disputants, drunken; yet seemed to have something noble about them. We dealt about the wit, or what passes for it after midnight, jovially. Of the quality called fancy I certainly possessed a larger share than my companions. Encouraged by their applause, I set up for a professed joker! I, who of all men am least fitted for such an occupation, having, in addition to the greatest difficulty which I experience at all times of finding words to express my meaning, a natural nervous impediment in my speech!

Reader, if you are gifted with nerves like mine, aspire to any character but that of a wit. When you find a tickling relish upon your tongue disposing you to that sort of conversation, especially if you find a preternatural flow of ideas setting in upon you at the sight of a bottle and fresh glasses, avoid giving way to it as you would fly your greatest destruction. If you cannot crush the power of fancy, or that within you which you mistake for such, divert it, give it some other play. Write an essay, pen a character or description,—but not as I do now, with tears trickling down your cheeks.

To be an object of compassion to friends, of derision to foes; to be suspected by strangers, stared at by fools; to be esteemed dull when you cannot be witty, to be applauded for witty when you know that you have been dull; to be called upon for the extemporaneous exercise of that faculty which no premeditation can give; to be spurred on to efforts which end in contempt; to be set on to provoke mirth which procures the procurer hatred; to give pleasure and be paid with squinting malice; to swallow draughts of life-destroying wine which are to be distilled into airy breath to tickle vain auditors; to mortgage miserable morrows for nights of madness; to waste whole seas of time upon those who pay it back in little inconsiderable drops of grudging applause,—are the wages of buffoonery and death.

Time, which has a sure stroke at dissolving all connections which have no solider fastening than this liquid cement, more kind to me than my own taste or penetration, at length opened my eyes to the supposed qualities of my first friends. No trace of them is left but in the vices which they introduced, and the habits they infixed. In them my friends survive still, and exercise ample retribution for any supposed infidelity that I may have been guilty of towards them.

My next more immediate companions were and are persons of such intrinsic and felt worth, that though accidentally their acquaintance has proved pernicious to me, I do not know that if the thing were to do over again, I should have the courage to eschew the mischief at the price of forfeiting the benefit. I came to them recking from the steams of my late over-heated notions of companionship; and the slightest fuel which they unconsciously afforded, was sufficient to feed my own fires into a propensity.

They were no drinkers; but, one from professional habits, and another from a custom derived from his father, smoked tobacco. The devil could not have devised a more subtle trap to re-take a backsliding penitent. The transition, from gulping down draughts of liquid fire to puffing out innocuous blasts of dry smoke, was so like cheating him. But he is too hard for us when we hope to commute. He beats us at barter: and when we think to set off a new failing against an old infirmity, 'tis odds but he puts the trick upon us of two for one. That (comparatively) white devil of tobacco brought with him in the end seven worse than himself.

It were impertinent to carry the reader through all the processes by which, from smoking at first with malt liquor, I took my degrees through thin wines, through stronger wine and water, through small punch, to those juggling compositions, which, under the name of mixed liquors, slur a great deal of brandy or other poison under less and less water continually, until they come next to none, and so to none at all. But it is hateful to disclose the secrets of my Tartarus.

I should repel my readers, from a mere incapacity of believing me, were I to tell them what tobacco has been to me, the drudging service which I have paid, the slavery which I have vowed to it. How, when I have resolved to quit it, a feeling as of ingratitude has started up; how it has put on personal claims and made the demands of a friend upon me. How the reading of it casually in a book, as where Adams takes his whiff in the chimney-corner of some inn in Joseph Andrews, or Piscator in the Complete Angler breaks his fast upon a morning pipe in that delicate room *Piscatoribus Sacrum*, has in a moment broken down the resistance of weeks. How a pipe was ever in my midnight path before me, till the vision forced me to realise it,—how then its ascending vapours curled, its fragrance lulled, and the thousand delicious ministerings conversant about it, employing every faculty, extracted the sense of pain. How from illuminating it came to darken, from a quick solace it turned to a negative relief, thence to a restlessness and dissatisfaction, thence to a positive misery. How, even now, when the whole secret stands confessed in all its dreadful truth before me, I feel myself linked to it beyond the power of revocation. Bone of my bone——

Persons not accustomed to examine the motives of their actions, to reckon up the countless nails that rivet the chains of habit, or perhaps being bound by none so obdurate as those I have confessed to, may recoil from this as from an overcharged picture. But what short of such a bondage is it, which in spite of protesting friends, a weeping wife, and a reprobating world, chains down many a poor fellow, of no original indisposition to goodness, to his pipe and his pot?

I have seen a print after Correggio, in which three female figures are ministering to a man who sits fast bound at the root of a tree. Sensuality is soothing him, Evil Habit is nailing him to a branch, and Repugnance at the same instant of time is applying a snake to his side. In his face is feeble delight, the recollection of past rather than perception of present pleasures, languid enjoyment of evil with utter imbecility to good, a Sybaritic effeminacy, a submission to bondage, the springs of the will gone down like a broken clock, the sin and the suffering co-instantaneous, or the latter forerunning the former, remorse preceding action—all this represented in one point of time.—When I saw this, I admired the wonderful skill of the painter. But when I went away, I wept, because I thought of my own condition.

Of *that* there is no hope that it should ever change. The waters have gone over me. But out of the black depths, could I be heard, I would cry out to all those who have but set a foot in the perilous flood. Could the youth, to whom the flavour of his first wine is delicious as the opening scenes of life or the entering upon some newly-discovered paradise, look into my desolation, and be made to understand what a dreary thing it is when a man shall feel himself going down a precipice with open eyes and a passive will,—to see his destruction and have no power to stop it, and yet to feel it all the way emanating from himself; to perceive all goodness emptied out of him, and yet not to be able to forget a time when it was otherwise; to bear about the piteous spectacle of his own self-ruins:—could he see my fevered eye, feverish with last night's drinking, and feverishly looking for this night's repetition of the folly; could he feel the body of the death out of which I cry hourly with feebler and feebler outcry to be delivered,—it were enough to make him dash the sparkling beverage to the earth in all the pride of its mantling temptation; to make him clasp his teeth,

and not undo 'em
To suffer WET DAMNATION to run thro' 'em.

Yea, but (methinks I hear somebody object) if sobriety be that fine thing you would have us to understand, if the comforts of a cool brain are to be preferred to that state of heated excitement which you describe and deplore, what hinders in your instance that you do not return to those habits from which you would induce others never to swerve? if the blessing be worth preserving, is it not worth recovering?

Recovering!—O if a wish could transport me back to those days of youth, when a draught from the next clear spring could slake any heats which summer suns and youthful exercise had power to stir up in the blood, how gladly would I return to thee, pure element, the drink of children and of child-like holy hermit! In my dreams I can sometimes fancy thy cool refreshment purling over my burning tongue. But my waking stomach rejects it. That which refreshes innocence only makes me sick and faint.

But is there no middle way betwixt total abstinence and the excess which kills you?—For your sake, reader, and that you may never attain to my experience, with pain I must utter the dreadful truth, that there is none, none that I can find. In my stage of habit (I speak not of habits less confirmed—for some of them I believe the advice to be most prudential), in the stage which I have reached, to stop short of that measure which is sufficient to draw on torpor and sleep, the benumbing apoplectic sleep of the drunkard, is to have taken none at all. The pain of the self-denial is all one. And what that is, I had rather the reader should believe on my credit, than know from his own trial. He will come to know it, whenever he shall arrive in that state in which, paradoxical as it may appear, *reason shall only visit him through intoxication;* for it is a fearful truth, that the intellectual faculties by repeated acts of intemperance may be driven from their orderly sphere of action, their clear daylight ministeries, until they shall be brought at last to depend, for the faint manifestation of their departing energies, upon the returning periods of the fatal madness to which they owe their devastation. The drinking man is never less himself than during his sober intervals. Evil is so far his good.[1]

[1] When poor M—— painted his last picture, with a pencil in

Behold me then, in the robust period of life, reduced to imbecility and decay. Hear me count my gains, and the profits which I have derived from the midnight cup.

Twelve years ago, I was possessed of a healthy frame of mind and body. I was never strong, but I think my constitution (for a weak one) was as happily exempt from the tendency to any malady as it was possible to be. I scarce knew what it was to ail anything. Now, except when I am losing myself in a sea of drink, I am never free from those uneasy sensations in head and stomach, which are so much worse to bear than any definite pains or aches.

At that time I was seldom in bed after six in the morning, summer and winter. I awoke refreshed, and seldom without some merry thoughts in my head, or some piece of a song to welcome the new-born day. Now, the first feeling which besets me, after stretching out the hours of recumbence to their last possible extent, is a forecast of the wearisome day that lies before me, with a secret wish that I could have lain on still, or never awaked.

Life itself, my waking life, has much of the confusion, the trouble, and obscure perplexity, of an ill dream. In the day-time I stumble upon dark mountains.

Business, which, though never very particularly adapted to my nature, yet as something of necessity to be gone through, and therefore best undertaken with cheerfulness, I used to enter upon with some degree of alacrity, now wearies, affrights, perplexes me. I fancy all sorts of discouragements, and am ready to give up an occupation which gives me bread, from a harassing conceit of incapacity. The slightest commission given me by a friend, or any small duty which I have to perform for myself, as

---

one trembling hand, and a glass of brandy and water in the other, his fingers owed the comparative steadiness with which they were enabled to go through their task in an imperfect manner, to a temporary firmness derived from a repetition of practices, the general effect of which had shaken both them and him so terribly

giving orders to a tradesman, etc., haunts me as a labour impossible to be got through. So much the springs of action are broken.

The same cowardice attends me in all my intercourse with mankind. I dare not promise that a friend's honour, or his cause, would be safe in my keeping, if I were put to the expense of any manly resolution in defending it. So much the springs of moral action are deadened within me.

My favourite occupations in times past now cease to entertain. I can do nothing readily. Application for ever so short a time kills me. This poor abstract of my condition was penned at long intervals, with scarcely an attempt at connexion of thought, which is now difficult to me.

The noble passages which formerly delighted me in history or poetic fiction now only draw a few tears, allied to dotage. My broken and dispirited nature seems to sink before anything great and admirable.

I perpetually catch myself in tears, for any cause, or none. It is inexpressible how much this infirmity adds to a sense of shame, and a general feeling of deterioration.

These are some of the instances, concerning which I can say with truth, that it was not always so with me.

Shall I lift up the veil of my weakness any further? —or is this disclosure sufficient?

I am a poor nameless egotist, who have no vanity to consult by these Confessions. I know not whether I shall be laughed at, or heard seriously. Such as they are, I commend them to the reader's attention, if he find his own case any way touched. I have told him what I am come to. Let him stop in time.

POPULAR FALLACIES.

I.—THAT A BULLY IS ALWAYS A COWARD.

This axiom contains a principle of compensation, which disposes us to admit the truth of it. But there is no safe trusting to dictionaries and definitions. We should more willingly fall in with this popular language, if we did not find *brutality* sometimes awkwardly coupled with *valour* in the same vocabulary. The comic writers, with their poetical justice, have contributed not a little to mislead us upon this point. To see a hectoring fellow exposed and beaten upon the stage, has something in it wonderfully diverting. Some people's share of animal spirits is notoriously low and defective. It has not strength to raise a vapour, or furnish out the wind of a tolerable bluster. These love to be told that huffing is no part of valour. The truest courage with them is that which is the least noisy and obtrusive. But confront one of these silent heroes with the swaggerer of real life, and his confidence in the theory quickly vanishes. Pretensions do not uniformly bespeak non-performance. A modest, inoffensive deportment does not necessarily imply valour; neither does the absence of it justify us in denying that quality. Hickman wanted modesty—we do not mean *him* of Clarissa—but who ever doubted his courage? Even the poets—upon whom this equitable distribution of qualities should be most binding—have thought it agreeable to nature to depart from the rule upon occasion. Harapha, in the "Agonistes," is indeed a bully upon the received notions. Milton has made him at once a blusterer, a giant, and a dastard. But Almanzor, in Dryden, talks of driving armies singly before him—and does it. Tom Brown had a shrewder insight into this kind of character than either of his predecessors. He divides the palm more equably, and allows his hero a sort of dimidiate pre-eminence:—"Bully Dawson kicked by half the town, and half the town kicked by Bully Dawson." This was true distributive justice.

II.—THAT ILL-GOTTEN GAIN NEVER PROSPERS.

THE weakest part of mankind have this saying commonest in their mouth. It is the trite consolation administered to the easy dupe, when he has been tricked out of his money or estate, that the acquisition of it will do the owner *no good*. But the rogues of this world—the prudenter part of them at least,—know better; and if the observation had been as true as it is old, would not have failed by this time to have discovered it. They have pretty sharp distinctions of the fluctuating and the permanent. "Lightly come, lightly go," is a proverb which they can very well afford to leave, when they leave little else, to the losers. They do not always find manors, got by rapine or chicanery, insensibly to melt away as the poets will have it; or that all gold glides, like thawing snow, from the thief's hand that grasps it. Church land, alienated to lay uses, was formerly denounced to have this slippery quality. But some portions of it somehow always stuck so fast, that the denunciators have been fain to postpone the prophecy of refundment to a late posterity.

III.—THAT A MAN MUST NOT LAUGH AT HIS OWN JEST.

THE severest exaction surely ever invented upon the self-denial of poor human nature! This is to expect a gentleman to give a treat without partaking of it; to sit esurient at his own table, and commend the flavour of his venison upon the absurd strength of his never touching it himself. On the contrary, we love to see a wag *taste* his own joke to his party; to watch a quirk or a merry conceit flickering upon the lips some seconds before the tongue is delivered of it. If it be good, fresh, and racy—begotten of the occasion; if he that utters it never thought it before, he is naturally the first to be tickled with it, and any suppression of such complacence we hold to be churlish and insulting. What does it seem to imply but that your company is weak or foolish to be moved by an image or a fancy, that shall stir you not at all, or but faintly? This is exactly the humour of the fine gentleman in Mandeville, who, while he dazzles his guests with the display of some costly toy, affects himself to "see nothing considerable in it."

IV.—THAT SUCH A ONE SHOWS HIS BREEDING.—THAT IT IS EASY TO PERCEIVE HE IS NO GENTLEMAN.

A SPEECH from the poorest sort of people, which always indicates that the party vituperated is a gentleman. The very fact which they deny, is that which galls and exasperates them to use this language. The forbearance with which it is usually received is a proof what interpretation the bystander sets upon it. Of a kin to this, and still less politic, are the phrases with which, in their street rhetoric, they ply one another more grossly;—*He is a poor creature.—He has not a rag to cover —— etc.;* though this last, we confess, is more frequently applied by females to females. They do not perceive that the satire glances upon themselves. A poor man, of all things in the world, should not upbraid an antagonist with poverty. Are there no other topics—as, to tell him his father was hanged—his sister, etc.——without exposing a secret which should be kept snug between them; and doing an affront to the order to which they have the honour equally to belong? All this while they do not see how the wealthier man stands by and laughs in his sleeve at both.

V.—THAT THE POOR COPY THE VICES OF THE RICH.

A SMOOTH text to the latter; and, preached from the pulpit, is sure of a docile audience from the pews lined with satin. It is twice sitting upon velvet to a foolish squire to be told that *he*—and not *perverse nature*, as the homilies would make us imagine, is the true cause of all the irregularities in his parish. This is striking at the root of free-will indeed, and denying the originality of sin in any sense. But men are not such implicit sheep as this comes to. If the abstinence from evil on the part of the upper classes is to derive itself from no higher principle than the apprehension of setting ill patterns to the lower, we beg leave to discharge them from all squeamishness on that score: they may even take their fill of pleasures, where they can find them. The Genius of Poverty, hampered and straitened as it is, is not so barren of invention but it can trade upon the staple of its own vice, without drawing upon their capital. The poor are not quite such servile imitators as they take them for. Some of them are very clever artists in their way. Here and there, we find an original. Who taught the poor to steal—to pilfer? They did not go to the great for schoolmasters in these faculties, surely. It is well if in some vices they allow us to be—no copyists. In no other sense is it true that the poor copy them, than as servants may be said to *take after* their masters and mistresses, when they succeed to their reversionary cold meats. If the master, from indisposition, or some other cause, neglect his food, the servant dines notwithstanding.

"O, but (some will say) the force of example is great." We knew a lady who was so scrupulous on this head, that she would put up with the calls of the most impertinent visitor, rather than let her servant say she was not at home, for fear of teaching her maid to tell an untruth; and this in the very face of the fact, which she knew well enough, that the wench was one of the greatest liars upon

the earth without teaching; so much so, that her mistress
possibly never heard two words of consecutive truth from
her in her life. But nature must go for nothing; example must be everything. This liar in grain, who never
opened her mouth without a lie, must be guarded against
a remote inference, which she (pretty casuist!) might
possibly draw from a form of words—literally false, but
essentially deceiving no one—that under some circumstances a fib might not be so exceedingly sinful—a fiction,
too, not at all in her own way, or one that she could be
suspected of adopting, for few servant-wenches care to be
denied to visitors.

This word *example* reminds us of another fine word
which is in use upon these occasions—*encouragement*.
"People in our sphere must not be thought to give encouragement to such proceedings." To such a frantic
height is this principle capable of being carried, that we
have known individuals who have thought it within the
scope of their influence to sanction despair, and give *éclat*
to—suicide. A domestic in the family of a county member lately deceased, from love, or some unknown cause,
cut his throat, but not successfully. The poor fellow was
otherwise much loved and respected; and great interest
was used in his behalf, upon his recovery, that he might
be permitted to retain his place; his word being first
pledged, not without some substantial sponsors to promise
for him, that the like should never happen again. His
master was inclinable to keep him, but his mistress
thought otherwise; and John in the end was dismissed,
her ladyship declaring that she "could not think of encouraging any such doings in the county."

VI.—THAT ENOUGH IS AS GOOD AS A FEAST.

Not a man, woman, or child, in ten miles round Guild
hall, who really believes this saying. The inventor of it
did not believe it himself. It was made in revenge by
somebody, who was disappointed of a regale. It is a

vile cold-scrag-of-mutton sophism; a lie palmed upon the palate, which knows better things. If nothing else could be said for a feast, this is sufficient—that from the superflux there is usually something left for the next day. Morally interpreted, it belongs to a class of proverbs which have a tendency to make us undervalue *money*. Of this cast are those notable observations, that money is not health; riches cannot purchase everything: the metaphor which makes gold to be mere muck, with the morality which traces fine clothing to the sheep's back, and denounces pearl as the unhandsome excretion of an oyster. Hence, too, the phrase which imputes dirt to acres—a sophistry so barefaced, that even the literal sense of it is true only in a wet season. This, and abundance of similar sage saws assuming to inculcate *content*, we verily believe to have been the invention of some cunning borrower, who had designs upon the purse of his wealthier neighbour, which he could only hope to carry by force of these verbal jugglings. Translate any one of these sayings out of the artful metonymy which envelopes it, and the trick is apparent. Goodly legs and shoulders of mutton, exhilarating cordials, books, pictures, the opportunities of seeing foreign countries, independence, heart's ease, a man's own time to himself, are not *muck*—however we may be pleased to scandalise with that appellation the faithful metal that provides them for us.

VII.—OF TWO DISPUTANTS, THE WARMEST IS GENERALLY IN THE WRONG.

OUR experience would lead us to quite an opposite conclusion. Temper, indeed, is no test of truth; but warmth and earnestness are a proof at least of a man's own conviction of the rectitude of that which he maintains. Coolness is as often the result of an unprincipled indifference to truth or falsehood, as of a sober confidence in a man's own side in a dispute. Nothing is more insulting sometimes than the appearance of this philosophic temper. There is little Titubus, the stammering law-stationer in Lincoln's Inn—we have seldom known this shrewd little fellow engaged in an argument where we were not convinced he had the best of it, if his tongue would but fairly have seconded him. When he has been spluttering excellent broken sense for an hour together, writhing and labouring to be delivered of the point of dispute—the very gist of the controversy knocking at his teeth, which like some obstinate iron-grating still obstructed its deliverance—his puny frame convulsed, and face reddening all over at an unfairness in the logic which he wanted articulation to expose, it has moved our gall to see a smooth portly fellow of an adversary, that cared not a button for the merits of the question, by merely laying his hand upon the head of the stationer, and desiring him to be *calm* (your tall disputants have always the advantage), with a provoking sneer carry the argument clean from him in the opinion of all the bystanders, who have gone away clearly convinced that Titubus must have been in the wrong, because he was in a passion; and that Mr. ———, meaning his opponent, is one of the fairest and at the same time one of the most dispassionate arguers breathing.

VIII.—THAT VERBAL ALLUSIONS ARE NOT WIT, BECAUSE THEY WILL NOT BEAR A TRANSLATION.

THE same might be said of the wittiest local allusions. A custom is sometimes as difficult to explain to a foreigner as a pun. What would become of a great part of the wit of the last age, if it were tried by this test? How would certain topics, as aldermanity, cuckoldry, have sounded to a Terentian auditory, though Terence himself had been alive to translate them? *Senator urbanus* with *Carruca* to boot for a synonym, would but faintly have done the business. Words, involving notions, are hard enough to render; it is too much to expect us to translate a sound, and give an elegant version to a jingle.

The Virgilian harmony is not translatable, but by substituting harmonious sounds in another language for it. To Latinise a pun, we must seek a pun in Latin that will answer to it ; as, to give an idea of the double endings in Hudibras, we must have recourse to a similar practice in old monkish doggrel. Dennis, the fiercest oppugner of puns in ancient or modern times, professes himself highly tickled with the "a stick," chiming to "ecclesiastic." Yet what is this but a species of pun, a verbal consonance ?

IX.—THAT THE WORST PUNS ARE THE BEST.

IF by worst be only meant the most far-fetched and startling, we agree to it. A pun is not bound by the laws which limit nicer wit. It is a pistol let off at the ear ; not a feather to tickle the intellect. It is an antic which does not stand upon manners, but comes bounding into the presence, and does not show the less comic for being dragged in sometimes by the head and shoulders. What though it limp a little, or prove defective in one leg?—all the better. A pun may easily be too curious and artificial. Who has not at one time or other been at a party of professors (himself perhaps an old offender in that line), where, after ringing a round of the most ingenious conceits, every man contributing his shot, and some there the most expert shooters of the day; after making a poor *word* run the gauntlet till it is ready to drop; after hunting and winding it through all the possible ambages of similar sounds; after squeezing, and hauling, and tugging at it, till the very milk of it will not yield a drop further,—suddenly some obscure, unthought-of fellow in a corner, who was never 'prentice to the trade, whom the company for very pity passed over, as we do by a known poor man when a money-subscription is going round, no one calling upon him for his quota— has all at once come out with something so whimsical, yet so pertinent; so brazen in its pretensions,

yet so impossible to be denied; so exquisitely good, and
so deplorably bad, at the same time,—that it has proved a
Robin Hood's shot; anything ulterior to that is despaired
of; and the party breaks up, unanimously voting it to be
the very worst (that is, best) pun of the evening. This
species of wit is the better for not being perfect in all its
parts. What it gains in completeness, it loses in naturalness. The more exactly it satisfies the critical, the less
hold it has upon some other faculties. The puns which
are most entertaining are those which will least bear an
analysis. Of this kind is the following, recorded with a
sort of stigma, in one of Swift's Miscellanies.

An Oxford scholar, meeting a porter who was carrying
a hare through the streets, accosts him with this extraordinary question: "Prithee, friend, is that thy own hair
or a wig?"

There is no excusing this, and no resisting it. A man
might blur ten sides of paper in attempting a defence of
it against a critic who should be laughter-proof. The
quibble in itself is not considerable. It is only a new
turn given by a little false pronunciation to a very common though not very courteous inquiry. Put by one
gentleman to another at a dinner-party, it would have
been vapid; to the mistress of the house, it would have
shown much less wit than rudeness. We must take in
the totality of time, place, and person; the pert look of
the inquiring scholar, the desponding looks of the puzzled
porter: the one stopping at leisure, the other hurrying
on with his burden; the innocent though rather abrupt
tendency of the first member of the question, with the
utter and inextricable irrelevancy of the second; the
place—a public street, not favourable to frivolous investi-
gations; the affrontive quality of the primitive inquiry
(the common question) invidiously transferred to the
derivative (the new turn given to it) in the implied
satire: namely, that few of that tribe are expected to
eat of the good things which they carry, they being in
most countries considered rather as the temporary trustees

than owners of such dainties,—which the fellow was beginning to understand; but then the *wig* again comes in, and he can make nothing of it; all put together constitute a picture: Hogarth could have made it intelligible on canvas.

Yet nine out of ten critics will pronounce this a very bad pun, because of the defectiveness in the concluding member, which is its very beauty, and constitutes the surprise. The same person shall cry up for admirable the cold quibble from Virgil about the broken Cremona;[1] because it is made out in all its parts, and leaves nothing to the imagination. We venture to call it cold; because, of thousands who have admired it, it would be difficult to find one who has heartily chuckled at it. As appealing to the judgment merely (setting the risible faculty aside), we must pronounce it a monument of curious felicity. But as some stories are said to be too good to be true, it may with equal truth be asserted of this biverbal allusion, that it is too good to be natural. One cannot help suspecting that the incident was invented to fit the line. It would have been better had it been less perfect. Like some Virgilian hemistichs, it has suffered by filling up. The *nimium Vicina* was enough in conscience; the *Cremonae* afterwards loads it. It is, in fact, a double pun; and we have always observed that a superfœtation in this sort of wit is dangerous. When a man has said a good thing, it is seldom politic to follow it up. We do not care to be cheated a second time; or, perhaps the mind of man (with reverence be it spoken) is not capacious enough to lodge two puns at a time. The impression, to be forcible, must be simultaneous and undivided.

X.—THAT HANDSOME IS THAT HANDSOME DOES.

THOSE who use this proverb can never have seen Mrs. Conrady.

[1] Swift.

The soul, if we may believe Plotinus, is a ray from the celestial beauty. As she partakes more or less of this heavenly light, she informs, with corresponding characters, the fleshly tenement which she chooses, and frames to herself a suitable mansion.

All which only proves that the soul of Mrs. Conrady, in her pre-existent state, was no great judge of architecture.

To the same effect, in a Hymn in honour of Beauty, divine Spenser *platonising* sings:—

——— Every spirit as it is more pure,
And hath in it the more of heavenly light,
So it the fairer body doth procure
To habit in, and it more fairly dight
With cheerful grace and amiable sight.
For of the soul the body form doth take:
For soul is form, and doth the body make.

But Spenser, it is clear, never saw Mrs. Conrady.

These poets, we find, are no safe guides in philosophy; for here, in his very next stanza but one, is a saving clause, which throws us all out again, and leaves us as much to seek as ever:—

Yet oft it falls, that many a gentle mind
Dwells in deformed tabernacle drown'd,
Either by chance, against the course of kind,
Or through unaptness in the substance found,
Which it assumed of some stubborn ground,
That will not yield unto her form's direction,
But is performed with some foul imperfection.

From which it would follow, that Spenser had seen somebody like Mrs. Conrady.

The spirit of this good lady—her previous *anima*—must have stumbled upon one of these untoward tabernacles which he speaks of. A more rebellious commodity of clay for a ground, as the poet calls it, no gentle mind—and sure hers is one of the gentlest—ever had to deal with.

Pondering upon her inexplicable visage—inexplicable, we mean, but by this modification of the theory—we have come to a conclusion that, if one must be plain, it is better to be plain all over, than amidst a tolerable residue of features to hang out one that shall be exceptionable. No one can say of Mrs. Conrady's countenance that it would be better if she had but a nose. It is impossible to pull her to pieces in this manner. We have seen the most malicious beauties of her own sex baffled in the attempt at a selection. The *tout-ensemble* defies particularizing. It is too complete—too consistent, as we may say—to admit of these invidious reservations. It is not as if some Apelles had picked out here a lip— and there a chin—out of the collected ugliness of Greece, to frame a model by. It is a symmetrical whole. We challenge the minutest connoisseur to cavil at any part or parcel of the countenance in question; to say that this, or that, is improperly placed. We are convinced that true ugliness, no less than is affirmed of true beauty, is the result of harmony. Like that, too, it reigns without a competitor. No one ever saw Mrs. Conrady without pronouncing her to be the plainest woman that he ever met with in the course of his life. The first time that you are indulged with a sight of her face, is an era in your existence ever after. You are glad to have seen it —like Stonehenge. No one can pretend to forget it. No one ever apologised to her for meeting her in the street on such a day and not knowing her: the pretext would be too bare. Nobody can mistake her for another. Nobody can say of her, "I think I have seen that face somewhere, but I cannot call to mind where." You must remember that in such a parlour it first struck you like a bust. You wondered where the owner of the house had picked it up. You wondered more when it began to move its lips—so mildly too! No one ever thought of asking her to sit for her picture. Lockets are for remembrance; and it would be clearly superfluous to hang an image at your heart, which, once seen, can never be out of it. It is not a mean face either; its entire originality precludes that. Neither is it of that order of plain faces

which improve upon acquaintance. Some very good but
ordinary people, by an unwearied perseverance in good
offices, put a cheat upon our eyes; juggle our senses out
of their natural impressions; and set us upon discovering
good indications in a countenance, which at first sight
promised nothing less. We detect gentleness, which had
escaped us, lurking about an under lip. But when Mrs.
Conrady has done you a service, her face remains the
same; when she has done you a thousand, and you know
that she is ready to double the number, still it is that
individual face. Neither can you say of it, that it would
be a good face if it were not marked by the small-pox—a
compliment which is always more admissive than excusa-
tory—for either Mrs. Conrady never had the small-pox;
or, as we say, took it kindly. No, it stands upon its own
merits fairly. There it is. It is her mark, her token;
that which she is known by.

XI.—THAT WE MUST NOT LOOK A GIFT HORSE IN THE MOUTH:

Nor a lady's age in the parish register. We hope we
have more delicacy than to do either; but some faces
spare us the trouble of these *dental* inquiries. And what
if the beast, which my friend would force upon my acceptance, prove, upon the face of it, a sorry Rosinante, a
lean, ill-favoured jade, whom no gentleman could think
of setting up in his stables? Must I, rather than not be
obliged to my friend, make her a companion to Eclipse or
Lightfoot? A horse-giver, no more than a horse-seller,
has a right to palm his spavined article upon us for good
ware. An equivalent is expected in either case; and,
with my own good-will, I could no more be cheated out
of my thanks than out of my money. Some people have
a knack of putting upon you gifts of no real value, to
engage you to substantial gratitude. We thank them for
nothing. Our friend Mitis carries this humour of never
refusing a present to the very point of absurdity—if it

were possible to couple the ridiculous with so much mistaken delicacy and real good-nature. Not an apartment in his fine house (and he has a true taste in household decorations), but is stuffed up with some preposterous print or mirror—the worst adapted to his panels that may be—the presents of his friends that know his weakness; while his noble Vandykes are displaced to make room for a set of daubs, the work of some wretched artist of his acquaintance, who, having had them returned upon his hands for bad likenesses, finds his account in bestowing them here gratis. The good creature has not the heart to mortify the painter at the expense of an honest refusal. It is pleasant (if it did not vex one at the same time) to see him sitting in his dining parlour, surrounded with obscure aunts and cousins to God knows whom, while the true Lady Marys and Lady Bettys of his own honourable family, in favour to these adopted frights, are consigned to the staircase and the lumber-room. In like manner, his goodly shelves are one by one stripped of his favourite old authors, to give place to a collection of presentation copies—the flour and bran of modern poetry. A presentation copy, reader—if haply you are yet innocent of such favours—is a copy of a book which does not sell, sent you by the author, with his foolish autograph at the beginning of it; for which, if a stranger, he only demands your friendship; if a brother author, he expects from you a book of yours, which does sell, in return. We can speak to experience, having by us a tolerable assortment of these gift-horses. Not to ride a metaphor to death— we are willing to acknowledge that in some gifts there is sense. A duplicate out of a friend's library (where he has more than one copy of a rare author) is intelligible. There are favours, short of the pecuniary—a thing not fit to be hinted at among gentlemen—which confer as much grace upon the acceptor as the offerer; the kind, we confess, which is most to our palate, is of those little conciliatory missives, which for their vehicle generally choose a hamper—little odd presents of game, fruit, perhaps wine—though it is essential to the delicacy of the latter, that it be home-made. We love to have our friend in the country sitting thus at our table by proxy; to apprehend his presence (though a hundred miles may be between us) by a turkey, whose goodly aspect reflects to us his "plump corpusculum;" to taste him in grouse or woodcock; to feel him gliding down in the toast peculiar to the latter; to concorporate him in a slice of Canterbury brawn. This is indeed to have him within ourselves; to know him intimately: such participation is methinks unitive, as the old theologians phrase it. For these considerations we should be sorry if certain restrictive regulations, which are thought to bear hard upon the peasantry of this country, were entirely done away with. A hare, as the law now stands, makes many friends. Caius conciliates Titius (knowing his *goût*) with a leash of partridges. Titius (suspecting his partiality for them) passes them to Lucius; who, in his turn, preferring his friend's relish to his own, makes them over to Marcius; till in their ever-widening progress, and round of unconscious circum-migration, they distribute the seeds of harmony over half a parish. We are well-disposed to this kind of sensible remembrances; and are the less apt to be taken by those little airy tokens--impalpable to the palate--which, under the names of rings, lockets, keepsakes, amuse some people's fancy mightily. We could never away with these indigestible trifles. They are the very kickshaws and foppery of friendship.

XII.—THAT HOME IS HOME THOUGH IT IS NEVER SO HOMELY.

HOMES there are, we are sure, that are no homes; the home of the very poor man, and another which we shall speak to presently. Crowded places of cheap entertainment, and the benches of alehouses, if they could speak, might bear mournful testimony to the first. To them the very poor man resorts for an image of the home which

he cannot find at home. For a starved grate, and a
scanty firing, that is not enough to keep alive the natural
heat in the fingers of so many shivering children with
their mother, he finds in the depths of winter always a
blazing hearth, and a hob to warm his pittance of beer
by. Instead of the clamours of a wife, made gaunt by
famishing, he meets with a cheerful attendance beyond
the merits of the trifle which he can afford to spend.
He has companions which his home denies him, for the
very poor man has no visitors. He can look into the
goings on of the world, and speak a little to politics. At
home there are no politics stirring, but the domestic. All
interests, real or imaginary, all topics that should expand
the mind of man, and connect him to a sympathy with
general existence, are crushed in the absorbing consideration of food to be obtained for the family. Beyond the
price of bread, news is senseless and impertinent. At
home there is no larder. Here there is at least a show
of plenty ; and while he cooks his lean scrap of butcher's
meat before the common bars, or munches his humbler
cold viands, his relishing bread and cheese with an onion,
in a corner, where no one reflects upon his poverty, he
has a sight of the substantial joint providing for the
landlord and his family. He takes an interest in the
dressing of it ; and while he assists in removing the trivet
from the fire, he feels that there is such a thing as beef
and cabbage, which he was beginning to forget at home.
All this while he deserts his wife and children. But
what wife, and what children ! Prosperous men, who
object to this desertion, image to themselves some clean
contented family like that which they go home to. But
look at the countenance of the poor wives who follow and
persecute their good-man to the door of the public-house,
which he is about to enter, when something like shame
would restrain him, if stronger misery did not induce him
to pass the threshold. That face, ground by want, in
which every cheerful, every conversable lineament has
been long effaced by misery,—is that a face to stay at

home with? is it more a woman, or a wild cat? alas! it is the face of the wife of his youth, that once smiled upon him. It can smile no longer. What comforts can it share? what burthens can it lighten? Oh, 'tis a fine thing to talk of the humble meal shared together! But what if there be no bread in the cupboard? The innocent prattle of his children takes out the sting of a man's poverty. But the children of the very poor do not prattle. It is none of the least frightful features in that condition, that there is no childishness in its dwellings. Poor people, said a sensible old nurse to us once, do not bring up their children; they drag them up.

The little careless darling of the wealthier nursery, in their hovel is transformed betimes into a premature reflecting person. No one has time to dandle it, no one thinks it worth while to coax it, to soothe it, to toss it up and down, to humour it. There is none to kiss away its tears. If it cries, it can only be beaten. It has been prettily said, that "a babe is fed with milk and praise." But the aliment of this poor babe was thin, unnourishing; the return to its little baby tricks, and efforts to engage attention, bitter ceaseless objurgation. It never had a toy, or knew what a coral meant. It grew up without the lullaby of nurses, it was a stranger to the patient fondle, the hushing caress, the attracting novelty, the costlier plaything, or the cheaper off-hand contrivance to divert the child; the prattled nonsense (best sense to it), the wise impertinences, the wholesome lies, the apt story interposed, that puts a stop to present sufferings, and awakens the passions of young wonder. It was never sung to—no one ever told to it a tale of the nursery. It was dragged up, to live or to die as it happened. It had no young dreams. It broke at once into the iron realities of life. A child exists not for the very poor as any object of dalliance; it is only another mouth to be fed, a pair of little hands to be betimes inured to labour. It is the rival, till it can be the co-operator, for food with the parent. It is never his mirth, his diversion, his solace:

it never makes him young again, with recalling his young times. The children of the very poor have no young times. It makes the very heart to bleed to overhear the casual street-talk between a poor woman and her little girl, a woman of the better sort of poor, in a condition rather above the squalid beings which we have been contemplating. It is not of toys, of nursery books, of summer holidays (fitting that age); of the promised sight, or play; of praised sufficiency at school. It is of mangling and clear-starching, of the price of coals, or of potatoes. The questions of the child, that should be the very outpourings of curiosity in idleness, are marked with forecast and melancholy providence. It has come to be a woman,—before it was a child. It has learned to go to market; it chaffers, it haggles, it envies, it murmurs; it is knowing, acute, sharpened; it never prattles. Had we not reason to say that the home of the very poor is no home?

There is yet another home, which we are constrained to deny to be one. It has a larder, which the home of the poor man wants; its fireside conveniences, of which the poor dream not. But with all this, it is no home. It is—the house of a man that is infested with many visitors. May we be branded for the veriest churl, if we deny our heart to the many noble-hearted friends that at times exchange their dwelling for our poor roof! It is not of guests that we complain, but of endless, purposeless visitants; droppers-in, as they are called. We sometimes wonder from what sky they fall. It is the very error of the position of our lodging; its horoscopy was ill calculated, being just situate in a medium—a plaguy suburban mid-space—fitted to catch idlers from town or country. We are older than we were, and age is easily put out of its way. We have fewer sands in our glass to reckon upon, and we cannot brook to see them drop in endlessly succeeding impertinences. At our time of life, to be alone sometimes is as needful as sleep. It is the refreshing sleep of the day. The growing infirmities of age manifest themselves in nothing more strongly than in an inveterate dislike of interruption. The thing which we are doing, we wish to be permitted to do. We have neither much knowledge nor devices; but there are fewer in the place to which we hasten. We are not willingly put out of our way, even at a game of nine-pins. While youth was, we had vast reversions in time future; we are reduced to a present pittance, and obliged to economise in that article. We bleed away our moments now as hardly as our ducats. We cannot bear to have our thin wardrobe eaten and fretted into by moths. We are willing to barter our good time with a friend, who gives us in exchange his own. Herein is the distinction between the genuine guest and the visitant. This latter takes your good time, and gives you his bad in exchange. The guest is domestic to you as your good cat, or household bird; the visitant is your fly, that flaps in at your window and out again, leaving nothing but a sense of disturbance, and victuals spoiled. The inferior functions of life begin to move heavily. We cannot concoct our food with interruptions. Our chief meal, to be nutritive, must be solitary. With difficulty we can eat before a guest; and never understood what the relish of public feasting meant. Meats have no sapor, nor digestion fair play, in a crowd. The unexpected coming in of a visitant stops the machine. There is a punctual generation who time their calls to the precise commencement of your dining-hour—not to eat—but to see you eat. Our knife and fork drop instinctively, and we feel that we have swallowed our latest morsel. Others again show their genius, as we have said, in knocking the moment you have just sat down to a book. They have a peculiar compassionate sneer, with which they "hope that they do not interrupt your studies." Though they flutter off the next moment, to carry their impertinences to the nearest student that they can call their friend, the tone of the book is spoiled; we shut the leaves, and with Dante's lovers, read no more that day. It were well if the effect of intrusion were simply coextensive with its presence, but it mars all the good hours afterwards. These scratches in appearance leave an orifice that closes not hastily. "It is a prostitution of the bravery of friendship," says worthy Bishop Taylor, "to spend it upon impertinent people, who are, it may be, loads to their families, but can never ease my loads." This is the secret of their gaddings, their visits, and morning calls. They too have homes, which are— no homes.

XIII.—THAT YOU MUST LOVE ME AND LOVE MY DOG.

"GOOD sir, or madam—as it may be—we most willingly embrace the offer of your friendship. We have long known your excellent qualities. We have wished to have you nearer to us; to hold you within the very innermost fold of our heart. We can have no reserve towards a person of your open and noble nature. The frankness of your humour suits us exactly. We have been long looking for such a friend. Quick—let us disburthen our troubles into each other's bosom—let us make our single joys shine by reduplication.—But *yap, yap, yap!* what is this confounded cur? he has fastened his tooth, which is none of the bluntest, just in the fleshy part of my leg."

"It is my dog, sir. You must love him for my sake. Here, Test—Test—Test!"

"But he has bitten me."

"Ay, that he is apt to do, till you are better acquainted with him. I have had him three years. He never bites me."

Yap, yap, yap!—"He is at it again."

"Oh, sir, you must not kick him. He does not like to be kicked. I expect my dog to be treated with all the respect due to myself."

"But do you always take him out with you, when you go a friendship-hunting?"

"Invariably. 'Tis the sweetest, prettiest, best-conditioned animal. I call him my *test*—the touchstone by which to try a friend. No one can properly be said to love me, who does not love him."

"Excuse us, dear sir—or madam, aforesaid—if upon further consideration we are obliged to decline the otherwise invaluable offer of your friendship. We do not like dogs."

"Mighty well, sir,—you know the conditions—you may have worse offers. Come along, Test."

The above dialogue is not so imaginary, but that, in the intercourse of life, we have had frequent occasions of breaking off an agreeable intimacy by reason of these canine appendages. They do not always come in the shape of dogs; they sometimes wear the more plausible and human character of kinsfolk, near acquaintances, my friend's friend, his partner, his wife, or his children. We could never yet form a friendship—not to speak of more delicate correspondence—however much to our taste, without the intervention of some third anomaly, some impertinent clog affixed to the relation--the understood *dog* in the proverb. The good things of life are not to be had singly, but come to us with a mixture; like a school-boy's holiday, with a task affixed to the tail of it. What a delightful companion is * * * *, if he did not always bring his tall cousin with him! He seems to grow with him; like some of those double births which we remember to have read of with such wonder and delight in the old "Athenian Oracle," where Swift commenced author by writing Pindaric Odes (what a beginning for him!) upon Sir William Temple. There is the picture of the brother, with the little brother peeping out at his shoulder; a species of fraternity, which we have no name of kin close enough to comprehend. When * * * * comes, poking in his head and shoulder into your room, as if to feel his entry, you think, surely you have now got him to yourself—what a three hours' chat we shall have!
—but ever in the haunch of him, and before his diffident body is well disclosed in your apartment, appears the haunting shadow of the cousin, overpeering his modest kinsman, and sure to overlay the expected good talk with his insufferable procerity of stature, and uncorresponding dwarfishness of observation. Misfortunes seldom come

alone. 'Tis hard when a blessing comes accompanied. Cannot we like Sempronia, without sitting down to chess with her eternal brother; or know Sulpicia, without knowing all the round of her card-playing relations?— must my friend's brethren of necessity be mine also? must we be hand and glove with Dick Selby the parson, or Jack Selby the calico-printer, because W. S., who is neither, but a ripe wit and a critic, has the misfortune to claim a common parentage with them? Let him lay down his brothers; and 'tis odds but we will cast him in a pair of ours (we have a superflux) to balance the concession. Let F. H. lay down his garrulous uncle; and Honorius dismiss his vapid wife, and superfluous establishment of six boys: things between boy and manhood—too ripe for play, too raw for conversation—that come in, impudently staring his father's old friend out of countenance; and will neither aid nor let alone, the conference; that we may once more meet upon equal terms, as we were wont to do in the disengaged state of bachelorhood.

It is well if your friend, or mistress, be content with these canicular probations. Few young ladies but in this sense keep a dog. But while Rutilia hounds at you her tiger aunt; or Ruspina expects you to cherish and fondle her viper sister, whom she has preposterously taken into her bosom, to try stinging conclusions upon your constancy; they must not complain if the house be rather thin of suitors. Scylla must have broken off many excellent matches in her time, if she insisted upon all that loved her loving her dogs also.

An excellent story to this moral is told of Merry, of Della Cruscan memory. In tender youth he loved and courted a modest appanage to the Opera—in truth, a dancer—who had won him by the artless contrast between her manners and situation. She seemed to him a native violet, that had been transplanted by some rude accident into that exotic and artificial hotbed. Nor, in truth, was she less genuine and sincere than she appeared to him. He wooed and won this flower. Only for appearance sake, and for due honour to the bride's relations, she craved that she might have the attendance of her friends and kindred at the approaching solemnity. The request was too amiable not to be conceded; and in this solicitude for conciliating the good-will of mere relations, he found a presage of her superior attentions to himself, when the golden shaft should have "killed the flock of all affections else." The morning came: and at the Star and Garter, Richmond—the place appointed for the breakfasting—accompanied with one English friend, he impatiently awaited what reinforcements the bride should bring to grace the ceremony. A rich muster she had made. They came in six coaches—the whole corps du Ballet—French, Italian, men and women. Monsieur de B., the famous *pirouetter* of the day, led his fair spouse, but craggy, from the banks of the Seine. The Prima Donna had sent her excuse. But the first and second Buffa were there; and Signor Se—, and Signora Ch—, and Madame V—, with a countless cavalcade besides of chorusers, figurantes! at the sight of whom Merry afterwards declared, that "then for the first time it struck him seriously, that he was about to marry—a dancer." But there was no help for it. Besides, it was her day; these were, in fact, her friends and kinsfolk. The assemblage, though whimsical, was all very natural. But when the bride—handing out of the last coach a still more extraordinary figure than the rest—presented to him as her *father*—the gentleman that was to *give her away*—no less a person than Signor Delpini himself—with a sort of pride, as much as to say, See what I have brought to do us honour!—the thought of so extraordinary a paternity quite overcame him: and slipping away under some pretence from the bride and her motley adherents, poor Merry took horse from the back yard to the nearest sea-coast, from which, shipping himself to America, he shortly after consoled himself with a more congenial match in the person of Miss Brunton; relieved from his intended clown father, and a bevy of painted buffas for bridemaids.

XIV.—THAT WE SHOULD RISE WITH THE LARK.

AT what precise minute that little airy musician doffs his night-gear, and prepares to tune up his unseasonable matins, we are not naturalist enough to determine. But for a mere human gentleman—that has no orchestra business to call him from his warm bed to such preposterous exercises—we take ten, or half after ten (eleven, of course, during this Christmas solstice), to be the very earliest hour at which he can begin to think of abandoning his pillow. To think of it, we say; for to do it in earnest requires another half hour's good consideration. Not but there are pretty sun-risings, as we are told, and such like gawds, abroad in the world, in summer-time especially, some hours before what we have assigned ; which a gentleman may see, as they say, only for getting up. But having been tempted once or twice, in earlier life, to assist at those ceremonies, we confess our curiosity abated. We are no longer ambitious of being the sun's courtiers, to attend at his morning levees. We hold the good hours of the dawn too sacred to waste them upon such observances ; which have in them, besides, something Pagan and Persic. To say truth, we never anticipated our usual hour, or got up with the sun (as 'tis called), to go a journey, or upon a foolish whole day's pleasuring, but we suffered for it all the long hours after in listlessness and headaches ; Nature herself sufficiently declaring her sense of our presumption in aspiring to regulate our frail waking courses by the measures of that celestial and sleepless traveller. We deny not that there is something sprightly and vigorous, at the outset especially, in these break-of-day excursions. It is flattering to get the start of a lazy world ; to conquer Death by proxy in his image. But the seeds of sleep and mortality are in us ; and we pay usually, in strange qualms before night falls, the penalty of the unnatural inversion. Therefore, while the busy part of mankind are fast huddling on their clothes,

are already up and about their occupations, content to
have swallowed their sleep by wholesale; we choose to
linger a-bed and digest our dreams. It is the very time
to recombine the wandering images, which night in a
confused mass presented; to snatch them from forgetfulness; to shape, and mould them. Some people have no
good of their dreams. Like fast feeders, they gulp them
too grossly, to taste them curiously. We love to chew
the cud of a foregone vision; to collect the scattered rays
of a brighter phantasm, or act over again, with firmer
nerves, the sadder nocturnal tragedies; to drag into daylight a struggling and half-vanishing nightmare; to handle
and examine the terrors, or the airy solaces. We have too
much respect for these spiritual communications, to let
them go so lightly. We are not so stupid, or so careless
as that Imperial forgetter of his dreams, that we should
need a seer to remind us of the form of them. They
seem to us to have as much significance as our waking
concerns; or rather to import us more nearly, as more
nearly we approach by years to the shadowy world, whither
we are hastening. We have shaken hands with the world's
business; we have done with it; we have discharged ourself of it. Why should we get up? we have neither suit
to solicit, nor affairs to manage. The drama has shut in
upon us at the fourth act. We have nothing here to
expect, but in a short time a sick-bed, and a dismissal.
We delight to anticipate death by such shadows as night
affords. We are already half acquainted with ghosts.
We were never much in the world. Disappointment early
struck a dark veil between us and its dazzling illusions.
Our spirits showed gray before our hairs. The mighty
changes of the world already appear as but the vain stuff
out of which dramas are composed. We have asked no
more of life than what the mimic images in play-houses
present us with. Even those types have waxed fainter.
Our clock appears to have struck. We are SUPERAN-
NUATED. In this dearth of mundane satisfaction, we
contract politic alliances with shadows. It is good to

have friends at court. The extracted media of dreams seem no ill introduction to that spiritual presence, upon which, in no long time, we expect to be thrown. We are trying to know a little of the usages of that colony; to learn the language and the faces we shall meet with there, that we may be the less awkward at our first coming among them. We willingly call a phantom our fellow, as knowing we shall soon be of their dark companionship. Therefore we cherish dreams. We try to spell in them the alphabet of the invisible world; and think we know already how it shall be with us. Those uncouth shapes which, while we clung to flesh and blood, affrighted us, have become familiar. We feel attenuated into their meagre essences, and have given the hand of half-way approach to incorporeal being. We once thought life to be something; but it has unaccountably fallen from us before its time. Therefore we choose to dally with visions. The sun has no purposes of ours to light us to. Why should we get up?

XV.—THAT WE SHOULD LIE DOWN WITH THE LAMB.

WE could never quite understand the philosophy of this arrangement, or the wisdom of our ancestors in sending us for instruction to these woolly bedfellows. A sheep, when it is dark, has nothing to do but to shut his silly eyes, and sleep if he can. Man found out long sixes— Hail, candle-light! without disparagement to sun or moon, the kindliest luminary of the three —if we may not rather style thee their radiant deputy, mild viceroy of the moon! —We love to read, talk, sit silent, eat, drink, sleep, by candle-light. They are everybody's sun and moon. This is our peculiar and household planet. Wanting it, what savage unsocial nights must our ancestors have spent, wintering in caves and unillumined fastnesses! They must have lain about and grumbled at one another in the dark. What repartees could have passed, when you must have felt about for a smile, and handled a neighbour's cheek to be sure that he understood it? This accounts for the seriousness of the elder poetry. It has a sombre cast (try Hesiod or Ossian), derived from the tradition of those unlantern'd nights. Jokes came in with candles. We wonder how they saw to pick up a pin, if they had any. How did they sup? what a mélange of chance carving they must have made of it?—here one had got a leg of a goat when he wanted a horse's shoulder—there another had dipped his scooped palm in a kid-skin of wild honey, when he meditated right mare's milk. There is neither good eating nor drinking in fresco. Who, even in these civilized times, has never experienced this, when at some economic table he has commenced dining after dusk, and waited for the flavour till the lights came? The senses absolutely give and take reciprocally. Can you tell pork from veal in the dark? or distinguish Sherris from pure Malaga? Take away the candle from the smoking man; by the glimmering of the left ashes, he knows that he is still smoking, but he knows it only by an inference; till the restored light, coming in aid of the olfactories, reveals to both senses the full aroma. Then how he redoubles his puffs! how he burnishes!—there is absolutely no such thing as reading but by a candle. We have tried the affectation of a book at noon-day in gardens, and in sultry arbours; but it was labour thrown away. Those gay motes in the beam come about you, hovering and teasing, like so many coquettes, that will have you all to their self and are jealous of your abstractions. By the midnight taper, the writer digests his meditations. By the same light we must approach to their perusal, if we would catch the flame, the odour. It is a mockery, all that is reported of the influential Phœbus. No true poem ever owed its birth to the sun's light. They are abstracted works—

> Things that were born, when none but the still night,
> And his dumb candle, saw his pinching throes.

Marry, daylight—daylight might furnish the images, the

crude material; but for the fine shapings, the true turning and filing (as mine author hath it), they must be content to hold their inspiration of the candle. The mild internal light, that reveals them, like fires on the domestic hearth, goes out in the sunshine. Night and silence call out the starry fancies. Milton's Morning Hymn in Paradise, we would hold a good wager, was penned at midnight; and Taylor's rich description of a sunrise smells decidedly of the taper. Even ourself, in these our humbler lucubrations tune our best-measured cadences (Prose has her cadences) not unfrequently to the charm of the drowsier watchman, "blessing the doors;" or the wild sweep of winds at midnight. Even now a loftier speculation than we have yet attempted, courts our endeavours. We would indite something about the Solar System.— *Betty, bring the candles.*

XVI.—THAT A SULKY TEMPER IS A MISFORTUNE.

WE grant that it is, and a very serious one—to a man's friends, and to all that have to do with him; but whether the condition of the man himself is so much to be deplored, may admit of a question. We can speak a little to it, being ourself but lately recovered—we whisper it in confidence, reader—out of a long and desperate fit of the sullens. Was the cure a blessing? The conviction which wrought it, came too clearly to leave a scruple of the fanciful injuries—for they were mere fancies—which had provoked the humour. But the humour itself was too self-pleasing while it lasted—we know how bare we lay ourself in the confession—to be abandoned all at once with the grounds of it. We still brood over wrongs which we know to have been imaginary; and for our old acquaintance N——, whom we find to have been a truer friend than we took him for, we substitute some phantom —a Caius or a Titius—as like him as we dare to form it, to wreak our yet unsatisfied resentments on. It is mortifying to fall at once from the pinnacle of neglect; to forego the idea of having been ill-used and contumaciously treated by an old friend. The first thing to aggrandize a man in his own conceit, is to conceive of himself as neglected. There let him fix if he can. To undeceive him is to deprive him of the most tickling morsel within the range of self-complacency. No flattery can come near it. Happy is he who suspects his friend of an injustice; but supremely blest, who thinks all his friends in a conspiracy to depress and undervalue him. There is a pleasure (we sing not to the profane) far beyond the reach of all that the world counts joy—a deep, enduring satisfaction in the depths, where the superficial seek it not, of discontent. Were we to recite one half of this mystery—which we were let into by our late dissatisfaction, all the world would be in love with disrespect; we should wear a slight for a bracelet, and neglects and contumacies would be the only matter for courtship. Unlike to that mysterious book in the Apocalypse, the study of this mystery is unpalatable only in the commencement. The first sting of a suspicion is grievous; but wait—out of that wound, which to flesh and blood seemed so difficult, there is balm and honey to be extracted. Your friend passed you on such or such a day,—having in his company one that you conceived worse than ambiguously disposed towards you,—passed you in the street without notice. To be sure, he is something short-sighted; and it was in your power to have accosted *him*. But facts and sane inferences are trifles to a true adept in the science of dissatisfaction. He must have seen you; and S——, who was with him, must have been the cause of the contempt. It galls you, and well it may. But have patience. Go home, and make the worst of it, and you are a made man from this time. Shut yourself up, and—rejecting, as an enemy to your peace, every whispering suggestion that but insinuates there may be a mistake—reflect seriously upon the many lesser instances which you had begun to perceive, in proof of your friend's disaffection towards you. None of them singly was much to the purpose, but the aggregate weight is positive; and

you have this last affront to clench them. Thus far the
process is anything but agreeable. But now to your relief
comes the comparative faculty. You conjure up all the
kind feelings you have had for your friend; what you have
been to him, and what you would have been to him, if he
would have suffered you; how you defended him in this
or that place; and his good name—his literary reputation,
and so forth, was always dearer to you than your own!
Your heart, spite of itself, yearns towards him. You
could weep tears of blood but for a restraining pride.
How say you? do you not yet begin to apprehend a comfort?—some allay of sweetness in the bitter waters? Stop
not here, nor penuriously cheat yourself of your reversions.
You are on vantage ground. Enlarge your speculations,
and take in the rest of your friends, as a spark kindles
more sparks. Was there one among them who has not
to you proved hollow, false, slippery as water? Begin to
think that the relation itself is inconsistent with mortality.
That the very idea of friendship, with its component parts,
as honour, fidelity, steadiness, exists but in your single
bosom. Image yourself to yourself as the only possible
friend in a world incapable of that communion. Now the
gloom thickens. The little star of self-love twinkles, that
is to encourage you through deeper glooms than this. You
are not yet at the half point of your elevation. You
are not yet, believe me, half sulky enough. Adverting to
the world in general (as these circles in the mind will
spread to infinity), reflect with what strange injustice you
have been treated in quarters where (setting gratitude and
the expectation of friendly returns aside as chimeras) you
pretended no claim beyond justice, the naked due of all
men. Think the very idea of right and fit fled from the
earth, or your breast the solitary receptacle of it till you
have swelled yourself into at least one hemisphere; the
other being the vast Arabia Stony of your friends and the
world aforesaid. To grow bigger every moment in your
own conceit, and the world to lessen; to deify yourself at
the expense of your species; to judge the world—this is

the acme and supreme point of your mystery—these the true PLEASURES OF SULKINESS. We profess no more of this grand secret than what ourself experimented on one rainy afternoon in the last week, sulking in our study. We had proceeded to the penultimate point, at which the true adept seldom stops, where the consideration of benefit forgot is about to merge in the meditation of general injustice—when a knock at the door was followed by the entrance of the very friend whose not seeing of us in the morning (for we will now confess the case our own), an accidental oversight, had given rise to so much agreeable generalization! To mortify us still more, and take down the whole flattering superstructure which pride had piled upon neglect, he had brought in his hand the identical S——, in whose favour we had suspected him of the contumacy. Asseverations were needless, where the frank manner of them both was convictive of the injurious nature of the suspicion. We fancied that they perceived our embarrassment; but were too proud, or something else, to confess to the secret of it. We had been but too lately in the condition of the noble patient in Argos:—

> Qui se credebat miros audire tragœdos,
> In vacuo lætus sessor plausorque theatro—

and could have exclaimed with equal reason against the friendly hands that cured us—

> Pol, me occidistis, amici,
> Non servastis, ait; cui sic extorta voluptas,
> Et demptus per vim mentis gratissimus error.

NOTES.

RECOLLECTIONS OF THE SOUTH-SEA HOUSE.—P. 1.
(*London Magazine*, August 1820.)

CHARLES LAMB left Christ's Hospital in the year 1789, at the age of fourteen, and at some date within the next two years he obtained a situation in the South-Sea House. His father's employer, Samuel Salt, the Bencher of the Inner Temple, was a Deputy-Governor of the South-Sea House at the time, and it was doubtless by the influence of this kind friend that the appointment was obtained. Charles's elder brother, John, was already a clerk in the office. In the *Royal Calendar* for 1792 John Lamb's name appears as holding the position of Deputy-Accountant. Other of the names mentioned by Lamb in this Essay are also found in the official records of the day—John Tipp, on whose promotion to the office of Accountant (as "John Tipp, Esq."), John Lamb succeeded to the post just mentioned; W. Evans, Deputy-Cashier in 1791; Thomas Tame, Deputy-Cashier in 1793; and Richard Plumer, Deputy-Secretary in 1800. Lamb's fondness for gratuitous mystification is thus curiously illustrated in the insinuation towards the close of the Essay that the names he has recorded are fictitious, after all. Lamb's old colleague, Elia, whose name he borrowed, has not (as far as I am aware) been yet traced in the annals of the office. But he probably held, like Lamb himself, a very subordinate position.

A full account of the famous South-Sea Bubble will be found in Lord Stanhope's History, and also in Chambers's *Book of Days*. For an account of the constitution of the Company at the end of the last century, Hughson's *Walks through London* (1805) may be consulted. He says—"Notwithstanding the terms of the charter by which we are to look upon this Company as merchants, it is observable that they never carried on any considerable trade, and now they have no trade. They only receive interest for their capital which is in the hands of the Government, and £8000 out of the Treasury towards the expense attending the management of their affairs, which is done by a Governor, Sub-Governor, Deputy-Governor, and twenty-one Directors annually chosen on the 6th of February by a majority of votes." Pennant (who is referred to in this Essay, and wrote in 1790) says—"In this (Threadneedle) Street also stands the South-Sea House, the place in which the Company did business, when it had any to transact."

Henry Man, the Wit, etc.—The two "forgotten volumes"—"*Miscellaneous Works in Verse and Prose of the late Henry Man.* London, 1802"—are now before me. They contain a variety of light and amusing papers in verse and prose. The humour of them, however, is naturally still more out of date now than in Lamb's day. One of the epigrams found there may be said to have become classical,—that upon the two Earls (Spencer and Sandwich) who invented respectively "half a coat" and "half a dinner." Henry Man was Deputy-Secretary in 1793.

Rattle-headed Plumer.—Lamb had a special interest in the family bearing this name, because his grandmother, Mary Field, was for more than half a century housekeeper at the Dower House of the family, Blakesware in Hertfordshire. The present Mr. Plumer, of Allerton, Totness, a grandson of Richard Plumer of the South-Sea House, by no means acquiesces in the tradition here recorded as to his grandfather's origin. He believes that though the links are missing, Richard Plumer was descended in regular line from the Baronet, Sir Walter Plumer, who died at the end of the seventeenth century. Lamb's memory has failed him here in one respect. The "Bachelor Uncle," Walter Plumer, uncle of William Plumer of Blakesware, was most certainly not a bachelor (see the Pedigree of the family in Cussans' *Hertfordshire*). Lamb is further inaccurate as to the connection of this Walter Plumer with the affair of the franks. A reference to Johnson's *Life of Cave* will show that it was Cave, and not Plumer, who was summoned before the House of Commons. Walter Plumer, member for Aldborough and Appleby, had given a frank to the Duchess of Marlborough, which had been challenged by Cave, who held the post of Clerk of the Franks in the House of Commons. For this, Cave was cited before the House, as a Breach of Privilege.

In the passage on John Tipp, Lamb, speaking of his fine suite of rooms in Threadneedle Street, adds —"I know not who is the occupier of them now." When the Essay first appeared in the *London Magazine*, the note in brackets was appended. Thus we learn that John Lamb was still, in 1820, occupying rooms in the old building.

Mild, child-like, pastoral M——.—"Maynard, hang'd himself" (Lamb's "Key"). Mr. T. Maynard was chief clerk of the Old Annuities and Three per Cents from 1788 to 1793. His name does not appear in the almanacs of the day after this date.

OXFORD IN THE VACATION.—P. 10.

(*London Magazine*, October 1820.)

Lamb was fond of spending his annual holiday in one or other of the great university towns, more often perhaps in Cambridge. It was on one such visit, it will be remembered, that Charles and Mary first made the acquaintance of little Emma Isola. On its first appearance in the *London*, the paper was dated "August 5, 1820. From my rooms facing the Bodleian." A sonnet writen a year before at Cambridge, tells of the charm that University associations had for one who had been debarred through infirmity of health and poverty from a university education:—

> "I was not trained in Academic bowers,
> And to those learned streams I nothing owe
> Which copious from those twin fair founts do flow ;
> Mine have been anything but studious hours.
> Yet can I fancy, wandering 'mid thy towers,
> Myself a nursling, Granta, of thy lap ;
> My brow seems tightening with the Doctor's cap,
> And I walk *gownèd ;* feel unusual powers.
> Strange forms of logic clothe my admiring speech,
> Old Ramus' ghost is busy at my brain ;
> And my skull teems with notions infinite.
> Be still, ye reeds of Camus, while I teach
> Truths which transcend the searching schoolmen's vein,
> And half had staggered that stout Stagirite !"

"*Andrew and John, men famous in old times,*" quoted, quite at random, from *Paradise Regained*, ii. 7.

G. D. George Dyer (1755-1841), educated at Christ's Hospital and Emmanuel College, Cambridge. A compiler and editor and general worker for the booksellers, short-sighted, absent-minded, and simple, for whom Lamb had a life-long affection. He compiled, among other books, a *History of the University and Colleges of Cambridge*, and contributed the original matter (preface excepted) to Valpy's edition of the *Classics*. The account of him given by Crabb Robinson in his Diary well illustrates Lamb's frequent references to this singular character. "He was one of the best creatures, morally, that ever breathed. He was the son of a watchman in Wapping,

and was put to a charity school by some pious Dissenting ladies.
He afterwards went to Christ's Hospital, and from there was
sent to Cambridge. He was a scholar, but to the end of his
days (and he lived to be eighty-five) was a bookseller's drudge.
He led a life of literary labour in poverty. He made indexes,
corrected the press, and occasionally gave lessons in Latin and
Greek. When an undergraduate at Cambridge he became a
hearer of Robert Robinson, and consequently a Unitarian. This
closed the church against him, and he never had a fellowship.
. . . He wrote one good book—*The Life of Robert Robinson*,
which I have heard Wordsworth mention as one of the best
works of biography in the language. . . . Dyer had the kindest
heart and simplest manners imaginable. It was literally the
case with him that he would give away his last guinea. . . .
Not many years before his death he married his laundress, by
the advice of his friends—a very worthy woman. He said to
me once, 'Mrs. Dyer is a woman of excellent natural sense,
but she is not literate.' That is, she could neither read nor
write. Dyer was blind for a few years before his death. I used
occasionally to go on a Sunday morning to read to him. . . .
After he came to London, Dyer lived always in some very
humble chambers in Clifford's Inn, Fleet Street."

Give me Agur's Wish.—See the Book of Proverbs xxx. 10.

Our friend M.'s in Bedford Square.—M. was Basil Montagu,
Q.C., and editor of *Bacon*. Mrs. M. was of course Irving's
"noble lady," so familiar to us from Carlyle's *Reminiscences*.
"Pretty A. S." was Mrs. Montagu's daughter, Anne Skepper,
afterwards the wife of Mr. Procter (Barry Cornwall). In his
Memoir of Lamb, Mr. Procter significantly remarks that he
could vouch personally for the truth of this anecdote of Dyer's
absent-mindedness.

Still less have I curiosity to disturb the elder repose of MSS.—
In the *London Magazine* was appended the following note:—

"There is something to me repugnant at any time in written
hand. The text never seems determinate. Print settles it.
I had thought of the Lycidas as of a full-grown beauty—as
springing up with all its parts absolute—till, in an evil hour,
I was shown the original copy of it, together with the other
minor poems of its author, in the library of Trinity, kept like
some treasure, to be proud of. I wish they had thrown them
in the Cam, or sent them after the latter Cantos of Spenser,
into the Irish Channel. How it staggered me to see the fine
things in their ore! interlined, corrected! as if their words
were mortal, alterable, displaceable at pleasure! as if they
might have been otherwise, and just as good! as if inspiration
were made up of parts, and these fluctuating, successive, in-

different! I will never go into the workshop of any great artist again, nor desire a sight of his picture till it is fairly off the easel: no, not if Raphael were to be alive again, and painting another Galatea."

CHRIST'S HOSPITAL FIVE-AND-THIRTY YEARS AGO.
—P. 17.

(London Magazine, November 1820.)

The first collected edition of Lamb's Prose and Verse appeared in the year 1818, published by C. and J. Ollier. Among other papers it contained one entitled *Recollections of Christ's Hospital*. The Essay was a reprint from the *Gentleman's Magazine* for June 1813, where it originally owed its appearance to an alleged abuse of the presentation system in force at the Blue Coat School.

This earlier article on Christ's Hospital had been written in a serious and genuine vein of enthusiasm for the value and dignity of the old Foundation. Lamb now seems to have remembered that there were other aspects of schoolboy life under its shelter that might be profitably dealt with. The "poor friendless boy," in whose character he now writes, was his old schoolfellow Coleridge, and the general truth of the sketch is shown by Coleridge's own reference to his schooldays in the early chapters of his *Biographia Literaria*. "In my friendless wanderings on our leave-days (for I was an orphan, and had scarce any connections in London) highly was I delighted if any passenger, especially if he were dressed in black, would enter into conversation with me."

Lamb's love of mystification shows itself in this Essay in many forms. "Sweet Calne in Wiltshire" is a quite gratuitous substitution for Ottery St. Mary in Devonshire, the home after which young Coleridge did actually yearn. Coleridge did, however, reside for a time at Calne in later life. Moreover, as will be seen, the disguise of identity with Coleridge is dropped altogether towards the close of the Essay. The general account of the school here given it is interesting to compare with that given by Leigh Hunt in his autobiography.

L.'s governor (so we called the patron who presented us to the foundation) lived in a manner under his paternal roof.—It was under Samuel Salt's roof that John Lamb and his family lived, and as the presentation to Christ's was obtained from a friend of Salt's, Lamb considers it fair to speak of the old Bencher as the actual benefactor.

There was one H——.—Hodges (Lamb's "Key").

"*To feed our mind with idle portraiture,*" a line apparently extemporised by Lamb as a translation of the passage in Virgil to which he refers, "*animum picturâ pascit inani.*"

"'*Twas said*
He ate strange flesh."

As usual, a new quotation formed out of Lamb's general recollection of an old one. He had in his mind, no doubt, a passage in *Antony and Cleopatra* (Act I. Sc. 4):—

"It is reported thou didst eat strange flesh
Which some did die to look on."

Mr. Hathaway, the then Steward.—Perry was steward in Lamb's day (see the former Essay on Christ's Hospital). Leigh Hunt says of his successor :—"The name of the steward, a thin stiff man of invincible formality of demeanour, admirably fitted to render encroachment impossible, was Hathaway. We of the grammar school used to call him 'the Yeoman' on account of Shakspeare having married the daughter of a man of that name, designated as 'a substantial yeoman.'"

The Rev. James Boyer became upper master of Christ's in 1777. For the better side of Boyer's qualifications as a teacher, see Coleridge's *Biographia Literaria*, the passage beginning, "At school I enjoyed the inestimable advantage of a very sensible, though at the same time a very severe master." Elsewhere Coleridge entirely confirms Lamb's and Leigh Hunt's accounts of Boyer's violent temper, and severe discipline. Lamb never reached the position of Grecian, but it is the tradition in Christ's Hospital that he was under Boyer's instruction some time before leaving school.

The Rev. Matthew Field.—Some charming additional traits in this character, entirely confirming Lamb's account, will be found in Leigh Hunt's autobiography. "A man of a more handsome incompetence for his situation perhaps did not exist. He came late of a morning; went away soon in the afternoon; and used to walk up and down, languidly bearing his cane, as if it were a lily, and hearing our eternal *Dominuses* and *As in praesentis* with an air of ineffable endurance. Often he did not hear at all. It was a joke with us when any of our friends came to the door, and we asked his permission to go to them, to address him with some preposterous question wide of the mark; to which he used to assent. We would say, for instance, 'Are you not a great fool, sir?' or 'Isn't your daughter a pretty girl?' to which he would reply, 'Yes, child.' When he condescended to hit us with the cane, he made a face as if he were taking physic."

The Author of the Country Spectator.—For an amusing account of the origin of this periodical, see Mozley's *Reminiscences of Oriel College*, vol. ii. *addenda*.

Dr. T——e.—Dr. Trollope, who succeeded Boyer as headmaster.

Th ——.—Thornton (Lamb's "Key").

Poor S——.—"Scott, died in Bedlam" (Lamb's "Key").

Ill-fated M——.—"Maunde, dismiss'd school" (Lamb's "Key").

"*Finding some of Edward's Race
Unhappy, pass their annals by.*"

Adapted from Matt. Prior's *Carmen Sæculare* for 1700 (stanza viii.)—

"Janus, mighty deity,
Be kind, and as thy searching eye
Does our modern story trace,
Finding some of Stuart's race
Unhappy, pass their annals by."

C. V. Le G.—Charles Valentine Le Grice and a younger brother of the name of Samuel were Grecians and prominent members of the school in Lamb's day. They were from Cornwall. Charles became a clergyman and held a living in his native county. Samuel went into the army, and died in the West Indies. It was he who was staying in London in the autumn of 1796, and showed himself a true friend to the Lambs at the season of the mother's death. Lamb writes to Coleridge, "Sam Le Grice, who was then in town, was with me the three or four first days, and was as a brother to me; gave up every hour of his time to the very hurting of his health and spirits in constant attendance, and humouring my poor father; talked with him, read to him, played at cribbage with him." He was a "mad wag," according to Leigh Hunt, who tells some pleasant anecdotes of him, but must have been a good-hearted fellow. "Le Grice the elder was a wag," adds Hunt, "like his brother, but more staid. He went into the church as he ought to do, and married a rich widow. He published a translation, abridged, of the celebrated pastoral of Longus; and report at school made him the author of a little anonymous tract on the *Art of Poking the Fire*."

"*Which two I behold,*" *etc.*—This is Fuller's account of the wit-combats between Ben Jonson and Shakspeare.

The Junior Le G. and F.—The latter of these was named Favell, also a Grecian in the school. These two, according to

Leigh Hunt, when at the university wrote to the Duke of York to ask for commissions in the army. "The Duke good-naturedly sent them." Favell was killed in the Peninsula. His epitaph will be found on a tablet in Great St. Andrew's Church, Cambridge:—"Samuel, a Captain in the 61st Regiment, having been engaged in the expedition to Egypt, afterwards served in the principal actions in the Peninsula, and fell whilst heading his men to the charge in the Battle of Salamanca, July 21, 1812." We shall meet with him again, under a different initial, in the essay on *Poor Relations*.

THE TWO RACES OF MEN.—P. 31.
(*London Magazine*, December 1820.)

Ralph Bigod.—John Fenwick, editor of the *Albion*. See later essay on *Newspapers Thirty-five Years Ago*.

" *To slacken virtue and abate her edge*
Than prompt her to do aught may merit praise."
Paradise Regained, ii. 455.

Comberbatch, more properly *Comberback*, the name adopted by Coleridge when he enlisted in the 15th Light Dragoons, in Dec. 1793. He gave his name to the authorities as Silas Titus Comberback, with initials corresponding to his own, perhaps in order that the marks on his clothes might not raise suspicion. "Being at a loss when suddenly asked my name," he writes, "I answered Comberback; and, verily, my habits were so little equestrian, that my horse, I doubt not, was of that opinion."

Wayward, Spiteful K.—Kenney, the dramatist, who married a Frenchwoman and lived for some years at Versailles. Lamb visited him there in 1822.

" *Unworthy land, to harbour such a sweetness.*"
I have not been able as yet to trace this quotation to its source.

S. T. C.—Of course, Coleridge again. It is a good illustration of Lamb's fondness for puzzling that having to instance his friend, he indicates him three times in the same essay by a different *alias*. Coleridge's constant practice of enriching his own and other's books with these *marginalia* is well known.

NEW YEAR'S EVE.—P. 37.
(*London Magazine*, January 1821.)

It was probably this paper, together with that on *Witches and other Night Fears*, which so shocked the moral sense of Southey, and led to his lamenting publicly, in the pages of the *Quarterly*, the "absence of a sounder religious feeling" in the *Essays of Elia*. The melancholy scepticism of its strain would appear to have struck others at the time. A graceful and tenderly-remonstrative copy of verses, suggested by it, appeared in the *London Magazine* for August 1821, signed "*Olen.*" Lamb noticed them in a letter to his publisher Mr. Taylor, of July 30. "You will do me injustice if you do not convey to the writer of the beautiful lines, which I here return you, my sense of the extreme kindness which dictates them. Poor Elia (call him Ellia) does not pretend to so very clear revelations of a future state of being as 'Olen' seems gifted with. He stumbles about dark mountains at best; but he knows at least how to be thankful for this life, and is too thankful, indeed, for certain relationships lent him here, not to tremble for a possible resumption of the gift."

Lamb thinks that the verses may have been by James Montgomery, who was on the staff of the *London*, but I have not found them reprinted in any collected edition of Montgomery's poems.

"*I saw the skirts of the departing Year.*"

From the first strophe of Coleridge's "Ode to the departing Year," as originally printed in the Bristol edition of his poems in 1796. He afterwards altered the line to

"I saw the *train* of the departing Year."

"*Welcome the coming, speed the parting guest.*"

From Pope's translation of the *Odyssey*. (Book xv. line 84.)

Alice W———n.—According to Lamb's "Key," for *Winterton.* In any case the fictitious name by which Lamb chose to indicate the object of his boyish attachment, whose form and features he loved to dwell on in his early sonnets, Rosamund Gray, and afterwards in his essays. We shall meet her again later on.

"*Sweet assurance of a look.*"—From Lamb's favourite Elegy on Philip Sidney, by Matthew Roydon.

From what have I not fallen, if the child I remember was indeed myself.—The best commentary on this passage is that supplied by Lamb's beautiful sonnet, written as far back as 1795:—

"We were two pretty babes; the youngest she,
The youngest, and the loveliest far (I ween)
And *Innocence* her name: the time has been
We two did love each other's company;
Time was, we two had wept to have been apart.
But when, by show of seeming good beguiled,
I left the garb and manners of a child,
And my first love for man's society,

> Defiling with the world my virgin heart—
> My loved companion dropt a tear, and fled,
> And hid in deepest shades her awful head.
> Beloved! who shall tell me, where thou art?
> In what delicious Eden to be found?
> That I may seek thee, the wide world around."

MRS. BATTLE'S OPINIONS ON WHIST.—P. 41.
(*London Magazine*, February 1821.)

There is probably no evidence existing as to the original of Mrs. Battle. Several of Lamb's commentators have endeavoured to prove her identity with Mary Field, Lamb's grandmother, so long resident with the Plumer family; the sole fact common to them being that Lamb represents Mrs. Battle (in the essay on *Blakesmoor*) as having died at Blakesware, where also Mrs. Field ended her days. But any one who will read, after the present essay, Lamb's indisputably genuine and serious verses on Mrs. Field's death (*The Grandame*) will feel that to have transformed her into this "gentlewoman born" with the fine "last century countenance," would have been little short of a *mauvaise plaisanterie*, of which Lamb was not likely to have been guilty.

Mr. Bowles.—William Lisle Bowles brought out his edition of Pope in 1807.

Bridget Elia.—The name by which Lamb always indicates his sister in this series of essays.

A CHAPTER ON EARS.—P. 52.
(*London Magazine*, March 1821.)

Lamb's indifference to music is one of the best-known features of his personality. Compare the admirably humorous verses, "Free Thoughts on several Eminent Composers," beginning—

> "Some cry up Haydn, some Mozart,
> Just as the whim bites; for my part
> I do not care a farthing candle
> For either of them, or for Handel,—
> Cannot a man live free and easy
> Without admiring Pergolesi?
> Or through the world with comfort go
> That never heard of Dr. Blow?"

My friend A.'s.—Doubtless Lamb's friend, William Ayrton, the well-known musical critic of that day (1777-1858).

Party in a parlour, etc.—From a stanza in the original draft of Wordsworth's *Peter Bell*. The stanza was omitted in all editions of the poem after the first (1819).

My good Catholic friend Nov——.—Vincent Novello, the well-known organist and composer, father of Mde. Clara Novello and Mrs. Cowden Clarke (1781-1861).

—— *rapt above earth,*
And possess joys not promised at my birth.

—" As I thus sat, these and other sights had so fully possessed my soul with content that I thought, as the poet has happily expressed it,—

I was for that time lifted above earth ;
And possessed joys not promised at my birth."

—Walton's *Complete Angler*, Part I. chap. 4.

ALL FOOL'S DAY.—P. 58.

(*London Magazine*, April 1821.)

The crazy old church clock,
And the bewildered chimes.

—Wordsworth, "The Fountain : a Conversation."

Ha ! honest R.—According to Lamb's " Key," one Ramsay, who kept the " London Library" in Ludgate Street.

Granville S.—Granville Sharp, the abolitionist, died in 1813.

King Pandion, he is dead ;
All thy friends are lapt in lead.

—From the verses on a Nightingale, beginning—

"As it fell upon a day,"

formerly ascribed to Shakspeare, but now known to be written by Richard Barnfield.

A QUAKERS' MEETING.—P. 62.

(*London Magazine*, April 1821.)

" *Boreas and Cesias and Argestes loud.*"

—Milton, *Paradise Lost*, x. 699.

—— *sands, ignoble things,*
Dropt from the ruined sides of kings.

From " Lines on the Tombs in Westminster Abbey," by Francis Beaumont.

*How reverend is the view of these hushed heads,
Looking tranquillity !*

—A good example of Lamb's habit of constructing a quotation out of his general recollection of a passage. The lines he had in his mind are from Congreve's *Mourning Bride*, Act II. Scene 1 :—

> " How reverend is the face of this tall pile,
> Whose ancient pillars rear their marble heads
> To bear aloft its arched and ponderous roof,
> By its own weight made stedfast and immoveable,
> Looking tranquillity."

The writings of John Woolman.—" A journal of the life, gospel labours, and Christian experiences of that faithful minister of Jesus Christ, John Woolman, late of Mount Holly, in the Province of Jersey, North America " (1720-1772). Woolman was an American Quaker of humble origin, an "illiterate tailor," one of the first who had "misgivings about the institution of slavery." Crabb Robinson, to whom Lamb introduced the book, becomes rapturous over it. "His religion is love ; his whole existence and all his passions were love !"

" Forty feeding like one."

—From Wordsworth's verses, written in March 1801, beginning

> "The cock is crowing,
> The stream is flowing."

I have noted elsewhere Lamb's strong native sympathy with the Quaker spirit and Quaker manners and customs, a sympathy so marked that it is difficult to believe it was not inherited, and that on one or other side of his parentage he had not relations with the Society of Friends. His picture of the Quakerism of sixty years ago is of almost historical value, so great are the changes that have since divided the Society against itself.

THE OLD AND THE NEW SCHOOLMASTER.—P. 67.
(*London Magazine*, May 1821.)

My friend M.—Thomas Manning, the mathematician and explorer, whose acquaintance Lamb made early in life at Cambridge.

King Basilius.—See Sidney's *Arcadia*, Book i. (vol. ii. p. 17 of the edition of 1725.)

Even a child, that "plaything for an hour."—One of Lamb's quotations from himself. The phrase occurs in a charming poem, of three stanzas, in the *Poetry for Children* :—

> "A child's a plaything for an hour;
>   Its pretty tricks we try
> For that or for a longer space;
>   Then tire and lay it by.
>
> "But I knew one that to itself
>   All seasons could control;
> That would have mocked the sense of pain
>   Out of a grieved soul.
>
> "Thou straggler into loving arms,
>   Young climber up of knees,
> When I forget thy thousand ways,
>   Then life and all shall cease."

IMPERFECT SYMPATHIES.—P. 76.
(*London Magazine*, August 1821.)

Standing on earth, not rapt above the sky.—Quoted, not with perfect accuracy, from *Paradise Lost*, vii. 23.

John Buncle.—"The Life of John Buncle, Esq.; containing various observations and reflections, made in several parts of the world, and many extraordinary relations." By Thomas Amory (1756-66). Amory was a staunch Unitarian, an earnest moralist, a humorist, and eccentric to the verge of insanity—four qualifications which would appeal irresistibly to Lamb's sympathies.

A graceful figure, after Leonardo da Vinci.—This print, a present to Lamb from Crabb Robinson in 1816, was of Leonardo da Vinci's *Vierge aux Rochers*. It was a special favourite with Charles and Mary, and is the subject of some verses by Charles.

B—— would have been more in keeping if he had abided by the faith of his forefathers.—Braham, the singer. In a letter to Manning, Lamb describes him as a compound of the "Jew, the gentleman, and the angel."

"*To sit a guest with Daniel at his pulse.*"
—Slightly altered from *Paradise Regained*, Book ii. line 278.

I was travelling in a stage-coach with three male Quakers.—This adventure happened not to Lamb, but to Sir Anthony Carlisle, the surgeon, from whom Lamb had the anecdote.

WITCHES, AND OTHER NIGHT FEARS.—P. 85.
(*London Magazine*, October 1821.)

Headless bear, black man, or ape. From "The Author's Abstract of Melancholy," prefixed to Burton's *Anatomy of Melancholy.*

Dear little T. H.—Thornton Hunt, Leigh Hunt's eldest boy. This passage is interesting as having provoked Southey's violent attack on Leigh Hunt and his principles, in the *Quarterly Review* for January 1823.

"—— *names whose sense we see not
Fray us with things that be not.*"
—From Spenser's *Epithalamium*, line 343.

I have formerly travelled among the Westmoreland Fells.—See Lamb's letter to Manning, in 1802, describing his and Mary's visit to Coleridge at Keswick. "We got in in the evening, travelling in a post-chaise from Penrith, in the midst of a gorgeous sunset, which transmuted all the mountains into colours. We thought we had got into Fairyland. . . . Such an impression I never received from objects of sight before, nor do I suppose that I can ever again."

VALENTINE'S DAY.—P. 93.

(Leigh Hunt's *Indicator*, February 14, 1821.)

"*Brushed with the hiss of rustling wings.*"
—*Paradise Lost*, i. 768.

"*Gives a very echo to the throne where hope is seated.*"—Another of Lamb's adaptations of Shakspeare. The original is in *Twelfth Night* (Act II. Sc. 4.)

A little later on will be noticed a similar free-and-easy use of a passage from Wordsworth.

E. B.—Edward Francis Burney (1760-1848), a portrait-painter, and book-illustrator on a large scale. He was a cousin of Mde. D'Arblay, and not a half-brother as stated in Lamb's "Key." His name may be seen "at the bottom of many a well-executed vignette in the way of his profession" in the periodicals of his day. He illustrated for Harrison, the *World*, *Tatler*, *Guardian*, *Adventurer*, etc., besides the Arabian Nights, and novels of Richardson and Smollett.

MY RELATIONS.—P. 96.

(*London Magazine*, June 1821.)

In these two successive essays, and in that on the Benchers of the Inner Temple, Lamb draws portraits of singular interest to us, of his father, aunt, brother, and sister—all his near relations with one exception. The mother's name never occurs in letter or published writing after the first bitterness of the calamity of September 1796 had passed away. This was doubtless out of consideration for the feelings of his sister. Very noticeable is the frankness with which he describes the less agreeable side of the character of his brother John, who was still living, and apparently on quite friendly terms with Charles and Mary.

I had an aunt.—A sister of John Lamb the elder, who generally lived with the family, and contributed something to the common income. After the death of the mother, a lady of comfortable means, a relative of the family, offered her a home, but the arrangement did not succeed, and the aunt returned to die among her own people. Charles writes, just before her death in February 1797—" My poor old aunt, who was the kindest creature to me when I was at school, and used to bring me good things ; when I, schoolboy-like, used to be ashamed to see her come, and open her apron, and bring out her basin with some nice thing which she had saved for me,—the good old creature is now dying. She says, poor thing, she is glad she is come home to die with me. I was always her favourite." See also the lines " written on the day of my aunt's funeral " in the little volume of *Blank Verse*, by Charles Lloyd and Charles Lamb, published in 1798.

Brother or sister, I never had any to know them.—In this and the next sentence is a curious blending of fact and fiction. Besides John and Mary, four other children had been born to John and Elizabeth Lamb in the Temple, between the years 1762 and 1775, but had apparently not survived their infancy. Two daughters had been christened Elizabeth, one in 1762 and another after her death, in 1768. John and Mary Lamb are now to be described as cousins, under the names of James and Bridget Elia. Charles Lamb actually had relations, in that degree, living in Hertfordshire, in the neighbourhood of Wheathampstead.

James is an inexplicable cousin.—The mixture of the man of the world, dilettante, and sentimentalist—not an infrequent combination—is here described with graphic power. All that we know of John Lamb, the " broad, burly, jovial," living his bachelor-life in chambers at the old Sea-House, is supported and confirmed by this passage. Touching his extreme sensibility to the physical sufferings of animals, there is a letter of Charles to Crabb Robinson of the year 1810, which is worth noting. " My brother, whom you have met at my rooms (a plump, good-looking man of seven-and-forty), has written a book about humanity, which I transmit to you herewith. Wilson the publisher has put it into his head that you can get it reviewed for him. I daresay it is not in the scope of your review; but if you could put it into any likely train, he would rejoice. For, alas! our boasted humanity partakes of vanity. As it is, he teases me to death with choosing to suppose that I could get it into all the Reviews at a moment's notice. I!!!—who have been set up as a mark for them to throw at, and would willingly consign them all to Megaera's snaky locks. But here's the book, and don't show it to Mrs. Collier, for I remember she makes excellent eel soup, and the leading points of the book are directed against that very process."

Through the green plains of pleasant Hertfordshire.
— From an early sonnet of Lamb's.

MACKERY END, IN HERTFORDSHIRE.—P. 103.
(*London Magazine*, July 1821.)

Bridget Elia.—Mary Lamb. The lives of the brother and sister are so bound together, that the illustrations of their joint life afforded by this essay, and that on *Old China*, are of singular interest. They show us the brighter and happier intervals of that life, without which indeed it could hardly have been borne for those eight-and-thirty years. In 1805, during one of Mary Lamb's periodical attacks of mania, and consequent absences from home, Charles writes—"I am a fool bereft of her co-operation. I am used to look up to her in the least and biggest perplexities. To say all that I find her would be more than, I think, anybody could possibly understand. She is older, wiser, and better than I am; and all my wretched imperfections I cover to myself by thinking on her goodness." Compare also the sonnet written by Charles, in one of his "lucid intervals" when himself in confinement, in 1796, ending with the words—

"—— the mighty debt of love I owe,
Mary, to thee, my sister and my friend."

The oldest thing I remember is Mackery End, or Mackarel End.—The place, now further contracted into "Mackrye End," is about a mile and a half from Wheathampstead, on the Luton Branch of the Great Northern Railway. On leaving the Wheathampstead Station, the traveller must follow the road which runs along the valley towards Luton, nearly parallel with the railway for about a mile, to a group of houses near the "Cherry Trees." At this point, he will turn short to the right, and then take the first turning on his left, along the edge of a pretty little wood. He will soon see the venerable old Jacobean mansion, properly called Mackrye End, and close to it a whitish farmhouse, which is the one occupied by Lamb's relatives, the Gladmans, at the time of the pilgrimage recorded in this essay. The present writer has visited the spot, also in the "heart of June," and bears the pleasantest testimony to its rural beauty and seclusion. The farmhouse has had an important addition to it since Lamb's day, but a large portion of the building is evidently still the same as when the "image of welcome" came forth from it to greet the brother and sister. May I, without presumption, call attention to the almost unique beauty of this prose idyll?

> But thou that didst appear so fair
> To fond imagination.

—Wordsworth's "Yarrow Visited."

B. F.—Barron Field, who accompanied Lamb and his sister on this expedition. See the essay on *Distant Correspondents*.

Compare a letter of Lamb to Manning in May 1819. "How are my cousins, the Gladmans of Wheathampstead, and farmer Bruton? Mrs. Bruton is a glorious woman. 'Hail, Mackery End.' This is a fragment of a blank verse poem which I once meditated, but got no further."

MY FIRST PLAY.—P. 108.

(*London Magazine*, December 1821.)

The only landed property I could ever call my own.—Mrs. Procter informs me that a relative of Lamb's did actually bequeath to him a small "landed estate"—probably no more than a single field—producing a pound or two of rent, and that Lamb was fond of referring to the circumstance, and declaring that it had revolutionised his views of *Property*.

The first appearance to me of Mrs. Siddons in Isabella.—One of Lamb's earliest, perhaps his first sonnet, was inspired by this great actress. It was published, with some of Coleridge's, in the columns of the *Morning Chronicle* in 1794.

> As when a child, on some long winter's night
> Affrighted clinging to its grandam's knees
> With eager wondering and perturbed delight
> Listens strange tales of fearful dark decrees
> Muttered to wretch by necromantic spell;
> Or of those hags, who at the witching time
> Of murky midnight ride the air sublime,
> And mingle foul embrace with fiends of Hell:
> Cold Horror drinks its blood! Anon the tear
> More gentle starts, to hear the beldame tell

Of pretty babes that loved each other dear,
Murdered by cruel Uncle's mandate fell :
Even such the shivering joys thy tones impart,
Even so thou, Siddons, meltest my sad heart!

MODERN GALLANTRY.—P. 113.

(London Magazine, November 1822).

Joseph Paice, of Bread Street Hill, merchant.—Some very interesting particulars of the life and character of this generous and self-sacrificing person, in whom most unquestionably "manners were not idle," will be found in the *Athenæum* for the year 1841 (pp. 366 and 387), contributed by the late Miss Anne Manning. Thomas Edwards, author of *Canons of Criticism,* a very acute commentary upon Warburton's emendations of Shakspeare, was his uncle. Edwards was a mediocre poet, but his sonnets are carefully constructed on the Miltonic scheme, which perhaps accounts for Lamb's exaggerated epithet. The sonnet may be given here as at least a curiosity :—

To Mr. J. Paice.

Joseph, the worthy son of worthy sire,
Who well repay'st thy pious parents' care
To train thee in the ways of Virtue fair,
And early with the Love of Truth inspire,
What farther can my closing eyes desire
To see, but that by wedlock thou repair
The waste of death ; and raise a virtuous heir
To build our House, e'er I in peace retire?
Youth is the time for Love : Then choose a wife,
With prudence choose ; 'tis Nature's genuine voice ;
And what she truly dictates must be good ;
Neglected once that prime, our remnant life
Is soured, or saddened, by an ill-timed choice,
Or lonely, dull, and friendless solitude.

THE OLD BENCHERS OF THE INNER TEMPLE.—
P. 118.

(London Magazine, September 1821.)

Charles Lamb was born on the 10th of February 1775, in Crown Office Row, Temple, where Samuel Salt, a Bencher of the Inn, owned two sets of chambers. This was Lamb's home for the seven years preceding his admission into Christ's Hospital in 1782, and afterwards, in holiday seasons, till he left school in 1789, and later, at least till Salt's death in 1792. A recent editor of Lamb's works has stated that, with the exception of Salt, almost all the names of Benchers given in this essay are "purely imaginary." The reverse of this is the fact. All the names here celebrated are to be found in the records of the honourable society.

There when they came, whereas those bricky towers,
—Spenser's *Prothalamion*, stanza viii.

Of building strong, albeit of Paper hight.
—Paper Buildings, facing King's Bench Walk in the Temple. The line is doubtless improvised for the occasion.

That fine Elizabethan hall.—The hall of the Middle Temple. The fountain still plays, but "quantum mutatus."

Ah! yet doth beauty like a dial hand.
—Shakspeare's Sonnet, No. 104.

"*Carved it out quaintly in the sun.*"
—*III. Henry VI.*, ii. 5.

The roguish eye of J—ll.—Jekyll, the Master in Chancery. The wit, and friend of wits, among the old Benchers—the Sir George Rose of his day. Called to the Bench 1805; died 1837.

Thomas Coventry, nephew of William, fifth Earl of Coventry; of North Cray Place, Bexley, Kent.—Called to the Bench in 1766; died in 1797.

Samuel Salt.—Called to the Bench 1782; died in 1792. The Bencher in whom Lamb had the most peculiar interest. John Lamb, the father, was in the service of Salt for some five and forty years—he acting as clerk and confidential servant, and his wife as housekeeper. As we have seen, Mr. Salt occupied two sets of chambers in Crown Office Row, forming a substantial house. He had two indoor servants, besides John and Elizabeth Lamb, and kept his carriage. Salt died in 1792. By his will, dated 1786, he gives "To my servant, John Lamb, who has lived with me near forty years," £500 South Sea stock; and "to Mrs. Lamb £100 in money, well deserved for her care and attention during my illness." By a codicil, dated December 20, 1787, his executors are directed to employ John Lamb to receive the testator's "Exchequer annuities of £210 and £14 during their term, and to pay him £10 a-year for his trouble so long as he shall receive them," a delicate and ingenious way of retaining John Lamb in his service, as it were, after his own decease. By a later codicil, he gives another hundred pounds to Mrs. Lamb. These benefactions, and not the small pension erroneously stated, on the authority of Talfourd, in my memoir of Lamb, formed the provision made by Salt for his faithful pair of attendants. The appointment of Charles to the clerkship in the India House in 1792 must have been the last of the many kind acts of Samuel Salt to the family. Where the Lamb family moved to after Salt's death in 1792, and how they struggled on between that date and the fatal year 1796, is one of the unsettled points of Lamb's history. Mary Lamb's skill with her needle was probably used as a means of increasing the common income. Crabb Robinson tells us of an article on needlework contributed by her some years later to one of the magazines.

The unfortunate Miss Blandy. The heroine of a *cause célèbre* in the year 1752. Her whole story will be found, *apropos* of the town of Henley, in Mr. Leslie's charming book on the Thames, entitled *Our River*. Miss Blandy, the daughter of an attorney at Henley, with good expectations from her father, attracted the attention of an adventurer, a certain Captain Cranstoun. The father disapproved of the intimacy, and the Captain entrusted Miss Blandy with a certain powder which she administered to her father with a fatal result. Her defence was that she believed the powder to be of the nature of a love-philtre, which would have the effect of making her father well-affected towards her lover. The defence was not successful, and Miss Blandy was found guilty of murder, and executed at Oxford in April 1752.

Susan P——.—Susannah Pierson, sister of Salt's brother-Bencher, Peter Pierson, mentioned in this essay, and one of Salt's executors. By his second codicil, Salt bequeaths her, as a mark of regard, £500 ; his silver inkstand ; and the "works of Pope, Swift, Shakspeare, Addison, and Steele ;" also Sherlock's Sermons (Sherlock had been Master of the Temple), and any other books she likes to choose out of his library, hoping that, "by reading and reflection," they will "make her life more comfortable." How oddly touching this bequest seems to us, in the light thrown on it by Lamb's account of the relation between Salt and his friend's sister! What a pleasant glimpse, again, is here afforded of the "spacious closet of good old English reading" into which Charles and Mary were "tumbled," as he told us, at an early age, when they "browsed at will upon that fair and wholesome pasturage."

I knew this Lovel.—Lamb's father, John Lamb. The sketch of him given in Mr. Procter's memoir of Charles, taken doubtless from the portrait here mentioned, confirms the statement of a general resemblance to Garrick. Mrs. Arthur Tween, a daughter of Randal Norris, has in her possession a medallion portrait of Samuel Salt, executed in plaster of Paris by John Lamb. He published a collection of his verses, "Poetical Pieces on several occasions," in a rough pamphlet of quarto size. A few lines from the (rather doggerel) verses describing the life of a footman in the last century (doubtless reflecting his own experiences of the time when he wore "the smart new livery") may be given as a sample of his efforts in the manner of "Swift and Prior." The footman has just been sent on an errand to inquire after the health of a friend of his mistress who has lost her monkey :—

> "Then up she mounts—down I descend,
> To shake hands with particular friend ;
> And there I do some brothers meet,
> And we each other kindly greet ;
> Then cards they bring and cribbage-board,
> And I must play upon their word,
> Altho' I tell them I am sent
> To know how th' night a lady spent.
> 'Pho! make excuse, and have one bout,
> And say the lady was gone out ;'
> Th' advice I take, sit down and say,
> 'What is the sum for which we play ?'
> 'I care not much,' another cries,
> 'But let it be for Wets and Drys.'"

"*A remnant most forlorn of what he was.*"—One of Lamb's quotations from himself. It occurs in the lines (February 1797) "written on the day of my aunt's funeral :"—

> " One parent yet is left,—a wretched thing,
> A sad survivor of his buried wife,
> A palsy-smitten, childish, old, old man,
> A semblance most forlorn of what he was,
> A merry cheerful man."

John Lamb lingered till April 1799.

Peter Pierson.—Called to the Bench 1800, died 1808. It will be seen that Salt and Pierson, though friends and contemporaries at the Bar, were not so as Benchers. Salt had been some years dead when his friend was called to the Bench.

Daines Barrington.—The antiquary, naturalist, and correspondent of White of Selborne. Called to the Bench in 1777, died 1800.

Thomas Barton.—Called to the Bench 1775, died 1791.

John Read.—Called to the Bench 1792, died in 1804.

Twopenny.—There never was a Bencher of the Inner Temple of this name. The gentleman here intended, Mr. Richard Twopeny, was a stockbroker, a member of the Kentish family of that name, who, being a bachelor, lived in chambers in the Temple. On his retirement from business he resided at West

Malling in Kent, and died in 1809, at the age of eighty-two. Mr. Edward Twopeny of Woodstock, Sittingbourne, a great-nephew of this gentleman, remembers him well, and informs me that he was, as Lamb describes him, remarkably thin. Lamb evidently recalled him as a familiar figure in the Temple in his own childish days, and supposed him to have been a member of the Bar. Mr. Twopeny held the important position of stockbroker to the Bank of England.

John Wharry.—Called to the Bench 1801, died in 1812.

Richard Jackson.—Called to the Bench 1770, died 1787. This gentleman was M.P. for New Romney and a member of Lord Shelburne's Government in 1782. From his wide reading and extraordinary memory he was known, beyond the circle of his brother-Benchers, as "the omniscient." Dr. Johnson (reversing the usual order of his translations) styles him the "all-knowing." See *Boswell*, under date of April 1776:—"No, Sir; Mr. Thrale is to go by my advice to Mr. Jackson (the all-knowing), and get from him a plan for seeing the most that can be seen in the time that we have to travel."

James Mingay.—Called to the Bench 1785, died 1812. Mr. Mingay was an eminent King's Counsel, and in his day a powerful rival at the Bar, of Thomas Erskine—according to an obituary notice in the *Gentleman's Magazine* of "a persuasive oratory, infinite wit, and most excellent fancy." His retort upon Erskine, about the knee-buckles, goes to confirm this verdict.

Baron Maseres.—Cursitor Baron of the Exchequer, a post which he filled for fifty years. Born 1731, died May 1824. He persevered to the end of his days in wearing the costume of the reign in which he was born.

R. N.—Randal Norris, for many years Sub-Treasurer and Librarian of the Inner Temple. At the age of fourteen he was articled to Mr. Walls of Paper Buildings, and from that time, for more than half a century, resided in the Inner Temple. His wife was a native of Widford, the village adjoining Blakesware, in Hertfordshire, and a friend of Mrs. Field, the housekeeper, and there was thus a double tie connecting Randal Norris with Lamb's family. His name appears early in Charles's correspondence. At the season of his mother's death, he tells Coleridge that Mr. Norris had been more than a father to him, and Mrs. Norris more than a mother. Mr. Norris died in the Temple in January 1827, at the age of seventy-six, and was buried in the Temple churchyard. Talfourd misdates the event by a year. It was then that Charles Lamb wrote to Crabb Robinson—"In him I have a loss the world cannot make up.

He was my friend and my father's friend all the life I can
remember. I seem to have made foolish friendships ever since.
Those are the friendships which outlive a second generation.
Old as I am waxing, in his eyes I was still the child he first
knew me. To the last he called me Charley. I have none to
call me Charley now."

GRACE BEFORE MEAT.—P. 130.

(*London Magazine*, November 1821.)

C——.—Coleridge.

C. V. L.—Charles Valentine le Grice, Lamb's schoolfellow
at Christ's Hospital. See the Essay on that Institution.

Some one recalled a legend.—Leigh Hunt tells the story in
his account of Christ's Hospital:—"Our dress was of the
coarsest and quaintest kind, but was respected out of doors,
and is so. It consisted of a blue drugget gown, or body, with
ample skirts to it; a yellow vest underneath in winter time;
small clothes of Russia duck; worsted yellow stockings; a
leathern girdle; and a little black worsted cap, usually carried
in the hand. I believe it was the ordinary dress of children in
humble life during the reign of the Tudors. We used to flatter
ourselves that it was taken from the monks; and there went a
monstrous tradition, that at one period it consisted of blue
velvet with silver buttons. It was said, also, that during the
blissful era of the blue velvet, we had roast mutton for supper;
but that the small clothes not being then in existence, and the
mutton suppers too luxurious, the eatables were given up for the
ineffables."

The following beautiful passage from the *Recreations and
Studies by a Country Clergyman of the Eighteenth Century* (John
Murray, 1882), shows that others, besides Lamb, had thought
the main thought of this essay. The writer is describing, in
1781, the drive from Huddersfield, along the banks of the
Calder:—"I never felt anything so fine: I shall remember it
and thank God for it as long as I live. I am sorry I did not
think to say grace after it. Are we to be grateful for nothing
but beef and pudding? to thank God for life, and not for
happiness?"

DREAM CHILDREN; A REVERIE.—P. 137.

(*London Magazine*, January 1822.)

The mood in which Lamb was prompted to this singularly
affecting confidence was clearly due to a family bereavement, a
month or two before the date of the essay. I may be allowed

to repeat words of my own, used elsewhere, on this subject. "Lamb's elder brother John was then lately dead. A letter to Wordsworth, of March 1822, mentions his death as even then recent, and speaks of a certain 'deadness to everything' which the writer dates from that event. The 'broad, burly, jovial' John Lamb (so Talfourd describes him) had lived his own easy prosperous life up to this time, not altogether avoiding social relations with his brother and sister, but evidently absorbed to the last in his own interests and pleasures. The death of this brother, wholly unsympathetic as he was with Charles, served to bring home to him his loneliness. He was left in the world with but one near relation, and that one too often removed from him for months at a time by the saddest of afflictions. No wonder if he became keenly aware of his solitude." The emotion discernible in this essay is absolutely genuine ; the blending of fact with fiction in the details is curiously arbitrary.

Their great - grandmother Field. — Lamb's grandmother, Mary Field, for more than fifty years housekeeper at Blakesware, a dower-house of the Hertfordshire family of Plumers, a few miles from Ware. William Plumer, who represented his county for so many years in Parliament, was still living, and Lamb may have disguised the whereabouts of the "great house" out of consideration for him. Why he substituted Norfolk is only matter for conjecture. Perhaps there were actually scenes from the old legend of the Children in the Wood carved upon a chimneypiece at Blakesware ; possibly there was some old story in the annals of the Plumer family touching the mysterious disappearance of two children, for which it pleased Lamb to substitute the story of the familiar ballad. His grandmother, as he has told us in his lines *The Grandame*, was deeply versed "in anecdote domestic."

Which afterwards came to decay, and was nearly pulled down. —The dismantling of the Blakesware house had therefore begun, it appears, before the death of William Plumer. Cussans, in his *History of Hertfordshire*, says it was pulled down in 1822. Perhaps the complete demolition was not carried out till after Mr. Plumer's death in that year. The "other house" was Gilston, the principal seat of the Plumers, some miles distant. See notes on the essay *Blakesmoor in Hertfordshire*.

And then I told how, when she came to die.—Mrs. Field died in the summer of 1792, and was buried in the adjoining churchyard of Widford. Her gravestone, with the name and date of death, August 5, 1792, is still to be seen, and is one of the few tangible memorials of Lamb's family history still existing. By a curious fatality, it narrowly escaped destruction in the great gale of October 1881, when a tree was blown down across it, considerably reducing its proportions.

John L.—Of course John Lamb, the brother. Whether Charles was ever a "lame-footed" boy, through some temporary cause, we cannot say. We know that at the time of the mother's death John Lamb was suffering from an injury to his foot, and made it (after his custom) an excuse for not exerting himself unduly. See the letter of Charles to Coleridge written at the time. "My brother, little disposed (I speak not without tenderness for him) at any time to take care of old age and infirmities, had now, with his bad leg, an exemption from such duties."

I courted the fair Alice W—n.—In my memoir of Charles Lamb, I have given the reasons for identifying Alice W—n with the Anna of the early sonnets, and again with the form and features of the village maiden described as Rosamund Gray. The girl who is celebrated under these various names won the heart of Charles Lamb while he was yet little more than a boy. He does not care to conceal from us that it was in Hertfordshire, while under his grandmother's roof, that he first met her. The Beauty " with the yellow Hertfordshire hair —so like my Alice," is how he describes the portrait in the picture gallery at Blakesmoor. Moreover, the "winding wood-walks green " where he roamed with his Anna, can hardly be unconnected with the " walks and windings of Blakesmoor," apostrophised at the close of that beautiful essay. And there is a group of cottages called Blenheim, not more than half a mile from the site of Blakesware House, where the original Anna, according to the traditions of the village, resided. "Alice W—n" is one of Lamb's deliberate inventions. In the key to the initials employed by him in his essays, he explains that Alice W—n stood for Alice Winterton, but that the name was "feigned." *Anna* was, in fact, the nearest clue to the real name that Lamb has vouchsafed. Her actual name was, I have the best reason to believe, Ann Simmons. She afterwards married Mr. Bartram, the pawnbroker of Princes Street, Leicester Square. The complete history of this episode in Lamb's life will probably never come to light. There are many obvious reasons why any idea of marriage should have been indefinitely abandoned. The poverty in Lamb's home is one such reason ; and one, even more decisive, may have been the discovery of the taint of madness that was inherited, in more or less degree, by all the children. Why Lamb chose the particular *alias* of Winterton, under which to disguise his early love, will never be known. It was a name not unfamiliar to him, being that of the old steward in Colman's play of the *Iron*

Chest, a part created by Lamb's favourite comedian Dodd. The play was first acted in 1796, about the time when the final separation of the lovers seems to have taken place.

In illustration of Lamb's fondness for children, I have the pleasure of adding the following pretty letter to a child, not hitherto printed. It was written to a little girl (one of twin-sisters), the daughter of Kenney the dramatist, after Lamb and his sister's visit to the Kenneys at Versailles in September 1822. The letter has been most kindly placed at my disposal by my friend Mr. W. J. Jeaffreson, whose mother was the Sophy of the letter. At the close of a short note to Mrs. Kenney, Lamb adds:—"Pray deliver what follows to my dear wife, Sophy:—

"My dear Sophy—The few short days of connubial felicity which I passed with you among the pears and apricots of Versailles were some of the happiest of my life. But they are flown!

"And your other half, your dear co-twin—that she-you—that almost equal sharer of my affections—you and she are my better half, a quarter apiece. She and you are my pretty sixpence, you the head, and she the tail. Sure, Heaven that made you so alike must pardon the error of an inconsiderate moment, should I for love of you, love her too well. Do you think laws were made for lovers? I think not.

"Adieu, amiable pair.
"Yours, and yours,
"C. LAMB.

"*P.S.*—I inclose half a dear kiss apiece for you."

DISTANT CORRESPONDENTS.—P. 142.

(*London Magazine*, March 1822.)

B. F.—Barron Field. Born October 23, 1786. He was educated for the Bar and practised for some years, going the Oxford Circuit. In 1816 he married, and went out to New South Wales as Judge of the Supreme Court at Sydney. In 1824 he returned to England, having resigned his judgeship; but two or three years afterwards he was appointed Chief-Justice of Gibraltar. He died at Torquay in 1846. His brother, Francis John Field, was a fellow-clerk of Charles Lamb's at the India House, which was perhaps the origin of the acquaintance. Barron Field edited a volume of papers (*Geographical Memoirs*) on New South Wales for Murray, and the appendix contains some short poems, entitled *First-Fruits of Australian Poetry*.

Some papers of his are to be found in Leigh Hunt's *Reflector*, to which Lamb also contributed.

One of Mrs. Rowe's superscriptions.— Mrs. Elizabeth Rowe (1674-1737), an exemplary person, and now forgotten moralist in verse and prose. Among other works she wrote, *Friendship in Death—in Twenty Letters from the Dead to the Living*. The following are from the "superscriptions" of these letters:— "To Sylvia from Alexis;" "From Cleander to his Brother, endeavouring to reclaim him from his extravagances;" "To Emilia from Delia, giving her a description of the invisible regions, and the happy state of the inhabitants of Paradise."

The late Lord C.—The second Lord Camelford, killed in a duel with Mr. Best in 1804. The day before his death he gave directions that his body should be removed "as soon as may be convenient to a country far distant! to a spot not near the haunts of men, but where the surrounding scenery may smile upon my remains. It is situated on the borders of the lake of St. Lampierre, in the Canton of Berne, and three trees stand in the particular spot." The centre tree he desired might be taken up, and his body being there deposited immediately replaced. At the foot of this tree, his lordship added, he had formerly passed many solitary hours, contemplating the mutability of human affairs.—*Annual Register* for 1804.

*Aye me! while thee the seas and sounding shores
Hold far away.*

—*Lycidas*, quoted incorrectly, as usual.

J. W.—James White, Lamb's schoolfellow at Christ's Hospital. Died in 1820.

THE PRAISE OF CHIMNEY-SWEEPERS.—P. 148.
(*London Magazine*, May 1822.)

*A sable cloud
Turns forth her silver lining on the night.*
—Milton, *Comus*, line 223.

My pleasant friend Jem White.—James White, a schoolfellow of Lamb's at Christ's Hospital, and the author of a Shaksperian squib, suggested by the Ireland Forgeries "Original Letters, etc., of Sir John Falstaff and his friends, now first made public by a gentleman, a descendant of Dame Quickly, from genuine manuscripts which have been in the possession of the Quickly family near four hundred years." It was published in 1795, and Southey believed that Lamb had in some way a hand in it. The Preface in particular bears some traces of his peculiar vein, but Lamb's enthusiastic recommendation of the book to his friends seems to show that it was in the main the production of James White. The *jeu d'esprit* is not more successful than such parodies usually are. White took to journalism, in some form, and was at the time of his death in March 1820 an "agent of Provincial newspapers." His annual supper to the little climbing-boys was imitated by many charitable persons in London and other large towns.

Our trusty companion, Bigod.—Lamb's old friend and editor John Fenwick, of the Albion. See Essay on the *Two Races of Men*.

Golden lads and lasses must.
—*Cymbeline*, Act iv. Sc. 2.
Golden lads and girls all must,
As chimney-sweepers, come to dust.

It is curious that in this essay Lamb does not even allude to the grave subject of the cruelties incident to the climbing-boys' occupation—a question which for some years past had attracted the attention of philanthropic persons, in and out of Parliament. A year or two later, however, he made a characteristic offering to the cause. In 1824 James Montgomery of Sheffield edited a volume of Prose and Verse—*The Chimney-Sweeper's Friend, and Climbing-boy's Album*, to which many writers of the day contributed. Lamb, who had been applied to, sent Blake's poem —*The Chimney-Sweeper*. It was headed, " Communicated by Mr. Charles Lamb, from a very rare and curious little work" --doubtless a true description of the *Songs of Innocence* in 1824. It is noteworthy that, before sending it, this incorrigible joker could not refrain from quietly altering Blake's " Little Tom Dacre" into " Little Tom *Toddy*."

A COMPLAINT OF THE DECAY OF BEGGARS,

IN THE METROPOLIS. P. 156.
(*London Magazine*, June 1822.)

Each degree of it is mocked by its "neighbour grice." A reference, apparently, to *Timon of Athens*, iv. 3.
——" every grise of fortune
Is smoothed by that below."

Unfastidious Vincent Bourne (1697-1747).—The "dear Vinny Bourne" of Cowper, who had been his pupil at Westminster.

Cowper, it will be remembered, translated many of Bourne's Latin verses.

B——, *the mild Rector of* ——.—In Lamb's "Key" to the Initials, etc., used in his essays, this is affirmed to be a quite imaginary personage.

A DISSERTATION UPON ROAST PIG.—P. 164.
(*London Magazine*, September 1822.)

The tradition as to the origin of cooking, which is of course the salient feature of this essay, had been communicated to Lamb, he here tells us, by his friend M., Thomas Manning, whose acquaintance he had made long ago at Cambridge, and who since those days had spent much of his life in exploring China and Thibet. Lamb says the same thing in one of his private letters, so we may accept it as a literal fact. The question therefore arises whether Manning had found the legend existing in any form in China, or whether Lamb's detail of the Chinese manuscript is wholly fantastic. It is at least certain that the story is a very old one, and appears as early as the third century, in the writings of Porphyry of Tyre. The following passage, a literal translation from the Treatise *De Abstinentiâ* of that philosopher, sets forth one form of the legend:—

"Asclepiades, in his work on Cyprus and Phœnice, writes as follows :—' Originally it was not usual for anything having life to be sacrificed to the gods—not that there was any law on the subject, for it was supposed to be forbidden by the law of nature. At a certain period, however (tradition says), when blood was required in atonement for blood, the first victim was sacrificed, and was entirely consumed by fire. On one occasion, in later times, when a sacrifice of this kind was being offered, and the victim in process of being burned, a morsel of its flesh fell to the ground. The priest, who was standing by, immediately picked it up, and on removing his fingers from the burnt flesh, chanced to put them to his mouth, in order to assuage the pain of the burn. As soon as he had tasted the burnt flesh he conceived a strange longing to eat of it, and accordingly began to eat the flesh himself, and gave some to his wife also. Pygmalion, on hearing of it, directed that the man and his wife should be put to death, by being hurled headlong from a rock, and appointed another man to the priest's office. When, moreover, not long after this man was offering the same sacrifice, and in the same way ate of the flesh, he was sentenced to the same punishment. When, however, the thing made further progress, and men continued to offer sacrifice, and in order to gratify their appetite could not refrain from the flesh, but regularly adopted the habit of eating it, all punishment for so doing ceased to be inflicted."

'Manning may have been aware of this passage, and have told the story in his own language to Charles Lamb. It is worth noticing that in 1823, the year following the appearance of this essay, Thomas Taylor, the Platonist, published a translation of certain Treatises of Porphyry, including the *De Abstinentiâ*. It is possible that Manning may, on some occasion, have learned the tradition from Taylor.

Recent editors of Lamb have asserted, without offering any sufficient evidence, that he owed the idea of this rhapsody on the Pig to an Italian Poem, by Tigrinio Bistonio, published in 1761, at Modena, entitled *Gli Elogi del Porco* (Tigrinio Bistonio was the pseudonym of the Abate Giuseppe Ferrari). Mr. Richard Garnett of the British Museum, to whom I am indebted for calling my attention to the passage in Porphyry, has kindly examined for me the Italian poem in question, and assures me that he can find in it no resemblance whatever to Lamb's treatment of the same theme. There is no affectation in Lamb's avowal of his fondness for this delicacy. Towards the close of his life, however, Roast Pig declined somewhat in his favour, and was superseded by hare, and other varieties of game. Indeed Lamb was as fond of game as Cowper was of fish; and as in Cowper's case, his later letters constantly open with acknowledgments of some recent offering of the kind from a good-natured correspondent.

> *Ere sin could blight or sorrow fade,*
> *Death came with timely care.*

From Coleridge's *Epitaph on an Infant*. It must have been with unusual glee that Lamb here borrowed half of his friend's quatrain. The epitaph had appeared in the very earliest volume to which he was himself a contributor—the little volume of Coleridge's poems, published in 1796, by Joseph Cottle, of Bristol. The lines are there allotted a whole page to themselves.

It was over London Bridge.—The reader will not fail to note the audacious indifference to fact that makes Lamb assert in a parenthesis that his school was on the other side of London Bridge, and that he was afterwards "at St. Omer's."

ON THE BEHAVIOUR OF MARRIED PEOPLE.—P. 172.

(*London Magazine*, September 1822.)

The essay had previously appeared, in 1811, in Leigh Hunt's *Reflector*.

ON SOME OF THE OLD ACTORS.—P. 180.

(London Magazine, February 1822.)

This essay was originally one of three which appeared in the *London* under the title of *The Old Actors*. When Lamb collected and edited his essays for publication in a volume in 1823, he abridged and rearranged them under different headings. Many of Lamb's favourites, here celebrated, had died or left the stage almost before Lamb entered manhood, showing how early his critical faculty had matured.

Bensley, whose performance of Malvolio he has analysed in such a masterly way, retired from his profession in 1796, and Palmer in 1798. Parsons died in 1795, and Dodd in the autumn of 1796, three months after quitting the stage. Suett survived till 1805, and Mrs. Jordan till 1816.

ON THE ARTIFICIAL COMEDY OF THE LAST CENTURY.—P. 192.

(London Magazine, April 1822.)

Originally the second part of the essay on *The Old Actors*. This essay is noteworthy as having provoked a serious remonstrance from Lord Macaulay, in reviewing Leigh Hunt's edition of the Restoration Dramatists. Lamb's apology for the moral standards of Congreve and Wycherley is simply an exercise of ingenuity, or rather, as Hartley Coleridge pointed out, is an apology for himself—Charles Lamb—who found himself quite able to enjoy the unparalleled wit of Congreve without being in any way thrown off his moral balance. It is in a letter to Moxon on Leigh Hunt's proposed edition that Hartley Coleridge's comment occurs. He writes: "Nothing more or better can be said in defence of these writers than what Lamb has said in his delightful essay on *The Old Actors;* which is, after all, rather an apology for the audiences who applauded and himself who delighted in their plays, than for the plays themselves. . . . But Lamb always took things by the better handle."

ON THE ACTING OF MUNDEN.—P. 201.

(London Magazine, October 1822.)

Cockletop.— In O'Keefe's farce of *Modern Antiques; or, The Merry Mourners.*

—— *There the antic sate
Mocking our state.*

Adapted from *Richard II.*, Act iii. Sc. 2

THE LAST ESSAYS OF ELIA.

THE Second Series of Elia was published in a collected form by Mr. Moxon in 1833. It was furnished with a Preface, purporting to be written by "a friend of the late Elia," announcing his death, and commenting freely on his character and habits. This Preface (written, of course, by Lamb himself) is placed in the present edition at the beginning of the volume. Elia is here supposed to have died in the interval between the publication of the First and Second Series. From the opening sentences we should conclude that it was at first intended as a postscript to the First Series, and indeed it originally appeared in the *London Magazine* for January 1823. But this design, if ever entertained, was not carried out.

I have spoken in my Introduction of the estimate here pronounced by Lamb himself on his own writings, as in my memoir of Lamb I had occasion to deal with the same Preface as throwing light on the causes of his unpopularity. In each case he shows a rare degree of self-knowledge. If they stood alone they would entirely account for Carlyle's harsh verdict. "Few professed *literati* were of his councils," and he would be little disposed to show the serious side of himself, still less the better side of his humour, to such as Carlyle. To the evidence of such friends as Hood, Patmore, and Procter, confirming Lamb's own account, I may here add a piece of fresh testimony from Hazlitt. It occurs in the essay "On Coffee-House Politicians," one of the *Table-Talk* series:—

"I will, however, admit that the said Elia is the worst company in the world in bad company, if it be granted me that in good company he is nearly the best that can be. He is one of those of whom it may be said, *Tell me your company and I'll tell you your manners.* He is the creature of sympathy, and makes good whatever opinion you seem to entertain of him. He cannot outgo the apprehensions of the circle, and invariably acts up or down to the point of refinement or vulgarity at which they pitch him. He appears to take a pleasure in exaggerating the prejudices of strangers against him, a pride in confirming the prepossessions of friends. In whatever scale of intellect he is placed, he is as lively or as stupid as the rest can be for their lives. If you think him odd and ridiculous, he becomes more and more so every minute, *à la folie*, till he is a wonder gazed at by all. Set him against a good wit and a ready apprehension, and he brightens more and more—

> 'Or like a gate of steel
> Fronting the sun, receives and renders back
> Its figure and its heat.'"

BLAKESMOOR IN H——SHIRE.—P. 205.
(*London Magazine*, September 1824.)

Blakesmoor, as has been already observed, was Blakesware, a dower-house of the Plumers, about five miles from Ware, in Hertfordshire. If there were ever any doubt on the subject, Lamb's own words are decisive. In a letter to Bernard Barton, of August 10, 1827, occurs the following charming passage:— "You have well described your old-fashioned paternal hall. Is it not odd that every one's recollections are of some such place? I had my Blakesware ('Blakesmoor' in the *London*). Nothing fills a child's mind like a large old mansion, better if un- or partially-occupied: peopled with the spirits of deceased members of the county and justices of the Quorum. Would I were buried in the peopled solitudes of one with my feelings at seven years old! Those marble busts of the emperors, they seemed as if they were to stand for ever, as they had stood from the living days of Rome, in that old marble hall, and I to partake of their permanency. Eternity was, while I thought not of time. But he thought of me, and they are toppled down, and corn covers the spot of the noble old dwelling and its princely gardens. I feel like a grasshopper that, chirping about the grounds, escaped the scythe only by my littleness."

In face of this letter, it might seem strange that most of Lamb's editors have unhesitatingly asserted that the original of Lamb's Blakesmoor was Gilston, the other seat of the Plumers, near Harlow, in the same county. The origin of the mistake is to be found in the history of the Plumer property, after the death of Mr. William Plumer, the member for Higham Ferrers, in 1822. Mr. Plumer died without children, and left his estates at Blakesware and Gilston to his widow. The house at Blakesware, which, as we have seen, had been partially dismantled in Mr. Plumer's lifetime, was now pulled to the ground —its principal contents having been already removed to the

other house at Gilston. It was after its final demolition that
Lamb paid the visit here recorded, to look once more on the
remains of a place associated with so many happy memories.
The widow, Mrs. Plumer, not long after her first husband's
death, married Commander Lewin of the Royal Navy, and
finally, after his death, married for the third time, in 1828, Mr.
Ward, author of the once popular novel *Tremaine*. On marrying
Mrs. Plumer Lewin Mr. Ward received the royal permission to
take and use the name of Plumer as a prefix to that of Ward.
Mr. and Mrs. Plumer Ward continued to live at the family
residence of the Plumers at Gilston.

Mr. P. G. Patmore — the father of the present Mr. Coventry
Patmore — made the acquaintance of Mr. Plumer Ward in 1824,
and in a book, entitled *My Friends and Acquaintance*, published in 1854, gave an interesting account of Mr. Ward,
together with a full description, supplied by that gentleman
himself, of the furniture and general arrangements of Gilston
House. Among these appear the Twelve Cæsars and the
Marble Hall, and other features of the old house at Blakesware,
familiar to readers of Charles Lamb, which had been in fact
removed from the one house to the other. Mr. Patmore, apparently ignorant of the existence of any other residence belonging to the Plumers, at once assumed that Gilston had been the
house celebrated by Lamb, and announced the discovery with
some natural exultation. From that time Mr. Patmore's version
of the facts has been generally accepted. Gilston House was
pulled down in 1851. The contents, except such as were used
for the new house erected at a short distance, were sold by
auction. The Twelve Cæsars, and many other things, went to
Wardour Street.

Nothing remains of Blakesware save the "firry wilderness"
and the faint undulations in the grassy meadow, where the
ample pleasure garden rose backwards in triple terraces. But
the rural tranquillity of the surrounding country is still unchanged, and that depth and warmth of colouring in the foliage
that gives to the Hertfordshire landscape a character all its
own. It is a day well spent to make an excursion from the
country town of Ware, and wander over the site of the old
place, and among the graves of Widford churchyard. It will
be felt then how, with this "cockney of cockneys," the beauty
of an English home—a "haunt of ancient peace"—had passed
into his life and become a part of his genius and himself.

I was the true descendant of those old W———s.—Lamb disguises the family of Plumer under this change of initial. He
certainly did not mean the Wards—Mr. Ward not having
become connected with the family of Plumer till several years
later than the date of this essay.

So like my Alice!—See notes on *Dream Children* in the first series of the essays.

Compare with this essay Mary Lamb's story of "the Young Mahomedan" in *Mrs. Leicester's School*. Blakesware is there again described, as remembered by Mary Lamb when a child.

POOR RELATIONS.—P. 210.
(London Magazine, May 1823.)

Richard Amlet, Esq., in the play.—See Vanbrugh's comedy, *The Confederacy*.

Poor W——.—The Favell of the essay, *Christ's Hospital Five-and-thirty Years Ago*. Lamb, in his "Key" to the initials used by him, has written against the initial F., there employed: "Favell left Cambridge, because he was asham'd of his father, who was a house-painter there." He was a Grecian in the school in Lamb's time, and when at Cambridge wrote to the Duke of York for a commission in the army, which was sent him. Lamb here changes both his friend's name and his University.

Like Satan, "knew his mounted sign—and fled."—See the concluding lines of *Paradise Lost*, Book iv., of which this is a more than usually free adaptation. In the incident referred to, the angel Gabriel and Satan are on the point of engaging in struggle, when

"The Eternal, to prevent such horrid fray,
Hung forth in heaven his golden scales."

Satan's attention being called to the sight,

"—— The fiend looked up, and knew
His mounted *scale* aloft: nor more: but fled
Murmuring, and with him fled the shades of night."

DETACHED THOUGHTS ON BOOKS AND READING.
—P. 218.
(London Magazine, July 1882.)

The wretched Malone.—This happened in 1793, on occasion of Malone's visit to Stratford to examine the municipal and other records of that town, for the purposes of his edition of Shakspeare.

Martin B——.—Martin Charles Burney, the only son of Admiral Burney, and one of Lamb's life-long friends. Lamb dedicated to him the second volume of his collected writings in

1818 in a prefatory sonnet, in which he says—

"In all my threadings of this worldly maze
(And I have watched thee almost from a child),
Free from self-seeking, envy, low design,
I have not found a whiter soul than thine."

Martin Burney was originally an attorney, but left that branch of the profession for the Bar, where, however, he was not successful. Mr. Burney died in London in 1852.

A quaint poetess of our day.—Mary Lamb. The lines will be found in Charles and Mary Lamb's *Poetry for Children.*

STAGE ILLUSION.—P. 225.
(*London Magazine*, August 1825.)

TO THE SHADE OF ELLISTON.—P. 229.
(*Englishman's Magazine*, August 1831.)

Up thither like aërial rapours fly.

—A parody of the well-known description of the Limbo of Vanity in the third book of the *Paradise Lost.*

ELLISTONIANA.—P. 231.
(*Englishman's Magazine*, August 1831.)

G. D.—George Dyer.

Sir A—— C——.—Sir Anthony Carlisle, the surgeon.

These two papers were prompted by the death of the popular comedian in July 1831.

THE OLD MARGATE HOY.—P. 237.
(*London Magazine*, July 1823.)

Charles and Mary Lamb had actually, as here stated, passed a week's holiday together at Margate, when the former was quite a boy. In his early days of authorship Charles had utilised the experience for a sonnet, one of the first he published—"written at midnight by the sea-side after a voyage." It is amusing to note these two different treatments of the same theme :—

> "O winged bark! how swift along the night
> Passed thy proud keel; nor shall I let go by
> Lightly of that dread hour the memory,
> When wet and chilly on thy deck I stood
> Unbonneted, and gazed upon the flood."

> "*For many a day, and many a dreadful night,
> Incessant labouring round the stormy Cape.*"

—Thomson's *Seasons*—"Summer," l. 1002.

> "*Be but as buggs to fearen babes withal,
> Compared with the creatures in the sea's entral.*"

—Spenser, *Fairy Queen*, Book ii. Canto xii.

"*The daughters of Cheapside and wives of Lombard Street.*"—Imperfectly remembered from the *Ode to Master Anthony Stafford*, by Thomas Randolph (1605-1635):—

> There from the tree
> We'll cherries pluck, and pick the strawberry;
> And every day
> Go see the wholesome country girls make hay,
>   Whose brown hath lovelier grace
>   Than any painted face
>   That I do know
>   Hyde Park can show.
> Where I had rather gain a kiss than meet
>   (Though some of them in greater state
>   Might court my love with plate)
> The beauties of the Cheap, and wives of Lombard Street.

THE CONVALESCENT.—P. 246.

(*London Magazine*, July 1825.)

Lamb had an illness of the kind here described in the winter of 1824-25, and the condition in which it left him seems to have been one of the causes of his proposed retirement from the India House. As with all the other essays which savour of the autobiographical, the freshness and precision of the experience is one of its great charms.

SANITY OF TRUE GENIUS.—P. 251.

(*New Monthly Magazine*, May 1826.)

"*So strong a wit,*" says Cowley. From Cowley's fine lines—a true "In Memoriam"—*On the death of Mr. William Hervey*.

The common run of Lane's novels.—Better known as the novels of the Minerva Press, from which Lane the publisher issued innumerable works.

That wonderful episode of the Cave of Mammon.—See *Fairy Queen*, Book ii. Canto vii., the Legend of Sir Guyon.

CAPTAIN JACKSON.—P. 254.
(*London Magazine*, November 1824.)

It has been suggested that this exquisite character-sketch may have been taken from Lamb's old friend Mr. Randal Norris, of the Inner Temple. An obvious objection to this theory— that Mr. Norris was still living when the sketch appeared (he did not die till 1827)—is not so conclusive as it might seem. Lamb was in the habit of describing living persons with a surprising frankness. The account of James Elia, for example, in *My Relations*, was written and published in his brother's lifetime. Mr. Norris had two daughters, and although Sub-Treasurer to the Inner Temple, was never apparently in very flourishing circumstances. The very unlikeness of most of the incidents here recorded to those of Randal Norris's actual life, is quite after Lamb's custom. Mr. Norris lived and died in the Temple; he was *not* "steeped in poverty to the lips," and his wife was not a Scotchwoman, but a native of Widford, in Hertfordshire, and a friend of old Mrs. Field. Lamb may have introduced the significant reference to the wedding-day on purpose to amuse his sister. When Randal Norris was married (his daughter tells me) Mary Lamb was bridesmaid, and the happy pair, in company with Miss Lamb, spent the day together at Richmond.

When we came down through Glasgow town.
—From the beautiful old ballad, a special favourite with Lamb,

"Waly, waly, up the bank,
And waly, waly, down the brae."

THE SUPERANNUATED MAN.—P. 259.
(*London Magazine*, May 1825).

An account, substantially true to facts, of Lamb's retirement from the India House. This event occurred on the last Tuesday of March 1825, and Lamb, after his custom, proceeded to make it a subject for his next essay of Elia. He here transforms the directors of the India House into a private firm of merchants. The names Boldero, Merryweather, and the others, were not those of directors of the company at the time of Lamb's retirement. Lamb retired on a pension of £450, being two-thirds of his salary at that date. Nine pounds a year were deducted to assure a pension to Mary Lamb in the event of her surviving her brother. "Here am I," writes Charles to Wordsworth shortly afterwards, "after thirty-three years' slavery, sitting in my own room at eleven o'clock, this finest of all April mornings, a freed man, with £441 a year for the remainder of my life, live I as long as John Dennis, who outlived his annuity and starved at ninety."

> —— *that's born and has his years come to him,*
> *In some green desert.*

—Inaccurately quoted from Middleton's *Mayor of Queenboro'*, Act i. Sc. 1. It should be "in a rough desart."

A Tragedy by Sir Robert Howard.—The lines are from *The Vestal Virgin, or the Roman Ladies*, Act v. Sc. 1. Sir Robert Howard (1626-1698) was Dryden's brother-in-law, and joint author with him of the *Indian Queen.*

As low as to the fiends.—From the dramatic fragment, concerning Priam's slaughter, declaimed by the player in *Hamlet.*

Of Lamb's fellow-clerks in the India House, referred to here by their initials, Ch—— was a Mr. Chambers, Pl—— was W. D. Plumley, the son of a silversmith in Cornhill, and Do—— a Mr. Henry Dodwell, evidently one of Lamb's most intimate friends in the office. Their names occur together in an unpublished letter of Lamb's to Mr. Dodwell, now lying before me. It is addressed "H. Dodwell, Esq., India House, London. (In his absence may be opened by Mr. Chambers.)" The letter is so characteristic that I may be allowed to quote some passages. It is written from Calne in Wiltshire, where Lamb was spending his summer holiday, in July 1816:—

"My dear Fellow—I have been in a lethargy this long while and forgotten London, Westminster, Marybone, Paddington; they all went clean out of my head, till happening to go to a neighbour's in this good borough of Calne, for want of whist-players we fell upon *Commerce*. The word awoke me to a remembrance of my professional avocations and the long-continued strife which I have been these twenty-four years endeavouring to compose between those grand Irreconcileables—Cash and Commerce. I instantly called for an almanack, which, with some difficulty was procured at a fortune-teller's in the vicinity (for the happy holiday people here having nothing to do keep no account of time), and found that by dint of duty I must attend in Leadenhall on Wednesday morning next, and shall attend accordingly.... Adieu! Ye fields, ye shepherds and—herdesses, and dairies and cream-pots, and fairies, and dances upon the green. I come! I come! Don't drag me so hard by the hair of my head, Genius of British India! I know my hour is come—Faustus must give up his soul, O Lucifer, O Mephistopheles! Can you make out what all this letter is about? I am afraid to look it over.   Ch. Lamb.

"Calne, Wilts. Friday, July something, Old Style, 1816. No new style here—all the styles are old, and some of the gates too for that matter."

THE GENTEEL STYLE IN WRITING.—P. 267.

(*New Monthly Magazine*, March 1826.)

This essay, as originally published, formed one of the series of *Popular Fallacies*—with the title, "That my Lord Shaftesbury and Sir William Temple are models of the Genteel Style of Writing."

My Lord Shaftesbury.—Anthony Ashley Cooper, the third Earl of Shaftesbury, and author of the *Characteristics*. In his essay on *Books and Reading* Lamb had said, "I can read anything which I call *a book*. Shaftesbury is not too genteel for me, nor Jonathan Wild too low." The essays of Temple here cited are those *Of Gardening, Of Health and Long Life, The Cure of the Gout by Moxa,* and *Of Poetry.*

BARBARA S——.—P. 272.

(*London Magazine*, April 1825.)

The note appended by Lamb to this essay, as to the heroine being named Street, and having three times changed her name by successive marriages, is one of the most elaborate of his fictions. The real heroine of the story, as admitted by Lamb at the time, was the admirable comedian, Fanny Kelly, an attached friend of Charles and Mary Lamb, who has just died (December 1882) at the advanced age of ninety-two. In the year 1875 Miss Kelly furnished Mr. Charles Kent, who was editing the centenary edition of Lamb's works, with her own interesting version of the anecdote. It was in 1799, when Fanny Kelly was a child of nine, that the incident occurred, not at the old Bath Theatre, but at Drury Lane, where she had been admitted as a "miniature chorister," at a salary of a pound a week. After his manner, Lamb has changed every detail—the heroine, the site of the theatre, the amount of the salary, the name of the treasurer. Even following Charles Lamb, Miss Kelly has told her own story with much graphic power.

Miss Kelly, with the "divine plain face," was a special favourite of Lamb's. See his sonnets "To Miss Kelly," and "To a celebrated female performer in *The Blind Boy*."

She would have done the elder child in Morton's pathetic afterpiece to the life.—This is an ingenious way of intimating that Miss Kelly *did* play the elder child in the *Children in the Wood*. The drama was first produced in 1793. The incident of the roast-fowl and the spilt salt, recorded later on, occurs in the last scene of this play. The famished children, just rescued from the wood, are fed by the faithful Walter with a roast-chicken, over which he has just before, in his agitation, upset the salt-box.

When she used to play the part of the Little Son to Mrs. Porter's Isabella.—See Crabb Robinson's version of this anecdote (*Diaries*, iii. 19).—"She (Miss Kelly) related that when, as Constance, Mrs. Siddons wept over her, her collar was wet with Mrs. Siddons's tears."

THE TOMBS IN THE ABBEY.—P. 278.
(London Magazine, October 1823.)

The concluding paragraphs of Lamb's letter to Southey, remonstrating with him for his remarks upon certain characteristics of Lamb's writings. The *Quarterly Review* for January 1823 contained an article by Southey on Bishop Gregoire and the spread of the Theo-philanthropists in France. The first series of Elia was then on the point of being published in book form, and Southey thought to do the book a good turn by paying it an incidental compliment. Having to deal with the spread of free-thought in England, Southey went on to say that unbelief might rob men of hope, but could not banish their fears. "There is a remarkable proof of this," he added, "in Elia's essays, a book which wants only a sounder religious feeling, to be as delightful as it is original," and proceeded to quote from the essay on *Witches and other Night Fears* Lamb's account of the nervous terrors of "dear little T. H."—known to be Thornton Hunt, Leigh Hunt's eldest boy. The moral drawn by Southey may be easily guessed. These nervous terrors were the natural result of the absence of definite Christian teaching in the systems of Leigh Hunt and others of the Radical set.

Lamb was hurt by the attack on himself, but still more by the reflections on his friends; and the greater part of his letter is employed in defending Leigh Hunt and William Hazlitt. The breach with Southey was soon healed, and the old affectionate intercourse renewed. If only for this reason, it is intelligible why Lamb did not care to reproduce the entire letter when he published the *Last Essays of Elia* in a collected form. I have dealt with the subject at some length in my memoir of Lamb.

AMICUS REDIVIVUS.—P. 251.
(*London Magazine*, December 1823.)

For an account of G. D.—George Dyer—see notes to the essay, *Oxford in the Vacation*. The incident had actually occurred a few weeks only before the date of this essay. Mr. Procter supplements the account here given with some amusing particulars:—"I happened to go to Lamb's house, about an hour after his rescue and restoration to dry land, and met Miss Lamb in the passage in a state of great alarm; she was whimpering, and could only utter, 'Poor Mr. Dyer! Poor Mr. Dyer!' in tremulous tones. I went upstairs, aghast, and found that the involuntary diver had been placed in bed, and that Miss Lamb had administered brandy and water, as a well-established preventive against cold. Dyer, unaccustomed to anything stronger than the 'crystal spring,' was sitting upright in the bed perfectly delirious. His hair had been rubbed up, and stood out like so many needles of iron-gray. 'I soon found out where I was,' he cried out to me, laughing; and then he went wandering on, his words taking flight into regions where no one could follow."

And could such spacious virtue find a grave.

—Lamb had headed this essay with an appropriate quotation from Milton's *Lycidas*. He now cites a less famous poem from the collection of tributary verse in which *Lycidas* made its first appearance—the little volume of *Elegies* on the death of Edward King, published at Cambridge in 1638. The couplet here quoted is from the contribution to this volume by John Cleveland, the Cavalier. It runs thus in the original:—

"But can his spacious vertue find a grave
Within th' imposthumed bubble of a wave."

The sweet lyrist of Peter House.—The poet Gray.

The mild Askew.—Anthony Askew, M.D.—See *Dyer's Poems*, 1801, p. 156 (note):—"Dr. Anthony Askew, formerly a physician in London, once of Emmanuel College, well known in this and foreign countries for his acquaintance with Greek literature, and his valuable collection of Greek books and MSS.: a particular friend and patron of the author's early youth."

SOME SONNETS OF SIR PHILIP SIDNEY. -P. 286.

(*London Magazine*, September 1823.)

In the year 1820 William Hazlitt delivered a course of lectures at the Surrey Institution on the Literature of the Age of Elizabeth. In the sixth lecture of the course he dealt, among other writers, with Sidney, on whose *Arcadia* he made an elaborate onslaught. "It is to me," he says, "one of the greatest monuments of the abuse of intellectual power upon record. It puts one in mind of the Court dresses and preposterous fashions of the time, which are grown obsolete and disgusting. It is not romantic, but scholastic; not poetry, but casuistry; not nature, but art, and the worst sort of art, which thinks it can do better than nature. Of the number of fine things that are constantly passing through the author's mind, there is hardly one that he has not contrived to spoil, and to spoil purposely and maliciously, in order to aggrandise our idea of himself"—with much more in the same strain. In the course of his remarks he describes the sonnets inlaid in the *Arcadia* as "jejune, far-fetched, and frigid," the very words cited by Lamb in his essay; and it is clear that Hazlitt's lecture was the immediate cause of the present paper.

It is a lesson of high value to contrast Lamb's and Hazlitt's estimate of Sidney. Hazlitt possessed acuteness, wide reading, and had command of an excellent style, but he was (through political bias, among other causes, as Lamb suggests) out of sympathy with his subject. Moreover, Lamb was a poet. His few sentences beginning, "But they are not rich in words only," are truer and more satisfying than the whole of Hazlitt's minute analysis.

I am afraid some of his addresses ("*ad Leonoram*" *I mean*) *have rather erred on the other side.*—Cowper translated most of Milton's Latin poems in skilful intimation of the Miltonic verse. It is significant that he "drew the line" at this exorbitant piece of flattery, which remains untranslated by him.

Lord Orford.—The "foolish nobleman," just before mentioned. Sidney was grossly insulted by the young earl in a tennis-court, where they had met for play. According to Fulke Greville, the earl called Sidney "a puppy"—the "opprobrious thing" alluded to by Lamb. It is worth noting that two centuries later another earl (Horace Walpole) made an equally memorable and insolent attack upon Sidney. See the notice of Fulke Greville in Walpole's *Royal and Noble Authors*.

There is a touching incident associating Lamb's last days with those of Sidney. The last letter written by Lamb before the fatal issue of his accident was to Mrs. George Dyer, concerning the safety of a certain book belonging to Mr. Cary of the British Museum, which Lamb had left by accident at her house. The book was the *Theatrum Poetarum* of Edward Phillips, Milton's nephew. On the recovery of the volume it was found that the page was turned down at the notice of Philip Sidney. It was on this incident that Cary wrote his charming lines:—

> "So should it be, my gentle friend;
> Thy leaf last closed at Sidney's end.
> Thou too, like Sidney, would'st have given
> The water, thirsting, and near Heaven;
> Nay, were it wine, fill'd to the brim,
> Thou hadst looked hard—but given, like him."

NEWSPAPERS THIRTY-FIVE YEARS AGO.—P. 295.

(*Englishman's Magazine*, October 1831.)

The title of this essay was first given to it when it appeared in the *Last Essays of Elia* in 1833. The date, therefore, to which it refers is the year 1798, or thereabouts. Lamb's connection with the newspaper world began even earlier than this. He seems to have owed his first introduction to it to Coleridge, who published some of his own earliest verse in the columns of the *Morning Chronicle*. Coleridge was contributing sonnets to this paper as early as the year 1794, and among them appeared Lamb's sonnet (perhaps a joint composition with his friend) on Mrs. Siddons. After this period, until Coleridge's return from Germany at the end of 1799, we have no means of tracing Lamb's hand in the newspapers; but from 1800 to 1803 frequent mention is made in Lamb's correspondence of his employment in the capacity described in this essay. It was his time of greatest poverty and struggle, when the addition of an extra fifty pounds a year to his income was of the greatest importance. Coleridge appears to have introduced Lamb to Daniel Stuart, the editor of the *Morning Post*. He was writing in the same year for the *Albion*, the final collapse of which, by the help of Lamb's epigram, is here described. "The *Albion* is dead," he writes to Manning on this occasion, "dead as nail in door—my revenues have died with it; but I am not as a man without hope." He had now got an introduction, through his friend George Dyer, to the *Morning Chronicle*, under the editorship of Perry. In 1802 he was trying an entirely new line of writing in the *Morning Post* turning into verse prose translations of German poems supplied by Coleridge. A specimen of Lamb's work of this kind has been preserved—Thekla's song in *Wallenstein*. "As to the translations," he writes to Coleridge, "let me do two or three hundred lines, and then do you try the nostrums upon Stuart in any way you please." His connection with the newspapers came to an end in 1803. "I have given up two guineas a week at the *Post*," he writes to Manning, "and regained my health and spirits, which were upon the wane. I grew sick, and Stuart unsatisfied. *Lusisti satis, tempus abire est*. I must cut closer, that's all."

Daniel Stuart—who lived till 1846- published in the *Gentleman's Magazine* for June 1838 an account of his dealings with Coleridge, Wordsworth, and Lamb. It is amusing to hear the other side of the story. He says, "As for good Charles Lamb, I could never make anything of his writings. Coleridge repeatedly pressed me to settle him on a salary, but it would not do. Of politics he knew nothing; and his drollery was vapid when given in short paragraphs for a newspaper." Certainly no style was ever less fitted for journalism, in any department, than Lamb's.

Bob Allen—our quondam schoolfellow.—He was a Grecian at Christ's Hospital in Lamb's time. See the story of him, and his handsome face, in the essay on the *Blue Coat School*.

John Fenwick.—The Ralph Bigod of the essay, *The Two Races of Men*.

An unlucky, or rather lucky, epigram from our pen.—The alleged apostasy of Sir James Mackintosh consisted in his having accepted, at the hands of Mr. Addington, the office of Recorder of Bombay in 1804. His *Vindiciæ Gallicæ* were published in 1791. Lamb's epigram was the following:—

> "Though thou'rt like Judas, an apostate black,
> In the resemblance one thing dost thou lack;
> When he had gotten his ill-purchased pelf,
> He went away, and wisely hang'd himself:
> This thou may do at last, yet much I doubt
> If thou hast any bowels to gush out!"

BARRENNESS OF THE IMAGINATIVE FACULTY IN THE PRODUCTIONS OF MODERN ART.—P. 303.

(*The Athenæum*, January and February 1833.)

Apropos of what Lamb writes in this essay on the Titian in the National Gallery, it is not unamusing to find the following sentence in a letter to Wordsworth of May 1833:—

"Thank you for your cordial reception of Elia. *Inter nos*, the 'Ariadne' is not a darling with me; several incongruous things are in it, but in the composition it served me as illustrative."

THE WEDDING.—P. 315.

(*London Magazine*, June 1825.)

Sarah Burney, the daughter of Admiral Burney, married her cousin John Payne in April 1821, and her father died in November of the same year. Her age was between twenty-seven and twenty-eight. This is the foundation of fact on which this idyllic little story is built up. It is at least a curious coincidence that, when Lamb revised the essay for the *Last Essays of Elia*, he was himself looking forward to a bereavement strictly parallel to that of the old admiral. He and Mary were about to lose, by marriage, one who had been to them as an only child. Emma Isola married Mr. Moxon in July 1833. Lamb might indeed have said of himself, "He bears bravely up, but he does not come out with his flashes of wild wit so thick as formerly . . . the youthfulness of the house is flown." Did he perchance remember, as he quoted his favourite Marvell, that the poet was bidding good-bye to one who had been his pupil, as Emma Isola had been Lamb's? In the lines on Appleton House, Marvell predicts the marriage of Mary Fairfax -

"While her glad parents most rejoice,
And make their destiny their choice."

REJOICINGS UPON THE NEW YEAR'S COMING OF AGE.—P. 321.

(*London Magazine*, January 1823.)

OLD CHINA.—P. 327.

(*London Magazine*, March 1823.)

This beautiful essay tells its own story - this time, we may be sure, without romance or exaggeration of any kind. It is a contribution of singular interest to our understanding of the happier days of Charles and Mary's united life.

Dancing the hays.—The hays was an old English dance, involving some intricate figures. It seems to have been known in England up to fifty years ago. The dance is often referred to in the writers whom Lamb most loved. Herrick, for example, has—

"On holy-dayes, when Virgins meet
To dance the Heyes, with nimble feet."

THE CHILD ANGEL; A DREAM.—P. 333.

(*London Magazine*, June 1823.)

Thomas Moore's *Loves of the Angels* had appeared in the year 1823. Lamb, as we may well believe, was not in general attracted to this poet, but there were reasons why this particular poem may have been an exception to the rule. It was based upon the translation in the Septuagint of the second verse in the sixth chapter of Genesis—"Angels of God" instead of "Sons of God." "In addition to the fitness of the subject for poetry," Moore writes in his preface, "it struck me also as capable of affording an allegorical medium, through which might be shadowed out the fall of the soul from its original purity—the loss of light and happiness which it suffers in the pursuit of this world's perishable pleasures—and the punishments, both from conscience and Divine justice, with which impurity, pride, and presumptuous inquiry into the awful secrets of God are sure to be visited." This vein of thought had a strange fascination for Lamb, as we know from his reflections in *New Year's Eve*, and his beautiful sonnet on *Innocence*. The topic, in short, may have attracted him, rather than Moore's fluent verse and boudoir metaphysics. It may be doubted whether he meant his sequel to the poem to be in any sense an allegory. It is probably fantastic merely.

CONFESSIONS OF A DRUNKARD.—P. 336.

(*London Magazine*, August 1822.)

In the year 1814 Basil Montagu compiled a volume of miscellaneous extracts on the subject of temperance, under the title *Some Enquiries into the Effects of Fermented Liquors. By a Water Drinker*. The contents were taken from the writings of physicians, divines, poets, essayists and others who had pleaded the temperance cause. The volume was arranged in sections, and to that headed *Do Fermented Liquors contribute to Moral Excellence?* Lamb furnished (of course anonymously) his *Confessions of a Drunkard*. It was illustrated by an outline engraving of the Correggio drawing so powerfully described in the essay. A second edition of the book appeared in 1818.

In the *Quarterly Review* for April 1822 appeared an article on Dr. Reid's treatise on *Hypochondriasis and other Nervous Affections*. These *Confessions of a Drunkard* were there referred to, as "a fearful picture of the consequences of intemperance," which the reviewer went on to say, "we have reason to know is a true tale." I may be allowed to finish the story in words used by me elsewhere. "In order to give the author the opportunity of contradicting this statement, the paper was reprinted in the *London* in the following August, under the signature of Elia. To it were appended a few words of remonstrance with the *Quarterly* reviewer for assuming the literal truthfulness of these confessions, but accompanied with certain significant admissions that showed Lamb had no right to be seriously indignant. 'It is indeed,' he writes, "a compound extracted out of his long observation of the effects of drinking upon all the world about him; and this accumulated mass of misery he hath centred (as the custom is with judicious essayists) in a single figure. . We deny not that a portion of his own experiences may have passed into the picture (as who, that is not a washy fellow, but must at some time have felt the after-operation of a too generous cup?); but then how heightened! how exaggerated! how little within the sense of the review, when a part in their slanderous usage must be understood to stand for the whole.' The truth is that Lamb, in writing his tract, had been playing with edge-tools, and could hardly have complained if they turned against himself. It would be those who knew Lamb, or at least the circumstances of his life, best, who would be most likely to accept these confessions as true." There is, in short, a thread of fact running through this paper, though with exaggerations and additions in abundance. The reference to the excessive indulgence in smoking we have too good reason for accepting as genuine. When some one watched him persistently emit dense volumes of smoke during the greater part of an evening, and asked him how he had contrived to do it, he answered, "I toiled after it, sir, as some men toil after virtue." Compare his *Ode to Tobacco*.

————*and not undo 'em
To suffer wet damnation to run thro' 'em.*

From the *Revenger's Tragedy*, by Cyril Tourneur. Vindici is addressing the skull of his dead lady:—

"Here's an eye,
Able to tempt a great man—to serve God;
A pretty hanging lip, that has forgot how to dissemble.
Methinks this mouth should make a swearer tremble;
A drunkard clasp his teeth, and not undo 'em,
To suffer wet damnation to run through 'em."

POPULAR FALLACIES.—P. 346.

(*The New Monthly Magazine*, January to September 1826.)

Lamb writes to Wordsworth in 1833, when the volume was newly out:— "I want you in the *Popular Fallacies* to like the 'home that is no home,' and 'rising with the lark.'" The former of these naturally interested Lamb deeply, for it contains a hardly-disguised account of his own struggles with the crowd of loungers and good-natured friends who intruded on his leisure hours, and hindered his reading and writing. There is little to call for a note in these papers. The pun of Swift's criticised—with rare acumen—in the Fallacy, "that the worst puns are the best," was on a lady's mantua dragging to the ground a Cremona violin. Swift is said to have quoted Virgil's line—

"Mantua væ miseræ nimium vicina Cremonæ."

THE END

Printed by R. & R. CLARK, LIMITED, *Edinburgh.*

www.ingramcontent.com/pod-product-compliance
Lightning Source LLC
Chambersburg PA
CBHW021232300426
44111CB00007B/511